CANOE AND CANVAS

Life at the Encampments of the
American Canoe Association, 1880–1910

Canoe and Canvas

*Life at the Encampments of the
American Canoe Association, 1880–1910*

JESSICA DUNKIN

UNIVERSITY OF TORONTO PRESS
Toronto Buffalo London

© University of Toronto Press 2019
Toronto Buffalo London
utorontopress.com
Printed in Canada

ISBN 978-1-4875-0476-2

∞ Printed on acid-free, 100% post-consumer recycled
paper with vegetable-based inks.

Library and Archives Canada Cataloguing in Publication

Title: Canoe and Canvas : life at the encampments of the American Canoe
Association, 1880–1910 / Jessica Dunkin.
Names: Dunkin, Jessica, 1981– author.
Description: Includes bibliographical references and index.
Identifiers: Canadiana 20190094990 | ISBN 9781487504762 (hardcover)
Subjects: LCSH: American Canoe Association – History – 19th century. |
LCSH: American Canoe Association – History – 20th century. | LCSH:
Canoes and canoeing – Social aspects – United States – History – 19th
century. | LCSH: Canoes and canoeing – Social aspects – United States –
History – 20th century.
Classification: LCC GV783 .D86 2019 | DDC 797.1220973–dc23

This book has been published with the help of a grant from the Federation
for the Humanities and Social Sciences, through the Awards to Scholarly
Publications Program, using funds provided by the Social Sciences and
Humanities Research Council.

University of Toronto Press acknowledges the financial assistance to its
publishing program of the Canada Council for the Arts and the Ontario
Arts Council, an agency of the Government of Ontario.

Canada Council   Conseil des Arts
for the Arts   du Canada

ONTARIO ARTS COUNCIL
CONSEIL DES ARTS DE L'ONTARIO
an Ontario government agency
un organisme du gouvernement de l'Ontario

Funded by the   Financé par le
Government   gouvernement   Canada
of Canada   du Canada

MIX
Paper from
responsible sources
FSC® C016245

Contents

List of Illustrations vii

Preface ix

Introduction 3
1 Organizing 15
2 (Dis)Placing 33
3 Navigating 51
4 Governing 72
5 Domesticating 96
6 Inhabiting 117
7 Competing 137
8 Working 160
Conclusion 183

Appendix: Dates and Locations of the American Canoe Association Encampments, 1880–1910 191

Notes 193

Bibliography 259

Index 281

Illustrations

0.1 Map of American Canoe Association encampments, 1880–1910 4
1.1 Area map of the 1895 encampment on Lake Champlain 28
1.2 Site map of the 1901 encampment on Mudlunta Island 30
2.1 "The bottle of rum closed the deal," 1930 49
3.1 "Mrs Snedeker and Karl," 1891 52
3.2 "'Medora' at Muskoka with American Canoe Association on board," 1900 59
3.3 "Jabberwock Canoe Club Cruise to Lake Champlain Meet," 1887 61
3.4 "SS Valeria arriving at Sugar Island," 1905 69
4.1 "Headquarters from Dock," 1897 76
4.2 "Squaw Point Flag" 81
4.3 Course map from the 1889 meet on Stave Island 85
4.4 "Group at the American Canoe Association Camp at Stave Island," 1889 87
4.5 "Mixed Drinks," 1887 92
5.1 "Toronto Canoe Club Camp," 1889 99
5.2 "Dinner Time in the Mess Tent," 1898 101
5.3 "Ubique Canoe Club Mess," c. 1886 103
5.4 "Official Headquarters," 1886 104
5.5 "A Typical ACA Squaw Camp," 1890 108
5.6 "A Tent Interior," 1891 109
5.7 "Squaw-Land" 112
6.1 "The Camp Fire at Squaw Point," 1890 122
6.2 "At Bala Falls," 1900 128
6.3 "Grindstone Island, Thousand Islands," c. 1896 129
6.4 "Three of the Performers in Seavey's Circus," 1889 134
7.1 "Start of the ACA Paddling Trophy Race," 1890 138
7.2 "Lake George, ACA at Crosbyside," 1882 154
7.3 "Watching the Races," 1891 155

8.1	"Work and Fun in Camp," 1887	161
8.2	"Joe"	169
8.3	"The Sneak-Box Mess: Camp of the Brooklyn Canoe Club," 1887	169
8.4	"Arrival of the Coon Band," 1890	178
8.5	"De Wattah Mellin Growin' on de Vine," 1890	178
8.6	"Keys, Kanoe, Kaptor, and Kowboy," 1887	181
9.1	"Packing Up – Sad Day in Camp," 1888	184

Preface

In February 2014, a colleague and I travelled to the New York State Historical Association (now the Fenimore Museum) in Cooperstown, New York, to consult the photographic collection of the American Canoe Association (ACA). As we thumbed through the albums and loose images, I was reminded of my first encounters with the association as a doctoral student in 2008. ACA members were notorious pranksters and loved any opportunity to play dress-up; I often found myself smiling at their antics. I also recognized something of myself in the "knights of the paddle": a love for the outdoors, a desire to visit and paddle in new places, a certain contentment that comes with ending the day by a campfire. I have spent part of most summers since I was young paddling canoes and sleeping in tents, first on South Lake near our farm north of Gananoque and at our family cottage in Muskoka, then at summer camps around Ontario, and most recently north of 60.

As I came to know the ACA and its members, I also felt a sense of historical and cultural distance. Who were these men and women sporting sugarloaf hats, racing sailing canoes, performing gymnastic feats on their small craft, and dressing in blackface? I read broadly to make sense of both the playful and troubling aspects of association life in the late nineteenth century, though my dissertation was weighted to the latter in no small part because my awareness of the politics of sport developed in tandem with the research. The final result was a text that denounced many of the practices that occupied the members of the ACA. Members of my defense committee understood my critical stance, but they also encouraged me to think in more nuanced ways about the canoeists and the encampment. The question that lingered in the wake of the defense was: How can we as historians write about our subjects in ways that respect their humanity and personal circumstances, but are still attuned to their prejudices and the inequities that both enabled and proceeded from their lifestyles?

The question of representation was never far from my mind as I worked on this book manuscript. It was given greater urgency when I was invited to look at photograph albums of the encampments by a grandson of an early and prominent ACA member in the summer of 2014. The experience of poring over the albums with Bob MacKendrick, his wife Margie, and two of their friends was profoundly moving. Not only did it make the members of the ACA more human to me, but it also introduced a degree of accountability to my research that had not previously existed.

I have done my best in *Canoe and Canvas* to evoke the colourful, fun-loving canoeists who attended the ACA's annual encampments and to recreate the world of outdoor sport and recreation to which they were drawn, while also attending to the ways in which prejudice and inequity were part of the events. While I am respectful of the experiences of those who attended the yearly encampments, I do not shy away from asking difficult questions of the organization and its members.[1]

And what of my place in this narrative? As I mentioned, I have long been an avid canoeist. Although I was born a century after the ACA was established, I have benefitted from many of the same policies and ideologies as the organization and its members. For a good portion of my life, I gave little thought to the origins of the canoe or its implication in the settler colonial project called Canada. Researching the ACA has given me ample time and opportunity to understand the colonial history of the canoe, and to reflect on what it means to be a white settler paddler. Increasingly, I see the points of connection between my story and that of the ACA, rather than the distance. As I work to develop an ethical canoeing practice, I strive to lay bare the role of the canoe in the establishment and expansion of the colonial state and extractive capitalism and to subvert romantic narratives of the canoe as a national symbol of cooperation and unity.[2] Equally important has been supporting projects that enable Indigenous nations and people to revitalize their relations with the canoe. For all of the time I have spent reflecting on what it means to paddle against the colonial current, I have much to learn.

Canoe and Canvas owes a great deal to my doctoral supervisor, John C. Walsh, who has taught me so much about being a good historian, writer, teacher, and human. I am so thankful for his continued presence in my life and scholarship since I moved north. I have also been fortunate to call Dimitry Anastakis a mentor and a friend since I was an undergraduate student at Trent University. I can always count on Dimitry for frank advice and a laugh. I am especially appreciative of his assistance throughout the publishing process. Many of the changes I made as I developed this manuscript were inspired by feedback I received from Andrew Johnston, Mary Louise Adams, Emilie Cameron, and Joanna Dean. I have also benefitted from the time, attention, and support of Dominique Marshall, Nancy Bouchier, Russell Field, Alan MacEachern, Graeme Wynn, Finis Dunaway, Kevin Siena, and Janet Miron.

I had the good fortune of meeting a number of smart, engaged scholars while in graduate school who have continued to inspire me long after convocation, including Bryan Grimwood, David Banoub, David Tough, and Tina Adcock. I want to offer a special thanks to my dear friend and colleague, Sara Spike. I am so grateful for your ceaseless encouragement, keen editorial skills, and patient counsel, whether we are discussing academic life or tramping through the bush admiring wildflowers and trees.

I have presented different parts of this work over the years at conferences and workshops hosted by, among others, the Canadian Historical Association (CHA), the American Society for Environmental History (ASEH), the Network in Canadian History and Environment (NiCHE), the Canadian Association of Geographers (CAG), and the Research Centre for Sport in Canadian Society. Questions and conversations that stemmed from those presentations helped to refine my thinking on a number of subjects including governance, colonialism, and space. Thanks are also due to the editors of *Moving Natures*, *Labour/Le travail*, and *Lifestyle Mobilities and Corporealities*, who published aspects of my ACA research and provided feedback on the same.

I am grateful for the support of the Canadian Canoe Museum and canoeing scholars and enthusiasts like James Raffan and Dale Standen. Ken Brown deserves special mention for passing along old newspaper articles about the ACA. I had the pleasure of giving community lectures about the association in Gravenhurst and Port Carling thanks to my Muskoka agent, Andrew Watson. It was through these lectures that I was introduced to Bob and Margie MacKendrick. Flipping through the MacKendrick photograph albums in the shadow of the cottage that Bob's grandfather Jack MacKendrick built in 1901 was one of the highlights of researching this book. *Canoe and Canvas* benefitted immensely from the generosity of the MacKendricks.

Another highlight of studying the ACA was visiting repositories large and small on both sides of the border. At the New York State

Historical Association Library (now part of the Fenimore Museum) in Cooperstown, NY, I wish to thank Sarah, Joanne, and Wayne for their gracious assistance and for always making me feel at home in the lovely reading room overlooking Lake Otsego. More recently, Jennifer Griffiths helped with photographic reproductions and permissions. At the Adirondack Museum (now Adirondack Experience) in Blue Mountain Lake, NY, I am indebted to Hallie Bond and Jerry Pepper for their early interest in this project and their help in locating suitable archival materials and a place to sleep. A special thanks to Hallie for inviting a lonely graduate student to her daughter's Christmas concert on a snowy evening in December. Ivy Gocker has been invaluable in arranging images from the Adirondack Experience's collection. Thanks are also due to the staff at the Mystic Seaport Collections Research Center in Mystic, CT, and the Antique Boat Museum in Clayton, NY. Finally, I would like to extend my gratitude to Mary Margaret Johnston-Miller for her assistance with photographic materials at Library and Archives Canada, and the staff of Carleton University's Interlibrary Loan Department, who tracked down a steady stream of obscure published sources for me.

The research for this book was enabled by the financial support of the Social Science and Humanities Research Council of Canada (SSHRC), the Carleton Department of History, and Carleton University. A SSHRC Postdoctoral Fellowship in the Department of Kinesiology and Health Studies at Queen's University gave me the time and space to prepare the book manuscript. The Awards to Scholarly Publications Program, also an initiative of SSHRC, made the dream of publishing this book a reality. Many thanks to the team at the University of Toronto Press who have shepherded *Canoe and Canvas* from manuscript to book, including Len Husband, Kate Baltais, Lynn Fisher, and Frances Mundy. The index was prepared by Stephen Ullstrom.

In 2015, I accepted a job as the On the Land Programs Consultant with the NWT Recreation and Parks Association and I relocated to Sǫmba K'è (Yellowknife) in Chief Drygeese Territory (Treaty 8), home of the Yellowknives Dene First Nation. In that capacity and now as the Director, On the Land Programs, I support Indigenous communities and organizations across the territory who are delivering land-based programs. Working in community has been both a pleasure and instructive, making tangible my accountabilities to others and the land. I am routinely humbled by the brilliance and generosity that surrounds me and feel so fortunate to be able to live and learn alongside Dene, Inuvialuit, and Métis. A special thanks to the Executive Director of the NWTRPA, Geoff Ray, for his graceful leadership and support for this book project, and for finding ways for me to be a historian while working in recreation.

I have been able to continue to think with the canoe since moving north because of invitations from Michael Dawson, Catherine Gidney, and Donald Wright, and from Bruce Erickson and Sarah Krotz, to attend workshops in Fredericton and Winnipeg, respectively. I have been particularly fortunate to be able to work and write with Dr John B. Zoe, a Tłı̨chǫ philosopher and cosmologist who has played an important role in creating opportunities for Tłı̨chǫ to travel their ancestral waterways by canoe through programs like Wha Dǫ Ehtǫ K'è (Trails of Our Ancestors). The Tłı̨chǫ are one of a growing number of Indigenous nations who are reclaiming the canoe through canoe building projects and canoe journeys. This book makes clear that the canoe was a symbol and tool of colonialism, but as examples like Wha Dǫ Ehtǫ K'è demonstrate, in the hands of its original architects, the canoe is also a symbol and tool of resurgence and sovereignty.

My family and friends have supported me in myriad ways as I journeyed from student to academic to northerner, but also through the publishing process. An enormous thank you is due to my parents, Diane Gagné and Stephen Dunkin, and their respective partners, Lee Gagné and Susan Dunkin, my brother and sister-in-law, Matthew Dunkin and Victoria Boomgaardt, and my nephew and niece, Griff and Molly, for their unceasing love and encouragement. Matt deserves special mention for being (to my knowledge) the only person not in the room at my defense to have read my dissertation in its entirety. What a pleasure it has been to share the world of the ACA with my brother and fellow canoe nerd, especially when we were able to do so with paddles in hand. I would not have made it through the dissertation, postdoc, or the early work of preparing this manuscript without the support and culinary skills of Paul Nelles. And thank you, Elliot, Audrey, and Peter, for providing a welcome escape from the stress of writing a book, and for all of the ways in which you inspire me as you make your way in the world. Finally, I am grateful to my dear friends in Ottawa and beyond who have been cheering me and this project on for more than a decade, including Katelyn Friendship, Sarah Posthuma, Britt Gregg-Wallace, Colleen Sutton, Lisa Kilner, Jenna Murdock-Smith, Robert Muir, Emma Mason, and Neale McDonald.

Moving north reignited my passion for canoe travel. I have had the pleasure of undertaking a number of canoe trips since relocating to the NWT in Yellowknives Dene, Tłı̨chǫ, Dënesųłıné Dene, Gwıch'ın, and Métis territory with a colourful cast of new friends, including Jill, Keith, Chris, Alyssa, Susan, Eric, Thomsen, Kajsa, Ryan, Shin, Tee, and Janna.

A special thanks to the students and staff of Chief Paul Niditchie School in Tsııgehtchıc for inviting me to travel Tsııgèhnjık with them in June 2018. It was breathtaking to watch young Gwıch'ın come to know their river through the canoe. I have particularly enjoyed sharing a canoe with Michael Gilday and look forward to many more trips together under the midnight sun. More than a paddling partner, you have kept me grounded through the long and arduous process of seeing this book come to fruition. I look forward to celebrating its publication on the shores of Walsh Lake. Thank you, Pam and David, for your love and support, and for gifting us a canoe.

Canoe and Canvas is dedicated to my dear friend, Deborah Simmons. Deb is a model of rigorous and respectful community-based research and practice. I could not have asked for a better mentor as a mola and scholar living and working on Dene land. Máhsı, Deb, for your generosity of spirit, knowledge, books, meals, wine, and laughter.

CANOE AND CANVAS

Life at the Encampments of the
American Canoe Association, 1880–1910

Introduction

In June 1880, the *New York Times* informed readers that "to the various political booms, must now be added a canoe boom." The newspaper traced the origins of this boom to the recreational pursuits of John "Rob Roy" MacGregor, a Cambridge-educated lawyer turned social reformer, who, having piloted the waterways of Europe by canoe in 1865, "stirred up hundreds of his countrymen to follow his example." Although the sport had been "naturalized" in the United States in the early 1870s – with the founding of the New York Canoe Club, in 1871 – the *Times* claimed that its subsequent expansion had been slow because "the American mind was imbued with the belief that a canoe was a 'birch,' and could not by any possibility be anything else."[1] In spite of this impediment, the article noted, the New York club was growing, other canoe clubs had been founded, and there were now half a dozen canoe builders in the United States.

Not two months after the "The Canoe Boom" appeared in the *New York Times*, a small group of men gathered on Lake George in the Adirondack Mountains for the purpose of creating a national canoeing organization.[2] The American Canoe Association (ACA) was founded with the aim of bringing together enthusiasts from across the continent, thereby furthering "an interchange of opinion" and increasing "the range of fraternity and good fellowship amongst the knights of the paddle."[3] To this end, the organization decided to hold a yearly encampment. Each August, canoeists from the United States and Canada would gather to race canoes, sleep under canvas, and socialize. For the first three years, these events of three or four days were held on Lake George. Between 1883 and 1902, the annual meets, which had grown to two weeks in length, took place at different locations in New York, Ontario, and New England. In 1903, the organization established a permanent encampment on Sugar Island in the St Lawrence River; that site remains in use to this day.

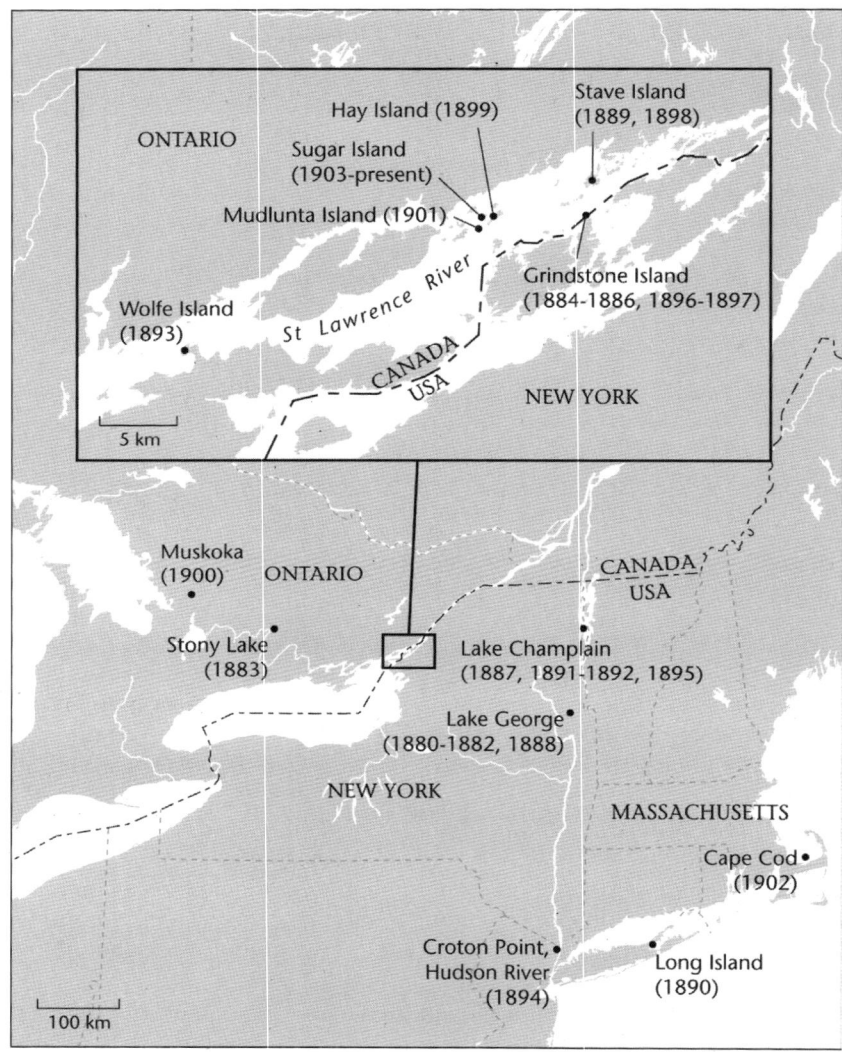

0.1 Map of American Canoe Association encampments, 1880–1910. Map prepared by Eric Leinberger.

Canoe and Canvas is a close reading of the annual encampments of the American Canoe Association from 1880 to 1910.[4] It follows the temporal arc of organizing and attending a meet each year from the identification of a site to the dismantling of the tents, considering the locations the canoeists chose, the ways in which they organized their encampments, and the activities that occupied them during their time together. As a series of temporally and spatially bound events that took place at a distance from traditional centres of power, the annual gatherings of the American Canoe Association offer a unique site for exploring cultures of sport and leisure in late Victorian society.

The encampments were popular events that drew visitors from near and far. Early meets attracted between thirty and one hundred campers. By the late 1880s, several hundred canoeists were typically in residence with many more spectators making their way to the site for the regattas – newspaper reports suggest that at some of the annual gatherings upwards of two thousand people watched the canoe races. Attendance declined somewhat through the 1890s. After 1900, there were usually between one and two hundred campers on site each year. There are a few possible explanations for waning participation, not the least of which was competition from other recreational pursuits. Recessions and depressions may have also contributed; economic downturns plagued industrialized countries in the early-to-mid 1890s and, arguably, right through to the First World War. The founding of the Canadian Canoe Association in 1900 could have also been a factor.

The American Canoe Association encampments were not just well attended, they also drew campers back year after year. Canoeists were enticed by the promise of spending time with old friends, seeing the latest developments in canoe technology, competing in the races, and visiting new locales. They appreciated the fact that the encampments took place away from urban centres, their "natural" location providing a welcome escape from the city during the hot summers. No less appealing was the relatively relaxed approach to dress and decorum and the seemingly flexible schedule. Perhaps most importantly, the encampments were fun. Pranks, excursions, and impromptu gatherings were commonplace, and the schedule was filled with dances, spectacles, campfires, and novelty races, in addition to the daily pleasure of canoeing with friends.

Although they were certainly spaces of fun and frivolity, the encampments also invite a more critical reading. My first intimation of this came when I learned that, ten years after the organization was founded, the American Canoe Association instituted races for women. At a time when women were rarely imagined as competent athletes, what did it mean for a canoeing association to provide opportunities for women to engage in formal competition? As I looked more closely at the meets, other elements of encampment life came to the fore that begged for deeper analysis, including the presence of Indigenous paddlers, the emphasis placed on order and good governance, the popularity of minstrel shows, and the role of paid labour.

A social history of sport, *Canoe and Canvas* is particularly concerned with how gender, class, and race shaped the social, cultural, and physical landscapes of the ACA encampments. Although there was an ever-expanding arena of opportunity for leisure and sport in the late nineteenth century, as the example of the ACA makes clear, not all were granted equal access. Most of the members of the American Canoe Association and the majority of the campers at the annual meets were white, middle-class men. White women were extended partial membership in 1882, and beginning the following year, they were allowed to camp on site. White women were extended full membership in the ACA, including the right to vote and hold office, only in 1944. The formal place of women in the association did not necessarily reflect their experiences of the encampments. If anything, the annual gatherings appear to have provided a more egalitarian social environment than was on offer elsewhere in the same period.

The organization never explicitly prevented working-class enthusiasts or people of colour from joining; however, the social networks that sustained the American Canoe Association, the time and money required to actively participate, and contemporary cultures of leisure all worked to create a visibly white, middle-class, and male organization. That said, the encampments were not absent of Black, Indigenous, and working-class people: these were the people hired to landscape, cook, clean, and entertain. Although their presence was often obscured in the documentation of the yearly meets, which served to reinforce the image of the ACA as white and middle class, as we shall see, people of colour and working-class folks were indispensable to the smooth functioning of these events.

Canoe and Canvas contributes to a number of historical fields, including the history of travel and tourism, environmental history, gender history, and the history of labour. Chiefly, however, this book is a social history of sport and leisure. *Canoe and Canvas* builds on the work of scholars such as Colin Howell, Nancy Bouchier, Russell Field, and Gillian Poulter, all of whom attend to the ways in which sport organizations and enthusiasts are embedded in webs of power and privilege, shaped by contemporary relations of gender, race, and class, while simultaneously constituting those webs and relations.[5] More often than not, sport has reproduced the social divisions and hierarchies that have historically privileged white, middle- and upper-class men to the exclusion of white women, the working class, and people of colour, although occasionally sport and sport organizations have provided an arena for contesting social inequalities. As we shall see, the American Canoe Association is no exception.

What sets *Canoe and Canvas* apart from previous scholarship is its geographical orientation. First, there is the location of the events in "wild places." Most sport history is concerned with urban sporting spaces, cultures, and events from baseball leagues and hockey arenas to gymnastics classes and athletics associations. This book is about sport beyond the city limits. As an example of extra-urban sport tourism, the American Canoe Association encampments have some parallels in other forms of nature-based leisure, such as wilderness vacations and summer camps. Certainly, my understanding of the encampments has been enriched by the work of Patricia Jasen, Leslie Paris, Sharon Wall, and Jocelyn Thorpe, among others.[6] The annual gatherings of the ACA are unique, however, for their emphasis on competition, their size, the age of those in attendance, and their enduring ephemerality – a term meant to capture both the impermanence of the meets and their persistence in memory. Second, spatial theory is critical to my analysis and understanding of the ACA encampments, particularly ideas of placemaking, the uses and meaning of space, and the ways in which different bodies constitute and experience space. As we shall see, the ACA meets were *spaces of leisure*: they attracted white, middle-class women and men with the promise of a two-week holiday of socializing and amusement. The encampments were also *spaces of sport*: the second week of the annual gathering featured races lasting anywhere from three to seven days that were billed as national canoeing championships. Moreover, the ACA encampments were *spaces of work*: some came, not to play, explore, relax, and compete, but to exchange their labour for wages or to sell goods and services. Even within these two broad categories of canoeist and worker, there was no singular experience of these gatherings. Rather, gender, class, race, and marital status all contributed to the ways in which workers and members of the American Canoe Association moved through and occupied the campsites and interacted with the community of canoeists.

There is a tension running through this book between the aims of the organizers and the everyday practices of the canoeists. Drawing on the technologies and techniques of the late nineteenth-century state, the American Canoe Association worked hard to structure the space and experience of the annual encampments, to control access to the sites, and to regulate the behaviour of the canoeists. Order was an important, if unattainable, objective. Not surprisingly, some of the people at the encampments resisted these efforts at control, making clear to organizers that bodies in motion could not be managed in ways that bodies on paper could. My understanding of the regulatory regime and power relationships that structured encampment life owes much to Michel

Foucault. Of particular utility is his later writing, which extends the idea of government beyond political administration to include management of the household, the family, and the self.[7] Whereas other forms of rule employ the fear of physical punishment to regulate behaviour, Foucault argues that a governmental mentality rules through the self-management of desire. Individuals in a field of governmentality perform in ways that satisfy state, community, or organizational ends in order to realize personal aspirations for pleasure, success, security, and even a basic sense of fulfilment.

Organizers structured the social and physical space of the encampments to effect particular ends, and frequently their strategies proved successful. This, however, is only part of the story of the ACA encampments. Michel de Certeau's writing on the practices of everyday life is useful here for thinking about the disparities between organizers' prescriptions and canoeists' behaviour, the intersections between regulation and resistance.[8] De Certeau maintains that it is through the "dispersed, tactical, and makeshift creativity" of daily practices – his examples include activities such as walking and cooking – that individuals challenge the institutional order and "reappropriate the space organized by techniques of sociocultural production."[9] His description of consumers beautifully illustrates this point: "Their trajectories form unforeseeable sentences, partly unreadable paths across a space. Although they are composed with the vocabularies of established languages ... and although they remain subordinated to the prescribed syntactical forms ..., the trajectories trace out ruses of other interests and desires that are neither determined nor captured by the systems in which they develop."[10] Likewise, canoeists' experiences of the yearly meets were shaped by both organizational expectations and their own desires.

As the efforts to order the campsite and the campers, what Henri Lefebvre calls "representations of space," intersected with the canoeists' desires and trajectories, "spatial practices" in Lefebvrian parlance, they produced what the French philosopher referred to as lived space, or place.[11] Lived space, Lefebvre argues, is the space of human experience. The story of the ACA encampments, in other words, is a story of *placemaking*: each year, the organizers and canoeists, sometimes in harmony and sometimes at odds with one another, transformed the chosen site through their expectations and activities into an encampment, a recognizable place for canoeing enthusiasts to race, sleep, and socialize. The story of the ACA encampments is, therefore, also a story of community formation – which always has a spatial component.[12] Through invitation and exclusion, organizers and participants alike worked to create a visible and cohesive group of canoeists. The themes of placemaking and community formation provide a unifying thread in this book, linking topics like colonialism, domesticity, competition, and work.

Members of the ACA appropriated Indigenous technologies and practices as they camped and canoed at the annual meets. Occasionally, they acknowledged their debt to Indigenous designers, but mostly they claimed their boats and styles of camping bore little resemblance to the "crank" craft and rudimentary living arrangements of "Indians," both having been improved, in their eyes, by modern materials and methods. The canoeists did not just benefit from the ingenuity of Indigenous peoples, they were also beneficiaries of the colonial system that sought to contain, assimilate, and eradicate the continent's original inhabitants. In particular, colonial policies and structures worked to ensure that white folks had places to play that were free of Indigenous peoples. Informed by the work of scholars like Edward Said and Paige Raibmon, this book explores how colonialism as a set of state policies and a cultural milieu enabled and structured the spaces and practices of encampment life and the subject position of the canoeist.[13]

The American Canoe Association was from the start a transnational organization largely peopled and administered by Americans. The existing scholarship on the canoe, however, is remarkably Canadian, written in and about Canada.[14] Much of this work celebrates the canoe's practical contributions – the canoe was critical to the expansion of the fur trade and also to surveying the territory that would become Canada – and its symbolic contributions to nation-building. As Jamie Benidickson has shown, the canoe is ubiquitous in Canadian culture, appearing on everything from wine bottles and clothing to cigarettes and milk boxes.[15] More recently, scholars like Bruce Erickson and Misao Dean have used critical theory to produce more complex histories of the canoe and to call into question the romantic association between the canoe and Canada.[16] I have benefited greatly from this critical canoeing scholarship; I am, however, less interested in the representational qualities of the canoe than I am with the social formations that have emerged in and around the canoe. In light of the Canadian orientation of contemporary canoeing scholarship, the example of the American Canoe Association is particularly interesting for the ways in which it challenges the nationalist narratives of canoeing. How do we understand the canoe and cultures of canoeing differently when we take the ACA encampments as our starting point?

Canoeists from both sides of the Canada-US border recounted the pleasures of attending the American Canoe Association encampments in book-length travelogues, magazine pieces, and memoirs. They photographed the meets, sometimes gathering these images into albums.

They assembled collections of flags and trophies, homages to fondly remembered holidays spent in canoes and under canvas, some of which survive in personal and institutional repositories. I have used these various personal sources, as well as minutes of meetings, yearbooks, encampment circulars, and newspaper articles to reconstruct the world inhabited by the canoeists. In the 1880s, the American Canoe Association was a novel institution, and the annual encampments were unusual events that attracted significant attention in big city dailies and small town newspapers alike. Stories about the encampments appeared in periodicals across the continent, although they were more often seen in American newspapers and magazines. With time, coverage declined, albeit unevenly. By the first decade of the twentieth century, media accounts of the gatherings were spare, focusing almost exclusively on the results of the races. I suspect that the diminishing coverage was a result of the routinization of the encampments and waning interest in canoeing.

The most remarkable aspect of the ACA archive is the rich photographic collection. Much of this collection was once the property of C. Bowyer Vaux, a founding member of the ACA and, along with his wife Agnes Marion Chipp, a familiar face at the annual encampments.[17] The almost five hundred images Vaux collected and eventually donated to the New York State Historical Association, now the Fenimore Museum, document the encampments between 1880 and 1899. The photographic collection at the Fenimore also includes a series of scrapbooks covering the period 1880–1940 produced by former Commodore Fred Saunders, as well as personal scrapbooks belonging to Thomas J. Hale (1885–1900) and Walwin Barr (c. 1905–date unknown).[18] Other photograph albums and scrapbooks were accessed at the Canadian Canoe Museum and the Archives of Ontario, and in the personal collections of Bob and Marge MacKendrick, of Milford, Connecticut, and Windermere, Ontario. Following Joan Schwartz and James Ryan, I understand photographs simultaneously as "records of visual facts and as sites where those visual facts are invested with, and generate, meaning."[19] Particularly important for this project are the ways in which, to borrow from Allan Sekula, photographic practices and images "serve to legitimate and normalize existing power relationships."[20]

Canoe and Canvas is structured around the annual rhythms of organizing and attending an ACA encampment. Even as it watches the annual event unfold chronologically, this book is arranged thematically; successive chapters consider organizing, governing, inhabiting, and so on. Given this blended structure, I occasionally move back and forth in time to address thematic concerns. Chapter 1 examines two distinct but related iterations of organizing: the creation and administration of the American Canoe Association and the activities that organizers and canoeists performed throughout the year to prepare for the summer encampment. In chapter 2, I take a closer look at the locations of the ACA meets in the period between 1880 and 1910. This chapter demonstrates how hegemonic sporting practices contributed to the displacement and dispossession of Indigenous peoples, while also affecting the lives and livelihoods of white rural dwellers. The ACA encampments, like mega-sporting events more generally, required that attendees travel long distances to participate, whether as spectators or competitors. This travel was not incidental, but central to the experience of attending a meet. Chapter 3 enquires about the ways in which travel by train, steamer, and canoe variously shaped encounters with the places and people passed along the way.

The efforts of organizers and the executive committee of the American Canoe Association to order, discipline, and govern the encampments and the campers are the subject of chapter 4. This chapter also considers two particular challenges organizers faced as they pursued an orderly campsite: visitors and alcohol. Chapters 5 and 6 are concerned with how the canoeists inhabited the campsites, and thus, contributed to the production of the encampments as spaces of sport and sociability. Chapter 5 considers how the canoeists domesticated the sites through the organization of the encampment and also through decoration. Chapter 6 examines how daily routines and special events like excursions and spectacles transformed the campsites into meaningful places. Chapter 7 centres on the biggest spectacle of all: the regattas. In chapter 8, I question the framing of the encampments as exclusively recreational spaces through a consideration of workers hired by the ACA and the commercial vendors who sold their goods and services on site. The ACA encampments, this chapter makes clear, were simultaneously spaces of leisure and labour, of production and consumption.

The late nineteenth century witnessed an explosion in canoeing as sport, recreation, and leisure. Increased leisure time and greater disposable income created the material conditions for the canoe boom, while anxieties about the effects of industrial capitalism on the bodies of middle-class men offered an ideological rationale.[21] Nature and exercise were perceived as two of the most potent antidotes to the stresses of modern life, making canoeing an attractive recreational option for Victorians. Their guide in this pursuit was John MacGregor and in particular his 1866 memoir, *A Thousand Miles in a Rob Roy Canoe*.[22] MacGregor's account of travelling through the canals and rivers of Europe in a decked craft modelled on kayaks he had seen while visiting North America in 1859 was a bestseller.[23] His exploits started a "fashionable craze" in England, where "thousands of gentleman amateurs [took] to the water in imitation," including the Prince of Wales.[24] *A Thousand Miles* also found fertile soil on this side of the Atlantic, where it was eagerly read as a serial in *Harper's Weekly*, and the Rob Roy canoe was adapted to suit the conditions of North American waterways.[25]

The most prominent and prolific of the early disciples of "modern" canoeing in North America was William L. Alden, an editor at the *New York Times*.[26] Alden put the resources of the *Times* to use to celebrate the canoe, penning a number of editorials and articles on the subject in the 1870s.[27] As important as Alden's editorials were the travelogues of enthusiasts such as Nathaniel Holmes Bishop and George Washington Sears, who wrote under the pen name Nessmuk.[28] Their books and articles about travelling across the continent and traversing the Adirondacks in canoes whet the appetite of a generation of North American women and men. The growth of canoeing was also facilitated by builder boosters such as J.H. Rushton and William P. Stephens, who provided the canoes necessary to fulfil the public desire to sail or paddle, while also promoting the sport as healthful recreation.[29]

These early proselytizers had a difficult task before them. In the mid-nineteenth century, the canoe remained tethered in the minds of many white, middle-class Americans and Canadians to the Indigenous cultures to which it owed its existence. An 1865 advertisement for Wheeler and Wilson sewing machines is instructive. The advertisement claimed that the company's machines were "the boon of health and independence" for the widow and the seamstress, a welcome alternative to hand sewing, which the author conflated with "carding, spinning, weaving, and grinding corn by hand; *paddling a canoe*, fishing with bone hook, and inhabiting a hovel."[30] Enthusiasts worked hard to revision the canoe as a civilized craft worthy of middle-class attention. Borrowing from David Roediger, we might think of this process as the "whitening of the canoe."[31] In part, this was a linguistic and conceptual exercise that sought to rhetorically distance the "modern" canoe from its Indigenous past. For example, the organizers of a canoeing exhibition in New York in May 1886 endeavoured "to remove the impression that canoeing is a barbarous if not a crazy recreation, and to show that it is a sport in every way worthy of civilized and sane human beings."[32] Whitening the canoe was also about materially reimagining and reconstructing the "crank" canoe (e.g., dugout, birch) using techniques (e.g., rib and batten, lap-streak) and products (e.g., wood, tin, and copper) associated with modernity, and ultimately with civilization.[33] The American Canoe Association was integral to this project of whitening the canoe, as the following excerpt from the *New York Times* illustrates: "Little of this development from the canoe of the Indian could have taken place if every canoeist had paddled by himself. It was only through organization and the yearly exchange of new ideas that the evolution of canoeing became possible. The active agent was the American Canoe Association."[34]

Recreational canoeing in the late nineteenth century was a remarkably urban pursuit. Inspired by the broader association movement, urban enthusiasts came together in clubs.[35] The first of these was the New York Canoe Club, founded in 1871. By the turn of the century, communities large and small on both sides of the Canada-US border boasted similar organizations, which provided a physical location for storing boats, as well as spaces and opportunities for gathering and socializing with like-minded individuals. C. Bowyer Vaux, writing in 1890, described how "all manner of devices are resorted to continually to make [the club feeling] still stronger – meetings, dinners, regattas, short cruises, camp fires, 'smokers,' lectures, anything, everything, to bring the men together, for then canoe talk always follows."[36]

Canoe clubs, like sport more broadly, were largely the preserve of white, middle-class men.[37] This reflected their financial and social capital, as well as gendered understandings of sporting ability. However, canoeing was never exclusively a bourgeois masculine pursuit. Newspapers and magazines such as the *New York Times* and *Outing* occasionally included columns for women canoeists, and most canoe clubs had an associate or honorary member category that enabled white women to join, although their participation was often restricted.[38] For those without canoes or access to canoe clubs, boat liveries, such as those at Sunnyside Beach in Toronto and on the Charles River in Boston, rented canoes and rowboats at hourly and daily rates.[39] In doing so, they made canoeing accessible to the wider population of working-class people and immigrants capable of engaging in "cheap amusements," but barred from joining exclusive sporting clubs.[40]

Beyond the site-specific activities of clubs and liveries, canoeing enthusiasm also extended to "canoe cruising," a term that described journeys beyond urban areas lasting one or more days that typically married paddling or sailing with camping. Cruising was one expression of the wilderness ideal that celebrated the regenerative power of nature for bodies and minds wearied by modern urban life.[41] Cruises provided opportunities to escape the urban environments perceived as detrimental to the body, while also engaging in healthful recreation.

Out of this milieu the American Canoe Association emerged in 1880. Motivated in part by the sporting clubs and associations of the late nineteenth-century city, as well as the wilderness ideal, the association, as we shall see, was a hybrid that married home and away, domestic and wild, public and private. The organization drew on and contributed to the growing interest in both urban and wilderness canoeing manifest in canoe liveries, canoe clubs, and "cruises." We begin to uncover these connections in the following chapter by considering the formation of the American Canoe Association and the work of planning for the annual encampments.

Chapter One

Organizing

In the winter of 1880, readers of *Forest and Stream* and the *New York Times* were informed that a "general convention of canoeists" was to be held at Caldwell, New York, on Lake George in early August. The purpose of the event was "to perfect the organization of a national canoe club" and "to take such further action in the interests of the pastime as may be deemed expedient." In addition to the meetings planned for the "canoe congress," the gathering would feature sailing and paddling races. All with an interest in canoeing were invited to attend, "whether owning canoes or not." Invitations were also extended to enthusiasts in England and Canada. Interested parties were asked to send their names to Nathaniel Holmes Bishop, Esq., of Lake George.[1]

The inaugural meeting of the American Canoe Association took place six months later at Crosbyside Park on the shores of Lake George. The primary goal of the four-day gathering – to establish an American canoeing organization – was achieved on the first day. The remaining time was devoted to a regatta, which drew spectators from the local community as well as from the lakeside resorts.[2] Although most of the thirty to forty canoeists in attendance were Americans, it was a Canadian, Mr Wallace, who took first place in two of the races.[3] The campers pitched their tents adjacent to Nathaniel Bishop's cottage on the eastern side of the lake.[4] As would become commonplace at subsequent meets, they passed their evenings by the campfire, where "many a rollicking tale of adventure and many an anecdote" were shared. The gathering closed with a dinner catered by local hotelier Francis G. Crosby "at which ladies were present, and speeches were in order."[5] Small numbers aside, the first encampment was deemed a success.[6]

This chapter provides an introduction to the American Canoe Association and its annual summer encampments by considering the theme of organizing in three different but related ways. First, I explore the origins of the association, its administrative structure, and its organizational practices. To make sense of the encampments, we must understand the association to which they owe their existence. I situate the American Canoe Association within the nineteenth-century, middle-class impulse to form associations and clubs, an impulse that led Alexis de Tocqueville to call the United States a "nation of joiners."[7] Although a canoeing association served different interests than a mutual aid society or a temperance union, they often shared members, institutional structures, and values. Next, this chapter focuses on the practices of organizing that occurred throughout the year to bring the summer encampments to fruition. Although I am as interested in the routines of member canoeists as with the efforts of the organizing committees, the archive is weighted towards the latter. Third, I examine how information about the annual gatherings was organized and disseminated. Circulars, yearbooks, and previews in periodicals all played an important role in imagining the American Canoe Association and the annual encampment, which, in turn, shaped the canoeists' experiences of the event. As we shall see, besides a concern for organization, what connects these different activities – the creation of the ACA, the preparations undertaken for the annual encampment, and the information circulated to guide canoeists' planning – are the entwined themes of placemaking and community formation.

The newly minted American Canoe Association had all the trappings of a nineteenth-century voluntary association, including a well-defined and hierarchical administrative structure, a constitution and bylaws, and a public character, which Leonore Davidoff and Catharine Hall define as the property of being "open and visible to all."[8] The ACA also had a similar member profile to the voluntary associations described by Davidoff and Hall, Gerald Gamm and Robert D. Putnam, and Darren Ferry.[9]

The American Canoe Association boasted a hierarchical administrative structure that echoed both the form and some of the nomenclature of canoe clubs, yachting clubs, and naval squadrons.[10] At the helm of the organization was the commodore, who was assisted by a vice-commodore, rear-commodore, and secretary.[11] These positions, like membership more broadly, were open to canoeists from Canada and the United States; Canadians held the commodoreship seven times between 1881 and 1910.[12] Positions were for a one-year term. Although nothing prevented the incumbent from running for a second term, it was a rare occurrence.[13] The commodore was the public face of the organization, practically speaking; however, the secretary was the more important. This individual was responsible for the membership rolls, the publication of the yearbook, and organizational finances. The importance of the secretary is underscored by the fact that the position was the only one with an honorarium, a generous yearly allowance of 150 dollars, instituted in 1883.[14] Of course, election to any office heightened a canoeist's status within the ACA and could be used to strengthen an individual's social position outside of the organization as well.[15]

Three different sets of rules governed various organizational aspects of the American Canoe Association. The constitution and bylaws – first drafted at the 1880 meet and published annually in the ACA yearbook – outlined the roles and responsibilities of the officers, the definition of a canoe, annual dues, regulations for the design and bearing of club and personal signals (flags), and the timing of the yearly encampment. In the fall of 1880, a second set of rules was developed for the races; I consider these in more detail in chapter 7. Briefly, however, this set of rules declared who was eligible to participate, described the classification system for canoes, defined right of way and fouling (touching a buoy or another canoe), and laid out the timing and organization of the regatta. A third set of rules (described in chapter 4) was adopted in 1886 to structure and regulate the campsite.[16] Among other things, these rules advised campers of the hours for quiet, governed movement around the campsite, and outlined expectations for cleanliness. The three sets of rules were not static. Rather, they were constantly being expanded and revised to address new challenges facing the administration of the association, races, and campsites.

The structural organization of the American Canoe Association changed somewhat in the mid-1880s with the establishment of geographical divisions.[17] In part, this reorganization was initiated for "the convenience of government."[18] Divisions relieved the executive committee of some administrative work including membership applications and the payment of dues, making these tasks the responsibility of divisional executives. The institution of divisions also reflected the understanding that, although the annual encampment was the most important part of the association's calendar, it was impractical for most canoeists to attend the general meet.[19] Thus, each division was expected to host an annual meet within its own region similar to the yearly ACA gathering. The introduction of divisions may well have also been an attempt to entice the Western Canoe Association, organized in 1885, into joining the American Canoe Association.[20] At least one canoeist publicly opined that the ACA was "remodeled on a Federal basis to prevent any more secessions."[21] Certainly, the existence of the Western Canoe Association undermined the ACA's claim to be the representative national body for canoeing enthusiasts. Much as in federal Canadian politics, however, there was more interest in amalgamation from those in the east than from the western canoeists, who had banded together in part because they did not feel adequately represented by the ACA.[22] It was fourteen years before the Western Canoe Association agreed to join the American Canoe Association.

The institution of divisions created new administrative positions. The American Canoe Association as a whole remained under the watchful eye of the commodore and the secretary, but now each division elected a vice-commodore (who served as the divisional commodore), rear-commodore, and purser (the divisional secretary).[23] The commodore, secretary, and representatives from each of the divisions (usually the vice-commodores) formed the ACA's executive committee.[24] Additional efforts to represent the various constituents of the organization included rotating the commodoreship (this formalized an existing practice) and the location of the annual encampment between the divisions, although a division could (and occasionally did) waive the right to one or both of these privileges.[25] The structural changes were intended to improve the government of the ACA; however, the introduction of divisions also limited the democratic tenor of the organization. From 1886 onwards, it was not the membership that elected the ACA's officers, but the executive committee.[26] The affairs of the majority were now squarely in the hands of a minority, much as in a corporation.[27]

Further administrative change came in 1893 with the creation of a board of governors,[28] charged with overseeing the organization's finances and encouraging fiscal accountability. The board was but one aspect of the public character of the American Canoe Association.[29] Like other voluntary organizations in the period, the association also published the dates, times, and locations of the annual meetings in the club's official organs and in periodicals across the continent.[30] Minutes were taken at meetings and, as early as 1887, were printed in the yearbook, and usually in the pages of the official ACA organs as well. The organization's accounts were made public through similar means. Further to this, the American Canoe Association employed "experts" to audit its financial accounts and assess its dealings.[31] These practices of transparency, which were borrowed from contemporary business and political culture, were meant to signal the trustworthiness of the association, but particularly the organization's accountability to its membership.[32] They were also important tools of legitimation and performances of power. Public character was not just claimed by the leadership, it was also expected by the membership. Consider the following submission to the executive committee in 1890 regarding a change in sail rules: "In our opinion the passage, without due *publicity*, of any rule that antagonizes a considerable number tends to destroy the confidence that has always been placed in the executive committee."[33]

The American Canoe Association shared more than structural and bureaucratic features with other voluntary associations of the period. Its membership rosters also looked similar. Membership in the association was ostensibly open to "all persons of respectable character, of any age, who possess a true love of Nature, and are in earnest sympathy with the brotherhood of cruising Canoeists, whether owners of canoes or not."[34] In practice, most of the members were white, middle-class men. Like the amateur athletic associations studied by Nancy Bouchier, the American Canoe Association primarily "excluded by design."[35] A prospective member had to be able to afford the one-dollar initiation fee and yearly dues – of one dollar before 1888 and two dollars thereafter.[36] Although this was a pittance compared with the fees charged at other boating and sport clubs in the period (in 1880, the Narragansett Boat Club in Providence, Rhode Island, charged an entrance fee of 5 dollars and an annual fee of 20 dollars), it would have represented a day's wages to most manual labourers.[37] Perhaps more importantly, the association appeared to offer little to its members beyond an "official" place in the imagined community of canoeists and the opportunity to attend the yearly encampment.[38] Except for the meets in the association's first three years, these gatherings required a good two weeks' holiday, the means to travel a great distance, and additional fees.[39] In 1901, the *Watertown Daily Times*, for example, estimated that a trip to the encampment that year at Mudlunta Island in the St Lawrence River could be made for 30 dollars, and would likely cost less than 50 dollars for two weeks, including rail fare from New York or Boston – which would have further encouraged those with limited incomes to self-select.[40] Then there is the matter of canoe ownership. Although it was not necessary to have a canoe to attend an encampment, it was certainly encouraged.

The application for membership provided another opportunity to police the boundaries of the American Canoe Association. Prospective members submitted applications to the executive committee accompanied by a recommendation from a member in good standing, a requirement that reinforced existing social networks.[41] Following the advertisement of the candidate's name in the official organs of the association, a practice that allowed the broader membership to offer feedback, the application was put to a vote at a meeting of the executive committee. A three-fifths majority was required for acceptance.

I have found few instances in which an application for membership was rejected. Nevertheless, an example from 1889 is telling. This case survives because the applicant, Mr Haag, appealed the association's decision to reject his application. According to the minutes of the executive committee meeting, Haag was rejected because he was "not a proper person" with neither "the education [nor] the manners of a gentlemen."[42] Amy Milne-Smith in her work on private London clubs makes clear that social status was paramount in gaining entrance to a club. Equally important, however, were "sociability and amiability," because the "type of men who joined determined the character of the club."[43] Following Haag's appeal, Commodore Lieutenant-Colonel Henry Cassady Rogers of Peterborough, Ontario, reviewed the case. Rogers gave the executive committee the opportunity to produce evidence to support their allegations.[44] But the men only reiterated their initial position and reminded the commodore that they themselves were members in good standing. Commodore Rogers responded with the following decision, which is comparatively generous and inclusive:

> I do not wish to offer an interpretation of the word gentleman in Art. III of the constitution, although it certainly means more than male person, and I should be sorry to be the means of admitting to membership in the Association anyone who in thought and in deed did not come within the proper meaning of the term. There may be matters of personal feeling or questions as to social position, which would render it unpleasant for one man to associate with another in the close relationship of a club, but it is one of the advantages of the Association that it is broad enough and strong enough to find a place for men from all parts of the continent, in all ranks, and conditions of life, only requiring from its members that they shall be gentlemen in spirit and in conduct.[45]

Haag's case reveals that the term "gentleman" was not merely a substitute for men, but was also informed by ideas of respectability, which as historians of empire have made clear, was a deeply classed and racialized ideal.[46] Rogers suggested that one could perform this identity; the rest of the executive committee, however, remained unconvinced. Ultimately, they rejected the commodore's decision, and Mr Haag was not admitted to the American Canoe Association. Here, we see the failure of transparency and accountability. Victorian liberalism, Patrick Joyce has demonstrated, gave the appearance of fairness and objectivity, but remained influenced by partisan behaviour and, in some cases, petty interpersonal feelings.[47]

As the ACA's membership lists do not include occupations, it is difficult to produce a precise class profile for the organization. A random sample of members, however, indicates that most, particularly those who remained involved with the association over a long period of time, were middle class, numbering in their ranks medical doctors, clergy, lawyers, publishers, civil servants, and businessmen. More prominent members, including the officers, were of the upper reaches of this class, although only a few could be described as wealthy.

The first constitution of the American Canoe Association did not address the question of women members. Certainly, sport and outdoor recreation remained a largely, if not exclusively, male domain in 1880.[48] The reference to the "brotherhood of cruising Canoeists" in the original constitution might have also signalled to women their place (or lack thereof) in the organization. Women, nevertheless, wished to join the American Canoe Association, and in 1882 an honorary member category was created.[49] This change allowed white women to claim membership in the association and to attend the annual encampments. There were, however, clear limits to their participation. Women were prevented from voting or holding office.[50] There were also different rules for their membership applications. Whereas male applicants needed only a three-fifths majority, women required unanimous support from the executive committee to be admitted as members of the American Canoe Association.[51] The constitution also stipulated that the list of women members could be "revised at any time," effectively enabling the executive committee to strike women from the membership rolls at will, a provision that did not exist for men.[52] At the same time that women were officially granted honorary membership status, the membership clause in the constitution was amended so that the word "gentleman" replaced "person," thus officially limiting full membership to men.[53] It was only in 1944 that the association extended full membership to white women. The situation of women echoes Darren Ferry's observation that "initial attempts to incorporate women and ethnic minorities within voluntary associations were extremely problematic, for despite encouraging the *indirect* participation of women, men of colour and natives, voluntary associations clearly resisted their participation as equals."[54]

In addition to being middle class and male, the vast majority of the ACA membership was of Euro-American or -Canadian descent. The notable exception was the "Indian poetess" Pauline Johnson, who became an honorary member of the American Canoe Association in

1893.[55] Although the membership of the ACA was visibly white, employees of the association were not, a fact that troubles the characterization of the encampments as exclusively white spaces. As I explore in more detail in chapter 8, the history of ACA encampments includes Indigenous canoeists who performed for visitors at the 1880 and 1881 meets, the "Coon Band" who entertained campers at the 1890 meet at Jessup's Neck on Long Island, and the Black and French-Canadian men who served as cooks and valets on an ongoing basis.[56]

Finally, a word on age. Early descriptions of the encampments emphasized the generational diversity of the American Canoe Association. In an 1882 article, "About Canoeing," the *Lowell Daily Courier* reassured older canoeists: "It may be said that [while] canoeing is a manly, invigorating pastime," it is not "by any means monopolized by boys or young men." Rather, the ACA "embraces among its members men of all ages and even ladies."[57] In practice, most members of the ACA and most campers at the annual meets were between the ages of eighteen and forty, with a smaller constituency of older canoeists.[58] Children were not absent from the encampments, but particularly in the 1880s and 1890s, their numbers were small.[59] With the new century, the summer meets became more clearly family camps, although this change largely took place after the period covered by this study, so my remarks on children are necessarily limited. In this way, the ACA encampments departed from camping more broadly in the late nineteenth century, as they were not "child-centred experiences."[60]

The American Canoe Association bore many of the hallmarks of nineteenth-century associational life including a clearly defined hierarchy, multiple, overlapping lists of rules, a public character, and a commitment to respectability. Don Doyle argues that these bureaucratic structures and routines made voluntary associations "all the more suitable as schools of group discipline and parliamentary procedure," a point I explore in more depth in chapter 4.[61] Like other associations of the day, the American Canoe Association, by design, was largely peopled by white, middle-class men. But the ACA was also different from other voluntary associations. Most notably, the annual meets aside, members rarely met face to face; there were none of the weekly or biweekly meetings typical of local organizations.[62] Moreover, the American Canoe Association was without a physical headquarters. This and the rotation of the commodoreship and encampments between the different divisions guaranteed that the association represented not just one set of local circumstances, but a number of them.[63] Thus, although the American Canoe Association, as the existence of the Western Canoe Association makes clear, was never a national organization, it did represent a broad geography of interests. In the next section, we turn our attention to the preparations that organizers undertook to create a place for the canoeists travelling from points distant.

Official preparations for the inaugural encampment, which took place on Lake George from 3 to 6 August 1880, were relatively limited. Most of Nathaniel Bishop's time was likely spent advertising the meet, drawing up a regatta program, and arranging a campsite. Only three years later, however, *Forest and Stream* observed, "Instead of a small scouting party, self-contained and independent, we have an army to provide for, and must have some system, a place prepared in advance, a definite source of supplies, drinking water, sanitary arrangements, transport for a large number of boats and more or less baggage, that rob the meet of its free and extempore character."[64] By 1910, the organization of the ACA encampment was undertaken by five committees with three to five members each.[65] The expansion in the organizational bureaucracy started with the 1883 meet at Stony Lake. Whereas the three preceding meets were three or four days long, the gathering at Juniper Island lasted for two weeks. Perhaps in an effort to attract visitors and to keep them comfortable and occupied for the extended period of time, Commodore Elihu Burritt Edwards, a young Canadian lawyer, introduced a number of conveniences, including a camp store and local transportation.[66] My discussion of these preparatory practices will be necessarily brief here as I explore each of them in more detail in later chapters.

Much of the work of preparing for the encampments was conducted not by the association's brass, but by a separate organizing committee appointed when the executive committee gathered in the fall. Initially comprised of three members, at least one of whom was local to the chosen site, the organizing committee eventually expanded to include subcommittees responsible for the campsite, regatta, transportation, ladies' camp, and entertainment and music. Most of these committees had members from both sides of the Canada-US border, yet another attempt to represent the interests of the broader membership and further evidence of the organization's transnational character.[67] It was only with the creation of the ladies' camp committee in 1898 that women were formally involved in the organization of the annual encampment, although even then the committee chair was always a man.[68] The organizing committee's first official order of business was to choose a campsite. Committees, as I detail in chapter 2, were inclined towards spaces that embodied romantic aesthetics, while also offering the canoeists a certain range of amenities, including transportation routes and reliable supply chains. The designation of a site was typically performed in the fall, although occasionally it was delayed until the winter.

The winter months were given over to the surveying of the chosen campsite and the racecourses, as well as the acquisition and storage of ice. Although the latter received but cursory treatment in accounts of the meetings, surveying was more often discussed, perhaps because as a symbol of scientific rationality it underlined the organization's "modern" character.[69] A note from an 1891 Regatta Committee Report to the executive committee stresses the importance of the survey to the organization's reputation: "As the ACA is the head and front of canoeing in this country its record of performance should be in every way standard. That this may be assured it is recommended that the courses, especially the paddling courses be accurately surveyed and the surveying attested."[70]

The best account of surveying survives from the Stony Lake meet at Juniper Island.[71] In March 1883, the Canadian members of the organizing committee, E.B. Edwards and Robert Tyson, along with Provincial Land Surveyor James W. Fitzgerald, travelled north from Peterborough in a sleigh driven by Joe Vasseur, "a shrewd, good-humored French Canadian, and an excellent teamster." The group also included two local farmers, Mr McCracken and Mr Crow, and Crow's son, Willie, who likely served as axe- and chainmen for Fitzgerald.[72] With late winter still all around them, they moved between the snow-covered islands and frozen water of Stony Lake using the compass and chains to take bearings and measurements and mark off distances. These practices, which made Juniper Island and its environs visible and knowable to the organizing committee, enabled Fitzgerald to produce maps of the campsite and racecourses that were later circulated to potential visitors.[73] Here, the organizers were following the very same formula that the government and local land companies had used since the 1820s to settle this southern edge of the Canadian Shield.[74] They were also using the same personnel. James Fitzgerald had surveyed the Burleigh Colonization Road (1860–1), which facilitated white settlement in the area north of Peterborough.[75] That some of the visitors to the encampment would later purchase land on Stony Lake for cottages reinforces this connection between tourism and colonization.[76] The surveys and maps served practical purposes, but as we shall see in the chapters on (dis)placement and governance, neither practice was benign. The surveyor, to borrow from J.B. Harley, "replicates not just the environment in some abstract sense but equally the territorial imperatives of a particular political system."[77]

The winter months were also used to make travel arrangements, the subject of chapter 3. The organizing committee aided travel in a number of ways. It produced circulars, which provided prospective visitors with route, schedule, and fare information. It arranged reduced fares for passengers and facilitated the passage of canoes as freight. It worked with federal customs agencies to ease border crossings, a yearly reality for a transnational organization. Lastly, the committee coordinated local travel by arranging for the existing steamer service to include the camp wharf in its itinerary or hiring private boats or wagons to complete the last leg of the journey.

Finally, winter was the perfect opportunity to revise the regatta program and the racing rules, upon which I elaborate in chapter 7. Most programs were modelled on the previous year's schedule of events, but there were always adjustments to be made based on new technologies and the success or failure of particular races. New racing rigs also prompted revisions of the rules, as did participants' efforts to bend existing regulations to increase their chances of success.

With the ice off the waterways and the frost out of the ground, the work of "improving" the campsite began in earnest.[78] The amount and kind of improvements varied from year to year. In addition to clearing underbrush and digging wells, organizers arranged for the construction of paths and the installation of camp infrastructure.[79] The latter included tent platforms, a wharf, sanitary arrangements, and temporary buildings such as the camp store and kitchen. Much of this work, as we shall see in chapter 8, was performed not by ACA officials, but by local labourers. Members of the organizing and/or executive committees typically travelled to the site in advance of the meet to oversee these improvements.[80] It was not unusual, however, for the organization to hire someone locally to manage the work.[81]

Members also had to prepare for the annual encampments. In general, as the organizers' responsibilities expanded over this period, the campers' preparations decreased. This was the result of a growth in available transportation routes, the move to a permanent encampment in 1903, and the ACA's decision to rent tents, floors, cots, and blankets to members. On the whole, travel, especially from larger centres, became routinized, while duffle size shrank. For the canoeists, readying themselves for the ACA encampments was likely part of the more general wintertime preparations they performed in anticipation of the canoeing season. As one reporter for the *New York Times* noted in late March 1883, "Canoeing on the water does not fairly begin until May, but a vast deal of delightful canoeing is now in progress on dry land."[82] Such off-season "canoeing" included canoe upkeep, poring over catalogues, planning cruises (using maps and timetables), gathering at the clubhouse, and taking short cruises when the weather permitted.[83] Pauline Johnson's "Canoe and Canvas" series captures the longing that filled the canoeist's winter months as they waited for the weather and waterways to be amenable to their sails and paddles.[84] Presumably, for those who planned to cruise to the annual meet, the winter months were also the perfect time to gather maps and read the accounts of others who had undertaken similar journeys.

As August approached, the canoeists had to finalize their travel plans, acquire the necessary equipment, and organize their "outfits."[85] Individual ACA members and canoe clubs also employed the spring and early summer to ready their entries for the regatta.[86] Although the American Canoe Association decried the intensive training regimens associated with professional athletes, it soon became apparent that success in the regattas could not be guaranteed without some preparation. By 1885, the *New York Times* contended, "No man who is not an expert has now the slightest chance of winning in a regatta, and the combination of nerve, quickness, and technical skill shown by our best canoe sailors need only be witnessed to convince any one that canoeing is a worthy sister of yachting."[87]

The canoeists' preparations were facilitated by the information assembled and circulated by the organizing committee. Members of the ACA were kept apprised of arrangements in the pages of the association's official organs and other prominent periodicals; through circulars that arrived to their homes in the spring; and in the yearbook, which was usually delivered in early summer.[88] Together these methods of communication provided members new and old with the practical information necessary to prepare for and travel to the summer meets. Circulars and yearbooks, however, were more than tools for travel. Like the Old Home Week programs of the early twentieth century, which are the subject of John Walsh's research, ACA literature also "sought to educate the eye and ... frame the meaning of what people saw and experienced in the landscape even before they saw (or in some cases re-encountered) it."[89] Although the information communicated was tailored somewhat depending on space restrictions and the perceived audience, organizers routinely reproduced the same information in multiple locations. Organizers understood the circular, yearbook, and accounts in periodicals to be working together. For example, the site description in the circular for the 1902 Cape Cod meet advised readers, "See sketch of Camp Site in Year Book."[90] As the circulars typically offered a comprehensive overview of the association's activities and were widely accessible, they will centre this discussion of organizing and disseminating information about the meets.

Circulars functioned as guidebooks for the yearly meets of the American Canoe Association. They located the encampment in time and space, providing event dates and descriptions of the broader situation of the campsite, including notable natural and cultural features. They also located and described the main sites of the camp, namely, the headquarters, main camp, ladies' camp, and the mess tent, as well as campsite amenities such as the dark room, post office, and repair tent. Circulars provided ACA members with practical information about travelling to and from the encampments, including routes, times, and fares, as well as information about renting tent floors or camping equipment for their stay. Finally, the inclusion of sample schedules, descriptions of activities, and occasionally word pictures of camp life gave readers ideas about how they might spend their time at the summer gathering.

Photographs were rare in the circulars. More common were maps. Patrick Joyce reminds us that maps are things and "things shape and limit the way actions can be done, and doing affects knowing. Precisely because they are material, things carry meanings at the level of the habitus, the level of implicit and habitual practice."[91] Maps in conjunction with the text of the circulars organized the landscape of the encampments into readily identifiable and consumable pieces – headquarters, wharf, mess tent, camp store, main camp, ladies' camp – each with its own "conditions of possibility," which afforded particular experiences and hindered others.[92] Of course, even as maps are suggestive of certain understandings and practices, they are not deterministic. Maps, Jeff Oliver argues, are "things 'of-the-moment,' made for specific purposes but then dispersed and used in other contexts."[93] The canoeists' encounters with maps, like their encounters with the social and physical landscapes of the encampments were varied, at times dovetailing with and at other times departing from organizers' prescriptions.

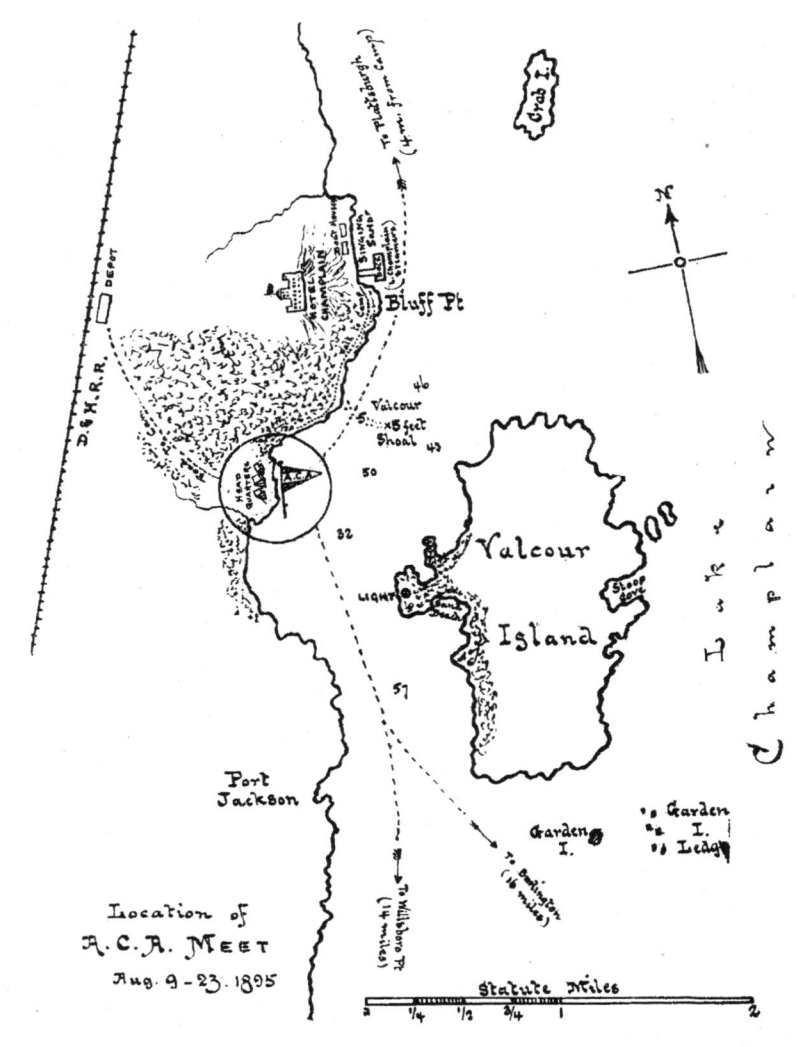

1.1 Area map of the 1895 encampment on Lake Champlain. There were two main types of maps that appeared in the meet circulars: area maps and site maps. Area maps like this one took a broader perspective, positioning the campsite vis-à-vis local landmarks, such as the stately Hotel Champlain, and nearby cities like Burlington, Vermont. Area maps made it easier for prospective canoeists to imagine the location of the encampment. They also subvert the assumption that the annual gatherings happened in wild locations. Charles E. Cragg, ed., *American Canoe Association Yearbook* (Port Henry: Press of Essex County Publishing, 1895), 10.

There was significant variation in the maps produced for the circulars, likely a reflection of the inclinations of the mapmaker or map chooser. Area maps, such as figure 1.1, employed a larger scale to indicate the location of the campsite, usually representing the site in relation to urban centres and rail lines or stations. Area maps were often reproductions of maps made for other purposes (figure 1.1 is an exception).[94] The map in the 1891 yearbook, for instance, was borrowed from the Delaware and Hudson Railroad Company, while the map included in the circular for the 1900 meet was a popular cartographic representation of Muskoka originally produced for a tourist guidebook.[95] By contrast, site maps, those maps that zeroed in on the encampment space, were almost always hand-drawn. As only two of the site maps are signed – the 1900 and 1901 maps were sketched by Commodore William Gordon MacKendrick and Secretary Herb Begg, respectively – it is difficult to know their origins.[96] We can reasonably assume, however, that they were produced by a member of the organizing committee or a surveyor such as James Fitzgerald. Some of the site maps are spare, indicating only the key parts of the campsite. Others are more detailed such as the representation of Mudlunta Island drawn by Herb Begg (figure 1.2). In addition to noting the location of different parts of the camp, this map offers descriptions of the landscape. Squaw Point (the organization's moniker for the ladies' camp) is described as "nicely shaded every tent overlooking river."[97] Many site maps named locations in the vicinity of the encampment including bays, points of land, and nearby islands.[98] The map for the 1893 encampment at Brophy's Point on Wolfe Island, for example, made note of Abraham Head, McDonnell's Bay, Knapp's Point, and Milton Island.[99] The presence of these names makes clear that the American Canoe Association encampments never took place in uninhabited wilderness, but rather in places with longer human histories, a subject I explore more fully in the next chapter.

Of course, as Patrick Joyce has observed, maps are "of interest for what they leave out as well as what they put in."[100] With the exception of the map produced for the 1900 encampment in Muskoka, at Birch Point on Lake Rosseau, none of the site maps include representations of the sanitary arrangements. This is surprising given that sanitation was a very public matter in the late nineteenth century.[101] Less surprising is the absence of any indication of where servants or workers were accommodated. As we shall see, they were an important, if largely invisible component of camp life.

Even as the circulars provided canoeists with practical information about travel, accommodations, and food services, they also endeavoured to shape the experiences of campers attending the meets by

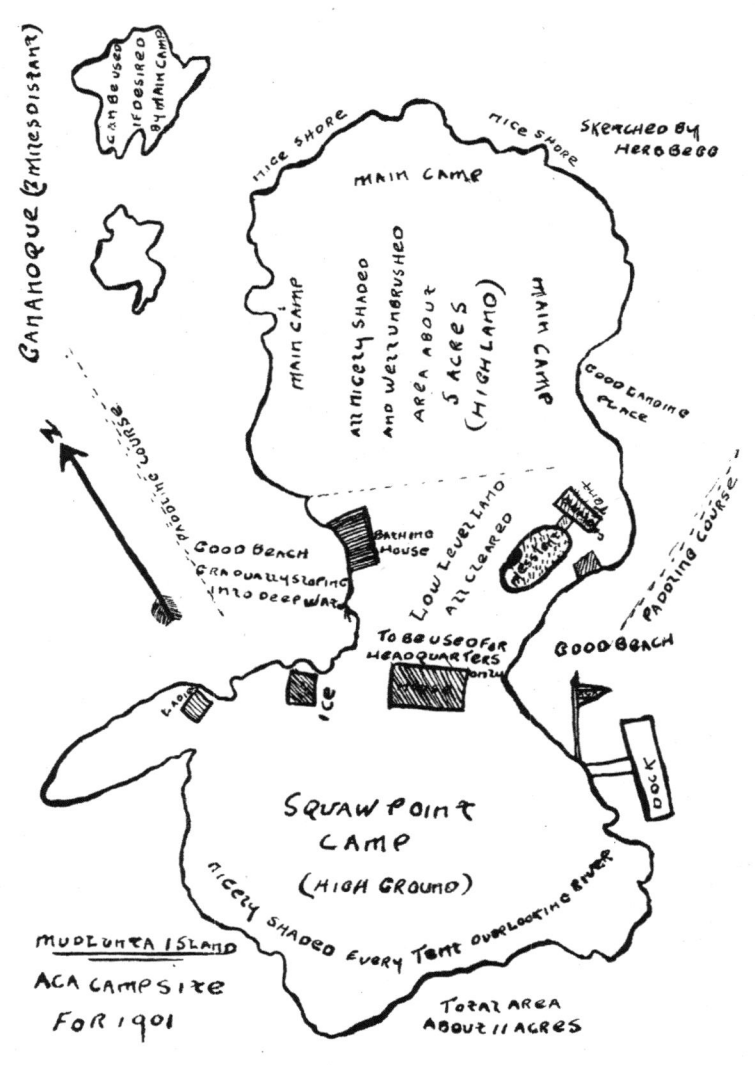

1.2 Site map of the 1901 encampment on Mudlunta Island. With the exception of locating Gananoque "2 miles distant," the 1901 map focuses exclusively on the campsite, making it an example of a site map. It is also notable for being one of the more expressive drawings, including evaluative descriptions of different parts of the site. The "good" beach, for example, is described as "gradually sloping into deep water." Maps such as this one were part of the ACA's attempts to entice prospective members. Herb Begg, ed., *American Canoe Association Yearbook* (New York City: Forest and Stream Publishing, 1901), 10.

preparing them to know, see, and inhabit the spaces of the encampments in particular ways. Of course, the canoeists also encountered unofficial information about encampment life as they spoke to friends and relatives, and read book, magazine, and newspaper accounts of the yearly events. These alternative sources may have worked at cross-purposes to the objectives of the organizers, or they may have reinforced official expectations. As Cecilia Morgan notes, tourists' "accounts make it clear that ... they also brought their own needs, fantasies, and desires to bear on the meanings that they attributed to such attractions. These were not uncomplicated processes."[102] What's more, the canoeists did not necessarily read the official information as intended. To borrow from Roger Chartier, "cultural consumption ... is at the same time a form of production, which creates ways of using that cannot be limited to the intentions of those who produce."[103] The consequences of these varied and at times conflicting understandings of participation in an ACA encampment will be considered in chapter 6, on inhabiting.

Founded in 1880 on the shores of Lake George in the Adirondack Mountains, the American Canoe Association was at once a novel institution and an unremarkable one. The first (trans)national canoeing organization in the world, it was nevertheless of a piece with other voluntary associations of the late nineteenth century, including political societies, philanthropic institutions, and arts and science associations. All shared similar institutional structures, values, and practices. Sporting clubs and associations, like other voluntary institutions, were never only about the things they purported to be about, in this case, canoeing, fresh air, and socializing. The organizational activities of the American Canoe Association, which drew heavily from contemporary political culture, made the organization "suitable as schools of group discipline and parliamentary procedure," a theme I explore in chapter 4, and membership practices produced an exclusive community that normalized the rule and privileges of white, middle-class manhood.[104] White, middle-class women were offered a place in the organization, albeit not one of equality, while working-class folks and people of colour were always at the margins. This at once mirrored and reinforced the existing social order in late nineteenth-century North America.

The annual encampment was the most important event in the American Canoe Association's calendar. Although the meet only occupied two weeks in August, preparations began long before the canoeists stepped onto the wharf, and the memory of the encampment lingered well after the last tent had been packed away. The association, in the form of the organizing committee, identified a location, facilitated transportation, and prepared the campsite. Individual canoeists also participated in "organizing" by learning about the destination, packing their duffle, and arranging for travel, which in some cases included planning a canoe cruise. The information produced and distributed by the organizing committee and gathered by enthusiastic campers as they readied themselves for the summer gathering shaped how canoeists imagined and constructed the encampment as a social and physical space. The dialogue between official descriptions, ancillary accounts, and canoeists' own imaginings represented an important part of the ongoing and contested process of placemaking, just as disputes over access to the American Canoe Association and the encampment served to shape the community of canoeists. Neither of these processes was geographically dislocated. Rather, they were rooted in specific places. In the next chapter, I consider the different locales and campsites in greater detail, using sources contemporary to the period to offer some sense of the historical and material landscapes that visitors to the encampments encountered, as well as of the colonial politics of placemaking.

Chapter Two

(Dis)Placing

In 1930, almost three decades after the American Canoe Association acquired a permanent encampment in the St Lawrence River, the evening entertainment at the annual meet included a "re-enactment" of the 1901 purchase of Sugar Island. In front of an audience of fellow ACA members, two "white traders" negotiated with four "Indians."[1] The Indians, which included a "Squaw," a "Brave," a "Chief," and "a Medicine Man," were clothed in stereotypical and historically inaccurate costumes: dark blankets, multicoloured face paint, and, in the case of the chief, a headdress reminiscent of the people of the Plains, not the Nishinaabeg or Haudenosaunee on whose territory they were gathered. Although the dress and narrative were historically inaccurate – the ACA purchased the island from the Canadian government, not directly from an Indigenous nation – there was no attempt to conceal those who were displaced by the exchange. If anything, the performance legitimized the purchase and further confirmed the ACA's right to the land.

This chapter attends to questions of space and place, bringing to the fore the relationship between sport, geography, and colonialism.[2] The American Canoe Association encampments were not located just anywhere; as we shall see, the sites were chosen (and debated over) for specific reasons. These contests over the placing of the yearly meets resonated beyond the narrow confines of the association. As Edward Said reminds us, every act of possession is an act of dispossession.[3] In colonialism, to borrow from Cole Harris, "one human geography [is] superseded by another, both on the ground and in the imagination."[4] The ACA encampments are no exception. As the organization occupied islands and points of land on the St Lawrence River, in the Adirondacks, and on Long Island, it contributed to the displacement of both Indigenous inhabitants and white settlers. The American Canoe Association was complicit in a larger colonial project well underway on both sides of the Canada-US border in the late nineteenth century that sought to isolate, assimilate, and, ultimately, to eradicate Indigenous peoples.[5] It was also part of a colonizing tourist industry that transformed spaces of production into spaces of consumption, writing local lives and livelihoods out of the landscape and replacing them with more convenient and profitable – to the ACA – fictions.[6]

Following a discussion of the debate over a mobile or permanent encampment and the criteria employed in choosing a campsite, I describe the regions in which the American Canoe Association gathered between 1880 and 1910. I am interested in the physical and social geographies of these areas, but particularly their histories as Indigenous homeplaces and as tourist destinations. This part of the chapter sets the stage for the concluding section, which considers the politics of displacement effected by this particular manifestation of sport tourism.[7] Given the number of encampment locations, I restrict my commentary in this final section to the case of Sugar Island, the site of the organization's permanent encampment. Nevertheless, many of the principles and effects of occupation are relevant to the other locations where the ACA gathered for their summer encampment. Taken together, the sections in this chapter highlight the physical and psychical displacement caused by white, middle-class practices of sport and leisure. As we shall see, the American Canoe Association encampments, both mobile and permanent, contributed in a variety of ways to delimiting, displacing, and dispossessing Indigenous peoples and other rural dwellers.

At the time of its founding in 1880, it was assumed that the American Canoe Association would gather annually on Lake George in perpetuity. That fall, charter members Nathaniel Bishop, Nicholas Longworth, and Lucien Wulsin purchased three islands in the centre of the lake to be used for a permanent encampment.[8] Early appraisals of the Canoe Islands were positive. At the close of the 1881 meet, the *New York Times* pronounced these islands "as delightfully situated for a Summer camping-ground as any place imaginable."[9] Yet, already by the next year, a number of complaints had been made about the Canoe Islands.[10] The main island was deemed too small for the burgeoning organization, and the racecourse, which remained off the shore of the Crosbyside Hotel, was judged to be too far from the campsite.[11] The "flawy" winds were unsuited to sailing, and the journey to Lake George was unnecessarily arduous.[12] As one visitor noted, "Many and bothersome were the portages from railway to steamer, from steamer to railway, from railway car to express wagon, from wagon to boat; many were the lifts; many were the bumps and jolts and scratches that the canoes had to endure," and presumably their owners as well.[13] Finally, there was a growing sense the members of the association had become "amusers for hotel crowds," Lake George being a popular destination for tourists from New York City.[14] An invitation from the newly elected commodore, Elihu Burritt Edwards, to hold the 1883 meet in the Kawarthas, north of his hometown of Peterborough, Ontario, provided the perfect opportunity for the association to test another location.[15] Edwards's suggestion was taken up, the encampment on Juniper Island on Stony Lake was deemed a success, and so the executive committee, with the support of the membership, decided to try a third site for the 1884 meet rather than return to Lake George.

The decision, made in 1882, to abandon the Canoe Islands marked the beginning of twenty years of mobile encampments. Between 1883 and 1902, the summer gathering of the American Canoe Association was held in fifteen different locations in Ontario, New York, and New England.[16] A mobile encampment was appealing to ACA members for a number of reasons, not least because it provided them an opportunity to visit new places. Canadian canoeist Vincent Clementi was in "no doubt that the establishment of a permanent camp would be beneficial." Nevertheless, he pointed out, "It should not be lost sight of that when we go from home for a holiday in the summer ... we like to visit various localities, and pick up new ideas or 'notions.'"[17] For the ACA, a steady rotation of campsites had the potential to attract new adherents, a fact that was amply proven at the Stony Lake meet in 1883. As only members could erect tents on Juniper Island and compete in the races, ACA membership numbers spiked in the months leading up to the event: 450 members registered for the organization's first two-week encampment, a 200 per cent increase from the previous year.[18] Even as mobile encampments had their advantages, it was both expensive and time-consuming to find and establish new camps every year. Moreover, for some people, the mobile meet was too much like the lives of professional racing oarsmen, who "go on the road posting themselves before rival hotels."[19] Mobility among athletes in the late nineteenth century was associated with professionalism – the antithesis of respectable middle-class sport.

Discussions of a permanent home for the encampments took place intermittently through the 1880s and 1890s. Supporters, which included the editors of *Forest and Stream*, argued that a permanent campsite would enable the ACA to invest in improvements such as landings, storehouses, and stake boats that would make for more comfortable and efficient operations.[20] Furthermore, a permanent location would allow the organization to develop advantageous relationships with local transportation and supply companies, the benefits of which could be passed onto members. *Forest and Stream* also believed a permanent encampment could be "a part of a man's life that he looks both backward and forward to with increasing pleasure each summer," akin to the farm of his youth or his alma mater. A "short halting place, whence one departs younger, stronger, and better."[21]

On a handful of occasions, a committee was struck to investigate the feasibility of acquiring land for an ACA campsite, but with no visible result.[22] When, in 1894, the association held a vote to gauge support for a permanent encampment, the membership voted overwhelmingly in favour of mobile meets.[23] Former Commodore Charles Edward Britton, of Gananoque, admitted the difficulty of currying support among the members for an ACA camp. In a 1901 letter, Britton explained, "It has taken some years to work them up to a fixed place, many preferring the Bohemian mode of moving from place to place."[24] In spite of opposition from the general membership, another committee was struck in 1900 to search for a permanent camp.[25] This time, the committee fulfilled its mandate, purchasing an island on the St Lawrence River from the Dominion Department of Indian Affairs.[26] That the committee appears not to have consulted the membership may go some way in explaining its success.

Prior to the acquisition of Sugar Island – located near to the community of Gananoque, which today bills itself as the "Gateway to the Thousand Islands" – the task of choosing a campsite was an important, if largely unregulated, component of preparing for the annual meet of the American Canoe Association. The executive committee would hear site suggestions and supporting arguments at its fall meeting. Campsite recommendations were welcomed, if only occasionally solicited.[27] Some members sent in their proposals by mail, others wrote letters to the editors of the official ACA organs, still others made their pitches in person.[28] If a site was not agreed upon at the fall meeting, the executive committee charged the organizing committee to investigate particular locations and report back. In such cases, the location was announced in the wintertime.

There were no official ACA criteria for choosing a site for the encampment, though not just any site would do.[29] The general feeling was that the encampment should be "far enough away from hotels and summer travel destinations to preserve the privacy and independence of the camp,"[30] while still being accessible and well-serviced.[31] An accessible location would have ample transportation routes at hand and be close to the Canada-US border. Within a few short years of the ACA's founding, rising Canadian membership meant the ideal camp was one located close to, although not necessarily in, the Dominion of Canada.[32] While the 1883 Stony Lake and the 1900 Muskoka camps were certainly enjoyed, there was a sense they were too far from the clubs on the eastern seaboard that furnished the American Canoe Association with the bulk of its membership. This sentiment was clearly manifested in the dismal attendance numbers at the 1900 meet: only 175 of the ACA's almost 4,000 members visited Birch Point on Lake Rosseau in Muskoka.[33] Poor attendance was not limited to inland Canadian encampments. The Camp Site Committee Report for the 1902 meet on Cape Cod, located in the Eastern Division, is replete with the chairman's frustration with participant numbers. The site had been chosen to appeal to those from away, but most of the canoeists who attended that year were from the area. Had the chairman known this would be the case, he declared, a site could have been chosen that was more attractive to members of the Eastern Division.[34] The best-attended encampments were located in the borderlands such as those on the St Lawrence River. Accessibility also referred to the ease with which the organizers could acquire the necessary goods to outfit the camp and feed the campers. For many years thereafter, the 1890 encampment at Jessup's Neck served as a cautionary tale of inadequate supply lines.[35]

Equally important to the choice of location were aesthetics; the site had to be attractive. What was meant by attractive, however, is somewhat perplexing. In the same breath, the 1900 camp at Birch Point was praised for being picturesque and derided for being too rough.[36] More congenial to the ACA membership were the "cultivated" sites of Grindstone Island in the St Lawrence River and Long Island on Lake George. The former was a farmer's field, although there were small woodlots adjacent to the main camp, while the latter was described as "delightfully wooded with cedars and other trees, and yet afford[ing] ample clear, open ground and grassy glades for camping."[37] Of course, sites could be reformed, as in the case of Jessup's Neck, whose "wild and roughly wooded shore" required "a great deal of work to be done" in order to "be made fit for a large camp."[38] Wild but not too wild appears to have been the consensus.

Other points of consideration for the organizing committee were more practical, such as the availability of fresh water, the terms of occupancy and rental fees, and the suitability of the site for racing. Occasionally, the American Canoe Association paid to rent the space for the annual encampment. This was true of the Muskoka meet.

Most years, however, the land was free.[39] The experience of the 1890 organizing committee brought into stark relief the importance of good relations with the site's owners. In the pages of that year's circular, the committee revealed that their work had been "seriously complicated by a long and vexatious course of negotiations among the owners."[40] Racecourses posed an additional challenge for the organizing committee because the regatta featured both paddling and sailing contests. Whereas paddling races were best conducted on calm water, sailing competitions required wind. In practice, it was difficult to accommodate both types of races successfully.

Given the importance attached to the site and the ACA's proclivities for regulation, it is surprising there were never any formal criteria established for choosing an encampment location. Perhaps officials felt the somewhat informal bid-style process afforded ample oversight. Regardless, the choice of location was not entirely without direction. In particular, it was shaped by practical concerns, aesthetic considerations, and accessibility, broadly understood. With these factors in mind, the ACA's executive committee identified what it judged to be suitable locations for a gathering of canoeing enthusiasts.

From its origins amid the weathered mountains of the Adirondacks to the rocky, wooded shorelines of the Canadian Shield and the deciduous forests of the St Lawrence Lowlands to the soaring Palisades of the Hudson River and the coastal communities of Cape Cod and Long Island, the American Canoe Association gathered in a number of iconic landscapes in northeastern North America in the period covered by this study. The physical environment, which was regularly represented in admiring descriptions in the circulars and accounts of the encampments, was more than a backdrop for the annual meet. It was an integral part of the experience, a participant even in constituting the ACA encampments as places and the association as a community. There was more to these sites than their physical geography. Each also had long histories of human use and occupation, which the organization alternately acknowledged and ignored. In each location, the ACA contributed to the reimagination of the local landscapes as spaces of tourism and leisure. In places with an established tourist trade, the ACA was reinforcing an existing representation; in other locales, the encampments were an important catalyst in this transformation.

Lake George was the site of the first three encampments (1880, 1881, 1882), as well as the 1888 meet. "A little over 33 miles long, running north and south," and "nearly four [miles] wide at the broadest place," the lake boasted more than two hundred islands.[41] Although founding member Nathaniel Bishop had a summer residence there, Lake George was also a logical choice for the first encampment because of its location in the Adirondack Mountains, which had been a popular destination for outdoor enthusiasts since the 1860s.[42] Lured by the travel writing of "Adirondack" Murray and the photographs and guidebooks of Seneca Ray Stoddard, men and women from the eastern seaboard flooded into the area to pass the summer months under canvas or in one of the luxury hotels.[43] By 1880, Lake George was home to numerous resorts and private summer residences.[44]

Although visitors to the area conceived of the Adirondacks as untouched wilderness, in the late nineteenth century, the region was home to a diverse if scattered local population. After the American Revolution, the Adirondack region, which prior to Contact had been home to Algonquian peoples and Haudenosaunee (Iroquois), was populated by a "variety of newcomers" including Kanien'kehá:ka (Mohawk) from Akwesasne, Abenaki refugees from New England, French Canadians, and Yankees from Vermont.[45] There were no official reserves in the area, but census records and settler accounts from the late nineteenth century locate Native American inhabitants near Saranac Lake, Indian Lake, and Long Lake.[46] Reports found in the ACA archive indicate there was also an Indigenous encampment at Caldwell on the southern tip of Lake George.[47] More than likely, these would have been Abenaki and Kanien'kehá:ka families.[48] The census listed most of the inhabitants, Indigenous and otherwise, as farmers, although occupational plurality was a more likely reality for Adirondack residents. Tourism provided opportunities for men to work as guides and for women "to bring their domestic skills as cooks and housekeepers into the marketplace."[49] The tourist industry also placed further pressure on local resources and introduced new class divisions.

The first Canadian encampment and the first ACA meet away from Lake George was held on Juniper Island on Stony Lake, just north of Peterborough, Ontario, in 1883.[50] Situated at the confluence of the Canadian Shield and the St Lawrence Lowlands in the "long chain of lakes and water stretches known as the Trent Waters," Stony Lake boasted a rugged northern shoreline of granite and coniferous trees and a smooth southern shoreline dominated by deciduous forest.[51] This was and is Michi Saagiig Nishnaabeg (Mississauga) territory, though the Wendat and Haudenosaunee also have relations to this land.[52] Under pressure from the Crown, the Michi Saagiig signed Treaty 20, a land cession treaty, in 1818.[53] Eleven years later, they were relocated to three reservations, one of which, Mud Lake (now Curve Lake), was just north of Stony Lake.[54] The relocation of the Michi Saagiig made way for more intensive white settlement in the area around Peterborough.

Today, Stony Lake is primarily a cottaging community. Its development for tourism, however, did not begin in earnest until the turn of the twentieth century.[55] Before that time, a traveller was more likely to see the faces and dwellings of farmers and lumbermen on the lake's shores; it was only occasionally a destination for settler outings.[56] Susanna Moodie describes canoeing on Stony Lake in *Roughing It in the Bush*: "Oh, what a magnificent scene of wild and lonely grandeur burst upon us as we swept round the little peninsula, and the whole majesty of Stony Lake broke upon us at once, another Lake of the Thousand Isles in miniature, and in the heart of the wilderness! ... Never did my eyes rest on a more lovely or beautiful scene. Not a vestige of man, or of his works was there ... We beheld the landscape, savage and grand in its primeval beauty."[57] Commodore E.B. Edwards forewarned visitors that the lake, while "easily accessible" was "removed from the sophistications of civilizations": "Visitors to it must expect no summer resort hotels, no ball-rooms, banquets, or brass bands, but a backwoods camping-ground, with paddling and fishing for amusements in the daylight, and the song or tale around the camp-fire at night."[58] Steamer service had only just started when the 1883 encampment took place, and options for accommodations beyond a tent site were virtually non-existent.[59]

The American Canoe Association encampment drew attention to Stony Lake as a potential holiday destination.[60] Following the lead of Commodore Edwards and Lieutenant-Colonel Rogers, who had purchased Juniper Island from the Dominion Department of Indian Affairs (DIA) in anticipation of the ACA meet, some of the campers acquired lots on Stony Lake, upon which they later erected cottages and summer homes.[61] Although the area's original inhabitants had been sequestered on reserves by this point, early cottagers "recall Native women paddling from cottage to cottage with quill baskets and beadwork."[62] We can assume that Michi Saagiig would have been a visible presence on Stony Lake in 1883, although tellingly they do not appear in accounts of the ACA gathering.

Between 1880 and 1902, just under half of the American Canoe Association encampments took place in the Thousand Islands, the portion of the St Lawrence River stretching between Kingston and Brockville, Ontario, and Cape Vincent and Morristown, New York. The Thousand

Islands, which serve as the border between Ontario and New York, provided a transnational location for a transnational organization. In total, the American Canoe Association held ten encampments in the St Lawrence: five on Grindstone Island (1884–86, 1896–97), two on Stave Island (1889, 1898), and one on each of Wolfe Island (1893), Hay Island (1899), and Mudlunta Island (1901). The association's permanent encampment on Sugar Island is also located in the St Lawrence River.

Over the course of the nineteenth century, as Patricia Jasen has demonstrated, the introduction of rail travel and the expansion of steamer service transformed the Thousand Islands into a "mass tourist attraction."[63] Panoramic river cruises on the St Lawrence were in vogue in the first half of the century. By century's end, islands on the Canadian and American sides of the river were "dotted with fashionable hotels, cottages, camp grounds, and the mansions of American millionaires."[64] The settler occupation of the Thousand Islands was never just for tourism. A number of the larger islands such as Grindstone and Wellesley were farmed, and both shores of the St Lawrence River boasted "small-scale processing industries," "metal-fabricating plants," and "extractive industries" that produced everything from stoves and sandstone to meat and lawnmowers.[65]

At the time of the first ACA encampment on the St Lawrence, most of the Indigenous peoples that called the Thousand Islands home had been relocated to reserves, both near and far. The transborder St Regis–Akwesasne Reserve near Cornwall, Ontario, was now the official home of the region's Kanien'kehá:ka (Mohawk) people, while the Michi Saagiig Nishnaabeg had been relocated to the Alnwick Reserve (now Alderville First Nation) in Northumberland County.[66] The Kanien'kehá:ka, because of their location on the St Lawrence, were well established in the river's burgeoning tourist industry as boat captains and souvenir vendors by the time of the first Grindstone Island meet.[67]

To the south and west of the Thousand Islands was another popular ACA destination, Lake Champlain. Four encampments were held there: one at Bow Arrow Point (1887), two at Willsborough Point (1891 and 1892), and one at Bluff Point (1895). At Contact, the Champlain Valley was home to Kanien'kehá:ka, Mahican, and Western Abenaki.[68] For the Western Abenaki, the long narrow lake, which they call Bitawbagok, meaning "lake between," is the site of their creation stories.[69] Owing to war and disease, most of the Abenaki had relocated to southern Quebec by 1800, although members of that community returned to the lake seasonally.[70] In the late nineteenth century, Lake Champlain, which sits immediately to the north of Lake George, was perhaps best known for its involvement in the War of 1812.[71] However, by the time of the first ACA encampment in the area, in 1887, Fort Ticonderoga was but a shadow of its former glory, a "most picturesque old ruin" that featured prominently in local guidebooks.[72] Flanked to the west by the Adirondack Mountains and to the east by the Green Mountains, the shorelines of Lake Champlain were not characterized by steep cliffs, but by agricultural land. Steamers on the lake served the local farm families, as well as industries including lumber mills, marble quarries, and magnetite mines. Steamers also serviced the resort hotels that had developed over the latter part of the nineteenth-century century to accommodate the growing numbers of tourists.[73]

The first of the American Canoe Association's two saltwater encampments took place in 1890 on Jessup's Neck, a small point of land on Peconic Bay on the eastern end of Long Island. Many, many years before it was transformed into a fashionable tourist destination, Algonquian peoples inhabited Long Island. Shinnecock and Montauk made their home on the eastern tip of the island. The arrival of European settlers in the mid-seventeenth century had a profound effect on both Indigenous nations. However, contrary to the assumption that by the nineteenth century the Shinnecock and Montauk had all but disappeared, there remains an Indigenous presence on Long Island to this day.[74] In 1890, there were two reservations on the eastern end of the island: one for the Montauk at the tip and a second near Southampton for the Shinnecock. Indigenous families living in these communities, like their white neighbours, were mostly farmers and fishers whose produce appeared on the dinner tables of New York City.[75] The extension of the Long Island Railroad to Southampton in 1870 made the eastern tip of the island a mere two-and-a-half-hour train ride from the city, and prompted the development of resort tourism, as well as the construction of summer homes, which disrupted local economies and communities.[76]

The soaring and storied palisades of the Hudson River provided the backdrop for the 1894 meet at Croton Point. Richard Gassan locates the origins of American tourism in the Hudson River Valley – in the 1810s – as a result of "a confluence of historical accidents, including the valley's proximity to the most rapidly growing financial center in the United States, its remarkable scenery, and its geographical position as a waterway that connected some of the country's most sought-after destinations."[77] Along the river's banks, a waterway immortalized in ink and paint by author James Fenimore Cooper and artist Thomas Cole, "unfolded the whole gamut of picturesque imagery: wild mountains and gentle valleys, quaint farms and tidy villages, nature mixed with culture in ever-changing configurations."[78] The Hudson River was part of the American Grand Tour, an imitation of the European Grand Tour that included stops in Albany, Niagara Falls, Montreal, Quebec, and New England.[79] The Hudson was also a working river that serviced the many industries and towns along its shores. Canoeists travelling to the 1894 meet by train or boat would have found it hard to miss the sights and smells of the expansive brickmaking industry that employed more than 7,000 workers in 130 manufactories on the river's shores.[80]

It is unlikely that the canoeists would have encountered any of the Munsee, Mahican, or Mohican people that had historically called the Hudson River Valley home. The Algonquian-speaking peoples were a visible presence on the river until the early eighteenth century when they were forcibly removed to central New York State, Massachusetts, and Connecticut. Most of the Munsee and Mohican, now known as the Stockbridge-Munsee, were further removed to the Wisconsin Territory in the early nineteenth century, well before the ACA meet at Croton Point.[81] Inspired by Cooper's *The Last of the Mohicans*, most of the canoeists at the 1894 meet likely assumed that this particular line of "noble savages" had been extinguished.

Muskoka developed as a tourist destination later than its more southerly counterparts. Nevertheless, by the turn of the century, the region "was by far the most popular destination in Ontario for holidays of any length, and its reputation was still growing."[82] Located 150 kilometres north of Toronto, Muskoka boasted the lakes, windswept pines, and rugged shorelines characteristic of the Canadian Shield. The Robinson Treaty of 1850 deposed the Anishnaabeg (Ojibwe) that had long occupied the north and eastern shores of Lake Huron to make way for white industry and settlement.[83] If from the perspective of the state, Anishnaabeg title to the land had been extinguished, communities remained at Rama and Parry Island, and the Ojibwe continued to return each year to hunt and trap in the Muskoka region.[84] There was also a reserve at Gibson near Bala that was home to Haudenosaunee who had relocated from Oka, Quebec, to Muskoka in the 1880s.[85]

In the middle decades of the nineteenth century, much of the region's shoreline was remade by axe and plow, lumbering proving more successful than agriculture on the thin layer of nutrient-poor soil that overlay the Canadian Shield.[86] The islands, however, remained largely wooded and thus attractive to the "eager but ill-equipped nature seekers" that travelled north from Toronto.[87] As in other locales, the arrival of the railway to the lakeside community of Gravenhurst in 1875 prompted a rapid increase in the numbers of visitors.[88] Most of them tended to stay in the newly completed resorts like the Royal Muskoka or the Windermere, or they built their own cottages. As the lumber industry moved north and farming became increasingly untenable, most local people, including Anishnaabeg and Haudenosaunee, were drawn into the tourist industry both directly and indirectly.

Chatham on Cape Cod (1902), the site of the second of two saltwater encampments and the last mobile meet before the American Canoe Association settled on Sugar Island, offered visitors a markedly different landscape. Stunted trees, long grasses, and undulating sand dunes constituted the visual landscape, while the waves rolling in from the North Atlantic dominated the aural one. The canoeists referred to their encampment at Chatham as Camp Nauset. The Nauset were one of the Indigenous communities that had historically called Cape Cod home; they were part of what in the 1920s would come to be called the Wampanoag Nation, a confederation that also included the Mashpee. Around the turn of the century, the Mashpee occupied a reserve on the western end of the Cape, near the ACA campsite.[89]

Cape Cod at the time of the ACA meet in 1902 was an economically depressed region with a rudimentary tourist industry. The fishing and shipbuilding industries that had long supported the local population began a steady decline in the mid-nineteenth century, a trend mirrored in the local manufacturing sector by century's end.[90] Cape Cod had all the building blocks for a successful tourist industry including "sublime landscapes, native legends, the tales of weather-beaten 'old salts,'" and adequate transportation services; nevertheless, for much of the nineteenth century, it was "regarded as a kind of New England outback, inhabited by unschooled savages with almost no contact with the outside world."[91] The easterly tip of Massachusetts was not entirely foreign to travellers, having been the subject of Henry David Thoreau's posthumously published *Cape Cod* (1865).[92] However, Thoreau's characterization of the Cape as the "most uninviting landscape on earth" was not altogether flattering, and tourism remained sluggish until the interwar period.[93] It was the automobile that transformed Cape Cod into the tourist mecca it is today.

Many of the places visited by the American Canoe Association were either established vacation spots when the organization set up camp or the association played a part in drawing tourists to these locales. None of these places, however, was ever just a tourist destination. As Karl Jacoby writes about the Adirondacks, "It was a place of abandoned farms and of grand new estates, where daily rhythms were set by commercial timber operations and by subsistence agriculture, by wage labor and by household chores, by summer tourism and by winter trapping, foraging, and lumber camps."[94] Such economic and social richness also characterized the other locations where the annual ACA gatherings were held. This richness was rarely visible to the canoeists, however, in part because of the work of the contemporary tourism industry, but also because of Victorian bourgeois cultures of seeing that rendered Other lifeways invisible to them.

The American Canoe Association held its first summer gathering on Sugar Island from 7 to 21 August 1903, having purchased the site for a permanent encampment two years earlier. In the years that followed, the organization and its members bought all of the adjacent islands from the Department of Indian Affairs as well, "to keep [them] in the very best hands."[95] By 1907, the board of governors could declare that the ACA was "entirely free now from any outside interference that heretofore has been somewhat anticipated by those in authority."[96] With the move to Sugar Island, the association no longer had to engage in the yearly practices of choosing and preparing a site. Instead, the organizing committee could turn its attention to the seemingly more manageable task of maintenance. Likewise, for most ACA members, the annual pilgrimage to Sugar Island came to be characterized not by learning a new place, but by reconnecting with an old one.

The DIA archive claims that Sugar Island and "other islands in the immediate vicinity were surrendered to the Crown by the Indian owners on the 19th June, 1856 in order that such disposition might be made of the property as would be in the best interests of the Indian owners."[97] From the viewpoint of the Alnwick Band (now Alderville First Nation), this settlement only applied to mainland territory. There remained "a number of unceded islands located in the Bay of Quinte, South Bay, and Lake Ontario, and between Kingston and 'Guananoque,'" which the community continued to use for fishing at least until the 1880s.[98] Initially, the Crown, wishing to open the land to white settlement and use, pushed the Alnwick Band, and other Indigenous nations in the region, to surrender any remaining land forthwith.[99] Later, it simply denied the existence of unceded territory. The Alnwick Band passed a resolution in 1884 in which "it expressed its willingness to surrender almost all of these non-reserve lands for the sum of $80,000" with the proviso that it kept "the fishing islands in the Bay of Quinte, the St Lawrence, and Rice Lake, as well as 'any other islands belonging to the said Band' for their own exclusive use." Nine years later, the Crown finally responded by rejecting the claim "on the basis that the First Nations had already been compensated for all their surrender lands in the 1818 treaties."[100] Thus, at the same time that the American Canoe Association was hosting encampments in the St Lawrence, most notably on Grindstone Island, the Michi Saagiig were fighting for access to the very islands on which the organization was camped.

During this period of protracted "negotiation," Sugar Island was home to white inhabitants. James McDonald, the keeper of the Jack Straw and Narrows lighthouses, and his descendants occupied Sugar Island from 1827 until the mid-1880s.[101] The island also had more temporary residents. In 1885, George Keys, of Lansdowne, Ontario, applied to the Department of Indian Affairs for the right to pasture his cattle on the island.[102] Others used the land for similar purposes, if not always with permission.[103] Beginning in 1894, the DIA started to receive requests for Sugar Island from interested buyers. That the Department chose to have the area surveyed by Charles Unwin in January 1873 indicates that such requests had been anticipated.[104] Some of the neighbouring islands were purchased for summer retreats as early as that very year, but it would be two decades before Sugar Island was sold.[105]

The Department of Indian Affairs awarded possession of Sugar Island twice in 1894. In both instances, the recipients lost title for failure to comply with the terms of sale.[106] The DIA archive remains silent on the island's fate until 6 February 1901, when the department received a purchase request from Charles Edward Britton of the American Canoe Association. In a letter to the Canadian government dated 10 February 1901, Britton emphasized the economic benefits of the ACA encampments for local communities. This meet, he claimed, "gives employment to our labouring men, boatmen, tent makers, etc. and also largely increases the patronage of our River Boats and in many other ways increases business on the River." He added that if the camp were to be located in Canada, "all supplies must be purchased here or pay duty ... [and] in either case Canadians will reap the benefit."[107] However compelling Britton's economic arguments may have seemed, it soon came to light that four years earlier the DIA had agreed to allow Dr Bowen of Gananoque, Ontario, to "have charge of the Island," with the understanding that he would "look after it."[108] What now ensued was a battle between Bowen and the ACA for rights to the island, a contest in which both parties submitted numerous letters to the DIA and circulated petitions to local residents as expressions of support. In the end, the department ignored Dr Bowen's claim and awarded Sugar Island to the American Canoe Association. Minister Clifford Sifton appears to have been swayed by the organization's influence – Britton had included copies of the ACA yearbook and membership lists with one of his letters – and the potential benefit to the local area. In a letter to fellow bureaucrat J.A. Smart, the minister wrote, "I think it is an advantage to all the people on the Canadian side to have the Canoe

Association established on Sugar Island, as they hold an annual camp and spend a large amount of money every year."[109]

To possess is to dispossess, Edward Said writes in *Culture and Imperialism*, for "the earth is in effect one world, in which empty, uninhabited spaces virtually do not exist. Just as none of us is outside or beyond geography, none of us is completely free from the struggle over geography."[110] The history of Sugar Island reveals a series of dispossessions that began with the colonial state's purchase of the islands in the St Lawrence and the removal of the Michi Saagiig to the Alnwick Reserve, and continued with the loss of title by Dr Bowen. The American Canoe Association did not physically expel members of the Alnwick Band from their land. Nevertheless, the organization's purchase of Sugar Island, which was enabled by colonial technologies such as reserves and colonial institutions like the Department of Indian Affairs, put an end to the possibility that the Michi Saagiig might be able to reclaim the island. The purchase, in other words, bolstered colonial structures and deepened the effect of Indigenous displacement. Consider the following excerpt from the "patent" for Sugar Island: "WHEREAS the Lands hereinafter described are part and parcel of those set apart for the use of the Mississaugas of Alnwick Indians. And Whereas We have thought fit to authorize the sale and disposal of the Lands hereinafter mentioned, in order that the proceeds may be applied to the benefit, support and advantage of the said Indians, in such a manner as We shall be pleased to direct from time to time."[111] Even as the ACA was not responsible for the initial displacement of the Michi Saagiig, the association's desire for and purchase of Sugar Island was part of the impetus behind the initial acquisition of the land by the state and the confinement of Indigenous peoples to reservations. Colonizers framed acquisition as necessary because the land was being misused or wasted; at the core of these practices was the racist assumption of Indigenous inferiority and white superiority.[112]

Occasionally, descriptions of the campsites published in the circulars include mention of the longer human history of a site. The circular for the 1900 meet in Muskoka explained, "The Camp Site which we have leased for the ACA meet was formerly the meeting point for the Huron tribe of Indians who hunted and fished there before the white man's arrival."[113] The incorporation of pre-Contact Indigenous history into settler historical narratives was not unusual in this period.[114] As Sharon Wall argues in the case of children's summer camps, "Reminding [people] that they walked on what had previously been 'Indian land' was portrayed not as a matter of controversy, as the basis for a critique of colonialism or social redress, but, rather, as a mildly interesting (if unchangeable) anthropological fact."[115] Rarely, if ever, did the American Canoe Association acknowledge continued Indigenous presence, as the circular from the Muskoka meet makes clear. Accounts of the 1890 meet on Long Island are likewise silent on the fact that the campsite was located on the ancestral lands of the Shinnecock, who were presently confined to a reserve just across Peconic Bay.[116] That accounts of these meets say nothing of Indigenous co-inhabitants is perhaps a function of their physical and temporal proximity to the ACA campsites. Only with distance or invisibility could Indians be safely romanticized.

The canoeists were not ignorant of their participation in displacing Indigenous peoples when they settled in for an encampment. An 1891 article discussing the ACA meet at Willsborough Point on Lake Champlain included the following description: "a small colony of white tents greet the eye where years before the poor Indian pitched his wigwam and feasted his eyes upon the same grand scenery that now delights the canoeists and indeed the modern canoe now on the shore would turn those old time campers 'green with envy' for here we behold the finest specimen of the canoe."[117] However, few of the canoeists appear to have had any qualms about it. This should not surprise us. As Mark Simpson observes, the "prospect of Aboriginal disappearance" emerged as "hegemonic common sense" in the late nineteenth century, serving to "naturalize Native removal, resettlement, and containment."[118] This point was made directly in the *Watertown Re-Union* shortly after the sale of Sugar Island: "The island is one of the original groud [sic] ceded by the Canadian government to a certain Indian tribe to be used by them and their children forever. The tribe has since become extinct, or nearly so, and the islands are not inhabited by the descendants of the tribe."[119] It was inconceivable that such a traditional and ostensibly savage people could survive in the modern world, despite evidence to the contrary.

In the 1940s, Fred Saunders, a former commodore of the American Canoe Association, made a series of scrapbooks featuring photographs, articles, and ephemera documenting the first sixty years of the association. Included in the third scrapbook, which covers 1900 to 1940, are photographs of the 1930 re-enactment of the sale of Sugar Island introduced at the outset of this chapter. The final image in the series shows the two traders passing a rifle and bottle to the Indians (figure 2.1). The caption reads: "The bottle of rum closed the deal." Saunders, who played the role of the "Chief" in the skit, referred to the re-enactment as "typical ACA campfire entertainment."[120] The performance traded more in stereotypes than historical accuracy; however, it does reveal that the circumstances of the purchase were not shrouded in mystery, but were

(Dis)Placing 49

> Fiftieth Annual A.C.A. Meet and Camp, August 1-15, 1930, Sugar Island
> St. Lawrence River

> It was customary for the members of each Division to entertain the Camp one night during the Meet. While the six actors here shown are not all from the same Division, the picture shows a typical A.C.A. campfire entertainment.
>
> The scene represents the imaginary purchase of Sugar Island from the Indians by the White Traders. The bottle of rum finally closed the deal with Chief White Feather of the long reach.
>
> The White Traders -
> Jule F. Marshall   A.C.A. 5895   Atlantic Div.
> Dr. Howard Wakefield A.C.A. 8813   Western Div.
>
> Indians -
> Squaw, Alice Williams   A.C.A. Associate 189   Central Div.
> Brave, Oscar S. Tyson   A.C.A. 6314   Atlantic Div.
> Chief, A. Fred Saunders A.C.A. 6187   Central Div.
> Medicine Man, Arthur M. Callman A.C.A. 5073   Western Div.

2.1 "The bottle of rum closed the deal," 1930. This page from Fred Saunders's scrapbook documents a performance from the 1930 meet, in which members of the ACA re-enacted the sale of Sugar Island. The re-enactment, which was historically inaccurate and traded in well-worn stereotypes, ultimately celebrated Indigenous dispossession. Fenimore Museum, ACA Collection, box 1.5/3, Fred Saunders Scrapbook, Meets and Camps, 1900–40.

common knowledge among the ACA membership. More telling, we see in this performance, as well as in its documentation and inclusion in the ACA archive, the organization and its members celebrating the act of dispossession engendered by their purchase of Sugar Island.

Between 1880 and 1910, the annual encampments of the American Canoe Association were located at fifteen sites in Ontario, New York, and New England. There were differences among the sites, including the topography, patterns of local land use, and the degree to which they were imbricated in the tourist trade. There were also important similarities. Few of the locations were wild. Rather, these locations had long histories as landscapes of subsistence, commercial activity, and leisure. Although Indigenous peoples continued to be part of the diverse local populations and economies, they had long been the targets of assimilative colonial policies. More recently, tourism had begun to displace and reconfigure the lives of white settlers as well, even as it appeared to offer opportunities for economic and social gain. The ability of the ACA canoeists to occupy these locations was underpinned by the colonial politics of placemaking. Colonial structures and hierarchies enabled them to assume a right to the land and to its transformation. Even though many of the canoeists were conscious of the human histories that preceded their arrival at the campsites, these histories were understood as consumable elements of the landscape rather than as a challenge to their right to use the water, land, and wildlife for their own sport and leisure. In the next chapter, we explore how the canoeists travelled to the encampments.

Chapter Three

Navigating

In July 1891, Florence Watters Snedeker, together with her husband Rev. Charles Henry and their eldest son Karl, then aged seven, left their home in Poughkeepsie, New York, and set out for the American Canoe Association encampment that was to be held at Willsborough Point on Lake Champlain from 6 to 27 August (figure 3.1). The three Snedekers travelled in a single canoe, a decked craft they had christened *Gernegross* and loaded down with their camping outfit of "tins, tents, rubber beds, [and] blankets." During the first part of the journey up the Hudson River and along the Champlain Canal past Albany and Troy, the family alternated paddling with barge travel and tows from riverboats and shoreline animals. At Glens Falls, the Snedekers placed their boat on a cart and passed along the corduroy road to Lake George, which they traversed over a number of days with a sail hung from an improvised sapling mast. Arriving at the village of Ticonderoga, the family engaged a vegetable seller to convey *Gernegross* by wagon through town to Lake Champlain. After a few days rest on the southern end of the lake, they finally reached their destination by way of Burlington, Vermont, on the steamers *Vermont* and *Chateauguay*.[1]

Florence Watters Snedeker's travelogue, which appeared in print as *A Family Canoe Trip*, in 1892, is in many ways representative of narratives of American Canoe Association meets. Her account highlights the complex of motive technologies that underpinned long distance travel to the encampments, drawing attention to the varied experiences engendered by different routes and modes of travel, the diverse landscapes to which travellers were exposed, and the social nature of travel in the period. In contrast with other contemporary accounts of travel, Snedeker offers a more detailed description of "getting there and away." Her writing is particularly notable for the attention paid to the natural and human landscapes the family encountered on its way to the

"Curving to the heart of meadow and wood" [Page 16.]

3.1. "Mrs Snedeker and Karl," 1891. Florence Snedeker penned one of the few extant accounts of an ACA meet from a woman's perspective. Her book-length narrative, entitled *A Family Canoe Trip*, is focused primarily on the experience of the family's journey to the meet, not surprising given that she, her husband, and her son, travelled to Willsborough Point from Poughkeepsie, New York, in the decked canoe pictured here. Florence Watters Snedeker, *A Family Canoe Trip* (New York: Harper and Brothers, 1892).

meet. *A Family Canoe Trip* is all the more unique for being the product of a woman's pen. Even as women were well represented at the ACA encampments from 1883 onwards, very few wrote publicly about their experiences.

As we learned in the previous chapter, these annual gatherings took place at out-of-the-way if not wild spots in northeastern North America. The members of the American Canoe Association, by contrast, were predominantly city dwellers, calling urban locales such as Springfield, Philadelphia, Montreal, Ottawa, and New York City home. Thus, travel to the sites, which could take anywhere from an afternoon to a week, was an important part of the experience of attending an encampment. In this chapter on navigating, a concept I borrow from Michael Haldrup, I consider how the ACA canoeists, with the aid of the organizing committee, prepared for and made their way to the meets.

Haldrup conceives of navigating as one aspect of a complex of tourist mobilities that also includes inhabiting (the practice of home making) and drifting (the pleasure of movement). Navigating is the act of leaving behind known places and travelling "towards points and places at which arrival is anticipated." The movement becomes meaningful as this goal of arriving is achieved. Navigating, Haldrup argues, is structured and deliberate, requiring a "rigorous organization of time and space, in which places to visit are planned in advance, possible routes considered and times of arrival scheduled."[2]

Rather than conceiving of travel to the encampments as a "precondition for performing tourism," I argue that it was central to the experience of attending an American Canoe Association meet, not unlike watching and participating in the races or sleeping in a tent.[3] It is a truism in the mobilities literature that different modes of travel afford different kinds of experiences.[4] Mobility scholars have nevertheless tended to focus their attention on a single form of movement, such as walking, flying, or cycling.[5] This chapter, by contrast, situates three different technologies of travel – canoe, train, and steamer – alongside one another in order to highlight variations in experience and meaning. The evidence presented in this chapter also counters the tendency in much mobility theorizing towards the figure of the nomad, an isolated and "remarkably unsocial being ... unmarked by the traces of class, gender, ethnicity, sexuality, and geography."[6] The travellers we shall meet were, both by intent and happenstance, in constant contact with one another and with countless others along the way.

Travel in the northeastern United States and eastern Canada evolved rapidly over the course of the nineteenth century. Early on, roads of dubious quality were used for local transit, while riverboats of varying description enabled longer journeys. The arrival of the railroad in the 1830s and 1840s did not displace boats. Rather, it "extended freight traffic into regions that were not accessible to waterways."[7] By the late nineteenth century, a growing network of rail and steamship lines linked communities in the northeastern United States and Ontario/Quebec. This network was developed to move the raw materials and products of industrial capitalism, although it also allowed growing numbers of travellers to seek out new sights, sounds, and experiences. The emergence of travel agencies and the proliferation of guidebooks aided travellers as they negotiated what was often a complicated and inconsistent system of transport.[8] Despite the growing numbers of people crisscrossing the continent for pleasure, leisure travel remained the privilege of upper- and middle-class white people.[9] Travel, to borrow from Karen Jones, "is not a flimsy term encapsulated by leisure, freedom, romance, and adventure ... Instead it is a complex process harbouring distinct social, racial, pedagogic, and class functions."[10]

The American Canoe Association took advantage of this expanding transportation network to get canoeists to and from the annual encampments. After 1883, a dedicated transportation committee was responsible for facilitating member travel. Via circulars, yearbooks, and the official ACA organs, the committee provided the canoeists with schedule and fare information for routes linking the campsite to cities throughout the northeast. The transportation committee also arranged for concessions from the railways and occasionally from steamship lines. That these concessions usually applied only to first-class travel underscores the privileged circumstances of ACA members.[11] The committee was more directly involved in organizing transportation between the railway terminals and the campsite. Some years, this involved asking local steamers to adjust their existing routes and/or schedules to accommodate the meet.[12] In other years, the association hired a steamboat to ferry members to and from the campsite.[13] Almost without exception, the American Canoe Association passed the cost for this convenience on to the canoeist, and in some years, it used the chartered craft to generate revenue.[14]

Not only people needed to move from city to campsite, but things as well. Few of the campers, men or women, travelled lightly. In announcing the opening of the ACA encampment at Birch Point on Lake Rosseau in Muskoka, on 3 August 1900, the *Daily Mail* reported that the baggage for the Toronto Canoe Club delegation, which consisted of forty members, required "three large freight cars."[15] The transportation of canoes posed a particular challenge.[16] Not only was it expensive because of their bulk, but also railroad companies and freight enterprises were notorious for mistreating the delicate craft.[17] The ACA transportation committee simultaneously attempted to reduce or eliminate freight fares and to educate railroad companies (and by extension canoeists) about the right way to transport a canoe. These were seen as such important issues that in 1888, the American Canoe Association struck a committee on railways transportation.[18] While the transportation committee was usually successful on the first front – most years the cost of transporting canoes to the meets was waived by transportation companies – continued complaints about the handling of canoes suggest the latter was a losing battle.[19] Clubs and individuals found other ways to ensure the safety of their craft.[20] In 1884, a janitor for a New York club was made to ride in the special car at the forward end of the train to look after the members' canoes going to the ACA meet on Grindstone Island.[21] The following year, a canoeist returning home from Grindstone Island "rode in the baggage car from Clayton to Utica, keeping a close watch on his canoe" to ensure its integrity.[22]

Regardless of the location of the encampment, some ACA members had to cross an international boundary on their way to the meet. Organizers sought to ease border crossing by making arrangements in advance with customs agencies. At issue in most cases was not the movement of bodies, but rather of goods normally subject to duty. Usually, the organizers were able to secure duty-free entry for the members' canoes and camping outfits.[23] Most of the later meets in the Thousand Islands, including those on Sugar Island, had customs officers on site for the duration of the encampment, a convenience that saved the canoeists both time and travel.[24] In some cases, this individual was an existing customs official.[25] In other cases, a local proxy was employed by the state to fill the role. For example, Michael Delaney, the farmer from whom the ACA rented the Grindstone Island site, was appointed "inspector of customs" for the 1885 encampment.[26]

The work of the transportation committee certainly had practical advantages for the canoeists. In some cases, however, the committee's plans served to limit the members' travel choices. In 1884, having arranged for the "palatial steamer Puritan" to transport members to the meet, the organizing committee decreed that no other steamer would be permitted to land at the camp wharf on Grindstone Island without a permit.[27] Similarly, for the 1907 gathering on Sugar Island, a single steamboat was arranged to meet the train at the Clayton dock on the morning of 10 August and to return passengers to the same on 24 August. In this case, organizers appear to have been less concerned with controlling access to the encampment, although this may have been a consideration, than with "encouraging" members to stay for the duration of the event.[28]

Responses to the yearly arrangements were largely positive, although the ACA canoeists were not always satisfied with the work of the transportation committee. *Forest and Stream* asserted that the 1887 meet on Lake Champlain was plagued by the worst transportation arrangements in the organization's history. Not only were there just two trains per day arriving from Albany/New York City, but also the local steamer that was to link the train depot to the campsite only made one trip a day – before the trains had even arrived. As a result, visitors had to pass a night unexpectedly in Plattsburgh.[29] Not surprisingly, the 1887 meet at Bow Arrow Point served as an exemplar of poor travel arrangements for later ACA encampments.

To be clear, while the work of the organizing committee was intended to facilitate individual travel plans, it did not stand in for them. Assuming their clubs (or divisions in later years) had not made any special arrangements, canoeists interested in attending the American Canoe Association encampments still had to identify which lines they could/would take, choose their travel times, and purchase their passage. They also had to prepare their luggage and make arrangements for their baggage and canoes. Finally, they had to transport both themselves and their things from home to the station or wharf. To do so, canoeists made use of the meet circulars and transportation details provided by the organizing committee. As already mentioned, however, canoeists could make use of other sources of information to plan for and embark on the journey to the encampment, including guidebooks.[30]

Guidebooks, a subgenre of travel literature that appeared in North America in the mid-1820s, were well-established tools of touristic practice by the late nineteenth century.[31] As both "literal and imaginative guides," guidebooks (in)formed how travellers moved and saw.[32] They "preceded the tourist, making the crooked straight and the rough places plain for the tourist's hesitant footsteps."[33] They also "accompanied the tourist on the path they had beaten, directing gazes and prompting responses."[34] Guidebooks, in other words, afforded and encouraged certain experiences and interpretations, while precluding others. The guidebook industry in this period was dominated by texts produced by railway and steamship companies.[35] These included schedules and narrative descriptions of the routes taken and were to be used while the railcar or steamship was in motion.[36] Newspapers and magazines could also function as handbooks for the prospective traveller. A "special correspondent" offered the following counsel to travellers attending the 1891 meet at Willsborough Point on Lake Champlain from 6 to 27 August (a particularly long meet of three weeks' duration):

> The extremity is a full six miles from the railroad station at Willsborough, and is reached by wagon road from the station. Coming then from the south, it is better not to leave the train at Willsborough, but to keep on to the next station, Port Kent. After leaving the little hamlet from which the point takes its name, the train skirts the head of Willsborough bay, six miles long and a mile and a half wide, until after several minutes' run one can plainly see, opposite, the fine grove of trees which divides the main

camp from the ladies tents ... Port Kent lies a little north of the point, but it is an easy paddle or sail down to camp if the wind is right, and if it is wrong, a puffing and consequential steamer enables one to disregard it.[37]

In some cases, canoeists preparing for the American Canoe Association encampment actively pursued and shared travel information. Publications like the *American Canoeist* provided the perfect forum for inquiries about travel to and from the meets. In 1882, a Chicago-based canoeist interested in cruising to Lake George petitioned his fellow readers for routes from the Windy City.[38] The following year, Orange Frazer offered the following advice to canoeists travelling to Stony Lake: "Members entering Canada via Grand Trunk at Detroit, should go to the up-town office on Jefferson Ave, and the agent there will supply tickets at reduced rates, and a letter to conductors of the road, instructing them to carry canoes, etc., free." He also encouraged his audience to "Exchange [their] American for Canadian money before crossing the border, as US bank-notes are at one per cent discount, and silver coins twenty per cent."[39]

Travel preparations for the ACA encampments began long before the canoeists left home with their trunk and boat in tow, although adjustments to these plans could take place up to the point of departure and, in some cases, during the journey itself. The organizing committee, but particularly the transportation committee, functioned much like a travel agency, arranging for concessions and organizing services such as customs inspectors and shuttles between the railway terminal and campsites. The practices of preparing for the encampments were also structured by the available travel literature, which included meet circulars, guidebooks, and periodicals. Canoeists negotiated the advice these various sources of information provided both as they prepared to travel and once they were on their way.

The experience of travelling to the annual encampments of the American Canoe Association depended on the canoeist's location and means of travel. There was usually a small contingent of canoeists who resided close to the campsite. Members of the Lake George Canoe Club had but a short trip to the 1882 and 1888 meets on Lake George,[40] while Kingstonians and New Yorkers were able to commute daily to the 1893 and 1894 meets on Wolfe Island and Croton Point, respectively.[41] The ACA gatherings were near to the summer residences of some members, including Frank Taylor, whose cottage on Round Island was a stone's throw from the site of the Grindstone Island meets. Most visitors, however, had farther to go, especially when the encampments were at one of the extremes of the organization's boundaries such as Muskoka in 1900 or Cape Cod in 1902. Particularly in the early years of the encampments, it was not unusual for the trip from home to camp to take two days or more if travelling by rail. It was almost always longer by canoe.

As the canoeists travelled from doorstep to campsite, they made use of multiple transportation technologies. The bulk of long distance journeys was accomplished by "epochal" technologies such as the train and steamer; however, travelling shorter distances, from home to rail station or railway terminus to steamer wharf, involved more "mundane" technologies such as streetcars, stages, wagons, and barges.[42] These different modes of transport mediated how "places and landscapes [were] sensed and made sense of."[43] They also invited different social experiences, for, as John Urry reminds us, travel "result[s] in intermittent moments of *physical proximity* to particular peoples," or *co-presence*.[44] In the following paragraphs, I consider the environmental and social experiences that three transportation technologies – canoes, trains, and steamers – engendered as the canoeists made their way to the annual encampments and back again.

The journey between home and the meet was not a smooth corridor. For canoeists on both sides of the Canada-US border, travelling to the American Canoe Association encampments involved the negotiation of multiple intersecting networks of mobility that occupied different scales and moved travellers at different speeds.[45] Connections between these networks occurred in train stations, at wharfs, on street corners, and at shorelines. Most points of transition were likely unremarkable, but these nodes could also be lively ACA affairs. Such was the case of the Muskoka meet in 1900, for example, where members travelling by rail from various points converged at the steamer docks in the town of Gravenhurst while en route to Birch Point on Lake Rosseau.[46] Commercial photographer Frank Micklethwaite's panoramas of the Gravenhurst wharf (figure 3.2) depict a "scene of bustle and confusion."[47] Transitions were rarely quick. A visitor to the 1891 meet at Willsborough Point reported: "The connection with the trains from the south ... is hardly perfect, entailing a wait of nearly five hours at Port Kent. In the hurry and bustle of everyday life, a few hours of serious thought and deliberate introspection, communing with one's self as it were, are never thrown away. At the same time, one would hardly select the string piece of the Port Kent dock on an August morning for such mental discipline."[48] Delays also happened on the way.

3.2 Frank W. Micklethwaite, "Muskoka Navigation Steamer 'Medora' at Muskoka Wharf, with American Canoe Association on board, 1900." Beyond evoking the spectacle and gaiety articulated in written accounts, commercial photographer Frank Micklethwaite's well-composed panoramas (this is one of a series) capture the Gravenhurst Wharf as a node, or transition point, in the journey from home to the ACA meet. It was here on the shores of Lake Muskoka that the canoeists transferred from train to steamer, the final leg of their long journey to the encampment at Birch Point. Library and Archives Canada, Frank W. Micklethwaite Fonds, PA-068442.

A broken log boom slowed the steamer carrying the Knickerbocker Canoe Club of New York City to Stony Lake in 1883.[49] Ford Jones of Brockville, Ontario, arrived to the Jessup's Neck meet in August 1890 without a tent, bedding, or change of clothes because his train had been obstructed by a strike on the New York Rail Road, and he chose not to wait for its resolution.[50]

The Canada-US border represented another kind of transition, a threshold as canoeists moved from one national space to another. ACA membership certificates enabled the canoeists to cross the border without having to pay duties, but they did not eliminate wait times and searches. In 1890, Colonel Oliver Lyman Spaulding, then assistant secretary in the US Treasury Department, reminded the collectors of customs at a number of border crossings that "the customary examination should be made" of travellers to the encampments "to prevent any frauds upon the revenue."[51] I only encountered a handful of references to canoeists experiencing difficulties at the border, most associated with the 1889 meet at Stave Island, which was located in Canadian waters.[52] As a result of "abominable Customs regulations," canoeists arriving to Clayton, New York, from Boston or New York on the overnight trains were "obliged to wander around the rather prosaic town until noon or later before finding a steamer for camp."[53] The delay was a consequence of an American statute that prohibited Canadian vessels "to call at two American 'ports' in succession."[54] The relative ease with which the canoeists appear to have moved back and forth across the Canada-US border calls into question the meaningfulness of that boundary for bourgeois recreationalists in the late nineteenth century.[55]

Early circulars encouraged ACA members to make their way to the encampments by canoe, canoe travel offering a more "authentic" experience than modern forms of transportation.[56] Although there is no record of how many people completed the journey from home to the encampment (or vice versa) in the small craft, it was never a large number.[57] More common, but still rare, were the canoeists who paddled or sailed their canoes for a portion of the trip, usually the last leg between the railway terminus and the campsite.[58] Travelling by canoe took significantly longer than going by rail or steamer, one reason it was never wildly popular as a method of transportation to the ACA meets. For those with sufficient time, however, cruising afforded environmental and social opportunities not available on mass transport.

Most of these intrepid travellers were men, although not all as the example of Florence Watters Snedeker makes clear. Other women cruisers included Mrs Parmalee of Hartford, Connecticut, who paddled to at least one meet alongside her husband, and the three women canoeists who were part of the Jabberwock Canoe Club group that cruised from Springfield, Ohio, to Bow Arrow Point on Lake Champlain in 1887 (figure 3.3).[59] It was rare for a canoeist to make the trip on their own, although Dr Neide of Schuylerville, New York, undertook a solo journey to the meet on Grindstone Island in 1885.[60] More typical were pairs like Mr Miller and James Little who sailed to the Wolfe Island meet in 1893 or small groups like the Jabberwocks.[61] Most were experienced cruisers, although here too there were exceptions. Clytie and his companion from Lowell, Massachusetts, who travelled from Vergennes, Vermont, to Lake George in 1882 described themselves as "green."[62] Unlike wilderness canoe trips, which often depended directly on the labour of others, few if any of the people travelling to the ACA encampments by canoe appear to have taken a guide or servants with them.[63]

Those who travelled by canoe typically carried their "outfit" and camped along the way. Florence Snedeker recounted the daily task of

3.3 George Warder, "Jabberwock Canoe Club Cruise to Lake Champlain Meet," 1887. Most people who attended the ACA encampments went by train or steamer. A handful of intrepid travellers made the journey by canoe, including this group from the Jabberwock Canoe Club, who sailed and paddled from Springfield, Ohio, to Bow Arrow Point on Lake Champlain in 1887. Travelling to the encampments by canoe and camping along the way allowed for very different experiences of the landscapes by-passed en route than travel in a steamship or railcar. Fenimore Museum, ACA Collection, box 1.1/28.

setting up camp, including finding "a clearing" and "two trees for the tent."[64] Likewise, images from the Jabberwock cruise like figure 3.3 depict the campers cooking together over an open fire and sharing meals.[65] When the weather was bad or the canoeists desired a more comfortable repose, there were alternatives to tenting. The pair from Massachusetts took refuge from a storm at Robert's Rock Hotel on Lake George.[66] Supplies were acquired from stores and farmhouses along the way. Florence Snedeker reported purchasing fruit from farm children and treats such as "bananas, peanuts, gumdrops, and root-beer" from the lock stores on the canals.[67]

Those canoeing to the American Canoe Association encampments frequently availed themselves of other forms of transport. They typically did so to overcome some sort of obstacle, to make up time, or to avoid inclement weather. In 1884, Dr Neide and L.L. Coubert hired a man to carry their canoes between Lake Champlain and Lake George, members of the 1883 Stony Lake canoeing party used both trains and steamers to accommodate their rapidly depleting vacation time, and the Snedekers purchased passage on the *Vermont* and *Chateauguay* in 1891 because of disagreeable weather.[68] The Snedeker family also interrupted their paddling for social reasons. Accepting tows from canal boats, they claimed, allowed them to become "better acquainted" with their "fellow travellers."[69]

Florence Snedeker's account raises questions about the social experience of travelling by canoe. Clearly, cruising offered opportunities to interact with others. In addition to intersecting with the trajectories of other travellers, "cruisers" made contact with local people. Beyond the "boat people" with whom she travelled up the Hudson, Snedeker introduces readers to Dominic Dumas, the Irishman who manned one of the lock stores on the Champlain Canal; the "dark maidens" of the "Indian encampment" in Caldwell; and Mr Windham, who accommodated their tents on Lake George when there were no other available campsites.[70] With the exception, however, of a professor and his wife whom they met at Fort Ticonderoga on Lake Champlain, it is clear that Snedeker did not view these acquaintances as equals, but rather as curiosities. It is no coincidence that her account reads like an ethnography of rural upstate New York. As Joan Pau Rubies has shown, "the description of peoples, their nature, customs, religion, forms of government, and language," both in a systematic form and as series of "subjective musings," has been deeply embedded in travel writing since the sixteenth century.[71] The prominence of the ethnographic gaze was only amplified in the late nineteenth century by the popularity of anthropological inquiry.[72]

There are also the interpersonal dynamics of the cruisers to consider. How did the canoeists interact with one another while they cruised? Did they tire of each other's company? Did they feel isolated? It is difficult to provide precise answers to these questions because of the fragmented nature of the accounts of cruising. Clearly, there was an intimacy to the canoe trip experience because of the small size of the group and the length of the trip. An 1892 article in the *New York Times* hints at the peril of this situation, noting a "lifelong friend may become almost one's enemy after a few days of this cruising life."[73] Interactions between the canoeists were informed by the material circumstances of travel. Tandem canoes and paddling facilitated social intercourse – paddling allowed for greater control of the craft, but also the potential to stay close to other boats that were part of the group. Some canoeists welcomed the solitude afforded by solo canoes and sailing, while others, including a contributor to the *New York Times*, thought the canoe "too lonely to be popular." "Most people," that writer opined, "are gregarious. They like rowing together in a long boat, or sailing in a yacht."[74] Among mixed-sex parties, gender played a prominent role in shaping canoe trip experiences. Women participated in canoe trips, but rarely as equals with their male companions.[75] In tandem canoes, women were often relegated to the bow of the boat regardless of their ability, while men took charge of steering. Women were excluded from physically demanding activities such as portaging, although most of the ACA cruisers, men and women both, appear to have availed themselves of the labour of others to travel between bodies of water on their way to the encampments.

Travel by canoe engendered particular kinds of environmental experiences. In part, this was because canoes were open, offering few places to escape from a hot sun or driving rain. They were also small and sat close to the water, making them susceptible to high winds and waves. Canoeists frequently commented on the weather that impeded their progress and, occasionally, forced them to stop altogether.[76] It was not just meteorological conditions that dictated the shape of a journey; canoes were at the mercy of larger craft. On his trip from the Brooklyn Canoe Club to the train station in northeast Manhattan in anticipation of the 1893 meet on Wolfe Island, Paul Vernon gave wide berth to the "formidable" ships at anchor in the harbour and the ferryboats, whose waves "danced the canoe around more than was pleasant."[77]

Canoeists' environmental experiences were further mediated by their means of locomotion: sail or paddle. Most cruisers, but particularly the American canoeists who were more likely to sail, switched back and forth between paddles and sails depending on the conditions, so these were not isolated experiences. Provided there was ample wind, sails enabled the canoeist to cover distance quickly, while paddles provided greater control of the craft. Both sails and paddles "sensuously extended" the canoeists' capacities "into and across the physical world," producing particular configurations of body, technology, and environment.[78] By sensing the shifting tension in the ropes and the resistance of the water to the paddle blade canoeists came to physically know the paths they travelled on their way to the campsite. Travelling by canoe was characterized, in part, by physical strain and accommodation. This was certainly captured in Florence Watters Snedeker's account: "Paddling on, we thought of weariness; then forgot it, and, an hour after, found ourselves fresh again. That is the advantage of paddling. There is no strain. The muscles soon play themselves to the rhythm.

Each day there is less effort in the lazy motion, until one fancies one might fall asleep, and still keep paddling on."[79]

Although sailing tended to be faster than paddling, the pace of travel in a canoe was almost always slower than that of the train and steamer. As the following account of travel to the 1886 meet on Grindstone Island suggests, this was not unwelcome:

> The sterns of our canoes are finally allowed to slide off the end of the Cape Vincent pier, and our sails are spread for a twenty-mile sail down the St Lawrence, which at this point is so wide, that we barely make out the cattle on either bank, as we jump the waves in the current ... So we scud, passing one island after the other until, with the sun, the wind goes down, and forces us to paddle the last few miles between little rocky territories, bristling with evergreens and rocks, around which lap defiantly the clear waters of this wonderful river.[80]

Here, we see how the slow pace of the canoe afforded time to optically and aurally consume one's surroundings: to observe flora and fauna, to listen to sounds of the land and water. Given the relative speed of the journey, it follows that accounts of canoe travel would place a greater emphasis on the natural, cultural, and social landscapes encountered en route.

Those who travelled to the American Canoe Association encampments in canoes did not just have the time to make close observation of the landscape, they also had the freedom to stop in ways that other travellers did not. In contrast with train and steamer logs, canoeing accounts are littered with reports of visiting local sites of interest. On their way across Lake Champlain, ACA member Clytie and his companion stopped off at Crown Point and Fort Ticonderoga, both remnants of the War of 1812, while the Snedeker family paid visits to a lumber mill in Glens Falls and an iron mine near Plattsburgh.[81] The canoeists took breaks to perform more mundane tasks. Images from the Jabberwock cruise show the canoes drawn together in a raft for lunch.[82] Likewise, partway through their trip, Clytie and his friend spent a "pleasant forenoon ... occupied in lounging about, reading, writing and taking pictures."[83]

Travel by canoe afforded social and environmental experiences that greatly appealed to some canoeists. For the majority of ACA members, however, travel by canoe was an impractical mode of transport. Most commonly, the campers availed themselves of the continent's growing network of rail lines to arrive to the encampment. Trains, like airplanes and automobiles, have received much attention from mobilities scholars. Wolfgang Schivelbusch and Michael Freeman have shown how the coming of the railroad reshaped experiences of time and space in the nineteenth century.[84] Railways offered up "new vistas," expanding the potential spaces for consumption by the leisured classes.[85] At the same time, trains "annihilated and differentiated space," allowing passengers to cover longer distances in relatively short periods of time and to compare successive landscapes.[86] Railcars also afforded particular kinds of views, which further shaped how travellers encountered the landscapes outside of the car. Matt Johnston observes that the speed of the train offered a "shearing, tangential view," while the large glass windows provided a frame akin to paintings. This is in contrast to the panoramas made possible by the openness of the canoe and the decks of the steamer.[87]

Accounts of travel to the American Canoe Association encampments echo these conclusions regarding the social impacts of new forms of travel. The succession of views is encapsulated in the following description of travelling by train from New York to Muskoka in 1900:

> The trip is one of unsurpassed beauty and interest ... Such a diversity of scenery could hardly be equaled in a trip of the same length anywhere else on the continent. From New York the route was across the fertile farming lands of New Jersey, through the picturesque Delaware, Lehigh, and Wyoming Valleys – the Switzerland of America – then along the peaceful and placidly flowing Susquehanna and across the beautiful lake region of Central New York to Niagara and its majestic wonders. Then came the quiet shores of Lake Ontario, a glance at the bustling City of Toronto, and a dash across the rich farming lands of Ontario into the wild and rugged beauties of Muskoka.[88]

We see here how trains highlighted changing landscapes, and in the process, informed travellers' perceptions of the variety in rail-side environments. Equally remarkable are the allusions to the speed of the train, which support Schivelbusch's contention that train travel prevented any significant depth of engagement with the landscapes glimpsed through the plate glass windows. Accounts of overnight travel underscore how the railway contributed to the annihilation of space and time. Sleeping cars, C. Bowyer Vaux observed, allowed the "tired and run-down business man" to leave behind "the hot and dusty city at night," and wake up the following morning "on the river."[89]

In the cocoon of the railway car, the smells and sounds of the passing landscape were all but absent, while the train's speed curtailed visual perception, permitting only the "broadest outlines of the landscape" to be grasped.[90] That said, train travel did not offer a disembodied experience, void of sensual encounters, but rather a differently embodied experience. Even in the late nineteenth century, rail travel could be quite uncomfortable.[91] Describing a trip to Lake George in 1883 by way of the newly opened railway, a *New York Times* staffer remarked, "The locomotive had the asthma, and, I guess, the black vomit, too, from the way she covered us all with cinders."[92] Moreover, train cars could be unbearably hot in the summer months, just as canoeists were making their way to the ACA encampment.[93]

The experience of train transport was dependent on how one travelled. Assuming they took advantage of the discounts arranged by the transportation committee, the canoeists travelled to the ACA meets in first-class cars. Not only did first class provide comfortable seating and sleeping berths, it enabled well-heeled travellers to distance themselves from "Others," namely, working-class travellers and people of colour.[94] Of course, even within the confines of a Pullman, one could come up against difference.[95] Some canoe clubs, including the Toronto Club in 1900, avoided such situations by hiring entire cars for themselves.[96] After 1886, ACA divisions often made similar arrangements for their member clubs.[97] Although organizers cited convenience, we might also read these private cars, like the desire to have the encampments in out-of-way places, as part of the ACA's efforts to insulate itself from others. Private cars, unlike the typical first-class railway journey, which was more likely to be characterized by isolation and anonymity than social engagement, were interactive, even lively affairs.[98] In 1884, the *New York Sun* reported that "as the train bearing the New York delegates rolled out of the Weehawken depot, the notes of a bugle were heard, and the club broke into its chorus":

> A little canoe down the bay;
> Good-bye, my lover, good-bye.
> It bore the flag of the A.C.A;
> Good-bye, my lover, good-bye.[99]

By the end of the century, a transportation circular prepared by the association claimed, "The pleasure of being amongst ACA friends on this private car has always been one of the delights of going to camp."[100] Even those canoeists who did not make their way to the encampments in a private car typically travelled to the meets with other enthusiasts. This was especially true of women who, owing to late nineteenth-century notions of respectability, were expected to travel with family members and chaperones.[101] Pauline Johnson, who had spent much of the winter and spring of 1892–3 performing for audiences across Ontario, nevertheless travelled to the 1893 meet on Wolfe Island with her mother.[102]

Unlike those who paddled or sailed, the ACA members who travelled to the meets by train said very little about their activities en route. Presumably, they used the time to catch up with their companions or to anticipate the coming event. Other non-ACA travelogues in *Forest and Stream*, including an account of a trip to Lake Champlain, highlight the anticipatory nature of such travel: "Once seated in the cars and disencumbered of our luggage, we fell to talking over our journey, and refreshed ourselves with several bottles of ginger ale."[103] Those in public cars may have taken the opportunity to observe strangers, which Amy Richter argues was one of the chief amusements of train travel in the period.[104] Alternatively, railroad guides provided opportunities to "sightsee" as the train rolled onwards, although some travellers may have agreed with railroad commentators who believed reading while the car was in motion could have deleterious effects.[105] For those travelling with their canoes, the trip to the encampment was punctuated by the transfer points characteristic of nineteenth-century train travel.[106] Three men from New York en route to the Grindstone Island meet in 1884 found themselves outside the car with the baggage personnel at each transfer point negotiating the transmission and stowing of their canoes. They were able to "induce" the clerks at the first two transfer points to repack their canoes; however, at the final stop, in Cape Vincent, the three men were informed that neither the canoes nor the canoeists would be permitted to board the train for the last leg of the journey. They had no choice but to travel the twenty miles from Cape Vincent to the encampment by sail.[107]

Steamboats represented an earlier era in transportation technology, although they were used on the continent's waterways into the twentieth century.[108] While rail travel has provided much fodder for the imagination of scholars, significantly less has been written about journeys by steamer.[109] J.I. Little maintains that historians have tended to conflate the passenger experiences of steamboats and trains. His work on the tourist industry on Lake Memphremagog, however, suggests that unlike trains, steamers provided "ample opportunity for passengers who were so inclined to develop a spiritual affinity with their scenic surroundings." Little also suggests that steamers boasted a "convivial atmosphere" uncommon on trains.[110] Both of these observations ring true for ACA members travelling to the summer encampments, as the following examples neatly illustrate. In 1881, C. Bowyer Vaux and his companions left the "hot, dusty, and work-a-day city of New York on the Albany night boat." As the boat made its way up the Hudson River, the group "sat on the deck till late in the night, and saw one of the finest auroras that had been seen for years."[111] D.B. Goodsell, meanwhile, recalled that en route to the 1890 meet at Jessup's Neck, the steamer was a site of hijinks: "Harry Quick and Oxholm amused themselves and others too, by throwing pitchers of water into each others state-rooms on the journey out. Sleep there was not."[112]

Occasionally, longer journeys were made by steamship. More typically, however, long distance travel was by train. Nevertheless, given that the majority of the American Canoe Association encampments were located on islands or points of land not accessible by road, the last stage of the journey from railway terminus to the campsite was almost always undertaken by steamship, unless one canoed.[113] As the means by which the canoeists often arrived to the campsite, steamers played an important role in (re)introducing canoeists to camp life in three ways. First, steamers functioned as material reminders of earlier experiences. Some years, the steamer itself was part of reacquainting oneself with the encampment because it was the same boat that had brought the canoeists to the site in successive years. The *Valeria*, pictured in figure 3.4, plied the waters between Gananoque, Clayton, and the ACA encampments in 1898, 1901, 1904, 1905, and 1906.[114] Even if the steamer was different, the boat's contents usually signalled the destination to those on board. As Florence Watters Snedeker observed in 1891, "There was no need now to ask, Whither bound? Canoes filled the passageways, and young men in knickerbockers and blazers swarmed everywhere."[115] Whereas on trains, canoes and camping outfits were stowed away in the baggage car, on steamers, they lined the corridors and, in some cases, were spread across the railings (figure 3.4).

Second, steamers served as important sites of social interaction between the ACA canoeists in advance of arriving at their encampment. It was their journey on the steamer *Chateauguay* that truly introduced the Snedeker family to camp life. Shortly after boarding, the family struck up a conversation with a young couple from Canada who had attended the previous year's meet. Among other things, Florence Snedeker used the opportunity to inquire about whether there were "many ladies" at the events and "what kind of people" the members were.[116] Of course, steamships did more than introduce the canoeists to others of their kind. Because they often served multiple constituencies, steamers also brought canoeists into contact with local people and other travellers. Snedeker recalled that her family waited for and travelled on the "steamboat in company with a party of farmer folk, the women very natural and lovable in old-fashioned gowns and bonnetfuls of preposterous buttercups and poppies," as well as with others summering on

3.4 "SS Valeria arriving at Sugar Island," 1905. Given that most encampments were located on islands or isolated points of land, the last leg of the journey was often undertaken by steamer. Whereas railcars permitted gear and luggage to be hidden away in a baggage car, on the steamer, canoeing equipment was piled high, a signal to all of the preoccupations of the travellers. Anticipation grew as the steamer chugged its way to the ACA wharf. For those already in camp, the arrival of the steamer was an event, signalling a new batch of campers, some of whom could be old or prospective friends. This photograph and others like it appeared and reappeared in ACA publications throughout the period in question, a testament to the power of this part of the encampment experience for members. Fenimore Museum, ACA Collection, box 1.3/6.

the lake.[117] Here again, while steamers may have provided opportunities for travellers to encounter difference, these experiences likely did little more than reinforce established ideas about the Other.

Lastly, the steamer provided a first glimpse of the campsite. An attendee at the 1884 encampment on Grindstone Island described seeing the "smooth brown hill," the "tops of clustered trees peeping over the hill," and the "fringe of gleaming white tents along the base of the hill," as the "steamer *Puritan* emerged from the Cut, a narrow, rocky strait leading northward from ... Wellesley Island."[118] As Tim Youngs points out, "The way we imagine places is not simply a private, individual affair and our responses to them when we visit them are not independent but are mediated by the culturally constructed representations we have previously encountered."[119] Visitors to the American Canoe Association encampments were primed to encounter the campsite from the water. Year after year, accounts of the meets featured descriptions of this scene with remarkably little variation, regardless of location.[120]

The canoeists did not just travel to the encampment; they also travelled back home again. Most left as they had arrived, "in all sorts of conveyances – carriages, sloops, their own canoes, the Transportation Committee's launch, and the steamboat."[121] As with travel to the encampments, the route home was not always direct. At the close of the 1884 meet on Grindstone Island, for example, *Forest and Stream* reported that "some sailed on down the river to cruise further, some scattered among the islands, and others started direct for home."[122] Whereas the journey to the American Canoe Association encampment was one of anticipation, I suspect that travel home was filled with reminiscing about the time spent in canoes and under canvas and, assuming the event had been enjoyed, making plans for the following year.

In this chapter, our concern has been with navigating, the activities that enabled members of the American Canoe Association to prepare for and travel to the summer encampments. Travel involves a "rigorous organization of time and space."[123] This was particularly true of the ACA encampments, which took place at out-of-the-way locations and necessitated the movement of people and bulky luggage over long distances and across international borders. Travel of this sort entails "a multiplicity of objects such as maps, clocks and guidebooks, etc. to provide images and knowledge against which the knowledge gained *en route* can be matched up."[124] Transportation circulars, railway schedules, route maps, tourist guidebooks, and accounts in periodicals were all consulted as the canoeists prepared for and travelled to an ACA encampment. These did more than provide practical advice about the journey, they also shaped how the canoeists imagined and encountered the landscapes, physical and social, through which and to which they travelled.

To arrive at the encampments, canoeists employed a variety of transportation technologies. Although the objective of the various craft was the same – to convey people and freight from point A to point B – each of these modes of transportation provided particular kinds of encounters with local landscapes and people. They also afforded different experiences of time and space. The experience of train travel, which shielded travellers from the elements and distanced them from the passing landscapes, was in marked contrast to going by canoe, which placed bodies in close contact with their environments and gave cruisers time to sensually consume their surroundings. Steamer travel offered some combination of the two. Steamships travelled more slowly than trains and provided open spaces from which to consume the passing landscapes unimpeded. If, however, the canoeists were confronted with inclement weather, they could take themselves inside, away from the wind, rain, or cold. Travel to and from the American Canoe Association encampments, as these examples make clear, was not dead time. Rather, travel was a time of sociability and of opportunities for observation and encounters with new people and places. In the next chapter, we turn our attention to the physical and cultural work that was performed to ready the campsite for the arriving canoeists and to ready the arriving canoeists for the campsite.

Chapter Four

Governing

In August 1890, the *New York Times* remarked that the American Canoe Association encampments are "managed as strictly as is a military post or a yachting squadron, and everything has to be done decently and in order."[1] This was neither the first nor the last time that the yearly gatherings were described in this way. A reporter for the *New York Sun* compared the 1885 Grindstone Island camp to army life at Peekskill, a military academy on the Hudson River, while an account of the 1893 meet on Wolfe Island, near Kingston, Ontario, observed, "It is all very prim and military on the grassy open, and one would expect to see a regiment of red coats line up and salute."[2] In part, these references reflect the number of military officers attracted to the organization. The 1885, 1889, and 1893 encampments were all under the direction of military men: General Robert Shaw Oliver of Albany, New York, later assistant secretary of war (1903–13); Lieutenant-Colonel Henry Cassady Rogers of Peterborough, Ontario; and Colonel William H. Cotton of Kingston, Ontario.[3] The concern for order was also a function of broader cultural currents in this period. At a time when industrialization and urbanization were radically transforming social and physical landscapes, "people in all classes sought assurances that order existed or could be made to exist."[4]

Interestingly, descriptions of the quasi-military air of the encampments frequently appear alongside references to the "freedom" afforded by the ACA meets. Canadian poet Pauline Johnson, in the same breath, observed that the camps were run on a "semi-military basis" and celebrated the "happy Bohemianism of the Association."[5] She added, "The first week under canvas is a veritable period of lotus eating. You idle through the long, yellow August days, living a happy-go-lucky, vagabondish life, the very memory of which brings a certain care-freeness into your busy afterdays."[6] Similarly, Florence

Watters Snedeker thought the ACA encampment was "the freest place in the world."[7] Contrary to appearances, these claims to freedom, like the observations of order, were rooted in efforts to govern. Following Patrick Joyce, "To think about freedom as a mode of ruling people is to consider the absence of restraint as a form of restraint, which is something of a paradox." Freedom in the context of late nineteenth-century liberalism was, as Joyce makes clear, something that was increasingly "ruled *through*," a "formula for exercising power."[8]

This chapter considers the attempts of the encampment organizers and the executive committee of the American Canoe Association to order, discipline, and govern the campsites and the campers. To do so, they drew on a repertoire of techniques deployed by the late nineteenth-century state, including surveying and mapping, the government of the self, and policing. The encampments thus demonstrate the reach of liberal governance beyond the realm of formal politics. The creation of disciplined citizens was not reserved for schools or museums, but could also be undertaken at sporting events and vacation spots. The chapter begins with an examination of the layout of the encampments, as well as the organizers' prescriptions for how the sites were to be used by the canoeists. Here, I pay particular attention to prescribed gender roles, which themselves were gestures in governance. I then consider the mechanisms by which the organizers sought to enforce their expectations, or governance on the ground. Their practices ranged between disciplinary power in the form of policing and biopower, or government of the self.[9] Of course, the spaces of the encampment and the canoeists did not always conform to expectations; order was constantly under threat by disorder.[10] The chapter concludes with an examination of two particular issues that posed an ongoing challenge to campsite order: visitors and alcohol. Beyond these two examples, I only hint here at the ways in which campers' visions for the site and their practices intersected with organizers' expectations, as this is the explicit focus of chapters 5 and 6.

Although the American Canoe Association encampments were located in rural places, the organizers' approach to the campsites was informed by their urban experiences. Urban planning and architecture in the late nineteenth century were profoundly shaped by "moral environmentalism," the belief that "natural and built environments exert a profound influence over the ideals and inward capacities of those who experience or inhabit them."[11] Bourgeois Victorians, who equated beauty with morality and goodness, assumed that "beautiful and orderly environments morally influenced human behaviour and thought, and encouraged social uplift."[12] This kind of thinking reached its apogee in the City Beautiful Movement, which originated in response to the 1893 World's Fair in Chicago. Proponents of City Beautiful espoused the improvement of urban space, and by extension urban dwellers, through comprehensive city planning and the employment of classical aesthetics.[13] Likewise, the ACA organizers believed that an aesthetically ordered encampment cultivated morally sound and decorous campers.

Putting the camp in order meant a number of things to the leadership. First, it referred to the imposition of a physical plan on the designated site. Using the surveying and mapping technologies described earlier, the organizers located and then constructed the key locations of the encampments, such as the wharf, the mess tent, and the ladies' camp, on markedly different sites each year, a practice that made new locations familiar to returning canoeists. The acts of designation inherent in mapping also bound space to conduct, thereby regulating the possibilities of use.[14] Second, putting the camp in order signified "improvements" to the campground. Despite the ACA's claims that members were visiting wild places, much work was done to prepare the sites for their arrival: brush was cleared, a wharf built, paths graded, tent floors constructed, and outbuildings erected. In anticipation of the 1890 meet on Long Island, Mr Scoville, of Peconic Bay, agreed to "clear off all the objectionable underbrush during the early spring and have the grass burned in time to have a fresh crop for August ... to fill in a certain objectionable pool, to clear the shore of seaweed and riff-raff."[15] These improvements made the Jessup's Neck campsite more aesthetically pleasing for the canoeists who, as we saw in chapter 2, desired sites that were cultivated. They also made it more habitable. Trails, for instance, facilitated movement around the campsite. Like sidewalks in the city or paths through a park, trails also implied appropriate routes for navigating space.[16] Finally, putting the camp in order referred to efforts to encourage cleanliness. These included the creation of sanitation infrastructure such as wells, water closets/outhouses, and bathhouses, as well as the inclusion of daily cleanups in the camp schedule.

The American Canoe Association encampments were actively curated spaces. In addition to sculpting the aesthetics of the site, the organizers reproduced activity arenas devoted to the management of the event (headquarters), the accommodation of campers (main camp and ladies' camp), the provision of board (mess tent and camp store), sanitation, and competition (racecourses).[17] While the organization of the different sections of the camp varied, in general the organizers tended towards a mid-point between the straight-line aesthetic of a military encampment (visible in figures 4.1 and 5.1) and what Abigail Van Slyck calls "picturesque design principles" in which "pavilions [were] scattered throughout the wooded site in an irregular arrangement designed to complement the natural surroundings."[18] In other words, the ACA campsite boasted its own version of order that retained some romantic elements of disorder. This likely contributed to the campers' impressions of the campsites as spaces of freedom.

For most visitors, ACA members or otherwise, their official introduction to the encampment came at the wharf. A sign at the end of the dock announced to all who landed that the camp was a private one and that all visitors must report to the camp secretary to be vetted before gaining formal entry to the camp.[19] Much of the "freedom" of camp life was enabled by the gatekeeping that took place at the wharf and in the secretary's tent.

The secretary's tent was located at the headquarters, the practical and symbolic seat of power at the encampment. It was here that the annual meets were officially opened with a flag-raising and cannon ceremony, members and visitors alike came to register, the bulletin board broadcast the events of the day, and the regatta committee ruled on racing protests. The headquarters, such as the one in figure 4.1, typically consisted of three to six tents arranged in a line or semi-circle.[20] Ideally, the tents were of uniform size and shape. The names of the occupants were typically announced by a sign hanging from the tent or were painted on the tent stairs. Most years, the commodore's tent was situated in the centre, flanked by structures housing the secretary and regatta committee. Other committees and service providers such as customs agents, the camp surgeon, and the postmaster were located in adjacent tents.

The arrangement and style of the headquarters tents reflected the organizing committee's commitment to a social order defined as much by rank as function.[21] The camp cannon and tall flagpoles flying the colours of the American Canoe Association and the flags of the nations officially represented at the meet were positioned in front of the headquarters' tents.[22] The cannon was used to mark time; the flagpoles increased the visibility of the headquarters from points distant. The headquarters was also home to the camp bulletin board, a large board displaying neatly arranged notices of various shapes and sizes, including the site rules, the schedule of the day, "orders for the day," the location of nightly activities, and "racing, cruising and general notices."[23] The bulletin board was an ACA institution in this period and a primary means by which the organizers communicated the schedule and their expectations to the canoeists. The board also had a lighter side. One

4.1 H.C. Morse, "Headquarters from Dock," 1897. The ACA encampments developed their own aesthetic that included elements of order common to a military encampment and romantic disorder, described by Abigail Van Slyck as "picturesque design." As the practical and symbolic seat of power at the encampments, the camp headquarters, captured in this plate by amateur photographer H.C. Morse, tended to represent order. Fenimore Museum, ACA Collection, box 1.2/26.

post that found its way into the historical record advertised: "For sale cheap, a Bull Terrier Pup, with large capacious jaws, will eat anything, very fond of children."[24]

Whereas the camp headquarters was a space of authority and regulation, the camp mess (kitchen and dining tent) and camp store provided for the alimentary needs of the canoeists. Both were later additions to the site. At the early ACA encampments on Lake George, the canoeists cooked for themselves or took meals off site at the Crosbyside Hotel. In 1884, the Delaney family, owners of the Grindstone Island campsite, opened their home to canoeists desiring a home-cooked meal. The arrangement was a success, so the following year an official mess tent, overseen by Mrs Delaney, was added to the campsite. Guests wishing to eat at the mess purchased meal tickets from the secretary. Most years, three meals a day could be had for a dollar. More often than not, the dining room was a much larger version of the wall tents used by campers for sleeping. At the 1896 meet on Grindstone Island, however, campers took their meals in an eighty-foot circus tent, and at the 1887, 1891, and 1892 meets, the canoeists ate in wood-frame structures not unlike the dining pavilions common at summer camps.[25] Even as the mess served the very practical purpose of feeding the campers, it also signalled appropriate behaviour to them. Meals in the mess tent/shed were delivered on china by uniformed servers to cloth-covered tables adorned with flowers, all clear signals of the ACA's aspirations for respectability and expectations for decorum.[26]

Unlike at summer camps in this period, where young people often participated in meal preparation, the mess tent at the ACA encampments was more akin to a hotel dining room or a restaurant where food was prepared by hired help and hidden from view.[27] Accounts of the meets offer few specifics regarding the facilities available to the cooks. Likewise, I have yet to see a photograph of an encampment kitchen. Nevertheless, we know they were relatively simple affairs. Cooking facilities were usually housed in makeshift sheds and might feature iron stoves or portable baker's ovens.[28] The exception was the kitchen at the Jessup's Neck encampment, which was the "most extensive affair yet seen at a meet."[29] Although still within a wood frame structure, it featured an icehouse and storeroom. It also boasted hot and cold water together with ranges, broilers, and ovens that had been acquired from Delmonico's, a venerable New York restaurant.[30] Unfortunately, the upscale appliances appear not to have been used to full effect, for the 1890 meet had notoriously bad food.[31]

Not everyone ate in the mess tent. In recognition of this fact, a camp store was introduced in 1883 to provide those canoeists wishing to cook for themselves with the necessary supplies. Typically run by local merchants or the person in charge of the mess, the camp store featured fresh produce, milk, eggs, and bread ostensibly at "city prices."[32] One might also find other camping-related comestibles on the shelves, such as coal oil, candles, lanterns, fireworks, postage stamps, wood, and flags.[33] The quality of the store varied from year to year. Visitors to the 1889 meet on Stave Island complained that it was difficult to procure staples such as bread and milk.[34] The following year, the camp store was better equipped, if expensive.[35] The example of the camp store suggests that not everyone at the ACA encampments was well off, and that for those who found ways to attend on a limited budget reasonably priced foodstuffs were a necessity.

Prior to 1883, the American Canoe Association encampment was a largely if not exclusively homosocial masculine space. "Ladies Day" aside, women were absent from the Crosbyside and Canoe Island campsites, although they were present at the canoe races and closing banquets. The decision to include a "ladies' camp" at the Stony Lake in 1883 meet reconfigured the physical and imagined space of the encampment. What prompted the organization to invite women to stay on site is unclear. It is possible that women expressed a desire to participate. Certainly, when the announcement was made that the Stony Lake meet would accommodate women canoeists, parties were quickly formed to attend.[36] The decision may also have been a response to anxieties about the perceived respectability of the annual meet.[37] Respectability, which Lynne Marks refers to as an often "vaguely defined but clearly understood category" in the nineteenth century, was an important ideal that informed all manner of social interaction.[38] Colin Howell has documented how Atlantic Canadian promoters in the same period encouraged women's attendance at baseball games believing their presence in the stands "would have a civilizing effect" on what was considered a rowdy pastime.[39] Andrea Smalley likewise argues, "Male writers and editors ... asserted that women's participation would reform hunting, making it a modern, respectable recreation."[40] It is also possible that women's altered place within the ACA meet was part of, and in some ways anticipated, the shift towards heterosocial leisure spaces and practices in the early twentieth century.[41] Regardless of the initial motivation, most association members assumed that women would contribute to a more orderly encampment. Thus, the inclusion of women was also part of a larger strategy of governance.

A number of male canoeists publicly welcomed the change, including C. Bowyer Vaux who opined, "Why should the men enjoy the monopoly of the camping pleasures, the freedom, exercise, and sport of canoeing? Girls can swim – some of them – paddle and rest comfortably in tents, and a few of them can actually handle a canoe under sail. It is, after all, only a matter of training and practice."[42] Not everyone was so approving, however. One unnamed commentator did not want to imagine an annual meet without a ladies' camp. Yet, he was "sure that there were far too many squaws over the ridge at Stave Island" and that "nothing could be done in camp without more attention being paid to the necessities of the squaws than the wishes of the canoeists."[43] In addition to positioning women and canoeists as mutually exclusive categories, the same writer voiced a common concern of male ACA members, that women were somehow undermining the true purpose of the annual encampment. One of the organization's early secretaries was perhaps the most explicit in his opposition to having women on site. In the January 1884 issue of the *American Canoeist*, Dr Charles Neide issued a sweeping condemnation of the ladies' camp for being "detrimental to the best interests of the Association."[44] Canoeists were not alone in such feelings. Anxieties about the feminization of culture and everyday life were pervasive in nineteenth-century North America.[45] Historians have documented how such anxieties contributed to new religious movements like muscular Christianity, organizations such as the Boy Scouts and the Young Men's Christian Association, and recreational spaces like boys' summer camps.[46]

There was no question in 1883 that should women be allowed to camp at the annual meets, they would have to have their own space.[47] Initially, the organizers of the Stony Lake encampment intended to house the women on a separate island; ultimately, for reasons never articulated, the ladies' camp was sited on the southern tip of Juniper Island, a safe distance from the main camp.[48] The decision to segregate women stemmed from classed notions of respectability. As Cindy Aron reminds us, middle-class status in the nineteenth century "rested, in part, on claims to a *publicly recognized* respectability, a respectability gained by adhering to elaborate and complicated rules of etiquette that governed every minute aspect of life."[49] Heterosocial leisure, if increasingly commonplace in the decades around the turn of the century, nevertheless invited concern. Creating a separate ladies' camp may have also reflected a desire to "encourage women's entry into socially sanctioned areas" of public life.[50] Here, the ladies' camp had parallels in the ladies' reading rooms described by Abigail Van Slyck, who observes that ladies' rooms were "often considered an absolute necessity for encouraging respectable women to venture into the public library."[51] By the 1880s, women could for the same reasons find designated spaces in department stores and banks, hotels and restaurants, and on steamboats and railroad cars.[52]

The American Canoe Association's ambivalence about women canoeists is evident in its treatment of the newly formed ladies' camp. First, this space was more commonly referred to as "Squaw Point." "Squaw" at once exoticized the women's camp and undermined women's claim to the space of the encampment. Following Muriel Stanley Venne, "when a person is called a 'Squaw' she is no longer a human being who has the same feelings as other women. She is something less than other women."[53] The origins of the name are unclear. On a number of occasions, however, the occupants of the ladies' camp requested that the name be changed on account that it had been imposed on them; they preferred "Paradise."[54] The introduction of a Squaw Point flag (figure 4.2) in 1902 suggests the women eventually embraced the moniker. Designed by Mrs Peebles and produced by a sewing bee of "the Squaws" at the Cape Cod meet, the flag featured a red bust of a woman with long, thick braids and a feather extending backwards from the top of the head in profile on a white background.[55] Her gaze is directed towards the inside of the flag and the letters ACA are positioned vertically in decorative script. The existence of Squaw Point is evidence of the complex and intersecting currents of race and gender in late nineteenth-century North America. Patriarchy positioned all women as inferior to men. Whiteness, however, remained a privilege. To borrow from Anne McClintock, "White women were not the hapless onlookers of empire but were ambiguously complicit both as colonizers and colonized, privileged and restricted, acted upon and acting."[56]

The physical location of the two campsites is telling. The men's, or main camp, was typically situated at the heart of the encampment, close to the public spaces of the wharf and the headquarters. Like the rules that reserved full ACA membership and office for men, the location of the main camp was a physical reminder of men's favoured position at the core of the association. The women's camp, by contrast, was situated at the margins of the encampment, distant to the headquarters, echoing their lesser status within the ACA. The emplacement of both camps also recalled the separate spheres ideology so popular in the nineteenth century that associated men with public life and women with private, family affairs.[57] Whereas the main camp was best located out in the open, organizers sought out wooded and out-of-the-way locations for the women's camp.[58] That these sites were typically described as "quiet coves" or "a secluded grove" served to further distance the ladies' camp from the rest of the campsite.[59] Not only should men and women be separated, but the weaker sex should also be sheltered and protected. One visitor to the 1883 encampment on Stony Lake observed that "the ladies' camp is sacred ground, not to be lightly profaned, and is kept guarded with oriental exclusiveness."[60] This writer simultaneously conjures up images of convents and harems, framing women as pure and in need of protection, and as objects of desire. Anxieties about respectability were further manifest in the presence of official chaperones in the ladies' camp, typically, an older woman or couple.[61] Mrs E.J. Toker was responsible for the ladies' camp in 1884 and 1885, while Mr and Mrs Seavey were charged with seeing that "all are made comfortable" there in 1890.[62]

THE SQUAW POINT FLAG.

4.2 "Squaw Point Flag." Designed in 1902 by Mrs Peebles, this flag was raised annually thereafter at the ladies' camp, more commonly known as "Squaw Point." The flag speaks to the ambivalent place that women held in the organization. While white women were welcome at the encampments, they were associated with the figure of the squaw, a derogatory trope of Indigenous womanhood, that at once exoticized and othered the women canoeists. This flag and the moniker attributed to the ladies' camp are just two ways in which the ACA campers "played Indian." John Sears Wright, ed., *American Canoe Association Yearbook* (n.p., 1904).

Women were not just spatially cloistered. Their movements were temporally constrained as well. As Harry Eckford observed, "Those [women] who honor the meets with their presence are ... enjoined not to visit the main encampment till after eight in the morning, when the laziest canoeist is expected to have had his dip, made his toilet, and done breakfast."[63] Most years, women were not to visit the main camp until after ten in the morning. Nor were they to be in the men's camp after six in the evening, unless formally invited and accompanied by a chaperone. Likewise, single men were not to venture into the ladies' camp unaccompanied and without invitation. These regulations hint at some of the perceived threats that mixed-sex camping posed to middle-class respectability, not the least of which was bodily intimacy.

To be clear, "ladies' camp" is somewhat of a misnomer. Although it was routinely represented in ACA literature as exclusively for women and, thus, as having a different character than the men's camp, the ladies' camp also accommodated married couples and occasionally families with children. Whereas married women had to follow the same rules as single women as they navigated the spaces of the encampment, men's marital status rendered them immune to the regulations surrounding movement between the two camps. Ostensibly, marriage conferred a more stable maturity and respectability on men.

The organizers' efforts to police encounters between men and women existed alongside popular cultural references that routinely linked courting to canoes.[64] Thus, it should not surprise us that campers like Casper Whitney claimed that "the mingling of the sexes is one of the happiest features of the Meet" and "under no conditions is Cupid more artful than in a dancing canoe, silently guided by the wooer's cunning paddle."[65] Even organizers occasionally encouraged canoodling. Two descriptions of the Stony Lake campsite circulated by the organizing committee suggest the site was suitable for more than racing or cruising. The first painted Juniper Island as "a *charming* spot ... with a broken and indented coast line forming *delightful* little *coves* and *nooks*" with "smooth water" perfect for a canoe at rest, while the second claimed that "there are so many channels, sudden turns, and *secluded* nooks [around the island], that weeks may be spent in exploring them without monotony."[66] Such language produced a rudimentary geography of intimacy, which, as we shall see in chapter 6, was embellished by the practices of individual canoeists as they inhabited the campsite.

While the organizing committee was clearly concerned about the location of the ladies' camp within the larger encampment, it appears not to have spent much time on its internal organization, a fact that only reinforced the otherness of the women's camp. Flip, in her account of the 1887 meet on Lake Champlain, recalled arriving to the ladies' camp to find only "two tents up ... to identify the spot." She also remarked on the time it took to "find suitable places" for their tents, suggesting that the organizers had not pinpointed locations in advance of the meet.[67] The same could not be said of the men's camp. At the 1890 encampment at Jessup's Neck on Long Island, the organizers laid out two long parallel avenues along the edge of the bluff, connected at intervals by smaller streets.[68] The result of the organizers' labours recalled the cadastral grid employed by surveyors to rationalize landscapes, often for colonization.[69] That the connecting streets at the Jessup's Neck encampment "were not as numerous as they should have been" because some of the campers erected their tents in "spaces intended to be left open for passage" speaks to the tensions between order and disorder in the campsite.[70] It was not just campers that could upend the committee's system. Some years, the landscape itself foiled attempts to organize the site in particular ways. On Long Island in 1888, "none of the clubs [had] the same compact and well-arranged encampments that have sometimes been so prominent" because of the topography, but particularly the "uneven nature of the ground," which "scattered irregularly" the tents.[71]

Inspired perhaps by the mounting preoccupation with waste management in urban areas, the organizing committee made a series of arrangements and instituted a number of rules to encourage cleanliness in camp.[72] They dug wells for clean water, erected outhouses to contain bodily waste, and raised bathhouses for daily ablutions.[73] They also carved time out of the official schedule for bathing and cleaning. The former was to be undertaken before the morning meal, the latter, after breakfast, before the garbage cart began its rounds at 10:00 a.m.[74] Sanitation infrastructure and cleaning activities were motivated by a desire for order and concerns about health and sanitation, a point that is succinctly captured in the closing line of the 1886 camp rules: "Cleanliness and good order are indispensable for the general health and comfort [of the camp]."[75] Just as moral environmentalism explained how natural and built space could influence a person's moral well-being, it also linked physical health to the environment. Even as the organizers pursued healthy sites, undisciplined campers could undermine their healthfulness with bodily consequence. Linda Nash writes, "Nineteenth-century bodies, white and non-white, were malleable and porous entities that were in constant interaction with the surrounding environment ... Consequently, prospective settlers approached new environments with caution, recognizing that the land itself could be either a font of health or a source of illness."[76]

The final activity arena of the American Canoe Association encampment was the racecourse. The broad contours of the regatta landscape changed when the annual gathering was a mobile event; the shoreline of Long Island presented a different scene from that of Stony Lake. Even when the meets settled at Sugar Island, however, and there was greater continuity from year to year, the landscape was not static. Nevertheless, there were common elements to the various theatres of contest: water, land, and buoyed courses. With the exception of the 1880 meet, at Crosbyside Park on Lake George, the American Canoe Association regattas always featured a triangular sailing course and a straightaway paddling course.[77] These were usually surveyed in the winter months, along with the campsite. Surveys were expected to be accurate in order to ensure a level playing field, although the regatta committee appears to have not always been successful.[78] As with yachting races, the surveyed courses were marked off by buoys or stake boats.[79] These were placed during the first week of the encampment (if not before) so those in attendance could practice on the course.[80]

The positioning of the courses reflected a number of environmental and social concerns such as tides, current, winds, and spectators. Tides and currents were best avoided in both types of events, but the degree of wind was contest dependent. Sailing courses were typically situated out in the open water on the windward side of the campsite, while the paddling courses were placed closer to shore on the leeward side. While the committee could deliberately place the buoys, they could not, of course, control the wind and water. As we see in figure 4.3, some years the regatta committee created multiple courses in an effort to ensure amenable conditions. Equally important was the location of the course relative to the campsite. Races, and by extension the racecourses, were to be visible to spectators.[81] Paddling courses were often located parallel to the shoreline so the spectators could watch the contests with ease from start to finish.[82] Sailing races were harder to position because of the triangular shape of the course. Most committees placed the start/finish line near to the shore.

From the mid-1880s on, most of the American Canoe Association encampments had a wharf, headquarters, mess, camp store, men's camp, women's camp, sanitary arrangements, and racecourses. The physical act of reproducing these spaces on an annual basis made unfamiliar locations familiar for the returning canoeists. Of course, these were not perfect reproductions. The yearly changes in the organizing committee and the different circumstances of the designated site also shaped the built environment of the encampment. Equally important were the campers. Before considering how two forms of camper behaviour threatened campsite order, I explore how organizers sought to encourage particular uses of the encampment spaces and discourage others.

The regulation of camper conduct was as important to ensuring order during the ACA meet as organizing the space of the encampment.[83] In fact, the two were inextricably linked. Camp officials employed a number of related techniques to encourage campers to conform to their expectations; they instituted regulations to govern conduct, categorized the campers, arranged the "temporal space" of the encampment with a schedule, and policed the campsite. Some of these were on-site activities, but officials did not wait for the annual meet to make

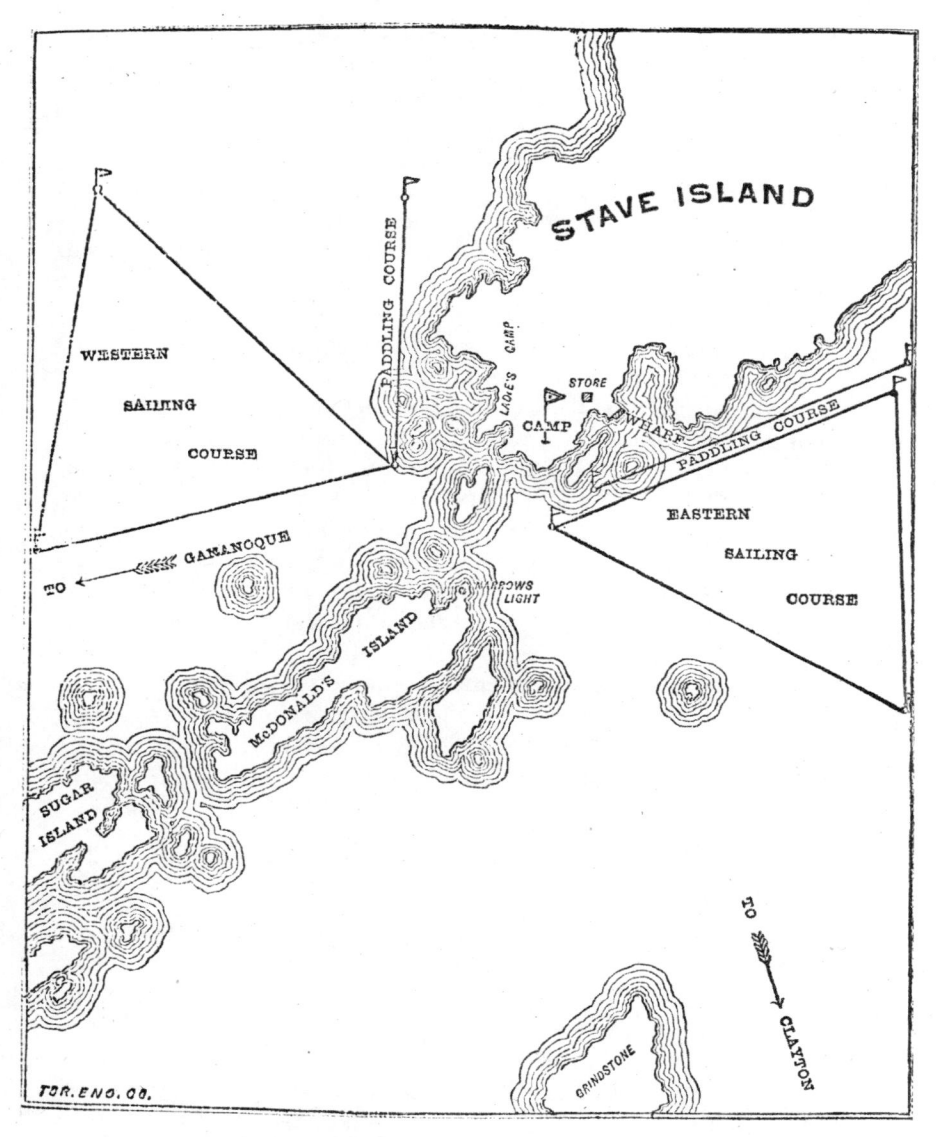

4.3 Course map from the 1889 meet on Stave Island. As important as the positioning of the camp buildings and tents was the layout of the racecourses. Organizers sought to mitigate the effects of environmental conditions such as wind and currents on the competition, while also affording spectators an adequate view of the course. Course maps appeared only occasionally in the circulars. Beyond previewing the courses, they signalled a commitment on the part of the organizers to a well-run regatta. Fenimore Museum, ACA Collection, box 1.6/12.

their expectations known. On the contrary, rules and schedules were included in the camp circulars and published in the official ACA organs in advance of the meets. For the benefit of campers not familiar with encampment life, copies of the rules and schedules were also posted on the camp bulletin board at the headquarters.

Three different sets of rules governed life at the ACA encampments: the constitution and bylaws, regatta regulations, and campsite rules. Some of the campsite rules, as I have alluded to already, controlled access to the encampments, movement around the site, and campsite cleanliness. Others governed particular activities like bathing. The organizers and officials often implied that rules were a necessity in order to afford the fun and frivolity that attendees desired. The circular for the 1886 meet at Grindstone Island opened with the following statement: "The bulletin board at the head of the dock will show the orders for the day, and all members are cautioned to observe the same for the general comfort and convenience."[84] This statement echoes Patrick Joyce's observation that, in the late nineteenth century, freedom functioned as a "technique of rule."[85] The rules were not static, of course. They evolved as new directives were added, others revised, and still others removed. What was considered orderly or disorderly shifted somewhat with the year, the site, and the ACA officials, although never drastically. The rules were also influenced to an extent by member behaviour. Perhaps the best example of this came in 1888 when the executive committee, recognizing that the campers would remain awake regardless, extended the hour for quiet from 10:00 p.m. to 11:30 p.m.[86] Ultimately, however, it was the administration that determined the rules.

The efforts of the American Canoe Association to regulate camper conduct were not limited to the campsite, although the ACA likely had a greater degree of control over this space. On the contrary, later additions to the campsite rules included notes about member behaviour while off site. In 1888, the camp bulletin board reminded all those who happened past, "The good repute of the ACA must be maintained by those who visit hotels in the neighbourhood."[87] As with behaviour on site, the organizers could not be assured that members would comply with their directives. At the 1899 meet on Hay Island, a special meeting of the executive committee was adjourned to discuss "disturbances in camp and [the] boisterous conduct of men in camp and at Gananoque."[88] There were clearly concerns about how such actions might appear to the public.

Regulations dictated that upon arrival to the American Canoe Association encampment all visitors had to register at the headquarters. Here, the secretary provided each individual with a coloured ribbon to

4.4 W.L. Scott, "Group at the American Canoe Association Camp at Stave Island," 1889. W.L. Scott's photograph of a Canadian contingent of canoeists at the 1889 meet on Stave Island illustrates the use of ribbons to govern the canoeists and, by extension, the encampment. In addition to the ACA ribbons, the individuals captured in this image are wearing ribbons that indicate their canoe club affiliation. Library and Archives Canada/William Louis Scott Fonds/PA-066627.

be worn while on site.[89] The ribbon featured the date and location of the meet, as well as the status of the camper: member, honorary/associate member, or visitor.[90] The ribbons, which functioned as visible reminders of a camper's place in the organizational hierarchy – it was literally marked on the body – governed participation and movement while at the encampment (figure 4.4). Visitors, for example, were only allowed on site during certain hours of the day and week, and they were barred from entering ACA races. Women, as I discussed earlier in this chapter, were also prevented from moving freely through the campsite.

The imposition of such categories was of a piece with efforts to rationalize the camp landscape. By grouping the campers into discrete and seemingly knowable quantities, they could be more easily "surveilled" as they perambulated through the encampment. Stephen Graham and David Wood assert, "Wherever there has been the creation and enforcement of categories, there has been surveillance."[91] Although divisions such as these "were largely appropriated from the logic of common perception, requiring no great exercise of imaginative powers," to borrow from Keith Walden, "they did reinforce the legitimacy of many of the cultural divisions of everyday life."[92]

Just as they ordered the physical space of the meets, the organizers arranged the "temporal space" of the encampment.[93] Much like at summer camps, "rigorously maintained mealtimes gave a clear and consistent structure to each day" at the ACA meets.[94] During the first week, the schedule might also include official excursions to local points of interest, campfires, or a "Divine Service." As an aside, the commitment to holding a weekly church service may have reflected genuine devotion, and certainly it met this need for some of the individual campers. We can, however, also read the inclusion of the Divine Service in the schedule as part of efforts to construct a respectable public image. Churchgoing was an important facet of middle-class respectability in the nineteenth century.[95] During the second week, the racing programming dominated the daily schedule.

Cannons, bells, and bugles were alternately used to wake the campers, to remind them of mealtimes, to signal the closing of the day, and finally, to call them to bed. At the 1900 meet on Lake Rosseau in Muskoka, there were even daily bugle calls to bring the sick to the camp surgeon.[96] One year, the liberal use of the horn earned the camp bugler the title of "dread dignitary," suggesting that such ordering was not always appreciated by the ACA's rank and file.[97] In 1890, the organization introduced a signal code to communicate with the canoeists. Pauline Johnson explains, "Twenty-one pennants, of various pattern and color, constituted the signal set adopted by the Association. All business notifications, meetings, weather signals, races and happenings of general interest were announced by a combination of several flags, the minute details of such matters being posted on the bulletin board below."[98] The cry of the bugle alerted campers to the changing of the signal.[99] Codebooks were sold at headquarters so ACA members could decipher the myriad combinations of pennants.[100] The sheer volume of signals made the code the target of jokes. In 1890, *Forest and Stream* quipped that the signal officer was "threatened with an attack of nervous prostration" because the code was so lengthy and changed so often.[101] This temporal ordering of the meet is a near-perfect illustration of E.P. Thompson's "time discipline."[102] Regardless of whether it stemmed from necessity or a fetish for efficiency, or both, this commitment to the camp schedule was, like the ordering of space at the camps, an exercise in governance.

Organizers hoped the campers would, with proper direction, regulate themselves. If this was not the case, the American Canoe Association had structures in place to "see that the rules [were] complied with."[103] As early as 1886, order in camp was the responsibility of an "Officer of the Day" appointed by the executive committee. The camp police, later referred to as "pickets," assisted the officer of the day by keeping watch over a particular part of the encampment.[104] All of the appointees wore badges to indicate their position.[105] Whereas the former was typically an established member of the ACA, the position of picket appears to have been farmed out to those who were new to the association. Thus, it is reasonable to assume their effectiveness was uneven.[106]

The officers and organizing committee deployed a variety of strategies to pursue order in the encampment. They crafted multiple sets of rules, which governed campers' movements and behaviour while on site; they visibly categorized the campers, so as to more easily monitor their comings and goings, and to remind them of their place in the association; they organized the temporal space of the encampment with a schedule communicated via bugles and flags; and they created a system of policing to encourage compliance with the ACA's policies. Just as the efforts to physically organize the encampment transformed the campsite into territory, these attempts to discipline the campers transformed them into subjects of rule.

The summer gatherings of the American Canoe Association were never spaces of perfect order. Rather, like the Industrial Exhibitions described by Keith Walden in *Becoming Modern*, disorder always lurked at the edges of the encampments.[107] Two aspects of camp life posed ongoing threats to order: visitors and alcohol.

"Visitors Days," or "Ladies Days" as they were known prior to 1883, were regular features of the meet schedule from the ACA's founding in 1880.[108] Most years, the association posted advertisements in area hotels and resorts inviting guests to visit the camp and/or watch the races.[109] The choice of location for these advertisements hints at the class of visitor desired by the organizers. Word also appeared in local and national newspapers.[110] In some cases, steamer lines or resorts took it upon themselves to arrange excursions to the campsite, a practice organization officials viewed with some concern, likely because they had less control over who might arrive on site.[111] Occasionally, churches and social reform organizations used excursions to the ACA encampments as fundraisers.[112] For all of their efforts to attract visitors to the site, the American Canoe Association was never entirely comfortable with having outsiders in camp: while they represented potential members, confirmed the popularity of the sport and the organization, and legitimized the meets as events, outsiders also posed a possible threat to the order of the campsite and the organization.

There was, quite clearly, a right and wrong kind of visitor. A report from the 1890 meet is instructive. It asserted that the American Canoe Association disdained "the ordinary type of country sightseers, without regard for anything," who arrived on site "armed with lunch baskets and paper parcels" and "settled down on the camp and made it their own." By contrast, "visitors from the yachts were always welcomed."[113] What separated the right and wrong type of visitor then appears to have been class, although presumably the camp was not open to non-white visitors, except as help or entertainment. Nevertheless, the best visitor was a friend to the association, that is, someone known to a member in good standing. Some years, visitor badges were only granted to those who had received an invitation from an on-site ACA member.

The American Canoe Association took a number of steps to limit the threat posed by visitors to the encampments. As noted earlier, visitors were always identified by a badge, making clear who did and did not belong to the association. Second, by designating visitors' days, the organizers implicitly suggested the encampment was not open to outsiders at other times. They also typically scheduled visitors' days during the week, which would have served to discourage the attendance of local working-class people, who continued to work six days a week in this period and had limited time for holidays.[114] Given that the encampments were typically located in rural areas, it is possible that farm families may have been able to attend. Certainly, the persistence of concerns about the class of people visiting the encampments suggests a more diverse citizenry was present than the organizers intended. A third strategy involved declaring in 1890, at the Jessup's Neck meet, that the headquarters should always be at the wharf.[115] Even as the new location was lauded for being more "accessible" to arrivals, it increased the officers' abilities to monitor the canoeists' comings and goings and to enforce campsite rules about visitors and fees. Likewise, the decision to move the camp store in 1907 was a response to concerns about outsiders on site. That year, the store was relocated from the headquarters, which was near to the wharf, to the mess tent, which was farther inland. Organizers hoped that the move would eliminate one of the more disagreeable elements of the camp store, namely, that it functioned as a meeting place for outsiders "who had no business being in camp."[116] Unfortunately, the organizers are not explicit about who these "outsiders" were. No solution was ever entirely satisfactory. As one observer noted, it was difficult to "keep out the ordinary sight-seer without discourtesy to friends of members, or others who would be welcome in camp."[117]

Part of policing the physical edges of the encampments was, like the membership process, about establishing the territorial and social boundaries of the ACA community. Such boundaries, however, were by no means impermeable. Undesirable visitors continued to find their way onto the campsite, where organizers claimed they disrupted the perfect order of the meets. More concerning, however, were the disturbances caused by drink, disturbances that were usually attributable to ACA members.

Officially, the American Canoe Association's encampments were dry spaces. Trees at an early meet on Lake George were affixed with signs proclaiming, "The sale and open use of intoxicating liquors is forbidden on this island."[118] In 1890, at Jessup's Neck on Long Island, despite requests by the membership that the caterer be allowed to serve beer and wine at meals, the ACA officers voted down the motion 13–4.[119] This decision was reaffirmed in 1904 at the annual meeting on Sugar Island, when the executive committee passed a motion prohibiting "the public sale of liquor ... at camp."[120] Journalistic accounts of the meets reinforced the image of the sober American Canoe Association. In 1885, Harry Eckford declared that "temperance is not only *courted*, but indispensable" at the ACA encampments.[121] The organization's public adherence to temperance should come as no surprise. Temperance, as Craig Heron has noted, was "a cornerstone of middle-class identities" in the late nineteenth century, one of the chief ways in which "growing numbers of professionals, businessmen, white-collar workers, master artisans, and their families differentiated themselves ... from the rougher elements of the manual workers below them and the decadent aristocracy above."[122]

Official rhetoric aside, there is explicit evidence that many canoeists were not teetotallers while in camp. In addition to photographs of the canoeists drinking, including George Warder's snap depicted in figure 4.5, we have textual accounts detailing their consumption of alcohol. The *British Daily Whig*, for example, reported that the arrival

4.5 George Warder, "Mixed Drinks," 1887. Publicly, the ACA encampments were dry spaces, a reflection of the association's commitment to respectability. In practice, the canoeists consumed alcohol on site. That amateur photographer George Warder was able to take such a playful approach to the subject of alcohol speaks to the place of drink at the ACA encampments. Fenimore Museum, ACA Collection, box 1.1/28.

of former Commodore Winne at the 1893 meet on Wolfe Island was celebrated with a case of champagne.[123] Likewise, D'Arcy Scott's 1896 description of a canoeist new to camp included the consumption of alcohol as part of the process of arriving at the Grindstone Island meet. According to Scott, "dealing out tin cups of ready-made cocktails" was a ritual of arrival that made the canoeist "one of the boys."[124] It was not just men who drank at the ACA meets, but women as well. Pauline Johnson expressed her delight with the Vesper Canoe Club campfire at the Brophy's Point meet on Wolfe Island, but particularly the "merry hosts, blazing bonfire and delicious claret cup."[125] This finding dovetails with Heron's assertion that not all in the middle and upper classes "bought into the dry life." To the contrary, some were "quite prepared to accept such vices as drinking, smoking, gambling, and other moral indiscretions provided that those pleasures were not excessive or socially dangerous."[126] What was important then was the optics of imbibing: "moderate consumption in genteel surroundings" emerged as the new ideal.[127]

Not everyone who drank at the ACA meets adhered to the principle of moderation. In his memoirs of the encampments, Paul Vernon introduces his readers to "Lipp," who, many nights, after attending campfires where "hospitality" was abundant, "made his bed for lack of personal transportation ability, by the fire's edge."[128] The 1893 Wolfe Island meet was particularly notable for its excesses of drink. One evening, Vernon arrived "to find a wild crowd surging around the inside of a ten by twelve tent much enthused by free quantity of cheer for the pleasure of slow assimilation seemed to be outweighed by the desire to reach a volume and a state of inebriety as rapidly as was physically possible."[129] D.B. Goodsell reported from the same meet, "Wiser of Prescott ... brought ... so many cases of Wiser's Canadian whisky that they filled all of one tent except for an aisle in the middle," and decorated sailor Paul Butler had a "bar tent, which he called the Midway."[130] It is likely no coincidence that these more explicit references to alcohol and drunkenness were included in memoirs written long after the fact.

Some of the organizers' anxieties about alcohol consumption appear to have been well founded, for overconsumption was not without consequence. On the final night of the infamous 1893 camp on Wolfe Island, "a gay group of men not desiring to take home any liquids they had brought with them, drank them all up." Then, "needing wood for a campfire, they appropriated the tent floors," which had previously been sold to the owners of the campsite, and "soon these pine boards were crackling, furnishing plenty of light and heat as they flamed skywards." As if this was not enough, the group then went looking for spectators for their blaze, carrying sleeping men on cots out of their tents to the fireside.[131]

The contradictory characterizations of the camp as both a dry and a wet space are perhaps best explained by concerns about middle-class respectability. Clearly, there were some people in camp who opposed consumption without qualification, suggesting a personal commitment to sobriety. Paul Vernon recalled being taken aside after the brewer's party by fellow club member Bob Wilkin and reprimanded for attending such a gathering. According to Wilkin, who was at least a few years senior, Vernon "would be classed as that kind" if he took part in such activities.[132] At the other end of the spectrum were those with little regard for keeping up appearances, including Lipp and Wiser. More common were those who participated in or condoned a drinking culture so long as it was kept away from the prying eyes of outsiders. Vernon recalled that at a meet on Sugar Island, "social refreshments at camps were taken behind the tents" – on account of the visitors.[133] Behaviour such as this enabled the maintenance of the American Canoe Association's public claim to respectability.

Speaking about the Industrial Exhibition, Keith Walden hypothesizes, "Perhaps because the grounds were a site where unusual degrees of transgression were permitted, a variety of agencies, both public and private, made special efforts to maintain high standards of rectitude."[134] These included church groups, temperance associations, and law enforcement officials. The American Canoe Association encampments, as spaces beyond the bounds of everyday existence with their own logics, also invited transgression, if not to the same degree as the exhibitions. Unlike the Industrial Exhibitions, efforts to curtail disorder at the ACA meets were undertaken not by outside agencies, but by onsite administrators. In the steps taken by the organizers and officials to promote order, however, we see attempts to shape the social landscape of the camp similar to those employed at the exhibitions. The camp schedule always included a Divine Service on Sundays, and men and women were to interact with the utmost propriety under the watchful gaze of chaperones. Temperance, to borrow from Harry Eckford, was "to be courted," indispensable as it was to the public respectability of the camp and its campers.[135] Finally, the rule of law was to prevail.

As these examples make clear, claims that the American Canoe Association encampments were spaces of freedom obscured the degree to which both the campsites and the campers were objects of governance.

As the organizers worked to order the encampments, they drew on the technologies of liberal government employed by the state in the same period. Most notable are efforts to rule through desire, or the conduct of conduct. Although there was a system of policing in place, the organizers hoped the campers would adhere to camp rules of their own volition, inspired by a personal desire for conformity rather than a fear of punishment. Of course, in spite of the myriad efforts to construct the encampments as spaces of order, the events were always disorderly at some level, a point that was particularly evident on visitors' days and in the evenings.

In this chapter, I explored the American Canoe Association encampments as "spaces of representation," a term used by Henri Lefebvre to describe spaces imagined and enacted by those in positions of power, in this case, the organizers and the executive committee.[136] In the next two chapters, my concern is with the ACA campsites as lived spaces, produced through the spatial practices of the campers themselves as they negotiated the expectations of the organizers. This desire to juxtapose governance with the practices of everyday life speaks to a more general concern in social history with the dialogic relationship between structure and agency. It also reflects my contention that the ACA encampments were more complex spaces then they appear at first glance: The American Canoe Association sought to create a particular kind of sporting space, while the participants often had different ends in mind.

Chapter Five

Domesticating

In 1896, American Canoe Association member D'Arcy Scott invited readers of *Massey's Magazine* to "follow a new-comer, as he arrives in camp":

> Landing from the steamer he doesn't look in the least like a canoeist, with his stiff, brown hat and neat, grey suit; but he must be, for the deck hands have just carried out a sort of overgrown coffin case ... which turns out to contain his canoe. He has not been on the wharf many minutes when he is taken charge by his friends ... Half an hour later we find the same individual decked out in flannels, with tennis shoes and a soft felt or flannel hat decorating his extremities, seated on a half-empty trunk in front of a tent just put up with the assistance of the camp carpenter and many willing and sunburnt hands, dealing out tin cups of ready-made cocktails, a couple of bottles of which he has been fortunate enough to bring with him. He's one of the boys now and has passed the ordeal of arriving in camp.[1]

Scott's description of the newcomer suggests that to arrive at the annual meet was also to "cross a threshold."[2] The ACA encampments, in other words, were liminal spaces, distinct from and yet connected to the spaces of home and work. This liminality was reinforced by the physical and temporal bounds of the annual meets: most encampments were on points of land only accessible by water, and they occupied a fixed length of time.[3] Crossing the threshold was about moving from the imagined community of canoeists into the material space of the encampment. This was a conceptual transition. It was also, as Scott's description makes clear, an embodied process that involved disembarking at the wharf, unloading baggage, visiting the secretary, donning camp clothes, and raising and outfitting a tent.

In this chapter, I explore these practices of "settling in" to better understand the transformation that campers underwent as they crossed the threshold, but also to make sense of the world they created at the encampments. The canoeists engaged in a number of verbal, mental, and physical acts of domestication most evident in the early days of the meet, but which continued until the last tent was taken down. I conceive of these acts as part of "creating a place in the world articulated via the home, that is, fashioning a space of belonging."[4] We might call this the making of domestic place or *placing domesticity*. Placing domesticity was at once a public and a personal gesture. It was a way for the campers to signal the character of the meets to outsiders, to present the encampment, the regatta, and even canoeing as white, middle-class forms of "proper" sport and recreation. It was also a labour of love, a reflection of the meaningfulness of the experience for members of the ACA. This chapter hinges on my belief that for two (or in some cases three) weeks the encampment functioned as a home away from home.[5] Borrowing from Alison Blunt and Robyn Dowling, I define home as "a place/site, a set of feelings/cultural meanings, and the relations between the two."[6] The "process of creating and understanding forms of dwelling and belonging" has both "material and imaginative elements ... [P]eople create home through social and emotional relationships. Home is also materially created – new structures formed, objects used and placed."[7]

In many respects, this aspect of encampment life is at odds with conventional understandings of outdoor recreation in the late nineteenth century – which suggest that white, middle-class men fled their homes for the "wilderness" and a temporary life of savagery in order to reinvigorate their masculinity and counter the physically debilitating effects of modern life.[8] In what follows, I propose that this class of men had a more complex relationship to home and domesticity than dominant constructions of Victorian masculinity allow. This chapter complements existing scholarship on male domesticity in homosocial locales such as clubs, lodges, and navy ships through a consideration of homemaking by white, middle-class men at leisure in wild environments inspired by, but never truly single-sex spaces.[9] Ostensibly, men went to the wilderness to escape the feminine space of the home, not to reproduce it. And yet, this is just what men who were members of the American Canoe Association did, in the presence of and at times in conjunction with women.

Most canoeists arrived at the American Canoe Association encampment by steamer. The toot of the boat's horn was "the signal for a grand turnout of the camp."[10] At the 1900 meet in Muskoka, "as soon as the gangway was run out there were many joyful meetings. Some of the old campers were literally received with open arms."[11] The gathered crowd usually offered assistance to the new arrivals. Canoes and trunks were carried off the boat and loaded onto wagons and carts.[12] Before they made their way to their campsites, the canoeists stopped at the secretary's tent at the headquarters. Whereas the wharf and waterfront functioned as the physical threshold of the encampment, enabling embodied passage from the outside to the inside much like a doorway, the headquarters was the practical threshold. It was here that those arriving at the campsite were either accepted into the fold and handed a camp badge, or turned away. This process of vetting arrivals constructed the American Canoe Association meets as bounded spaces and enabled the practices of domestication and sociability that defined encampment life for the canoeists.

Although the first campsites were fairly simple affairs, later encampments were more like small villages.[13] The organizers laid out "streets" to link the main sites of the camp, but also to act as thoroughfares within the men's and women's camps.[14] The streets were usually lined with strings of lanterns. At Croton Point on the Hudson River in 1894, lamp posts, some of which boasted electric light, were installed along the main road.[15] It was common practice for the campers to name the streets and to erect signposts such as those visible in figure 5.1.[16] Some of the street names cited particular clubs. "Knickbocker Avenue" and "Ianthe Avenue" referenced canoe clubs in New York and New Jersey, respectively. Others reproduced familiar urban locales such as "Madison Square" (New York) and "Rittenhouse Square" (Philadelphia) or thoroughfares like "Yonge Street" (Toronto) and "Beacon Street" (Boston). Finally, some of the names were tongue-in-cheek. "Baxter Street" was a well-known destination for immigrants arriving to New York in the late nineteenth century. It served as a stock image for social reformers wishing to "capture the horrors of 19th-century housing before tenement house reform."[17]

Street names, street signs, and lanterns reproduced the geographies of home by overlaying urban logics and objects on the natural topography of the campsite. Whereas the organization of the encampment, including laying out the streets, was typically initiated and overseen by the organizing committee, it was usually the campers who took responsibility for naming and erecting signs. In her work on Mina Hubbard's travels through Labrador, Wendy Roy argues that the attribution of names with private meaning to geographical features were a key part of Hubbard's "personalization and domestication of the landscape."[18] Of course, naming is also an act of power, a form of "spatial punctuation"

5.1 S.R. Stoddard, "Toronto Canoe Club Camp," 1889. For all of their efforts to escape the city for natural landscapes – a chief objective of outdoor recreation then and now – as we see in this photograph, the canoeists reproduced many of the features of urban life in their encampment, including streets, street signs, and streetlights. Fenimore Museum, ACA Collection, box 1.5/2.

that transforms space into "an object of knowledge, something that could be explored and read."[19] At once "material and metaphorical, substantive and symbolic," place names are "read, spoken, mapped, catalogued and written in the everyday intimate and official bureaucratic geographies of road signs, street names and addresses," making them central to "questions of power, culture, location and identity."[20] Naming streets at the ACA encampments was at once an affective act of domestication and a performance of colonial privilege.

Additional evidence of the village-like atmosphere of the encampments can be seen in the main camp, where the ordering of the tents was largely done on the basis of club affiliation. Here, the Brooklyn Canoe Club or Ottawa Canoe Club camps functioned as "neighbourhoods." With the move to Sugar Island in 1903, these neighbourhoods were inscribed on the landscape in a more enduring way, such that "every locality had its own camp. There was New York Bay with the New York men on one side and the Rochester men at Irondequoit Park on the other."[21] Eventually, these names appeared on official maps of the Sugar Island campsite.

The American Canoe Association encampment, like an urban locale, offered a number of amenities to those staying on site. During any given meet, the canoeists could visit the camp store, doctor's office, barbershop, post office, darkroom, repair tent, or customs office.[22] On a handful of occasions, the presence of art galleries reinforced the urbane air of the annual gatherings.[23] More often than not, these amenities were situated in the centre of the encampment, part of or near to the camp headquarters, which served as the high street to the residential quarters of the campsite.

After 1885, most of the encampments had a dining tent or shed. These represented points of contact between wildness and civilization. R.B. Burchard, referring to the 1896 mess on Grindstone Island, noted that on nice days "the canvas wall at one end was removed so that the diners could look upon the water and wooded shores beyond."[24] Dining tents rarely had a wood floor, so the canoeists ate with grass and dirt beneath their feet. It was not unusual for small creatures, such as mice or birds, to pass through the dining space. The wait staff were typically the daughters and wives of local farmers or fishers, presumably with little formal training or experience. Nevertheless, as the example of the 1898 Stave Island meet (figure 5.2) illustrates, the servers were uniformed, and the mess tent was decorated with strings of lanterns and flags, linen tablecloths, and china dishes. These decorations, many of which recall a Victorian dining parlour, hint at a desire for gentility at mealtimes. Abigail Van Slyck has identified a similar impulse at summer camps where mealtimes were important reminders of civilization for campers otherwise encouraged to embrace their inner savage.[25] The dining tent was a visible manifestation of efforts to domesticate the ACA encampment and to cultivate a sense of the place as "home."[26]

Perhaps the most striking examples of placing domesticity were the canvas abodes that housed the campers during the annual meet. Sleeping in a tent was understood to be part and parcel of attending the American Canoe Association encampment. Consider this excerpt from the *Syracuse Daily Standard*: "When canoeing at a canoe meet a man is supposed to live in a tent. Even upon Lake George where gorgeous hotels dotted the shores, the canoeists were banded by an unwritten law to live an Indian life ... to bring his own tent, pitch it and live in it."[27] In practice, not everyone who attended the meets stayed on site or slept in tents. Some boarded with local families, stayed in cottages near to the

5.2 A.A. Lewis, "Dinner Time in the Mess Tent," 1898. The mess tent at the 1898 meet on Stave Island with its oriental lanterns and centrepieces was one of the more elaborate of the encampment dining halls. Most, however, if not all of the encampment mess tents boasted the trappings of civilized dining, including tablecloths, china, and uniformed servers. Mess tents were at once manifestations of middle-class propriety and also carefully crafted home spaces. Fenimore Museum, ACA Collection, box 1.2/27.

campsite, or slept at neighbouring hotels.[28] Still others stayed in boats. The members of the Mohican Canoe Club of Albany, New York, were well known for their colourful canoe tents in the 1880s, and not a few canoeists passed the two weeks of the gathering in a houseboat moored off the wharf.[29] For the majority of participants, however, home away from home during the encampment was a canvas tent.

Tents at the early meets were relatively simple. Most of them were small A-frame structures covered with canvas and with a rubber ground sheet that accommodated one or two people. Some campers continued to make use of these compact constructions, but the trend was towards larger tents. To some extent, this was a matter of convenience; by the 1890s, campers would typically share a tent with fellow club members, family, or friends. However, a larger tent was also a matter of comfort and perhaps even of status. Larger tents had more space for entertaining, but also for displaying one's belongings. Wall tents became particularly popular after the 1886 encampment and remained the norm for the rest of the period covered by this study, a shift *Forest and Stream* attributed to the influence of English canoeist Warrington Baden-Powell, brother to Boy Scouts founder Robert Baden-Powell, who attended that Grindstone Island meet with fellow Englishman Walter Stewart.[30]

Wall tents were typically erected on a wooden base. The organizing committee arranged for carpenters to construct wooden floors in advance of the meet, passing the cost onto the campers. Once on site, some canoeists also hired the camp carpenters to raise their tents.[31] By the 1890s, most tents had a second "room" that served as a parlour. In some cases, this was enclosed; more often, it was open.[32] Also commonplace were folding camp cots. The shift towards tent floors and cots was underpinned by a desire for comfort. The popularity, however, of these amenities was likely also related to their perceived healthfulness. Sleeping bodies were considered particularly vulnerable.[33] Tent floors and cots removed the sleeping canoeist from the ground, which was believed to emit harmful vapours, and encouraged the movement of air within and beneath the tents. Circulating air, as Conevery Valencius has shown, was good air.[34]

Canoeists planning to cook for themselves, or even those who had hired a cook, constructed spaces near their tent sites for the preparation and consumption of food. "Kitchens" ranged from "a fireplace built of stones, over which hangs a pot on a cross-bar, supported by two upright, forked sticks" to "a shed of boards ... with an iron stove set up."[35] Most clubs erected a shared tent to serve as a dining room.[36] Some built tables and benches at which to take their meals and outdoor shelves to hold their dishes and foodstuffs, or they hired the camp carpenter to do the same.[37] As we can see in figure 5.3, these dining tables, like those in the mess tent, were usually covered with linen cloths and adorned with wild flowers.[38]

With their tents raised, the canoeists had space to change into their "camp togs." Clothing was an important signifier at the American Canoe Association encampments. The role of clothing in ordering the encampment is perhaps most visible in the cut of the officers' uniforms (figure 5.4). Their style, like the structure of the organization, was inspired by naval culture and dictated by the association's constitution: "The uniform of the officers of the ACA shall be of blue, with the letters

5.3 Ubique Canoe Club Mess, c. 1886. Even those campers who took meals at their tent site, prepared with their own hands or by a hired cook, employed the accoutrements of middle-class dining visible in this photograph of the Ubique Canoe Club's mess tent on Grindstone Island. This photograph, like figure 5.2, counters the image of the ACA encampments as wild locales, revealing the tensions between escaping and reproducing urban domesticity. MacKendrick Albums, Private Collection.

ACA embroidered in gold on the collar. The Commodore shall wear three rows of gold lace on each sleeve, the Vice-Commodore two, the Rear-Commodore one."[39] Robert J. Wilkin, writing in *Forest and Stream*, petitioned the "commanding officers of clubs" to attend the 1885 meet at Grindstone Island not as officers, but as ACA members. Too many commodores, Wilkin argued, would muddle the proper hierarchies and channels of power within the organization.[40] Jennifer Craik argues that the "adoption and retention of a military-influenced uniform," because of established links to order and discipline, "leant credibility and

5.4 "Official Headquarters," 1886. This photograph captures the ACA leadership in their military-inspired uniforms, revealing forms of self-representation that celebrate order, discipline, and hierarchy. The image is also of interest for the casual intimacy of the two men in the centre of the image. Such intimacy is not unusual in ACA photographs. Its very ordinariness subverts the stereotypical image of staid and restrained Victorians. It is also suggestive of homosocial intimacies at the encampments (chapter 6). Fenimore Museum, ACA Collection, box 1.1/18.

authority" to contemporaneous organizations, such as the Salvation Army. The American Canoe Association appears to have used uniforms in a similar way, as a means of legitimizing their fledgling project of a national canoe organization.[41] That said, uniforms were not mandatory in camp. The ACA constitution allowed for the "use of uniforms" to be at "the discretion of each officer."[42] At the very least, uniforms were worn during ceremonial occasions, which is also when visitors were most likely to be on site.

Clothing expressed belonging, most often signalling membership in a particular club. Full club uniforms were commonplace in the early years of the annual meets. At the 1884 Grindstone Island meet, members of the New York Canoe Club wore a hunter green Norfolk blouse, knee breeches, long stockings, and a cap of white linen duck embroidered with the club's insignia.[43] By the time of the 1888 meet on Lake George, this practice had fallen off to the disappointment of some: "While nothing is lost in picturesque effect, the change is rather to be regretted, as the effect of a club uniform was, as in the army, to unite the club, to heighten the *esprit de corps*, and to induce each club to make the best show that was possible."[44] Even with the decline in full uniforms, canoeists at the encampments continued to sport clothing such as sweaters and hats adorned with club insignia.[45]

Not everyone wore club clothing. For others, "the rule of dress" at the ACA meets was "to get as far away as possible from conventional patterns, and suit yourself exclusively."[46] The first Grindstone Island camp, in 1884, boasted a number of "oddities of costume," the most remarkable being the "tall-peaked, sugar-loaf straw hats ... ornamented with tassels and broad hat-bands of bright red."[47] The 1890 meet at Jessup's Neck was particularly notable for its unconventional attire. The *New York Times* reported: "Color runs riot in apparel [this year]. Nothing is too bright and no combination too startling for a canoeist to wear, and even a man who walks around in a bright yellow silk nightcap, a scarlet shirt, green knickerbockers, blue stockings, red shoes, and a spotted sash has yet caused a public uprising."[48] Diana Crane suggests that one of the consequences of new forms of work in America was the growing importance of clothing in signalling rank within the workplace, a shift that may have made abandoning convention particularly appealing.[49] Certainly, unusual outfits were cited as evidence of the freedoms afforded by life at the American Canoe Association encampments, but also of individuality. That the event could offer such apparent freedoms speaks to the organization's success in establishing the campsite as a safe space, an accomplishment that depended on the myriad gatekeeping practices the organization performed.

I do not want to overemphasize the degree to which the canoeists bucked trends and expectations in their clothing choices. If photographs of the annual gatherings are any indication, most of the men appear to have worn some variation on trousers or knickers and button-down shirts or wool sweaters for much of this period.[50] Even such quotidian fashion situated the ACA meet in relation to the home spaces the canoeists had temporarily left behind; the relatively informal clothing marked the space of the encampment as distinct from the more formal world of middle-class urbanity.

Contrary to expectation, accounts of the American Canoe Association encampments pay scant attention to what women were wearing. One exception was a dispatch from the 1894 meet at Croton Point that appeared in the *New York Sun*: "The canoe girl, as a rule, wears a Tam o' Shanter hat, dark blue serge or flannel dress, with an extremely light skirt, under which are Knickerbockers, heavy stockings, and rubber-soled shoes. The trousers are not due to the arguments of dress reformers, but to common sense. When a canoe girl capsizes she unhooks and discards her skirt, and can then move freely in righting her little ship. When inside her craft she puts the skirt on again, and when she sails home no one is the wiser."[51] It is worth highlighting the reporter's efforts to distance the dress choices of the women on site from "dress reform," a particularly contentious aspect of the women's movement that was gathering steam in the closing decades of the nineteenth century.[52] Nevertheless, the uniform described here was consistent with changes underway in women's fashion that released women from the strictures of Victorian apparel. Pauline Johnson was also attuned to the clothing women wore at the encampments. Following the 1893 meet on Wolfe Island, Johnson urged her fellow women canoeists to maintain their "reputation for healthy pastime" by rejecting "fashionable frills": "For the love of that most blessed of endowments given by your creator, health, don't mimic the cripple or quarrel with your better, most sensible self just because the little goddess fashion is whimsical and at times despises so wickedly the beauty of perfect form and health in the human body."[53]

These few examples aside, it was men's clothing that raised concerns for observers of the American Canoe Association encampments. In 1888, in a description of the gathering on Lake George, C. Bowyer Vaux opined: "The men seemed to think much more of dress than is usual at the meets, no doubt on account of the many ladies who camped on what in former years was known as Squaw Point."[54] In Vaux's lament, we see anxieties resurfacing about the presence of women in camp, but perhaps also concerns about the instability of masculinity. The attention paid to men's fashion suggests it was a fine line between respectability and the effeminacy associated with the contemporary figure of the dandy. In late nineteenth-century Britain, for example, Brent Shannon argues, "Antagonism toward effeminate behavior accelerated during an age in which rugged masculinity and athleticism were enthusiastically celebrated by popular culture. Any man who seemed to care too much about his appearance risked accusations that he was weak and womanish."[55] That such concerns emerged in a wilderness setting, a space seemingly divorced from urban life, is all the more interesting.

Given the power of clothing, it is no wonder those concerned with the public image of the American Canoe Association sought to police fashion.

Having raised their tents and donned their camp clothes, it was time for the canoeists to move into their temporary homes, which as we see in figures 5.5 and 5.6, was no small feat. The contents of the tents reflected both practical and aesthetic concerns.[56] Rugs and bearskins spread across the wood or earthen floors of the tent offered a homey defence against dampness and cold. Canvas cots put further distance between sleeping bodies and the ground, while heavy woollen blankets protected against cool August nights. Hastily built shelves and "bureaus" provided storage space for clothing, hygiene products, and trinkets. Camp chairs and trunks covered with shawls served as seats for entertaining. Hanging lanterns illuminated tent interiors, while mirrors affixed to tent poles facilitated grooming. Ice chests kept drinks and foodstuffs cold. Finally, brightly coloured flags, photographs and paintings, canoe paddles, and oriental lanterns personalized the space.

As they decorated their temporary living spaces at the American Canoe Association encampments, the canoeists employed conventions of bourgeois Victorian house design. Tents are perhaps best understood in relation to the parlour/living room. By the late nineteenth century, the parlour had become "a kind of stage upon which the family presented itself to visitors."[57] It increasingly featured "cozy corners" with overstuffed chairs and sofas intended to "invite repose and freedom from conventionality by offering a place to sprawl and lounge at ease."[58] Eventually, the parlour evolved into the living room – part of the "gradual transformation of the highly specialized and intensely private Victorian house into the open and unspecialized twentieth-century house." The living room not only collapsed distinctions between public and private, it was also explicitly devoted to "personal temperament and its self-expression."[59] Karen Halttunen attributes the move from parlour to living room and the emergence of a twentieth-century home type to changes in middle-class social life, but especially to the informal sociability characteristic of life at summer houses and while camping.[60] Cottages and tents frequently boasted an "outdoor parlor," adorned with "hammocks, large rockers, wicker tables and settees, rugs, decorative screens, and Japanese lanterns."[61] Restricted access made these spaces and the social practices they engendered possible. There was "no need for a front hall to exclude the undesirable or a parlor where claims to social position could be made through the formalities of the genteel performance, because those present at the summer home had already been screened."[62] The same was true at the ACA meets, where

5.5 "A Typical ACA Squaw Camp," 1890. Most of the people who attended the ACA meets did not rough it, as the tents depicted above and in figure 5.6 (opposite) make clear. To the contrary, many of the canoeists carefully crafted home spaces for themselves. Their tents served as representations of individual, club, and familial personalities. The decision to be photographed in or near to their tents is a further act of self-representation. Fenimore Museum, ACA Collection, box 1.1/19.

canoeists had been vetted during the membership process and again at the registration desk.

It is also useful to think about the canoeists' tents in relation to another room in the late Victorian home: the bedroom. Bedrooms were intimate spaces for dressing and sleeping. They were also, by the late nineteenth century, "known for their ability to convey *individuality*."[63] The bedroom, opined one contemporary design writer, "is the place for one's personal belongings, those numberless little things which are such sure indications of individual character and fancy ... the one room where purely personal preference may be freely exercised."[64]

Unlike bedrooms, however, tents did not ensure privacy.[65] Paul Vernon recalled of the 1893 encampment at Brophy's Point: "Colonel [William H. Cotton] was Commodore that year with a large white tent

5.6 S.R. Stoddard, "A Tent Interior," 1891. Fenimore Museum, ACA Collection, box 1.2/18.

in the center of camp. We noticed as we went past the first night that the Colonel's candle, as he retired furnished a perfect silhouette on the tent's side of his movements, showing all the actions of change, from his daily garb to the final hop into bed."[66] J.I. Little argues that the "minimum of privacy" afforded by tents is evidence of "the communal nature" of camp life.[67] Shared living, but particularly limited privacy, reinforced the bonds of community – for better or worse.

Photographic and textual accounts of the ACA meets routinely depict the canvas houses with their flaps pulled back, their "contents unblushingly revealed to the passer-by."[68] There were very practical reasons for keeping one's tent open, not least because canvas tents could be unbearably hot. Tents were also left open to "admit the sun and air." Contemporary science posited that sunshine killed harmful bacteria and provided the necessary energy to promote health.[69] Equally important to human health was clean air; bad air (miasma) was commonly understood to carry disease.[70] The canoeists also opened their tents for the visual consumption of others. Paige Raibmon argues that Victorians understood domestic spaces and domestic goods as "material markers of civilization," and as windows onto "the individual's soul and the family's moral state."[71] Thus, we might interpret this transformation of private domestic space into a public spectacle as part of individual self-fashioning made available for public consumption, a way for canoeists to demonstrate their morality, civilization, and perhaps also their gendered personality to fellow campers and to people visiting the ACA campsites. The display of tent interiors further reveals the reach of the emerging consumerist ethos of the day – and the belief that one's identity was intimately tied to one's possessions – beyond urban centres to "backwoods encampments."[72]

Tents did more than straddle the divide between public and private, between healthy and unhealthy, between rural and urban. Like cabins at children's camps, tents "represented points of contact between the natural world and domestic space."[73] In addition to allowing fresh air and sunshine to cross the threshold, accounts of the annual ACA gatherings reveal how the boundaries of tents were constantly breeched by insects and animals. At the 1890 meet at Jessup's Neck, the campsite was "full of a sort of field mouse, a very tame little animal that [ran] in and out of the tents and under the tent floors."[74] Not all creatures were received so congenially. The ubiquity of centipedes at the Juniper Island meet on Stony Lake in 1883 prompted one canoeist to sleep in his canoe rather than remain on land.[75]

Tents, including the mess tent, were also vulnerable to vagaries of climate. Heavy rains during the first week of the Stave Island meet in 1889 "searched out the weak places in the tents very effectively," leaving the campers wet and disgruntled.[76] Some tents were more susceptible to rain than others, especially the single-pole pavilion tents with their "striped sides, gaily painted poles and very flat roofs."[77] Few tents, however, could protect against cold. Paul Vernon recalled, "Being new to cot life in camp, I turned in the first night directly above the canvas of the cot to find I was damp and cold. As the only warm thing around was the oil lantern, I pulled it in to dry out the dampness, pulling it up and down on the canvas to ease the chill."[78] Vernon's body was accustomed to home beds, in which the "heavy hair-filled mattress keeps out the cold." He eventually adapted by layering blankets beneath him on the cot, but not before having a bad night's sleep and burning his foot on the oil lantern. Inhabiting a tent was not always a comfortable experience. Nevertheless, most of the ACA canoeists appear to have embraced the porous boundary between inside and outside, between civilization and nature.

Decorating extended beyond the walls of the tent to include the areas surrounding the canvas abodes. Whereas interior ornamentation balanced convenience and visual appeal, exterior decorating was largely about making the tent and its owner(s) identifiable to those passing by. The canoeists might raise flags or banners signalling their nationality. More typical were decorations that announced canoe club affiliation, suggesting that club membership was more important than citizenship. Also commonly seen was canoeing paraphernalia such as paddles, sails, and boats – marking the space as a canoescape and the camper as a serious canoeist. Finally, there were, occasionally, less conventional objects, such as the giant pocket watch that hung from the Brooklyn Canoe Club tent at one of the Grindstone Island meets.[79]

As much as exterior decorating had functional or ornamental ends, it also reveals how the canoeists understood themselves in relation to others. Consider, for example, the shell designs that adorned the grounds of the 1890 meet at Jessup's Neck, one of which is shown in figure 5.7. Visible along the main avenue on Long Island, the shell designs depicted club totems such as the Red Dragon, as well as touchstones in colonial American history, including the sailing craft that carried the early European settlers (Puritan Ship), the site of the Puritans' landing (Plymouth Rock), and the fabled location of the signing of the "treaty of friendship" between William Penn and the Shackamaxon Delawares (Treaty Elm) that provided the land for the city of Philadelphia.[80] Sydney Krause submits that the latter at once "memorializes a founding Quaker desire for amity between the races" and "testifies to an eventual erosion of that policy – predictably, the triumph in time of racial enmity over amity."[81] The shell drawings, in other words, recalled and celebrated white settlement. They also provided narrative justification for the presence of white canoeists specifically and white Americans generally on Indigenous land.

Other decorations were equally political. Beginning in 1902, at the Camp Cod meet, the tents at the women's camp stood under the Squaw Point burgee described in chapter 4. The flag was raised at a "pow wow" at which the women dressed as "Squaws" and arranged themselves around a campfire on blankets.[82] The Squaw Point flag was a visible reminder of the very people displaced by the encampments and white settlement more broadly. It is unlikely the women would have thought of their flag in these terms, but by the turn of the century, it was possible to romanticize Indigenous cultures in a way that was unimaginable a few decades earlier at the height of the "Indian Wars"

5.7 S.R. Stoddard, "Squaw-Land." In addition to their personal tents and the mess tent, the canoeists also decorated the encampment grounds. In 1890, at the meet on Long Island, this took the form of shell designs captured here in an image by commercial photographer Seneca Ray Stoddard. The composition of the photograph recalls the *tableaux vivants* (living pictures) popular in the late nineteenth century. Stephen Petersen (see "Tableaux," in *Encyclopedia of Nineteenth-Century Photography* [London: Routledge, 2013], 1373–5) argues that this genre was an important mechanism through which people in this period negotiated group and individual identities. Such scenes often drew on "historical or allegorical themes, or to recognizable moments from everyday life." In this case, the inhabitants of the ladies' camp and visitors are arranged in small groups, many of which are engaging with the shell design on the ground in the middle right of the photograph. The design depicts a teepee-style tent, perhaps an homage to Squaw Point. S.R. Stoddard, *Glimpses of the ACA* (Glens Falls, 1890).

when Indigenous peoples threatened American westward expansion.[83] In 1893, however, Frederick Jackson Turner, in a public address delivered at the Columbian Exposition, had declared the frontier closed.[84] It was at this historical moment, Paige Raibmon argues, "as political and economic conditions seemed to ensure the disappearance of Aboriginal people and culture, that non-Aboriginal fascination with romantic images of vanishing Indians flourished."[85]

No campsite was complete without strings of "oriental lanterns." Such lanterns, in the absence of electricity, served the practical purpose of illuminating the ACA encampments; they were also objects of "orientalism."[86] Late nineteenth-century culture was awash in decorative arrangements that drew inspiration from the Islamic, Indian, Japanese, and Chinese cultures that constituted "the Orient."[87] Orientalism appealed because it "hinted at something else, something perhaps not so urbane and genteel, even at something slightly impermissible – luxurious, to be sure, but also with touches of life's underside."[88] Edward Said maintains the appropriation of so-called oriental culture was not benign. Rather, orientalism, by presenting the "Other" as primitive, uncivilized, and childlike, provided the necessary ideological rationales for Western imperialism.[89] Imperial expansion was not just underwritten by representations; it was also effected through consumption. Kristin Hoganson has shown how as American consumers purchased tropical produce, ostrich plumes, and in this case, oriental lanterns, they were literally "buying into empire."[90] As we shall see in the next chapter, orientalism was not limited to campsite decorations, but was also evident in the spectacles on offer at the meets.

Descriptions of the ladies' camp are overrepresented in accounts of the American Canoe Association encampments, implicitly reinforcing the already established association between women, domestic space, and decoration and obscuring the degree to which men were enthusiastic participants in domesticating the campsite.[91] Historians have traditionally conceived of outdoor living as "offering the middle-class male an escape from domesticity and the opportunity to reassert his social dominance."[92] Men's participation in placing domesticity at the ACA meets calls such interpretations into question, suggesting men's relationship to domestic space was more complex. To borrow from Martin Francis, "If there was a 'flight from domesticity' in the late Victorian and Edwardian periods, it was unable to claim a monopoly over the masculine imagination, which was characterized by contradictory patterns of desire and self-identification." "Men," Francis contends, "were continually seeking to reconcile and integrate the contradictory impulses of domestic responsibility and escapism, both of which could, at various times, find sanction in the polyphonic voices of popular culture or politics."[93]

The American Canoe Association encampments are of particular interest because unlike those locales where historians have documented male domesticity – lodges, clubs, navy ships – the encampments were mixed-sex venues. To be fair, the ACA meets were not entirely unique as spaces of mixed-sex sociability in which men performed domesticity alongside women. J.I. Little's work on the Lake Memphremagog encampments of American social reformers in the late nineteenth century suggests their "camping experience ... elevated the domestic sphere," rather than trying to do away with it.[94] However, unlike the Memphremagog encampments, which Little characterizes as egalitarian, the ACA meets were not concerned with transforming the social order through domestic labour. If anything, these canoeing encampments reinforced the social hierarchies of late nineteenth-century life.

The impulse to domesticate for both men and women may have been a response to the very mobility of the encampments, and by extension to the canoeists' increasingly mobile lives. Angel Kwolek-Folland's work on Kansas homesteaders in the late nineteenth century is useful in thinking about the tensions between mobility and domesticity in this period of marked change and movement.[95] As Kwolek-Folland observes, "Late Victorian definitions of what it meant to be an American derived from a profound awareness of cultural and physical change and the perceived need to stabilize or standardize American social institutions." Mobility was one aspect of this rapidly changing world and one that Kwolek-Folland submits became a "conscious part of the national self-definition" in the wake of the 1880 census, which revealed the frequency with which Americans changed their dwelling. Domesticating temporary living spaces, be they a dugout or a rented room, through the careful placing of objects, was one way the women at the heart of Kwolek-Folland's study "created a stable home."[96]

My characterization of the tents as homes away from home would not be foreign to the ACA canoeists. They themselves frequently described their canvas dwellings using domestic nomenclature.[97] Not everyone in attendance, however, was comfortable with these practices of domestication. In 1888, when the meet was at Long Island on Lake George, a reporter for *Forest and Stream* claimed the character of the camp had changed "materially over the last three years"; each year the camp was "becoming less primitive and more civilized." The tents were now "double the size" and frequently furnished with "spring cots, rugs, chairs and tables"; board floors had become a necessity rather than a luxury; and the "large Saratoga [trunk] had replaced the modest camp chest."[98] The 1893 meet at Brophy's Point on Wolfe Island was particularly infuriating for "old-timers," with its "telegraph office, two pianos, a baggage wagon, a Custom House officer and Postmaster, steamboats making seven trips a day, bait and boats for hire for fishing, a dancing platform, a hotel and restaurant, a steamboat landing, a laundry agent, [and] a daily news service."[99] The canoeists, these critics make clear, trod a fine line between civilization and savagery.

The fact that the commentators referred to conveniences at the American Canoe Association encampments as "enervating" or "effeminate" hints at the complex of ideas that underpinned contemporary anxieties about domestication. "Enervating" makes specific reference to the threat of neurasthenia, a nervous ailment brought on by modern life and believed to only affect the white, middle classes.[100] "Effeminate," by contrast, highlights the ever-present concerns about the feminization of American culture. As Gail Bederman's work has demonstrated, these were not isolated concerns. Rather, gender and race were profoundly intertwined in this period within a hegemonic Western paradigm of civilization: "In the context of the late nineteenth century's popularized Darwinism, civilization was seen as an explicitly racial concept," which denoted "a precise stage in human racial evolution ... that only applied to whites.[101] Civilization was also a gendered concept: "One could identify advanced civilizations by the degree of their sexual differentiation ... The pronounced sexual differences celebrated in the middle class's doctrine of separate spheres were assumed to be absent in savagery, but to be an intrinsic and necessary aspect of higher civilization."[102]

Physical distance aside, the American Canoe Association encampments were tethered in both material and cultural ways to the world the canoeists ostensibly left behind. Although ACA members recognized the encampments as temporary, many went out of their way to domesticate the campsite, to (re)configure the landscape in ways that recalled the familiar spaces of home and the city. Not only did the campers reproduce elements of their Victorian homes (kitchens, dining rooms, parlours, bedrooms), they also decorated these spaces accordingly, employing design conventions that drew on objects and styles produced and circulated in the networks of colonial capitalism. They arranged the campsites to recall the layouts of urban neighbourhoods complete with street signs and lamp posts. Finally, the canoeists carried objects such as albums, linens, and rugs with them from their urban dwellings to the encampments, and they returned these experiences to the city in the form of flags and photographs. This exchange between home and the encampment was part of the reimagining of urban domestic space in the late nineteenth century that gave rise to living rooms.[103]

The desire to domesticate may have been inspired by the cultural meanings attributed to home and domesticity in the late nineteenth century, the rising spectre of consumerism, or a longing for rootedness in a rapidly changing world. We must, however, also consider these practices of homemaking as expressions of the deep meaning campers attributed to the ACA encampments. The care and concern with which they ordered the spaces of the encampments and recalled the geographies of home were testaments to the significance of the annual meets to the canoeists. Regardless of motivation, the practices of domestication, which formed a key part of the culture of the encampment, call into question the extent to which outdoor recreation was a rejection of domesticity, particularly for men. Rather, following Martin Francis, we are perhaps better suited to think of the tensions between the appeal of domesticity and a desire to escape as characteristic of the experience of white, middle-class men in late nineteenth-century North America. Placing domesticity was a series of practices central to placemaking and community formation at the ACA meets. In the next chapter, we turn our attention to other ways in which the canoeists inhabited the encampments.

Chapter Six

Inhabiting

Life at the American Canoe Association encampments was predictable. The morning bugle sounded at 7:00 a.m. to rouse the campers. Half an hour later, the camp gun was fired and the colours were run up at headquarters, marking the official start to the day. A morning dip was followed by breakfast, which, in turn, was followed by time for "house-keeping" and other "camp work." During the first week of the annual gathering, the rest of the day might be spent visiting, writing letters, exploring the campsite, calling at the post office, or heading out on an excursion. During the second week, races were the order of the day. Occasionally, the schedule was altered somewhat to accommodate a church service, visitors' day, or one of the many spectacles intended to amuse. If the canoeists were on site, lunch was taken at noon in the mess tent or at their campsite, and supper was served around six. Evenings were usually passed by the campfire. The flags were lowered with the setting of the sun, and the day officially drew to a close with taps, after which camp-wide silence was expected to prevail.[1]

In the previous chapter, I considered inhabiting as a series of practices campers performed to physically transform the ACA campsites. In this chapter, I examine how the canoeists inhabited the encampments through their daily activities. Like Michael Haldrup, I conceive of inhabiting not as a stationary activity, but as a mobile practice that involves multiple forms of movement.[2] The canoeists walked from their tents to the beach to bathe, bicycled to the mess shed for meals, and paddled along the shoreline to a campfire. Of course, not all movements were so utilitarian. The 1890 meet at Jessup's Neck on Long Island was appreciated for the "pleasant walks" afforded by the beaches and nearby woods.[3]

As they moved, the canoeists transformed the campsite into a meaningful place. Some of this movement was solitary, but far more of the canoeists' "micro-journeys" were undertaken with others.[4] Thus, these quotidian mobilities afforded encounters with the social landscape of the encampment, as well as the physical one. The importance of social encounters was brought into sharp relief at the 1891 meet at Willsborough Point on Lake Champlain. Organizers estimated that the site could accommodate upwards of six hundred people, although only half that many were in attendance. A reporter for *Forest and Stream* lamented that the dispersed nature of the encampment "interfere[d] greatly with the usual familiar, everyday intercourse of camp life."[5]

The first part of this chapter examines the daily routines that took the canoeists to different parts of the ACA campsite. We then turn our attention to the myriad excursions – day trips, fishing trips, picnics – that familiarized the canoeists with local landscapes, albeit in different ways depending on the mode of transport and the destination. Excursions took the canoeists away from the campsite for a brief period, which enabled them to return "home." Excursions, in other words, were an important part of constituting the encampments as home spaces. The chapter concludes with an examination of the many spectacles that occurred during the course of the American Canoe Association encampments: the Commodore's Review, the Illuminated Parade, historical re-enactments, circuses, and minstrel shows. Spectacles did more than amuse. As events that brought together large numbers of the campers, spectacles were a materialization of the imagined community of canoeists. As sites of shared experience, they reinforced the bounds and bonds of community.[6] They further reinforced the proper order of things, constituting the encampments as white, middle-class, and male space.

Unlike Haldrup, what I classify as inhabiting at the ACA encampments is not limited to the canoeists' daily practice, but also includes seemingly extraordinary activities: excursions and spectacles. By examining the banal alongside the spectacular, I suggest the extraordinary was as routine as the quotidian, in large part because, like the daily activities the canoeists performed, it conformed to temporal patterns established over the course of several encampments. This chapter makes clear the ACA encampment was shaped as much by uses of time as by uses of space. There were daily rhythms such as wake-up, mealtimes, and campfires. There were weekly rhythms that included visitors' days and church services. The canoeists could further expect other forms of entertainment such as an excursion, a minstrel show, a canoe parade, or a circus. Finally, there was the annual rhythm of the camp itself, a much anticipated and fondly remembered yearly event in the lives of members of the American Canoe Association.

With the tents raised and their baggage unpacked, the canoeists quickly settled into a routine. Much like at summer camps, "rigorously maintained mealtimes gave a clear and consistent structure to each day" at the ACA meets.[7] Most of the canoeists took their meals in the mess tent. Some, however, cooked for themselves or hired a cook (club mess). The preference for one method over another was informed by cost, time, and ability. In the 1880s, *Forest and Stream* estimated that a canoeist could meet their daily needs for 75 cents, while a good club mess ran upwards of 2 dollars per person per day.[8] With the exception of the Jessup's Neck meet in 1890, the mess tent provided canoeists with three meals a day for one dollar.[9] The competitive canoeists who used their time to prepare and compete in the races were less inclined to cook for themselves, while campers with limited experience in the realm of outdoor living might have chosen to frequent the mess tent for practical reasons. Still others had ideological motivations for choosing a personal mess over the camp kitchen such as a desire to "rough it."[10] Interestingly, accounts in periodicals and memoirs offer little about the contents of meals. Circulars, which previewed the mess tent offerings, suggest a relatively simple diet of grains (i.e., oats, hominy), meat, potatoes, and bread.[11] For dinner, the main meal of the day, there might also be vegetables, soups, and something sweet.[12] Those cooking for themselves likely had similar menus, although they appear to have relied more on canned goods because of their convenience.[13] Regardless of the fare, meals offered opportunities for social intercourse. This was particularly true if one was eating in the mess tent, where catered meals were often served on long wooden tables.

The time between meals was taken up with a variety of activities that brought campers to different locations around the campsite. Many of these activities took place on or near the water. At the early meets, bathing was more common as a practice of personal hygiene than as a recreational pursuit. For this reason, it happened before breakfast in areas near to the main camp for men or the ladies' camp for women.[14] By 1890, however, "ladies, as well as gentlemen" were being encouraged to bring their bathing suits to the annual gatherings.[15] By the time of the 1896 meet on Grindstone Island, the *Syracuse Evening Herald* could refer to bathing as "one of the principal amusements of the men's and women's camps."[16] The evolving place of swimming at the annual meets anticipated transformations underway elsewhere. As Jeff Wiltse demonstrates, swimming was, in the late nineteenth century, a "male activity" associated with "rowdy and indecent plebeians."[17] Modest bathing attire, the development of "proper" swimming facilities, and the emergence of formal swimming clubs all aided in recasting swimming as an acceptable middle-class pursuit.[18] That this transformation appears to have taken place earlier at the American Canoe Association encampments suggests these events were perceived as safe spaces that allowed for participation in otherwise morally questionable activities. To be sure, swimming at the annual meets was not without regulation. For much of this period, ACA members were prohibited from bathing while guests were in camp. They were also required to wear "proper bathing costume" at all times, an injunction that likely stemmed from swimming's historical associations with nudity and anxieties about the body, especially in a mixed-sex context.

Also popular at the American Canoe Association encampments was fishing.[19] There was particularly good fishing at the 1883 meet on Stony Lake.[20] The local paper reported that a group of "Waltonites" caught an 18.5 lb. muskellunge.[21] A week later, George Fitzgerald landed a 22.5 lb. fish of the same species.[22] It was not just men who took advantage of the fishing opportunities off Juniper Island. One "young lady ... covered herself with glory by gatting [sic] a 14 lb. monster."[23] Fishing excursions tended to take the campers further afield than bathing, creating opportunities for encountering local landscapes and local people. Occasionally, the canoeists hired resident guides to show them the choicest locales, particularly at the meets on the St Lawrence River, an area famed in the late nineteenth century for its muskie fishery.[24] Some fished for sport, but for others, "bass, pike and pickerel were lured and landed, to form substance for [their] frying pan."[25]

Canoes figured prominently in both activities, providing a means of accessing good fishing spots away from the campsite or serving as objects of play for swimmers.[26] Canoes also enabled the campers to explore the campsite environs.[27] For some, free time afforded the perfect opportunity to take to the water for a leisurely sail or paddle, or to go for a picnic by canoe. For others, free time was used to tinker with their canoes or to test new rigging.[28] Still others could be found perched on the shoreline watching a "scrub" or "scratch" race – the canoeists' terms for an informal contest – or taking part in the same.[29] Early on, such races enabled the canoeists to test the merits of a particular craft or technique. Increasingly, the week prior to the meet was used more explicitly for training.[30]

Canoe races were not the only sporting matches to provide amusement during the first week of the annual American Canoe Association gathering. The canoeists routinely brought baseball equipment and tennis racquets to the encampments.[31] Most commonly, they engaged in informal contests. Some years, however, the schedule might feature a camp-wide ball game or tennis tournament.[32] Despite the inroads made by women in ACA regattas (see chapter 7), they appear to have only been spectators in these other contests. Most of the other sporting activities popular at the encampments were respectable, although some of the canoeists engaged in "rough" sport as well. At the 1892 meet at Willsborough Point on Lake Champlain, *Forest and Stream* reported that one night, "after the return of the men to the headquarters, at 10:30 a couple of bouts with gloves took place, one very amusing one between two men of 139 lbs. and 206 lbs., the smaller man being the victor."[33] That boxing took place at night away from the prying eyes of women or visitors to the encampment makes its presence at the ACA meets more understandable. Boxing in the late nineteenth century had an unsavoury reputation.[34]

Time was also devoted to more leisurely forms of social intercourse. Paths around the site invited exploration on foot or by bicycle.[35] The area in front of tents provided the perfect space to learn more about new friends or get caught up with old ones, to share stories about one's canoeing exploits, and to compare recent innovations in canoeing technology.[36] On some occasions, the musical instruments that campers were encouraged to bring for the evening campfires were pulled out, and the time was passed singing songs or listening to music.[37]

During the day, the canoeists spread to the four corners of the campsite and beyond. When night fell, however, they could usually be found in one place: around the campfire (figure 6.1). To borrow from Pauline Johnson, "As the last atom of the sun's circle vanishes the sunset gun is heard at headquarters, and you turn to gaze on the myriad tents gathered at your feet, already a blaze of camp-fires here and there."[38] Every year, a handful of more formal and elaborate campfires were announced on the camp bulletin board. At the 1891 meet at Croton Point on the Hudson River, the committee on entertainments organized a fireside performance on a stage fitted with lanterns for footlights and the Mohican Canoe Club's war canoe sail for a curtain. There in the light of a large bonfire and oriental lanterns strung from the trees, the audience watched a series of tableaux directed by Lafayette Seavey and musical numbers that included a "touching solo" from Mrs Schuyler.[39]

Most ACA campfires were simpler affairs that saw the canoeists gather together to sing songs and tell stories. Where available, the music was enlivened by instruments that had been carried from home to camp.[40] At the meet on Wolfe Island in 1893, the canoeists were

6.1 *The Camp Fire at Squaw Point*, engraving, 1890. Campfires were a key part of encampment life; most of the campers ended their days around a campfire, a material reminder of the community of canoeists. This engraving hints at the romantic possibilities of the campfire as well. C.B. Vaux, "The Canoe Meet at Lake Champlain," *Harper's Weekly* 35, no. 1810 (1891): 664.

backed up by an "old rusty banjo, with no head" and a "three legged piano" that went "out of tune in the upper notes."[41] The ACA developed a repertoire of songs over the years that came to be associated with encampment life. These songs drew heavily on Black and French-Canadian folk melodies. "Alouette" and "En Roulant" were favourites at the 1884 meet on Grindstone Island, while the Jessup's Neck encampment in 1890 would "long be remembered for its famous 'Coon Band' of three darkies with their 'Watermelon Growing on the Vine,'" or "De Wattah Mellin Growin' on de Vine," in the canoeists' parlance.[42]

The appropriation of racialized folk melodies, like the Squaw Point flag and use of oriental lanterns, was inspired by the exoticism and otherness of the cultures ostensibly being represented and enabled by the privileged social position of the canoeists.

Campfires, while entertaining, also served as important sites for the materialization of community, much as they did at children's summer camps in the same period.[43] In bringing together canoeists from different parts of the campsite, campfires made the community of canoeists visible to itself. With the appropriate invitations and chaperones, campfires could and did accommodate both men and women. There were, however, a number of campfires just for men, a fact that speaks to the gendered tensions of life at the American Canoe Association encampments.[44] That campfires typically took place under the cover of darkness may have contributed to the abundance of single-sex campfires.

More universally mixed-sex venues were dances. Indeed, dances were held precisely because there were men and women present; they were not part of the homosocial world of the early ACA encampments on Lake George. Dances usually took place in the mess tent/shed. The addition of club flags, bunting, and oriental lanterns could transform the otherwise quotidian dining hall into a space for dancing.[45] Despite such efforts, the mess tent would never be a proper dance hall. Dancers at the Jessup's Neck meet "gyrating around in fine style one moment would catch the soles of their shoes against a swaying board a minute later and dance the next few steps on their knees or necks, while the spectators would laugh unfeelingly."[46] Observers remarked on the gender disparity among the dancers. However distant the American Canoe Association encampments may have been from formal society, it remained unthinkable in this context that men would dance with men, even as miners in California and British Columbia were known to do just that in the same period.[47]

As the campfire's flames weakened or the musicians played their final notes, the expectation was that the campers would drift off to their tents. In case they forgot, the camp bugler offered one final reminder that the day was done.[48] Nevertheless, some people remained around the fire, and if accounts are trustworthy, the vast majority of these were men. *Forest and Stream*, reporting from the Jessup's Neck meet, observed, "After the circle [of the campfire] has broken up and the ladies departed ... an extra bottle is emptied into the pail of punch on the embers ... the songs decrease in melody as they gain in force of expression, and ... those stupid tiresome and shameless old reprobates, the camp chestnuts ... come out for an annual airing in the darkness."[49] The cover of darkness encouraged behaviour few would categorize as respectable, including drinking and pranks.[50] At the meet in 1890, the "night owls" made their rounds of the main camp, turning over the beds of unsuspecting sleepers.[51] The night owls reappeared in 1893 at the Brophy's Point meet on Wolfe Island, where their efforts to play "God Save the Queen" on the whistle of the camp steamer succeeded in keeping their fellow campers from slumber.[52]

Sundays were quiet days at the American Canoe Association encampments.[53] In the morning, the mess tent or headquarters was transformed from a secular space into a sacred one. Although there were only ever two Sundays during the meets, Divine Services were an important part of the yearly ritual of the encampments.[54] Church services were markers of respectability. They were also another component of domesticating the campsite through the reproduction of the spaces and structures of home. We should not overlook the appeal, however, of the opportunity to worship "under a big oak tree, with a glorious view of the lake framed by braches of the trees." One attendee at the Divine Service at Bow Arrow Point in 1887 thought it "a noble church ... without four walls to hedge one's mind in."[55]

We have seen how the American Canoe Association sought to regulate heterosocial encounters at its annual meets by organizing the space of the encampment and the schedule in particular ways. In spite of such efforts, men and women found opportunities to spend time together. Most commonly, they took to the water in canoes. They also took advantage of ACA-sanctioned activities such as campfires (figure 6.1). Writing in 1900, D.J. Howell noted, "The uncertain light and the glamour of the night give opportunities for the growth of friendship that the most timid do not neglect."[56] In still other cases, couples found alternative spaces to meet. At the Jessup's Neck meet in 1890, the long camp wharf became "quite a fashionable promenade in the evening, being neutral ground between the forbidden precincts of Squaw Point and the main camp."[57] Although much emphasis was placed on keeping men and women apart except under the watchful eye of chaperones, there were clearly opportunities for couples to avoid the prying eyes of others.

At least a handful of romantic relationships blossomed at the ACA meets, perhaps fuelled by evening paddles and the dim light of the campfire. On 20 May 1900, the *New York Tribune* announced the engagement of Miss Clara Britton of Kingston, Ontario, and Louis H. May of New York City. The two had met "through a fondness in common for outdoor life in the camp of the American Canoe Association in the Thousand Islands."[58] Clara's sister Mary Alice had married a prominent canoeist, C. Valentine Schuyler, only a few years earlier.[59] Also married in 1894 were William J. Stewart and Miss Gertrude Fredericks, both residents of Newark, New Jersey, and members of the Ianthe Canoe Club.

The *New York Sun* reported that the two had attended ACA encampments together "for a number of years."[60] Walwin Barr and Gertrude Gard attended at least three meets together (at Sugar Island in 1905, 1906, and 1907) prior to their wedding in 1909.[61]

What of same-sex liaisons? None of the sources address this subject directly, although at least one is suggestive. Paul Vernon, in his account of the 1893 meet at Brophy's Point, refers to a "red headed, blue eyed Irishman" named Sparrow, "who was a plumber."[62] When another canoeist inquired about Sparrow, Vernon mused, "Thus I suppose desiring to reflect on the ancient and honorable vocation of wiping joints and going back for more tools, but little did the Brooklyn Club care and Sparrow's wit whether from pipes or fittings, was always welcome." Vernon's account could refer to occupational practices, although elsewhere the author claims that Sparrow died a few years later and "left a million dollars," suggesting the Toronto-based canoeist was not actually a plumber. Steven Maynard issued a call to labour historians in the late 1990s to take seriously the possibility that homosocial encounters occurred within the workplaces and between the people they studied. Reflecting on Ian Radforth's work on lumbering, Maynard supposes, "during a historical period in which homosexual activity did not necessarily confer a homosexual identity, perhaps some bushworkers, like many workingmen in early 20th-century New York City, had sex with other men without it calling into question their status as 'normal' men."[63] Or perhaps, there was a "camp equivalent (pun intended) to the city-based fairy" described by George Chauncey in *Gay New York*.[64]

Photographs of the American Canoe Association encampments reveal a casual intimacy between men. Figure 5.4, in which Secretary Dr Charles Neide lays in repose between the legs of the commodore, F.S. Rathbun (seated), is typical. It is difficult to disentangle the meanings of such photographs. As John Ibson's work has shown, it was common practice for men in the late nineteenth century to have their portraits taken together in a group.[65] More than this, it was in no way unusual for photographs to depict men sitting in one another's laps, holding hands, leaning into one another, and gazing fondly into each other's eyes. It is impossible to uncover the "emotional/erotic lives of subjects who are often anonymous." At the very least, Ibson believes men of this era were more comfortable showing affection for each other than were their successors. The corollary to this is that there was cultural space for such intimacies within the context of romantic friendships. But perhaps there is more to it than that. Even if the loving relationships depicted in these photographs were not realized, perhaps these photographic representations capture something of the subjects' unfulfilled desires.

We must, at the very least, entertain the idea that the American Canoe Association meets were spaces for heterosexual *and* same-sex encounters.[66] Certainly, the ACA encampments were, to a degree, homosocial spaces. Others have shown that same-sex institutions such as boarding schools, prisons, religious orders, and the navy were important in "fostering same-gender sexual networks."[67] In part, this stems from individuals living in close physical proximity to one another, sharing meals, personal grooming time, and perhaps most importantly, sleeping quarters. Some of the ACA campers slept alone, but it was more common for tents to be shared. Even the most palatial of tents were still cosy, offering little space for privacy. That most of the men who raised tents in the main camp were single, or at least unaccompanied, further increased the chances for sexual encounters. The women's camp was a more complicated space, as some of the tents housed couples and families, but even here, women, especially young, single women, enjoyed some degree of privacy, which may have enabled romantic liaisons.

As the canoeists went about their daily routines, their movements produced particular activity spaces and connected disparate parts of the camp landscape, giving shape to the American Canoe Association encampment as place. Their perambulations through the campsite brought them into contact with different people, encounters that further materialized the community of canoeists. Inhabiting, in other words, was a physical practice as well as a social one. As the example of sexuality makes clear, such movements were constrained by the specific expectations of camp organizers and broader notions of middle-class respectability. As they negotiated their own desires and social constraints, the campers constituted the community of canoeists and transformed the campsites into places. Alongside these everyday routines and practices of inhabiting were excursions and spectacles that, in addition to providing entertainment and excitement, played a complementary role in the processes of community formation and placemaking. It is to these activities that we now turn our attention.

Excursions were a regular feature of the schedule during the first week of the American Canoe Association encampments.[68] As they visited local sites of interest, ACA members were "doing" nineteenth-century tourism. Cecilia Morgan describes travel as a "performed art": "it was stylized, it was self-conscious, and it involved a repertoire that was repeated and reiterated, albeit with various levels of negotiation."[69] Michael Haldrup argues that day-trips, in particular, "derive their meaning through the 'collection' of particular places passed *en route*, in the form of souvenirs, photographs and vistas."[70] Excursions provided the canoeists with a wider field of vision of the encampment landscape. They also played an important role in constituting the campsite as home, by allowing the canoeists to leave for a short time and then return "home" again. As with the long distance travel discussed in chapter 3, excursions were made possible by a variety of mobile technologies, which shaped how landscapes were "sensed and made sense of." Most outings, however, happened in steamers and canoes.[71] The relative speed and openness of both craft made them ideal for sightseeing. Steamers were particularly favoured for the "conviviality" described by J.I. Little.[72]

The canoeists visited sites that appealed to a late nineteenth-century touristic sensibility.[73] "Natural" sites included the popular Au Sable Chasm, "a wonderful gorge of two miles" near Lake Champlain and Bala Falls at the 1900 meet in Muskoka (figure 6.2).[74] The canoeists also visited "historical" sites. Campers at the 1894 meet at Croton Point included the Old Van Cortlandt Manor, a veritable treasure trove of US history, in their itinerary. The basement still contained the "old embrasures" through which cannons "belched forth loads of grape and canister" during the American Revolution, a glass cabinet in the parlour housed thirty-two metal buttons from the coat of John Pauling of Sleepy Hollow fame, and in the library sat a small mahogany desk that once belonged to DeWitt Clinton, who served as a state and US senator and as mayor of New York City.[75] Patricia Jasen submits that the desire to frequent wild places was stimulated by the "emergence of the 'picturesque' and the 'sublime' as major aesthetic categories; the rising importance of landscape as an element of taste; growing links between the concepts of landscape, nationalism, and history; and a deepening fascination with aboriginal peoples."[76] Heritage tourism, by contrast, "emerged as part of the fin-de-siècle effort by American elites to define a cultural heritage for themselves apart from the European legacy that they had long revered and sought to emulate, yet to which they felt inferior."[77] Excursions to natural and historical sites, like the impulse to camp out and travel by canoe, may have fulfilled a desire to return to an earlier age.[78] One could argue that as the ACA canoeists travelled across space, they also imagined they were travelling back in time.

In addition to the handful of formal excursions that were arranged during the first week of the encampments, ACA canoeists also engaged in more informal outings. Picnics, leisurely paddles, and fishing trips in the general vicinity of the campsite were commonplace occurrences.[79]

6.2 "At Bala Falls," 1900. Interestingly, the surviving photographs of excursions at the meet, including those in personal collections, are almost exclusively of outings to natural sites such as Bala Falls, although the campers enjoyed visits to cultural sites and events as well. This may reflect the image of itself that the ACA and its members sought to construct: independent campers escaping the city for wild places. In Muskoka, these photographs suggest, wildness was best consumed in Sunday best. MacKendrick Albums, Private Collection.

Other outings took the canoeists farther afield. At the 1884 Grindstone Island meet, Frank Taylor bid the canoeists to pass the day at his cottage on nearby Round Island. About sixty or seventy canoes obliged.[80] The following year, a group of canoeists attended a lacrosse match in Brockville.[81] During the 1893 meet, Paul Vernon and friends made a visit to Kingston, "a good paddle from the camp" on Wolfe Island in order to "visit the sites."[82] One of the more memorable parts of that day

6.3 "Grindstone Island, Thousand Islands," c. 1896. This photograph and the previous one depict outings to natural places. They also highlight the social nature of encampment excursions. Getting away from camp afforded the canoeists time to consume local landscapes, but also opportunities for social intercourse. John R. Blake, ed., *American Canoe Association Yearbook* (Toronto: Bryant Press, 1897).

was their (unsuccessful) attempt to visit the penitentiary, a not uncommon destination for tourists in this period.[83]

As the canoeists visited local sites of interest, they were rarely alone. Figure 6.3, a photograph from the 1896 meet on Grindstone Island, is instructive. It depicts a mixed-sex group of excursionists stopped in a small cove. Three of the four canoes in the foreground are occupied. Behind the canoes, in various positions on a low rock face amid the trees, bushes, and mosses are four more women and two more men.[84] The environments of the ACA meets, in other words, were more than natural and cultural landscapes, they were social ones as well, produced (and consumed) in proximity to others.

One of the highlights of the American Canoe Association's camp schedule was the spectacles. If at first glance spectacles appear to be extraordinary events, they were, in fact, anticipated components of the encampment timetable. The organizing committee took responsibility for some of these events, but member canoeists were more likely to be in charge. The ACA membership also furnished much of the talent. Spectacles, while intended to amuse, were much more than this. They served the practical purpose of bringing the canoeists together en masse and making the ACA community visible to itself. They also joined the canoeists together in the act of watching.[85] They further provided opportunities for the canoeists to narrativize the American Canoe Association. A number of the performances were explicit celebrations of order. Even the spectacles that seemed to upset the proper order of things reinforced social hierarchies of race and gender. Drawing on Don Handelman's work, we may think of these public performances as "locations of community that convey participants into versions of social order in relatively coherent ways ... Their mandate is to engage in the ordering of ideas, people, and things."[86]

The Commodore's Review and the Illuminated Parade were celebrations of order. The Commodore's Review was typically scheduled during the second week of the ACA encampment in advance of the regatta. Spectators looked on as the commodore organized all of the canoes in camp into divisions – tandem paddling canoes, single paddling canoes, cruising sailing canoes, and racing sailing canoes – and then watched as they paraded in front of the camp.[87] Most of the participants in the review were men, but some women also took part.[88] Flip's participation in the 1887 review at Bow Arrow Point was the moment when she felt herself "to be a real canoeist."[89] A variation on the Commodore's Review, the Illuminated Parade, took place at night, occasionally during the regatta, but not necessarily.[90] The following account comes from the 1883 meet at Juniper Island on Stony Lake:

> A magnificent procession of canoes, decorated and illuminated, was held in the evening. Sixty-five canoes, by actual count, illuminated with Chinese lanterns, fastened up on the masts and on ropes, strung the whole length of the boats, were marshaled at the ladies' camp, under the command of Commodore Edwards, and as they slowly made their way in single line up the lake, the sight was beautiful ... The blending of colors, motion of the boats, and the reflection of the light from the waters, combined to give effect charming in the extreme.[91]

In the arrangement of the canoes, the display of the captains' healthy bodies, the authority of the commodore, the order of the procession, and the event's rituality, the Commodore's Review was an unambiguous display of the virtues of order and discipline, not unlike the "demonstrations of human coordination" prominent in contemporary exhibitionary culture.[92] The Illuminated Parade retained many of these elements, but also owed its appeal to the play of light and colour.

Minstrel shows were another enduring feature of the American Canoe Association encampments. During the period covered by this study, minstrelsy was "America's pre-eminent form of entertainment," being particularly popular among white, urban Americans in the northeastern states.[93] The ACA shows borrowed heavily from the form and content of mainstream minstrelsy. The actors arranged themselves in the semi-circle formation introduced by the pioneering Virginia Minstrels.[94] The cast included an interlocutor, "who was seated in the centre of the company and acted as the master of ceremony," and endmen, who, with "their seemingly endless store of riddles, puns, and one-liners," were known for their "raucous comedy."[95] Finally, the programs moved between jokes, tableaux, music, stump speeches, and monologues.[96] In chapter 8, I explore in more detail what performing at the ACA encampments may have meant for Black folks. The vast majority, however, of those who participated in the minstrel programs at the ACA meets were white canoeists. For this group, minstrelsy offered an opportunity to play the racial Other by applying face paint, dressing in "negro" clothing, and performing "blackness." What was the appeal of donning the trappings of the "negro"? There are likely parallels to children's summer camps here. As Leslie Paris's work demonstrates, "African Americans (and sometimes Africans) were ... made to stand in for pleasureable sensuality, freedom from modern industrial labor, and an authentic and natural state of being, as contrasted to the 'artificial' aspects of modernity."[97]

Even as the canoeists were ostensibly transgressing the racial divide, they were doing so for an audience of friends, or at the very least familiars; the wharf and headquarters had assured this. Moreover, at any point the performers could remove the blackface paint and other markers of racial inferiority. Rather than destabilize racial hierarchies, then, such performances reinforced the racial privilege of the white performers and spectators, and preserved the categories of racial difference. The audience was entirely in on the act, understanding the "rules" of blackface and the carefully guarded liminality it provided to both those onstage and off. As Greg Dening so compelling demonstrates, it is in the relationships between performers and audiences that meanings get worked out and that storytelling makes it effects felt and known.[98] For our purposes, then, we might argue that, besides providing a familiar form of entertainment, these minstrel shows also affirmed the whiteness of the American Canoe Association campsites and the racial privileges of the canoeists. Racial play, to borrow again from Leslie Paris, served to "establish the parameters of racial difference and of 'advanced' civilization."[99]

The most elaborate of the ACA spectacles were performed under the tutelage of Lafayette W. Seavey, a scene painter from New York City.[100] Although never a formal member of the administration or organizing committee, after joining the American Canoe Association in 1884, Seavey quickly became the camp's unofficial dramatist and director of amusements. Those years when he was not in attendance at the meet, his absence was palpable. Writing about the 1896 encampment on Grindstone Island, R.B. Burchard opined, "The camp was lacking in the humorous and picturesque spectacular effects and impromptu side-shows of which Mr Seavey was of old the chief promoter, and that gentleman's genial presence was missed by all who had been present at the earlier meets."[101] Seavey spared little expense in his spectacles, although it is unclear who funded the displays. For the tableaux of "As You Like It" at the 1892 gathering at Willsborough Point on Lake Champlain, not only was a large stage built in the grove, but also the "costumes and the little necessary scenery were sent from New York."[102]

Four of Seavey's spectacles lingered long in ACA memory. These spectacles are instructive for what they reveal about class, race, and gender at the encampments. The first took place at the showman's inaugural encampment on Grindstone Island in 1884.[103] Following the last day of races, several hundred campers and visitors gathered on Nob Hill for the performance, which opened with recitations, songs, and instrumental music. The highlight of the show was the arrival of a "band of Indians" in a birchbark canoe. This group presented a series of performances, including "an Indian wedding, funeral, hunt, capture and scalping of a white man, burning a captive at the stake and the war dance." The evening concluded with the singing of "God Save the Queen," presumably an homage to the Canadian hosts.[104] Whereas most of the evening's performers were canoeists, the account in the *New York Sun* suggests that the "Indians" were actually Indigenous participants, perhaps Kanien'kehá:ka from nearby Akwesasne.[105] Paige Raibmon's work on Indigenous performances at the Chicago World's Fair in 1893 offers insight into the complex of meanings and misunderstandings that such events engendered. Whereas spectacles provided opportunities for Indigenous performers to contest their absence in contemporary society and reaffirm their cultural integrity, for white audiences, such performances routinely reinforced existing stereotypes about the "dying race" and confirmed Indigenous culture "as a static relic of the past."[106]

At the 1889 meet on Stave Island, the "large three-pole tent" serving as the mess gave Seavey the idea for a circus.[107] In anticipation of the spectacle, a "ring was plowed in the sod under the tent, leveled off and 'sawdusted,'" and "rude benches were constructed around it for the spectators." The list of personalities that appeared in the ring was seemingly endless: "four clowns dressed in pajamas, and appropriately painted"; "Arabs"; "Indians, cowboys"; "Turks, wild men of Borneo, the hairy man, a bear and an elephant."[108] The performances were equally elaborate, featuring "bareback riding, tight-rope walking, gymnastics, contortion acts, bar performances, tumbling, turning, clown business, ringmaster, trick animals, heavy-weight lifting, barrel-turning, handsprings, somersaults, wild men and wild animals, a band, a big four-poled tent, sawdust ring, Deadwood coach, and all."[109] The star of the show was "Mlle Jabberwock" (figure 6.4), who "in true circus-rider costume, mosquito netting dress and all – barring a heavy mustache – rode a farm-horse, well tired out after a hard day's work." More than an opportunity for amusement, Janet Davis contends that the circus was "a powerful cultural icon of a new, modern nation-state" that "helped consolidate the nation's identity as a modern industrial society and world power."[110] Circus acts "articulated the instability of white racial identity through clownish caricatures of ethnic difference," while simultaneously reinforcing "a shared sense of white privilege" among the audience members.[111] Unlike at travelling circuses, ethnic differences at the ACA event were put on by white performers, much like the blackface of the encampments' minstrel shows. As the example of Mlle Jabberwock makes clear, spectacles like the circus also provided opportunities for the canoeists to transgress gender boundaries.

The third of Seavey's notable spectacles took place during the race for the Pecowisc Cup at the 1891 meet at Willsborough Point on Lake Champlain. As the sailing canoes rounded the buoys, there appeared a "strange and horrible monster." Observers reported that "as he came down, his eyes flashing fire, his huge jaws clashing together, and his many scaly coils rising above the water, the bravest quaked with fear, and the timid sought the shelter of the woods." The monster made its way towards the ladies' camp "in search of the beautiful maidens which all tradition tells us is the chosen food of dragons and sea serpents." Some of the canoeists sought to repel the beast with the guns on the cliff, but to no avail. Eventually, two men attacked it with "lances

6.4 "Three of the Performers in Seavey's Circus," 1889. Much like campfires, spectacles materialized community in a very tangible way by placing canoeists from around the camp in close physical proximity to one another and providing the circumstances for shared experiences. They also afforded opportunities to explore the boundaries of this community of white, middle-class canoeing enthusiasts: to represent and reflect on gender, race, and class in a controlled space. Fenimore Museum, ACA Collection, box 1.2/3.

and harpoons," finally managing to subdue the monster only a few feet from the ladies' camp. The beast, badly injured, was then dragged ashore at the pavilion dock. It measured a hundred feet.[112] The spectacle of the Lake Champlain monster, like the Commodore's Review, bolstered an envisioned order of things. Faced with a threat to the women, the men of the ACA rushed to the rescue, killing the beast and ensuring the safety and order of their encampment. Here, the gender binary was reaffirmed rather than transgressed.

Seavey's final spectacle, the "Storming of Taku Fort," was realized at 1900 meet on Lake Rosseau in Muskoka.[113] Midway through the encampment, a sizeable structure featuring a "pagoda and quaint turrets" was erected on a "little rocky island near the paddling course" under the direction of "Li Hung Chang" (Seavey). One evening, "allied fleets of war canoes and canoes of lighter draft" appeared on the waterfront, their "crews hurl[ing] a storm of rockets and Roman candles at the fort."[114] This spectacle was a recreation of a battle that took place during the Boxer Rebellion only a few months earlier. In 1901, William "Buffalo Bill" Cody produced an elaborate re-enactment of the same battle as part of his Wild West show.[115] John Haddad's analysis of this other performance is useful in understanding the ACA recreation. He argues that at the core of Cody's spectacle was a contest between civilization and savagery: "Americans viewed the Boxers as barbaric because [they] sought the eradication through violent means of the very things that signified 'progress' in the West – telegraph systems, railroads, mining projects, and Christian missions."[116] Haddad also sees the "The Rescue at Pekin" as a "rite-of-passage ritual that helped [Americans] reconcile their fondness for their rugged past with their necessary participation in the modern industrial state that America was fast becoming."[117]

A number of the spectacles at the American Canoe Association encampments were expressions or affirmations of order, including the Commodore's Review, the Illuminated Procession, and Seavey's water monster. Even those spectacles better suited to a midway, such as minstrel shows or circuses, did not dismantle social hierarchies.[118] If anything, they reinforced them by temporarily allowing the participants to don the dress and habits of "the Other." That the canoeists could engage in such transgressive behaviour is further evidence of the power of the threshold in constructing the campsites as safe spaces, but also of the shared roles of performer and spectator in the spectacles. Any fear the ACA canoeists may have felt when confronted with scalping Indians, lake monsters, or savage Boxers existed alongside the knowledge that they occupied a place and community that made such things safe. All of the performances assumed the presence of like-minded people, but more importantly people of a similar class and race. The spectacles, as events that attracted large numbers of campers, played an important role in constituting the community of the ACA. They provided another opportunity for the canoeists to see and be seen by one another. The spectacles were also important inscriptions of place at the annual gatherings, constituting the American Canoe Association encampments as white, middle-class spaces of order and play.

Throughout the two weeks of the American Canoe Association encampments, the canoeists were kept busy preparing and consuming meals; socializing with friends; visiting local sites of interest; engaging in recreational activities such as swimming, fishing, and baseball; and readying themselves for the regatta. The routine nature of camp life recalled the quotidian practices of home. The ACA canoeists' participation in these activities of inhabitation familiarized them with the spaces of the campsite, but also with their fellow campers. Going swimming or singing songs around the campfire were not just ways to pass the time or engage in pleasurable activities; as experiences shared with other canoeists, they reinforced the bonds of the American Canoe Association community. Excursions likewise provided opportunities for shared experience, while contributing to the production of the campsites as home places. Finally, the spectacles provided a safe and entertaining way to explore and occasionally transgress the social divisions of modern life. Such transgressions did not upset the "proper" order of things. If anything, the temporary space of the spectacle reaffirmed the class, gender, and racial privileges of the ACA canoeists. Performances of racialized Others, the most common boundary crossing at the meets, were ultimately celebrations of whiteness. This chapter considered a number of spectacles that took place at the American Canoe Association encampments. The biggest spectacle of all, however, is yet to come: the regatta. It is to this colourful event that we turn our attention in the next chapter.

Chapter Seven

Competing

On the opening day of the canoe races at the 1882 meet of the American Canoe Association on Lake George, the *New York Sun* reported, "New arrivals have swelled the number of canoes to 130, and these, with an immense number of rowboats collected off Crosbyside, present a *spectacle* full of animation and kaleidoscope changes."[1] The *Sun*'s choice of words was not accidental: as is visible in figure 7.1, the biggest spectacle of all at the ACA encampments was the regatta. For up to a week, the canoeists turned their attention away from the domestic spaces of the campsite and the recreational spaces of the surrounding waters and woods to focus on the space of competition: the racecourse. The optic and sonic landscapes of the camp reflected this reorientation with "hundreds of canoes of infinite variety, skiffs, sailing boats, steam yachts ... plying and flying in every direction," "flags of every fantastic device" unfurled, "whistles, horns and trumpets ... blowing," and "people shouting across the water to one another, and laughing."[2] Bodies also marked the shift in focus from socializing and recreation to competition. Pauline Johnson observed, "Men formerly given to immaculate flannels, gay blazers and nobby canvas shoes were arrayed in stingy bathing suits."[3] Women's dress, by contrast, became more elaborate and decorative – bright colours, parasols, and elegant hats were commonplace.[4] In general, the races, one observer argued, "did one thing and they did it well; they destroyed the enervating *dolce far niente* that had crept over the camp ... [T]he whole camp became, if not a hive of industry, at least an accumulation of activity."[5]

This chapter examines the regattas at the ACA encampments from three different but related perspectives. First, it considers the yearly races in relation to other nineteenth-century boating competitions, in particular military regattas and yachting and rowing races. Second, it reflects on amateurism and professionalism – two well-worn themes

7.1 S.R. Stoddard, "Start of the ACA Paddling Trophy Race," 1890. Stoddard's photograph of a paddling race at Jessup's Neck encapsulates the annual meets: it positions the encampments at the meeting point between water and land; it simultaneously makes visible the home spaces of the campers (tents), the spaces of order and discipline (headquarters), and the spaces of competition (racecourse); and it captures something of the occasion of the meets in the swell of the crowd and the ubiquity of flags. Fenimore Museum, ACA Collection, box 1.1/11.

in the history of sport – within the context of the ACA regattas. The example of the American Canoe Association reveals both similarities and differences to other sporting clubs and associations in this period, especially concerning the ambiguous meanings of professionalism and amateurism and the place of technology in sport. Third, this chapter examines the organization, delivery, and experience of participating in the canoe races. The regatta was a central component of the annual gatherings that confirmed the encampments as events and the American Canoe Association as a legitimate sport organization. Without it, the canoeists were little more than campers on holiday. Our understanding of the regattas as sporting events is enhanced if we think of them as a performance akin to a stage play.[6] In earlier chapters, we have seen how consistently officials staged the meets through careful planning and administration. The canoe races were no different.

Canoe racing was not an invention of bourgeois sport. Rather, it had a long history among the continent's First Peoples and later among fur traders.[7] Although different Indigenous groups were likely racing canoes long before Contact, the written history of Native canoeing contests was largely penned by European observers. In the 1830s, Anna Jameson watched as,

> Thirty canoes started, each containing twelve women, and a man to steer. They were to go round the little island in the centre of the bay, and return to the starting point, – the first canoe which touched the shore to be the winner. They darted off together with a sudden velocity, like that of an arrow from the bow. The Indians on the shore ran backwards and forwards on the beach, exciting them to exertion by loud cries, leaping into the air, whooping and clapping their hands; and when at length the first canoe dashed up to the landing place, it was as if all had gone at once distracted and stark mad.[8]

Canoe racing was also important in the world of the fur trade. Carolyn Podruchny argues that beyond play, canoe contests among the voyageurs provided a means for acquiring masculine capital, the measurement of wealth in a community that boasted a non-accumulation ethic.[9]

Racing canoes may have been a part of Indigenous and voyageur communities. Until the late nineteenth century, however, canoe racing was an anomaly among "gentlemen sports" in the urban centres of the industrializing northeast. One exception was Peterborough, Ontario, where beginning in the 1850s, wooden canoes were being manufactured and raced on local waterways.[10] The uneven popularity of canoe racing at mid-century can be partially explained by the fact that the canoe continued to be perceived as an Indigenous craft.

Although canoe races were rare, boating contests in the harbours of cities such as New York, Boston, Montreal, and Halifax were not. For the most part, these regattas featured yachts, skiffs, and rowing shells.

Occasionally, however, Indigenous contestants were called on to perform in a canoe race. As at snowshoe races in Victorian-era Montreal, the "Indian races" at these regattas were more likely a "crowd-drawing spectacle" than a test of paddling prowess.[11] White women's participation in regattas was constrained well into the twentieth century; however, it was not unusual for "Indian races" to feature Indigenous women.[12] This disparity is consistent with the complex social hierarchies of the nineteenth century produced through the intersections of gender and race.[13] That most "Indian races" were run for a purse – a necessity to ensure the participation of Indigenous athletes – contributed to the "common-sense" associations between professionalism and race in the late nineteenth century, a point I will return to shortly.

In Canada, early boating regattas were often organized by the local garrison, which as Peter Lindsay has shown were important institutions in the development of organized sport in Canada prior to Confederation.[14] Later in the nineteenth century, regattas became the responsibility of clubs like the Lachine Boating Club of Montreal or the Banook Canoe Club of Halifax.[15] Much of the pomp and circumstance of the garrison events lived on in the early regattas of Canadian boating and canoe clubs. At the turn of the century, orchestras might be hired by the host club to establish themselves near to the water, in some cases on floating pavilions, to play through the canoe races.[16]

In the United States, the shape and content of canoeing regattas owed much to rowing culture.[17] It is no coincidence that commentators often likened the scene of an American Canoe Association race day to events on the Thames or Charles rivers.[18] Both places, by the 1880s, were firmly established in the American imaginary as sites of rowing races. Also influential was the sport of yachting. First organized in the United States in the 1840s, by the late nineteenth century yachting clubs and regattas were a common feature of urban harbours along the eastern seaboard.[19] The creation of the ACA's International Challenge Cup in 1886 was directly inspired by the America's Cup, the pinnacle of nineteenth-century yachting races.[20]

Sport in the nineteenth century was shaped by an ongoing and vociferous debate over amateurism and professionalism, and canoeing was no exception.[21] Commenting on conditions at the ACA meet at Croton Point in 1894, one writer noted, "The great problem in racing is to make the sport interesting and popular, to induce men to work for the prize, and yet prevent such a rapid and unhealthy development as will lead a few men to give all their time and labor to securing every prize and shut out the great majority from the benefits that always follow from a general and open competition."[22] Given that rowing, yacht racing, and canoeing in England were all believed to be infected with the scourge of professionalism, many assumed it was only a matter of time before canoeists in North America would succumb. A small group of observers thought the sport of canoeing immune to professionalism, because "to be a canoeist a man must have that true love of nature and outdoor work which will enable him to regard the labor, inconveniences, discomforts, and occasional dangers of a canoe cruise as part of a delightful sport. The 'professional' is ready to work for money, but not for the mere pleasure of working, and there is not the slightest danger that he will ever be found in the cock-pit of a canoe."[23] Even as they claimed canoeing impervious, such writers acknowledged the ever-present spectre of the professional. Much as over-civilization lurked at the edges of ACA encampment life threatening to jeopardize the rejuvenating atmosphere of the annual meet, professionalism was a persistent concern for those committed to the amateur ideal.

Given the celebratory attitudes towards professionalization in the world of work in the late nineteenth century, what was so concerning about professionalism in sport?[24] First, sport was meant to be a haven from an individual's vocational toils; professionalism represented a breach of this boundary.[25] The irony is that these same sporting men did not object to the appearance of other elements of professionalization in their recreational organizations such as financial audits or a board of governors. Second, professionalism was associated with "playing for pay."[26] Wage labour was a contentious reality in this period. According to Clark Davis, "the dominant middle-class construction of occupational success had long glorified economic independence." By the late nineteenth century, however, most American men could expect to spend their lives as wage labourers, whether in factories or office buildings.[27] Third, professionalism made athleticism a commodity that could be bought and sold, much like wheat or gold, yet another manifestation of industrial capitalism. That opponents of professionalism in the wider world of sport often likened playing for pay to prostitution underscores the perceived moral bankruptcy of the professional athlete.[28]

The association of professionalism with the working class and visible minorities – two groups that rarely had the time or the means to participate intensively in sport without remuneration – was no coincidence. Amateurism, the counter of professionalism, was as much (if not more) a celebration of masculinity, whiteness, and middle-class status as it was an ideological stance on participation in sport. Amateurism centred on the assumption that one played for no other reason than the love of the game. Within the world of nineteenth-century sport, "amateur" and "gentleman" were often used interchangeably, at times coming together in reference to the "gentleman amateur."[29] Early amateur codes, as Bruce Kidd has shown, excluded on the basis of class and race, an attempt, he argues, of the upper classes "to reproduce the social hierarchies of Victorian England and the British Empire and to maintain the primacy of sports as an expression of manly honour and elegant display."[30] Even as "upper-class ostentation" gave way to an "ethos of sport as a field of 'civilized' contest and achievement," such hierarchies remained, albeit in a somewhat altered form.[31] New amateur codes required athletes to have the time to train, as well as the means to pay for equipment, travel, and club memberships. They did so, while preventing athletes from earning money from their performances.[32] Thus, amateurism, as Mary Louise Adams observes, had a circular quality to it: "National championships are institutionalized by upper-class sportsmen as amateur contests; members of the upper classes are the only ones able to expend the time and resources needed for training, and thus it is they who win the honours; once won, these honours come to signify the superiority of the upper classes and to justify the privileges, like freedom from work, that made it possible for them to compete in the first place."[33]

In spite of the assumed superiority of amateurism, adherence to the ideal was difficult, if not impossible. The American Canoe Association took a number of steps to counter what it saw as the ever-present threat of professionalism and to uphold the virtues of amateurism. Most directly, the ACA regulated who could enter association races, limiting participation to members, the vast majority of whom were white, middle-class men. Technically, participants also had to be amateurs, although the organization shied away from offering a clear definition of an amateur.[34] In 1890, Canadian canoeist John Noble MacKendrick drew attention to this oversight in a letter to the editor of *Forest and Stream*.[35] The editor concurred: "a definition of an amateur is certainly needed ... we have never yet seen one that was in any way perfect."[36] The difficulty of producing an adequate definition, which itself speaks to the slipperiness of the term, may explain the organization's inaction. In this way, the American Canoe Association differed from other sporting bodies that adopted explicit definitions of amateurs such as the oft-cited Montreal Pedestrian Club, which classified an amateur athlete as one who had "never competed in any open competition or for public money, or for admission money, or with professionals for a prize, public money or admission money, nor has ever, at any period of his life taught or assisted in the pursuit of Athletic exercises as a means of livelihood or is a laborer or an Indian."[37] Even the inclusion of an amateur clause in the ACA rules, however vague, was an act of boundary work. Because of the existence of clauses like that of the Montreal Pedestrian Club, by the late nineteenth century amateur was a deeply classed, gendered, and racialized social category that demarcated sporting clubs and amateur athletic associations as white, middle-class, and male institutions.

The decision to increase the duration of the encampments from four to fourteen days in 1883 was part of the American Canoe Association's offensive against professionalism. A longer encampment placed more emphasis on the annual ACA meet as a social and recreational space, and sought to curb the time and attention devoted to the races. Although some of the members responded positively to the new format by spending more time in camp, more common were the canoeists who arrived a day or two before the regatta. In limiting their time on site to the races, these campers made clear their interests and undermined the organizers' efforts to de-centre the regatta. In 1899, the executive committee mandated that ACA members wishing to compete be in camp for a prescribed amount of time before the races.[38] However, this clause was administered unevenly and eventually eliminated, suggesting a degree of ambivalence on the part of the officials. Encampment organizers also sought to frame the regatta as a space of friendly contest, rather than intense competition. Commodore E.B. Edwards pointed out that the races should "afford the means of testing in a friendly way the relative merits of various styles of canoes, rig, etc., and furnish a bit of pleasant sport at the end of the camp, rather than ... promote the fastest racing in the world, and thus give rise to personal jealousies."[39]

A central facet of the American Canoe Association's brand of amateurism was "generalism," which is to say the organization promoted the virtues of the canoeist and the canoe that could capably sail *and* paddle. In 1885, at Grindstone Island, organizers introduced "The Record," a contest meant to address the fact that "the paddlers were content to ... leave the sailing races alone, and the sailors left the paddling races alone."[40] To compete for The Record, canoeists had to enter a canoeing race, a sailing race, and a combined canoeing and sailing race. To place well, they had to be competent sailors and paddlers, thereby encouraging the development of generalist canoeists.

The Record was inspired, in part, by a concern that if canoeists continued to specialize, the result "would have been finally, paddling machines and sailing machines."[41] In other words, more than the payment of athletes threatened the amateur ideal. Equally concerning was the adulteration of the canoe itself. Consider the following excerpt from a *New York Times* account of the 1885 meet on Grindstone Island:

> The yearly meeting together of hundreds of canoeists has stimulated inventors in the effort to approach nearer to the ideal "perfect canoe." From year to year new rigs have been devised ... Improvements in the model, material, and fittings of canoes have constantly been made ... The best canoes of the association now seem to be beyond the reach of improvement ... No man who is not an expert has now the slightest chance of winning in a regatta, and the combination of nerve, quickness, and technical skill shown by our best canoe sailors need only be witnessed to convince any one that canoeing is a worthy sister of yachting.[42]

Early settler canoeing enthusiasts worked tirelessly to transform the canoe from an "Indian" craft into a respectable middle-class boat, a process I describe in the introduction to this volume as the whitening of the canoe. Canoeists also laboured to create the "perfect canoe," a project that included new materials, manufacturing techniques, and performance technologies.[43] This pursuit of perfection, much like the desire for progress that permeated late nineteenth-century society, was a "utopian statement about the future."[44] As the canoe was "improved," so too was the canoeist, and ultimately, society. Inspired by the language and tropes of evolutionary theory, this quest for technological perfection was not benign. As Robert Rydell demonstrates in the context of the fin-de-siècle World's Fairs, progress, in both a technological and socio-political sense, was "laced with scientific racism."[45]

Regattas, by providing opportunities for "determining the comparative merits of different models and different rigs," were central to the project of creating the perfect canoe.[46] Like scientific study – which was gaining purchase in the late nineteenth century – canoe races enabled the practices of observation and experimentation necessary for technological advancement.[47] However, regattas also revealed the deep contradictions of this project. They made clear that the perfect canoe was unattainable. The ideal sailing canoe was not suitable for a paddling contest, while the ideal cruising canoe was useless for racing of any kind.[48] In fact, specialized racing canoes of either type were good for little more than competition. If anything, the pursuit of the perfect racing canoe undermined the American Canoe Association's commitment to amateurism because it culminated in the creation of degenerate racing machines.[49] That racing canoes were cast in this light is evidence of anxieties about technological modernity. In the late nineteenth century, the machine, Alan Trachtenberg writes, "seemed the prime cause of the abundance of new products changing the character of daily life." However, the machine "also seemed responsible for newly visible poverty, slums, and an unexpected wretchedness of industrial conditions."[50] Even at the World's Fairs, which were unabashed celebrations of the mechanization of modern life, observers reported "bewilderment and fear" in the face of machines.[51] Anxieties about the machine appear not to have pervaded other forms of amateur sport in this period in the way they did canoeing; more frequently, amateur sport was constructed as antithetical to the technological imperative.[52] This disjuncture likely reflects the dependency of canoeing on such a sizeable instrument that could be manipulated in myriad ways.

The American Canoe Association primarily countered overmechanization by regulating the shape of canoes entered in the yearly regatta. Given that changes to the silhouette and the sail were intended to give canoes greater speed, the organization mandated that canoes entered into competition "must come within the prescribed limits" of sixteen feet in length and a beam of thirty inches, "decreasing the [maximum] length of the canoe one foot for every inch and a half of additional beam."[53] Sail sizes were similarly constrained with class A craft limited to fifty feet of sail and class B canoes to seventy feet.[54] Finally, the association instituted regulations pertaining to draft, keels, and centreboards, which, like boat and sail size, altered a canoe's performance.[55] To avoid disqualification, owners and boat builders alike were encouraged to "know the dimensions of [their] boat, and have her a fraction inside of the measurement, so as to avoid any possibility of dispute."[56] Commentators admitted that no one size was better than another; nevertheless, they judged it necessary to "secure a uniformity" to "greatly simplify the rules and lessen the labors of the regatta committee and measurers."[57] These changes served to discipline the boat choices of canoeists. By the time of the 1890 meet at Jessup's Neck, *Forest and Stream* could report that the "odd sizes [had] very nearly disappeared from the racing," with the vast majority of canoes measuring sixteen feet by thirty inches.[58] The American Canoe Association may have been successful in creating a standardized canoe; it was not, however, able to prevent the creation of racing machines: canoes good for little more than competition continued to appear at the annual meets.

Prizes for races at the American Canoe Association encampments were also contentious. At the earliest meets, canoeists competed for prizes donated by canoe manufacturers or individual members, such as canoes, sails, paddles, and flags.[59] Before too long, however, questions were being raised about the suitability of such rewards, given that "racing is not the end of the Association, but only a means of furthering an interest in the sport and improvements in the boats."[60] Thus, beginning in 1882, at the Canoe Islands meet on Lake George, the ACA regatta committee adopted flags as the official prizes. Such "simple and inexpensive" tokens, the commodore argued, were "not likely to tempt anyone to the systematic training necessary for an *oarsman's* race."[61] That the committee specifically requested homemade flags from the membership rather than "factory-made articles" suggests further ambivalence about the processes and products of industrial capitalism.[62] Even with the introduction of flags, more substantive awards were not immediately abandoned. At 1883 meet on Stony Lake, which Commodore Edwards had claimed would be free of prizes, competitors in the "impromptu races" held during the first week were rewarded with paddles and camping equipment donated by boat builders and canoe clubs.[63] Beginning at the 1886 Grindstone Island meet, there were also a number of expensive cups, acquired via subscription, for which the canoeists could compete. The most prominent of these was the International Challenge Cup, "a silver bowl, 12 inches high and 15 inches in diameter, ornamented around the base with the turtle, bears, frog and other club symbols."[64]

Like other late nineteenth-century athletic pursuits, canoeing was not immune to anxieties about amateurism and professionalism. The American Canoe Association waged the battle against professionalism on a number of fronts, targeting in various ways the competitors, the craft, and the contests. What stands out is the emphasis placed on equipment rather than training or payment for play, although these were also concerning for ardent amateurs. The dependency of canoe sport on such a sizeable tool stimulated anxieties about technological modernity and the increasing control of machines over different aspects of everyday life. Alan Metcalfe submits, "There never was a real difference between amateur and professional."[65] Rather, we can inquire after the manner in which and purpose for which these terms were deployed by sporting enthusiasts. In the case of the ACA canoeists, the use of amateur and professional were part of broader project of community formation that sought to include the right kinds of people, and exclude "Others." At the core of this boundary work was the question of fitness: Who was considered "fit" to attend and compete in the American Canoe Association regattas? And who was not? Practices of inclusion and exclusion reflected anxieties about the changing place of women, the working class, and immigrants in North American society. Also at the core of the debate between amateurism and professionalism was a tension between the mechanized culture of progress and the "antimodern" culture of fair play.⁶⁶ Clearly, there was no epistemological space at the American Canoe Association encampments for sport to be professionalized, mechanized, and "fair."

Commenting on the 1886 meet at Grindstone Island, a staff writer for *Forest and Stream* opined, "It is no light undertaking to manage a series of 20 races in three days, in which the entries aggregate no less than 350."⁶⁷ Like a theatrical performance, the American Canoe Association regatta had a program, which offered cues to the audience (spectators) about the drama unfolding between the various performers (contestants and officials) on the stage (racecourses), while the rules imposed on the competitors functioned as a kind of script, giving shape to the performance. From the early 1880s, a dedicated regatta committee was responsible for preparing and publishing the program, laying out and buoying the courses, organizing prizes, appointing officials, and ruling on protests.⁶⁸ In advance of the Cape Cod meet in 1902, the ACA further expanded the bureaucracy around the regatta with the creation of a racing board that had "full charge of all association racing and rules."⁶⁹

The first responsibility of the ACA's regatta committee was to set the program for the upcoming meet. A number of factors were considered. The success of a race virtually guaranteed its place in the next year's line-up. By contrast, it typically took a few years before the committee would drop a seemingly unsuccessful contest, perhaps to ensure that its failure was not an anomaly.⁷⁰ The program also sought to accommodate new trends in the sport of canoeing. For example, as canoe clubs began to purchase and race war canoes, the large craft were given their own place in the regatta program.⁷¹ Local circumstances were also important. During the inland Canadian meets and those hosted by the Northern Division, paddling races were more prominent, as were contests in open canoes.⁷² In part, this reflected the interests of Canadian canoeists. It may, however, have also represented efforts on the part of the smaller Canadian contingent to distinguish their regatta programs from those of their southerly neighbours. This suggests that the transnationality of the American Canoe Association did not preclude the existence and performance of national identities. Indeed, at times, it may have enhanced them.

Concerns about participation were particularly influential in crafting a program for the ACA regatta. At the 1886 meet on Grindstone Island, there were 323 entries for the races and 228 starters.⁷³ Five years later, at Willsborough Point, there were only forty names on the entry list.[74] As discussed in the introduction, there are a number of possible explanations for the decline in participation over the period covered by this study, including competition from other recreational pursuits, economic uncertainty, and the creation of the Canadian Canoe Association in 1900, although the departure of Canadian canoeists and clubs was more a slow leak than a mass exodus.[75] Regardless of the reasons for declining participation, most regatta programs were designed to encourage a broad field of competition with a variety of sailing, paddling, and novelty races.[76] New types of races were added to the program to inspire new contestants. A relay race was included in the 1898 Stave Island regatta in the hopes that "such an event [would] bring larger delegations of good paddlers to camp, and also increase club rivalry to a greater extent than now exists."[77]

The design of the regatta program was also intended to appeal to spectators. This is perhaps most evident in the numerous and varied novelty races. Typically, five to seven of the twenty-odd races were novelty contests that recalled schoolyard games or fair contests such as canoe tug-of-war, hurry-scurry, jousting, hand paddling, and canoe gymnastics.[78] Such competitions with their carnivalesque elements underscored the regatta as spectacle. Novelty races were not just for the spectators. They were also used by the regatta committee to offer a challenge to canoeists and, ultimately, to boost participation. Of course, catering to spectators and participants were not mutually exclusive ends, as the following comment about a proposed club relay race for the Grindstone Island meet in 1897 makes clear: "The event will surely prove one of the most interesting of the whole programme, from the spectators standpoint, and it can hardly fail in its purpose in increasing interest in the races generally."[79]

Finally, the addition of trophy and challenge races to the regatta program were acts of legitimation that also appealed to spectators. Intended as an assessment of national difference – observers claimed the appeal of the races was that they would "test the comparative merits of the radically different methods of sailing in vogue among American and English canoeists" – the International Challenge Cup was a highlight of the ACA meet in the late 1880s and early 1890s.[80] In addition to positioning the American Canoe Association as an organization of international repute, the race was also the kind of high-profile event that drew both competitors and spectators. In 1886, the presence of English canoeists Warrington Baden-Powell and Walter Stewart at Grindstone Island "brought to the meet many of the best sailors of the association to defend the cup," as well as excursionists from throughout the Thousand Islands.[81]

Although canoeists were always quick to offer advice as to how the regatta program could be improved, it was unusual for suggestions to be anything but civil. In 1899, however, the *New York Sun* reported from Hay Island that on a day of light wind the sailors "employed a portion of their spare moments in adverse criticism of the Regatta Committee" for "acting with undue obstinacy in adhering to its programme of races." The *Sun* blamed the intransigent regatta chairman "who seems to be neither in sympathy with the racing men nor willing to entertain their desires."[82] At issue was the committee's decision to forego the trial sailing race, which according to ACA rules, was to precede the trophy sailing race as a means of limiting the field of competition. The regatta committee maintained that the trial race was superfluous with such a small number of entries. On the day of the trophy race, hostilities reached a head, when "some of the canoeists formed themselves into a 'sailors' union,' protested, and went on strike."[83] We should not overlook the deep irony of the canoeists forming a union and going on strike in a period of labour unrest and volatile class relations, just as we cannot ignore the performances of race that were so popular at the American Canoe Association encampments.[84] The canoeists demanded the resignation of the regatta committee, a request that went unheeded. The race was a "flat failure owing to the refusal of the sailing fleet to enter any of the sailing races." In the end, Charles Archibald, of the Ottawa Canoe Club, much like a scab crossing a picket line, "sailed over the course alone and claim[ed] the handsome trophy" for his own.[85] The rest of the regatta program appears to have been run, although it is unclear how the dispute affected other entries. Perhaps the most visible protest with the farthest-reaching consequences was the founding of the Canadian Canoe Association. Unhappy with the fees charged to war canoe teams that may only have one or two races in which to compete at the annual ACA regatta, a group of Canadian paddlers started their own organization in 1900.[86]

That such examples of open antagonism between the canoeists and the organizing committee have survived suggests these were not isolated incidents, but part of an ongoing contest over the form and content of the regatta program. They are also further evidence of hierarchies of power within the American Canoe Association, despite its claims to egalitarianism. Finally, these challenges to the regatta program reveal the extent to which the "scripts" of the performances were prescriptive but not deterministic. In other words, programs and rules quite openly sought to structure the scenes of the regatta; however, both the actors (canoeists) and the audience (spectators) could and did play with the rules set down for them.

If the line-up of races was the program for the performance, then the theatre of contest was the racecourse. With the exception of the early meets on Lake George, there were always two courses at a meet: a triangular sailing course and a straightaway paddling course.[87] As we saw in chapter 4, the positioning of the courses reflected a number of environmental and social concerns such as tides, current, winds, and spectators. Buoys or stake boats, placed during the first week of the encampment (if not before), marked the surveyed racecourses.[88]

The cast of the American Canoe Association regattas was large, featuring at times upwards of 2,000 performers.[89] There were three broad roles available to participants: competitor, spectator, and official. These were not discrete entities; most competitors spent time as spectators, and officials often took part in the contests as racers were one of the few groups willing and able to officiate.[90]

Women almost exclusively played the role of spectator, although beginning in 1890 at Jessup's Neck, there were typically one or two opportunities on the regatta program for women to compete. This situation was not unique to the American Canoe Association. Over the course of the nineteenth century, sport generally "came to be forcefully and graphically depicted as the 'natural' province of males."[91] Women's marginal place reflected the related beliefs that women were not physically capable of demanding physical pursuits and that vigorous exercise would in some way imperil their femininity and/or reproductive capabilities, which in turn would spell "race suicide" for Anglo-North Americans.[92] Of course, the late nineteenth century was also the era of the "New Woman" and the "Gibson Girl," the former embodying physical and political independence and the latter representing a new ideal of beauty that was decidedly athletic.[93] Dress reform had begun to release women from the physical constraints of rigid corsets and voluminous petticoats.[94] There was also a growing cadre of physicians and physical educators who advocated for women to be physically active.[95] Perhaps not surprisingly, their support was often couched in the language and values of white, middle-class motherhood. "A reinvigorated motherhood," reformers argued, "would allow the 'fittest' race to expunge weaker strains and take its natural place atop the social order."[96] Even as opportunities to be physically active proliferated, women were encouraged to seek out "moderate and lady-like forms of exercise." Acceptable pursuits included croquet, figure skating, golf, and lawn tennis, activities in which "the 'grace and bearing' expected of 'ladies' could be maintained."[97] To do otherwise was to risk the coarsening effects of physical activity.[98]

We can only imagine what might have transpired to prompt the running of a women's race at the 1890 meet on Peconic Bay; the regatta report is spare, noting that "several extra events were called," including a ladies' paddling contest.[99] Based on extant accounts, we know the audience responded positively to the contest. The *New York Times* called the women's race "a most exciting and interesting one,"[100] in which "the ladies in the winning canoe paddled beautifully, with a powerful, even stroke from the start and deserved all the applause they got from the watching crowd."[101] The success of the race is also underscored by the fact that the next year, there were two races for women on the program: a tandem paddling race and single paddling race.[102] In the years that followed, races such as these or mixed events were a common if marginal part of the ACA regatta line-up.[103]

The American Canoe Association's treatment of women's races says much about the organization's perceptions of women as athletes, perceptions that fit neatly with contemporary associations between women and athletics. First, women's races often took place outside of the official race days; indeed, in some cases, they were scheduled after the meet.[104] Second, women's races were always classified as "Other" or "Novelty," alongside events such as the "upset race" or "hurry-scurry." This echoes baseball, where women's teams were "tolerated because of their 'novelty' or 'entertainment' value rather than from a sense of the legitimacy of their involvement in a more egalitarian social order."[105] Third, women's races were physically shorter than men's contests. A women's paddling race typically covered at most a quarter-mile, while men's paddling races were at least a half-mile. Finally, women's participation in the ACA regattas was limited to paddling races. Canoe sailing appears to have been perceived as a technically demanding sport to which women were ill-suited.

The vast majority of the competitors in the ACA regattas were not just men, they were also white. To date, I have found only a handful of exceptions. At the 1881 meet at Canoe Islands on Lake George, "an Indian race" in "real old birchbark canoes" was run off Crosbyside Park. An Abenaki man, Louis Tahamont, and Joseph Dufflin, whom the *New York Times* characterized as "a young Frenchman, who [had] grown up among the Indians," won the race and the purse. The *Times* maintained, however, that they did so "without showing extraordinary speed" and that there were "20 white canoeists on the lake who could easily beat them."[106] Such statements reassured the reader or spectator in the face of information that could subvert one's sense of the world and its seemingly "natural" hierarchies. Gillian Poulter has shown in the case of lacrosse how even as "Native players were admired for their skill and physical capacities," they were "considered inferior to white players since these were said to be innate abilities unrelated to intellect."[107] Like the women's races at later ACA meets, the "Indian race" was not part of the regular program.

Finally, a word on competitors with disabilities, a subject that has received limited attention in the sport history literature.[108] Although I have only found two explicit (and decidedly brief) examples of athletes with disabilities participating in the American Canoe Association regattas, it is imperative that these receive mention not only to begin the process of recovery, but also to counter sport's operation as a normative field of social relations with regards to ability. In the first example, visitors to the 1893 meet on Wolfe Island had the opportunity to watch a race involving Kenneth Cameron, "a one-armed man sailing a racing canoe with a big spread of muslin."[109] That the *New York Times* referred to the event as a spectacle reinforces the disabled body as anomalous, although Cameron's success also highlights his capabilities as an athlete. The second example is less an event than an individual. Paul Butler was a long-time member of the Vesper Boat Club in Lowell, Massachusetts, and a competitor in numerous ACA races in the 1880s and 1890s. Butler is perhaps best known for his creation of the "sliding-deck seat," an innovation that enabled him to transfer his weight further windward to accommodate his small stature.[110] Butler reportedly weighed 110 pounds, and photographs show that he was at least a head shorter than his fellow competitors.[111] Moreover, his stooped posture suggests he may have lived with scoliosis of some sort. W.P. Stephens described Butler as "a cripple (a hunchback)," who was "sadly handicapped against the agility of sailors like Vaux and athletes like Dr Heighway and W.G. MacKendrick."[112] Even as observers lamented his disability, the Lowell-based sailor was routinely lauded as a crack canoeist.[113]

The ACA archive is relatively silent on athletes like Kenneth Cameron and Paul Butler; however, contemporaries reported widely on the spectators who, not surprisingly, made up the largest contingent of the regatta cast (figures 7.2 and 7.3). At the 1890 meet at Jessup's Neck on Long Island, the meet captured in the photograph that opens this chapter (figure 7.1), *Forest and Stream* observed, "the waters in all directions were covered with sails before colors, and people crowded into camp from all directions; on foot, in carriages and wagons, in steam launches, sloops, catboats, and yachts."[114] The presence of spectators confirmed the races as events. Of the various members of the regatta's cast, the spectators were the most diverse socially, drawn as they were from the encampment, the surrounding resorts and cottages, and local communities. While the American Canoe Association sought to limit access to its encampments, it had little control over the watery landscape of the regatta. Thus, more than likely the audience included individuals who would have otherwise been unwelcome at the ACA meets. Surprisingly, for an organization that had separate lists of rules for members, campers, and racers, the American Canoe Association never issued a code of conduct for spectators.

Race officials constituted the third and final group of participants at the ACA regattas. Officials were a key feature of the bureaucracy of modern sport.[115] As Colin Howell notes, "Those who promoted sport and codified its rules recognized that players and audiences might lose control in the heat of the fray and that disinterested judges were therefore required."[116] In addition to functioning as arbiters of decorum, officials represented a more general fascination with technocracy, order, and time in the nineteenth century.[117] Much as the officer of the day and his pickets encouraged order in the ACA campsite, the race day officials pursued a similar end during the regatta.[118] At any given meet, the officials might include clerks of the course, judges, starters, timekeepers, entry clerks, buoymen, and measurers.[119] The clerk of the course organized the entries and kept the records of the regatta.[120] Timekeepers and buoymen were responsible, respectively, for timing the races and observing the boats as they passed the buoys, one of the prime sites for "foulings" (touching a buoy or another canoe).[121] According to *Forest and Stream*, buoymen were central to maintaining order on the course; they "insure more care in management of canoes in a race, a stricter regard to rules, and also avoid the disagreeable duty of one contestant lodging a protest against another on account of fouling."[122] Finally, there were measurers, whose job it was to guarantee that canoes conformed to the size regulations laid out in the racing rules.[123] The existence of an elaborate system of rules, as well as a cadre of officials responsible for overseeing the smooth running of the races suggests that the ACA regatta, like the encampment more broadly, was threatened by disorder. Certainly, canoeists were consistently finding ways to circumvent the rules, particularly in the sailing races, through the introduction of different riggings, sails, and the like.

With the scene set, the cast of characters in place, and the script posted on the bulletin board, the performance could begin. A typical day at the American Canoe Association regatta featured anywhere from one to seven races.[124] The different contests varied markedly in their temporal and physical length. The half-mile "paddling fours" at the 1897 meet at Grindstone Island lasted just over five minutes, while the winner of the nine-mile trophy sailing race at the 1896 meet crossed the finish line

7.2 S.R. Stoddard, "Lake George, ACA at Crosbyside," 1882. ACA organizers viewed spectators with some ambivalence. Spectators confirmed the regatta as an event. Thus, their presence was not just warranted, but encouraged through the circulation of information about the meets and the positioning of the racecourses to afford the best views. But spectators were also regarded with suspicion. In the early years, the canoeists were concerned they were nothing more than amusement for hotel guests on Lake George. Later, it was those at the bottom edge of the social ladder that posed a problem, their presence undermining the respectability of the encampment space. Adirondack Experience, 1975.020.0705.

after one hour, forty minutes, and fifty-five seconds.[125] That some of the sailing races had a three- or four-hour time limit indicates they could run even longer.[126] Whereas paddling races were run consecutively, the organizers often combined the long sailing races by staggering the starting times. The order of the races, unlike the content of the program, was largely the product of the weather, something no committee could predict. Thus, it was almost inevitable that the schedule of events would change during the meet. Despite pronouncements that "punctuality will be insisted upon," few programs ran on time.[127]

7.3 S.R. Stoddard, "Watching the Races," 1891. Adirondack Experience, 1975.052.0104.

By the time the first race was called, most canoeists had been at work for at least a couple of hours, preparing their canoes.[128] The best boats had been oiled down, the rigging perfected, and the captains warmed up.[129] The registered canoeists arrived to the starting line – at the 1894 meet at Croton Point, this was marked off by a barrel buoy and a rowboat[130] – decked out in their racing costumes, typically striped bathing suits.[131] Paddling races used a cold start.[132] Sailing canoes, by contrast, were already in motion when the gun sounded.[133] Competitors occupied a variety of different positions within the canoe during races. At the 1891 meet at Willsborough Point, M.F. Johnson, of Toronto, Ontario, paddled from standing; R.G. Muntz, also of Toronto, "knelt on one knee"; and Emil Knappe, of Springfield, Connecticut, sat in the bottom of his boat and used a foot stretcher.[134] Racing form was seen as indicative of national filiation. Canadian paddlers were associated with kneeling, while Americans were sitters. In sailing races, British canoeists could usually be found tucked in the cockpit of their canoes, while Americans were typically perched on the deck.

A racer's success was dependent on a number of different factors, not least of which was physical conditioning and form. *Forest and Stream* attributed Mr Johnson's first place finishes in a number of 1884 paddling races to his "admirable stroke, long and clean," his "high seat," and "his good condition and powers of endurance."[135] The boat and rigging were also important. A reporter in attendance at the 1885 regatta on Grindstone Island argued that C. Bowyer Vaux owed his first-place finish to his canoe's "splendid sea going qualities."[136] Of course, the most up-to-date equipment did not necessarily ensure success. At the 1883 meet at Stony Lake, the winner of the novice sailing race boasted "two lug sails and a jib, a rig seldom seen of late years."[137] In tandem or group paddling events, placing well hinged on teamwork.[138]

Favourable conditions never hurt a canoeist's chance of success. However, given that conditions were rarely favourable, more important was the ability to read the environmental situation on the course and respond appropriately. The regatta committee provided some assistance by posting "the course and conditions of each race on the bulletin board."[139] The ability to read conditions was a function of a canoeist's level of experience broadly, but also their knowledge of the specific course. For this reason, scratch or scrub races were an important part of a competitor's introduction to the racecourses during the first week of the encampment. Scrub races also provided canoeists with an opportunity to see their competition at work. It was disconcerting for the paddlers at the 1896 meet on Grindstone Island to come up against W.C. Mack of Detroit, "a new and uncertain quantity," because "his practice [was] not taken near the camp, and so the other paddlers [did] not know his gait."[140]

Regatta contestants faced a number of obstacles beyond the weather, both environmental and anthropogenic. During the club fours race at the 1902 meet on Cape Cod, the Winchester boat "got into trouble by a paddle being caught in the sea grass, cramping the boat until she went over and all hands were thrown into the water."[141] At the 1884 Grindstone Island meet, Mr Weller's entry was "run down by the steamer *E. Van Horne*, which came across the course as he finished the first round, deliberately running into him in spite of a warning from all on the bank." Thankfully for Weller, his craft "receiv[ed] but little damage," and he went on to win the race.[142] Given the chaotic scene of the regattas, it is understandable that the regatta committee found it hard to keep the courses clear of other craft, but also that some years they instituted police of the course.[143] It was not just spectators that posed a challenge, but one's opponents as well. In a single race at the 1886 Grindstone Island meet, the *Wraith* and *Peggy* collided, "carrying away the mainmast of each boat"; the "*Sofronia* had her rudder unshipped by a collision"; the "*Mona* broke her deck yoke"; the "*Pearl* was handicapped by her leakage"; and the *Nautilus* suffered a damaged rudder.[144] Such collisions occurred frequently in spite of the elaborate rules governing canoeists' behaviour in course.[145]

As they made their way around or along the course, the competitors were watched and, in some cases, cheered on by the spectators. Some people in the audience claimed "a much better view of the whole course could be gotten" on land; others complained about the difficulty of telling "which is which when the little bits of things are way off over the bay, rounding an outer mark."[146] Opera glasses were one solution.[147] Alternatively, spectators could take to the water to follow the action, both literally and figuratively.[148] At the early races on Lake George, accounts in periodicals suggest spectators were particularly engaged in the races. The diminutive C. Bowyer Vaux of New York City, received a standing ovation after he beat the "Giant," Dr A.E. Heighway of Cincinnati, Ohio, in the upset race.[149] Later accounts, by contrast, are relatively silent on the spectators' performances. This may have been a function of numbers. R.B. Burchard reported that at the 1900 meet in Muskoka, "scarce a dozen persons were attracted from the enjoyments of the camp to view the struggle," even though the races were "well contested and spirited."[150]

Not everyone who began a race finished. Usually, competitors bowed out because of injury to their boat or because they capsized. The latter was disappointing for a participant, of course, but it could be quite entertaining for the spectators.[151] The crowd at the 1883 meet on Stony Lake enjoyed watching the boats go "down like tenpins under the rude bowling of old Notus, until but three were left to go over the course."[152] There were also a number of infractions that could render a canoeist disqualified. These included accepting "pilotage or direction form any boat or from the shore" (something akin to coaching) and touching a buoy or another canoe ("fouling").[153]

Although there were officials in place to oversee the running of races, canoeists could lodge complaints if they felt unfairly treated. Complaints had to be presented in writing within one hour of the end of the race and accompanied by a dollar. Although the money was returned if the protest was successful, the fee discouraged objections, particularly as regatta committees were notoriously inflexible. The protest system functioned like a mini-judiciary. Before delivering a judgment, the regatta committee heard evidence from other contestants or spectators.[154]

If the committee's position was unanimous, the decision was final. However, if there was disagreement among its members, the canoeist could, with the payment of another dollar, appeal to the executive committee.[155] Despite the perception of transparency and equitability, not all protests were dealt with satisfactorily. At the 1890 meet at Jessup's Neck, the regatta committee, rather than posting the course for the paddling upset race – as dictated by ACA regulations – gave verbal instructions to the contestants. That "one-half of the men headed one way and the remainder the other" suggests their directions were not altogether clear.[156] Two of the competitors who had gone the wrong way made a verbal protest as soon as the winners' list was posted. That evening their club, the Ianthe of New Jersey, registered a formal protest. The regatta committee refused to acknowledge its error and honour the protests because the first had not been issued "prior to leaving the boat" and no written protest had been submitted in the hour after the race. The club made a second protest the following day, but once again, the committee declined to even consider the complaint. Whether fair or not, there was limited recourse for canoeists who felt slighted by the regatta committee.

The winners of a given contest could usually expect some immediate recognition of their feat. One of the spectators, Lorgnette, recalled "going to the cove" after the sailing trophy race to "congratulate the winner" in person.[157] The presentation of prizes, however, was typically saved for a banquet or campfire at the end of the regatta. Following a brief speech by the commodore, canoeists (usually women) bestowed flags, shields, or trophies on the successful contestants. Women's involvement here may have been a consequence of their role in producing flags. It may also have reflected the sense that women were better suited to the more decorative role of prize giving. It certainly positioned them as ancillary to competition rather than athletes in their own right.

If a curtain could have fallen on the performance that was the yearly regatta of the American Canoe Association, it would have done so following the presentation of the prizes. Instead, the campers either continued their campfire revelries, or they made their way to the fire pit from the mess tent as they did on so many other nights. The regatta was at once a unique and typical component of the American Canoe Association encampments. The onset of the races reconfigured the landscapes of the meet, introducing new forms of activity and patterns of movement and interaction among the campers. The scale of the races also set the regatta apart; none of the other spectacles lasted as long or drew as large a crowd. Yet, for many of the campers, these changes were familiar, part of the yearly ritual of attending the meets. Even those new to the ACA camp would have noticed that a number of the rhythms of encampment life such as meals and nightly campfires were little affected by the canoe races. The regatta, in other words, was as much a part of the "everyday life" of the ACA encampments as breakfast at the mess tent and taps following the evening campfire. The disciplinary structures in place to govern the encampments and the campers also remained during the regattas. If anything, efforts to order the encampments were amplified during the regatta with the addition of another set of rules to govern the canoeists' conduct. The canoe races thus reinforce the argument made in chapter 4 that sporting events and culture can serve as sites of governmental power relationships. The deployment of technologies and techniques of governance at the ACA regattas normalized similar practices in other aspects of everyday life. Finally, the regattas, while on a larger scale than the other spectacles, were still just spectacular performances, in which certain scripts were followed and certain characters allowed onstage. In this way, regattas were akin to the minstrel shows and parades described in the previous chapter. Like these other performative spaces, the regattas at the annual American Canoe Association encampments played an important role in affirming, reproducing, and defending both the bounds and bonds of community, making clear who belonged and who did not.

Chapter Eight

Working

Among the hundreds of photographs that are part of the American Canoe Association Collection at the Fenimore Museum in Cooperstown, New York, is an 1887 image by amateur photographer George Warder of Springfield, Ohio (figure 8.1).[1] Entitled "Work and Fun in Camp," the photograph depicts Robert W. Gibson of the Mohican Canoe Club of Albany, New York, attending to his canoe while at the Lake Champlain meet at Bow Arrow Point. The others in the frame are wrapped in flags and blankets and arranged in tableaux-like poses. Although its tone is tongue in cheek, the image simultaneously represents the ACA encampments as places of leisure and places of labour. However, it suggests a very narrow understanding of work, as preparation for the races. In other words, the image neglects the myriad other forms of labour that were necessary to the smooth functioning of the yearly gatherings.

This chapter examines the work and workers largely excluded from written and photographic accounts of the annual encampments of the American Canoe Association. The association never employed the teams of workers common at larger vacation enterprises such as the Saratoga Springs Resort.[2] Nevertheless, the ACA encampments would not have occurred or at the very least would have looked radically different without the carpenters, cooks, servers, performers, and general labourers responsible for construction, maintenance, and service. In turning our attention to work and workers, this chapter complicates the encampments as exclusively spaces of leisure.

Historians of sport have shown how the same activities can be defined as leisure or labour. Such definitions often reflect social position, namely, class, gender, and race. Perhaps the best example of this can be found in the literature on hunting, which explores the classed and racialized tensions between hunting as sport and subsistence, but also between white, middle-class male sport hunters and their guides,

8.1 George Warder, "Work and Fun in Camp," 1887. Warder was an amateur photographer affiliated with the Jabberwock Canoe Club of Springfield, Ohio. He produced a series of playful portraits, including this photograph, of his fellow club members at the 1887 meet. This photograph represents a very narrow understanding of work, preparing for the races and, in so doing, elides the many other forms of labour that enabled the encampments, labour that was typically performed by people of colour and by rural whites. Fenimore Museum, ACA Collection, box 1.1/24.

who were typically Indigenous people or rural white folks.[3] What has remained largely unexplored are the ways in which the sporting practices of the middle and upper classes, but particularly organized sport, have been made possible by the labour of "Others," including the working class, women, and people of colour.[4] This is the focus of the first half of this chapter. Nor has any significant attention been paid to other commercial endeavours associated with sport such as the souvenir trade or the sale of sporting equipment. In earlier chapters, I discussed the ways in which canoeists consumed vistas and experiences while at the encampments. However, campers were also consumers in a more material sense: they purchased handicrafts from local

Indigenous artists, produce and trinkets from the camp store, boat fittings from canoe builders, and images from commercial photographers. In the second half of this chapter, we turn our attention to those whose labour constituted the ACA encampment as a commercial space. The objective of this chapter, in other words, is to position the American Canoe Association encampments as spaces of leisure *and* work, of production *and* consumption.

This chapter seeks to show what other histories of work and sport are possible and, I believe, necessary, while recognizing the challenges that exist to meet such an end. Not least is the question of how to recover pasts seemingly without histories. In spite of their importance, workers exist, at best, on the margins of official accounts of the ACA meets; in most cases, they are altogether ignored. Unsurprisingly, I have yet to uncover accounts of the annual gatherings penned by a labourer. This makes it difficult to know with any certainty the extent or the exact ways in which workers contributed to encampment life. Other scholars in similar predicaments have turned to census material to determine, for example, the number and make-up of workers at hotels and resorts.[5] The women and men employed by the American Canoe Association were rarely in attendance for longer than a few weeks, which was not enough time to be counted and recorded by census takers. Likewise, efforts to uncover more, even about people who are named, have largely proven futile. Rather, I am forced to read against the grain of accounts in periodicals and canoeists' memoirs, and to pay close attention to those at the edges of photographs to tease out the web of workers and practices that enabled the canoeists to travel, camp, and compete.

Clearly, workers were not absent from the American Canoe Association encampments, but they and the work they performed were largely invisible. As Thomas G. Andrews notes, "It takes work to erase labor from a landscape," which he argues is a testament to the "two distinct but intertwined modes of constructing landscape: as built environments produced by physical labor and as representational spaces produced by cultural work."[6] What Andrews documents in the case of Colorado landscapes at the turn of the twentieth century was not isolated to the west, but was evident in other holiday destinations across the continent. Sites of labour and production were increasingly being recast as spaces of leisure and consumption, a process that continues today. Andrews writes, "It has become second nature for many of us to ignore the work that sustains our lives and the labor that constructs the landscapes we inhabit."[7] More than an act of recovery and replacement, then, this chapter also seeks to understand why workers and particular kinds of work are invisible in the archive of the ACA encampments.

Recovery of this labouring past is difficult and admittedly fragmentary; nevertheless, it is critical to this book's interest in the social and spatial politics of sport and leisure.

Accounts detailing preparations for the American Canoe Association encampments emphasize the labour performed by members of the organizing committee. They highlight revisions to the regatta program, letters written to government officials regarding international border crossings, correspondence with railway companies about travel discounts, and surveys made of the campsites and racecourses. What is largely occluded from these accounts is the extent to which the organizing committee depended on local resources, particularly local labourers, to prepare for the early meets.[8]

The site surveys were one of the first occasions that local people were called on to aid in the preparations. These usually took place in the winter months when the ice was still on the water. An article describing the survey undertaken for the 1883 meet at Juniper Island on Stony Lake is an unusually thorough account of labour performed by those outside the American Canoe Association.[9] According to author Robert Tyson, the regatta committee departed Peterborough, Ontario, at 6:15 a.m. on 30 March in a sleigh driven by Joe Vasseur, a "shrewd, good-humored French Canadian." Also in the sleigh was Crown Surveyor James W. Fitzgerald. The author had little to say about Fitzgerald who, given his occupation, was likely perceived as holding a similar class and race position to Tyson and the other ACA official in the sleigh, Commodore Elihu Burritt Edwards. However, a good-sized paragraph was devoted to describing Vasseur. Even as Tyson acknowledged the driver was an "excellent teamster," he painted him as simplistic and crude: his English was broken, his commentary obscene. He made special note of Vasseur's recreational pastimes, shooting a "saw-log slide" in "a narrow, log canoe" for "pure reckless fun," an ostensibly less rational and respectable canoeing activity than the cruises and races that appealed to members of the ACA.[10] Finally, Tyson called into question Vasseur's full humanity, by painting him as a "half-amphibious creature," a consequence of his time working as a river driver in the lumber industry. Tyson's description of Vasseur resonates with J.I. Little's observation that urban campers visiting Lake Memphremagog in the same period portrayed local men "not as heroic individualists," as was sometimes the case in hunters' accounts of guides, "but as rustic and often amusing folk figures."[11] Such representations established a certain distance between the canoeists and the people they employed, and underscored the otherness of workers.

Vasseur was not the only person the ACA organizing committee engaged that day. Before arriving at Juniper Island, they collected Mr McCracken, a farmer valued for his knowledge of the local environment, but particularly for his familiarity with the "unfailing springs of excellent water" near to the campsite. McCracken did more than share knowledge; he also lent his manual skills to the project by acting as surveyor's assistant to Fitzgerald. It is not clear if the farmer had performed these tasks before. However, Tyson observed, in the paternalistic parlance of contemporary labour relations, McCracken "proved himself a handy, willing, and cheerful worker."[12] Also assisting with the survey was another farmer, Mr Crow, and his son Willie; Tyson's report on these two individuals is cursory at best.

The attention paid to Vasseur and McCracken in this recounting of the 1883 surveying trip is uncharacteristic of ACA accounts, which more often record the activities of members than workers. In naming these men and describing the work they performed, Tyson was pulling back the cover of obscurity typically ascribed to the people whose work made the American Canoe Association encampments possible. How might we explain this anomalous account? Certainly, more attention is afforded to work and workers in the early years of the summer gathering, when detailed accounts of encampment life were the norm; later reports tend to focus exclusively on the regattas. This shift likely reflects the routinization of the organization, preparation, and execution of the annual meet. However, ultimately I think this is a story about the survey, which functions here as a tool of legitimation. Still in its infancy in 1883 when this account was published, the ACA could only have benefited from positive associations with the scientific tool, particularly as the organization sought to establish itself as *the* premier (inter)national canoeing organization. Local colour, which Vasseur, McCracken, and the Crows ostensibly offered in abundance, was necessary to properly tell the tale of the survey as a travelogue for readers of *The American Canoeist*.[13]

More common in the ACA archive are accounts that erase the work of Others altogether. This is perhaps most visible in descriptions of the campsite. Despite the ACA's claims that its members were visiting wild places, it took no small amount of work to produce these landscapes: trees had been cut down, brush removed, and paths graded. Yet, few accounts describe how this work was performed or who performed it. The fact that much of this landscaping was undertaken before the campers arrived on site would have contributed to its invisibility. That said, when it was not carried out to the satisfaction of the campers, notes were made and accusations levelled. The 1900 meet in Muskoka, for example, was derided for being "too rough."[14] Once judged and committed to "the record," poor performance made the invisible suddenly visible. This reinforces Thomas Andrews's point that if the "small armies of maids, waiters, cooks, and porters ... did their jobs properly," they could be overlooked.[15]

In addition to clearing underbrush, removing rocks, and laying out walking paths, labourers assembled the camp infrastructure: digging wells and sinks; constructing the camp wharf; erecting buildings for the mess, kitchen, and camp store; and building tent floors and landing stages for individual campers.[16] Whereas general labourers undertook landscaping duties, skilled carpenters appear to have performed this other work. With the move to Sugar Island, the number of labourers engaged in advance of the annual meet likely declined. Temporary structures were replaced with more permanent buildings, and landscaping became a matter of maintenance rather than yearly reinvention. Of course, there were always unexpected jobs to be performed. High water on the St Lawrence in 1908 caused a number of the ACA members' personal docks to be washed away. The organization reported, "It was necessary to do quite a little work to get the Island in shape."[17] We can assume that that much of this work was passed off to local labourers. The permanent encampment, and specifically concerns about leaving the association's property unattended for much of the year, also warranted a new position. In 1904, the organization hired a local lighthouse keeper, Manley Cross, to serve as the site's first caretaker. Cross was expected to watch over the site and perform general maintenance tasks. In the warmer months, he was also responsible for welcoming visiting canoeists to the site – Sugar Island was available to ACA members throughout the summer.[18]

Each stage of the journey from home to the encampment was facilitated by another's labour. At the front end, domestic servants assembled the luggage and kit of the ACA's well-to-do members.[19] Domestic service while on the decline at the turn-of-the-twentieth century was still a relatively common feature of middle-class life in Canada and the United States, and two weeks at a canoeing encampment required special preparations.[20] Some canoeists and clubs travelled to the American Canoe Association meets with domestic workers. The *British Daily Whig* reported that Alderman Skinner's valet filled a bathtub for him each day at the 1893 meet at Brophy's Point on Wolfe Island because he could not swim.[21] In the 1880s and 1890s, Paul Butler of the Vesper Boat Club of Lowell, Massachusetts, was accompanied to the encampments by "an old colored man, a body servant of [his father], whose duty it was to look after the sails."[22] I also found a photograph of the Knickerbocker Canoe Club at a division meet with an African-American boy seated in the foreground. Scrawled on the back of the image is the following note, "Rastus, the camp chore boy."[23] That there were domestic workers on site is also evident in the plans to include servants' quarters among the permanent buildings on Sugar Island.[24] These examples are exceptions in the ACA archive; domestic servants are otherwise absent from campers' accounts of the events. As a fact of life for many middle-class, and particularly upper-middle-class families, the presence of servants at the American Canoe Association encampments was likely unremarkable.

For journeys to the meets made by train, baggage handlers and porters were a necessity, if a frustrating one. Interactions between the canoeists and the baggage handlers were particularly fraught. The canoeists routinely complained about the poor treatment their beloved craft received in the baggage car.[25] This may explain why in 1884, one of the New York clubs had their janitor travel to Grindstone Island in a special car at the forward end of the train that carried the canoes, ostensibly to keep an eye on them, while not coincidentally keeping travellers' eyes free of him.[26] By contrast, accounts of travel to the American Canoe Association encampments are almost universally silent on the role of porters, in spite of the fact that they would have been present in the canoeists' first-class cars.[27] This should not surprise us. Thomas Andrews observes that, by the late nineteenth century, "luxury trains had become domestic spaces where pullman [sic] porters and other men performed precisely the types of feminized and racialized work that travelers were most likely to overlook."[28] Porters also cultivated invisibility as they worked, both at the behest of employers and for personal reasons. Invisibility, Beth Tompkins Bailey argues, could function as a protective mechanism and a strategy to attract tips.[29]

For those who travelled to the meets by canoe, the assistance of local people was less likely to be overlooked, although their labour was usually framed as an act of kindness rather than work. Travelogues describe the goods purchased from farms by-passed along the way, the local people contracted to transport canoes between waterways, the rental of land for tenting, and the appeal for assistance when the next stage of the journey was uncertain. Much like descriptions of the labourers at the encampments, the canoeists' accounts paint local people as "folk"-like.[30] They emphasize, for instance, the unfamiliar accents, the colourful vocabulary, and the perceived simplicity of their lives and personalities. Florence Watters Snedeker's slim volume, *A Family Canoe Trip*, is perhaps the best example of this. Early on, Snedeker observes of the roadside, "instead of Indians, there were lots of farmers' children offering us peaches and apples," who provided "choice pictures for our camera."[31] She also makes note of the mule drivers who worked along the canal: "We became acquainted with our fellow travellers ... In face they were less moral than the mules they drove: now a sallow Yankee with a hint of lost estate in his unquiet eyes; now an all-brutal, shaggy foreigner ... We found them civil, even obliging. But they whacked their beasts viciously."[32] Finally, Snedeker includes dialogue that, intending to capture the distinctive cadences of the speaker, universally constructs her subjects as uneducated and uncultured.[33] Ostensibly, travel brought the ACA canoeists into contact with difference, providing the opportunity for a readjustment of established assumptions about the Other. More often than not, however, such encounters reinforced cultural divisions. What's more, the labours of those they met were rarely interpreted as work, but rather as quaint performances of otherness.

Having arrived to the ACA meet, the canoeists turned their attention to settling into camp life. Cindy Aron observes that while early proponents of outdoor living highlighted the opportunities for relaxation that camping afforded, by the end of the nineteenth century, camping advocates were celebrating the work of outdoor life.[34] The American Canoe Association appears to have followed a somewhat different trajectory. By 1900, few of the canoeists did the work associated with camping out. Local carpenters built tent floors in advance of their arrival, and in some cases raised the canvas structures that would serve as the canoeists' homes away from home. Cooks and kitchen staff were hired to provide meals and wash dishes. Performers were engaged to amuse.

Although much of the work of readying the ACA campsite took place before the campers arrived, typically one or more of the carpenters remained on site during the annual meet to provide assistance. The few extant references to the "camp carpenter" suggest the indispensability of this individual. A visitor to the 1889 meet on Stave Island claimed, "Jackman was not only the carpenter, he was the flagpole raiser, fire builder and general utility man of the camp. He was an institution, and if he could be an annual institution that would be a good thing."[35] At the 1892 meet at Willsborough Point on Lake Champlain, handbarrows built by the camp carpenter were praised for aiding the canoeists as they moved boxes and bundles from tent to steamer.[36] There were also more general labourers on site who delivered firewood and carted goods around the encampment, although their efforts were rarely acknowledged.[37]

Some of the most visible work involved the planning, preparation, and service of food. Operating the camp mess was no easy feat, given that the cook and servers had to feed, in some cases, a few hundred campers three meals a day.[38] Early on, local people were responsible for the kitchen. The mess shed on Grindstone Island operated under the watchful eye of Mrs Delaney.[39] By the 1890s, the responsibility for meals was largely the purview of professionals, and also of men. D. McElveney and Sons, a well-known catering company from Albany, New York, managed the mess at a number of ACA encampments between 1897 and 1910.[40]

Even as the administration of the mess was professionalized, local people, the majority of whom were women, continued to work in the kitchen performing tasks consistent with their contributions to the family economy (figure 8.2).[41] With the exception of the 1890 meet at Jessup's Neck and the 1893 meet on Wolfe Island, the wait staff also appear to have been young white women like those pictured in the background of the photograph of the mess tent at the 1898 meet (figure 5.2).[42] Employment of female servers was out of step with other hotels and resorts in this period. LouAnn Wurst's research on Niagara Falls hotels has shown that waiters were typically men and domestics were women. She argues further that while most of the women workers were white, male staff were predominantly Black or mixed race.[43] The canoeists offer some other clues about the servers, hinting at a greater degree of contact between the servers and served than between ACA members and workers elsewhere on the site. For example, they note that most were teachers at nearby schools or the daughters of local farmers.[44] Certainly, some of the women workers appear to have been incorporated into the encampments in a way that male labourers, particularly those of colour, were not. In his memoirs of the American Canoe Association, D.B. Goodsell recalled "dances given for the waitresses of the mess tent."[45] According to R.B. Burchard, however, "woe to the luckless Johnny who attempted to be flirtatious," suggesting that some female workers maintained a sense of distance from the canoeists.[46]

Not everyone ate at the mess tent. In some cases, the ACA canoeists visited a nearby farmhouse for their meals, further strengthening dependencies on local farms and farmers.[47] Still others set up a "club mess" and hired a cook. Club cooks came from near and far. At the 1893 meet on Wolfe Island, the Brooklyn Canoe Club employed a man from neighbouring Kingston.[48] The previous decade, Frank Baker of the exclusive Down Town Club travelled from New York City to oversee the Brooklyn mess.[49] Some of the camp cooks had experience in lumber camps, where they would have "prepared and served three gigantic meals for forty to two hundred men."[50] Others were French Canadian, including the unnamed "presiding genius" of the Deseronto Canoe Club mess at Jessup's Neck in 1890.[51] Photographs indicate that some of the cooks were Black men. Figure 8.3 was produced by commercial photographer Seneca Ray Stoddard for the Brooklyn Canoe Club during the 1887 meet at Bow Arrow Point on Lake Champlain. Captioned the "Sneak Box Mess," a

8.2 "Joe." For some people, including cooks, kitchen staff, servers, carpenters, and entertainers, the ACA encampments were spaces of labour, not spaces of leisure. These two images are among a handful of extant photographs that capture the ACA workforce. This figure is unique for showing a worker mid-task, while figure 8.3 below stands out for depicting a person of colour at the meets. R.B. Burchard, "Back to Grindstone: The Canoe Camp," *Outing* 29, no. 2 (1896): 139.

8.3 S.R. Stoddard, "The Sneak-Box Mess: Camp of the Brooklyn Canoe Club," 1887. Fenimore Museum, ACA Collection, box 1.1/25.

reference to a canoe-like craft made prominent by founding ACA member Nathaniel Holmes Bishop, the photograph depicts five members of the club, four of whom are "seated in front of colored cook," to borrow from the note on the back of the image.[52] Even as the cook is visible and positioned somewhat above, if still behind the members, this unofficial caption speaks to the racial politics of the American Canoe Association encampments. Whereas the white canoeists are identified by name, signalling their full inclusion in the experience of the meets, the Black cook goes unnamed, leaving him beyond the imaginary bounds of the event, even as he occupies a physical place within it.[53] The profile of club cooks at the ACA meets echoes Abigail Van Slyck's findings researching children's summer camps in the United States in the decades around the turn of the century. She observes that lumber camp and sea cooks were favoured choices for overseeing dining halls, as were African Americans. Black cooks, in particular, "preserved the all-male environment while also reinforcing the idea that some kitchen chores were beneath the dignity of white males."[54]

The relative visibility of the club cooks, like the servers, suggests that not all labourers were perceived as "workers" (and ignored as such) in the same way. Even as the canoeists were more attentive to cooks in their accounts of encampment life, a good deal is left unsaid. In addition, they tend to present the cooks not as capable practitioners, but as sources of amusement, much as Robert Tyson portrayed Joe Vasseur, the driver for the 1883 survey delegation. The most notorious of the club cooks was "the venerable Sergeant Billings" who was in attendance at a number of American Canoe Association encampments, including the 1883 meet on Stony Lake and the 1888 meet on Lake George.[55] Following the Stony Lake camp, O.K. Chobee opined, "No one who camped with the A.C.A.'s on Juniper Island will forget the stentorian tones with which, each morning, Billings, the cook, strove to arouse the drowsy Mohican and Knickerbocker men who belonged to his mess: 'Breakfast, Morcans! Niggerboggers, breakfast! Dod rat them sleepy Yankees!'"[56] A loud, bossy cook from the shanties may have fulfilled the canoeists' desire for an authentic outdoor experience. Such representations, however, also reinforced the cook's position as Other within the white, middle-class world of the ACA encampments.

As the example of the cooks makes clear, the boundary that surrounded the encampments was a permeable one. Even as the canoeists sought to police membership in the association and limit visitors to the site, they allowed "Others" access to the meets as labourers. Framed in this way, the ACA encampments recall the situation of "peculiar tensions" that defined domestic service in the late nineteenth century.[57] Magda Fahrni submits that, on the one hand, "service was crucial to the creation of a respectable bourgeois home and lifestyle," a "hallmark" of middle-status.[58] On the other, servants, because of their class and race position, were perceived as "dubious intruders into the bourgeois domain." Domestic service, she concludes, was a "unique spatial process that transgressed the physical segregation of the classes perceived and defended in late-nineteenth-century Canada."[59] The American Canoe Association encampments also transgressed the physical segregation of the races.

Most of the individuals who traversed this boundary were engaged in various forms of manual labour. However, the campers also benefited from more artistic kinds of work. Whereas the majority of camp workers appear to have been rural whites, most of the entertainers were people of colour. At the 1884 meet on Grindstone Island, "a number of Indians" from the area "represented scenes of Aboriginal life" as part of Lafayette Seavey's annual spectacle.[60] Six years later, members of the ACA hired a "Coon Band,"[61] a group of three African-American men from nearby Sag Harbor to provide musical entertainment for the camp.[62]

The most famous of the ACA performers was E. Pauline Johnson.[63] Her appearance at the 1893 meet on Wolfe Island in full Indian costume was one of the most unusual and noteworthy aspects of that year's encampment.[64] Spectators watched as "this Indian girl, daughter of a Mohawk chief, stepped into the glare of the red lights, dressed in the ornamental garb of a Mohawk maiden ... and recited her own poem, wherein an Indian wife bids her warrior husband go to war with the whites."[65] The *New York Times* deemed the performance "all very stirring and tragic." Given the publicity of these performances, it is difficult to claim that performers were invisible. However, few of the canoeists likely perceived their contributions to encampment life as work.

Indigenous peoples were also called on to perform in canoe races. In this case, payment depended on the performance. At the 1881 meet on Lake George, spectators watched as canoes powered by local Indigenous men competed for a purse.[66] That "Indians" apparently leant some authenticity to early meets is evident in a letter penned by the meet organizer Nathaniel Bishop:

> Captain Lee Harris, the owner of the little steamer Owl, who is an Adirondack guide, and lives in Caldwell, will "enthuse" the Indians – some half dozen or more who live in the outskirts of the village. He will try to find them birch trees large enough to make canoes, and if we offer a prize for an Indian canoe race, we may coax them into dressing in savage style and putting on the war paint. As their leader is thoroughly Christianized, and the best member of one of our churches, it may require the persuasive eloquence of Rev. Mr H – ... but we must have an Indian canoe race on the Horicon of Cooper, if we have to import the Indians from Canada.[67]

Clearly, Bishop was not interested in the participation of Indigenous peoples on their own terms and as equals, but was more concerned with reproducing a mythological and quasi-historical stereotype that would lend some "authenticity" to the ACA meet.[68] This use of Indigenous peoples as a means of authenticating sporting events recalls Gillian Poulter's writing on lacrosse tours in the same period.[69]

The question of participation has long troubled historians studying Indigenous and Black performances for white audiences. Scholars in both fields tend to agree that participation in minstrel shows and World's Fairs, to name just two of the more popular venues for racialized performers at the end of the nineteenth century, offered economic benefits.[70] Sabine Milz's work shows that it was stage recitals, not publications that sustained Pauline Johnson.[71] Performances also provided Black and Indigenous performers opportunities to affirm their culture and "reverse stereotypes" constructed by whites.[72] In some cases, groups "performed with more irony than their white audiences appreciated, enjoying their status as tricksters by performing expected roles and subverting them."[73] In this way, performances were more than "capitulation to the forces of popular consumer culture"; they were a "form of political activism," an opportunity "to challenge the racial status quo and thus participate in the creation of modern discourse."[74] Of course, white audiences rarely if ever recognized the complexity of such performances. Rather, they functioned as confirmations of pre-existing assumptions about the racialized Other. Writing about Kwakwaka'wakw participation in the 1893 World's Fair in Chicago, Paige Raibmon notes that even as the performers "ingeniously combined cultural affirmation and adaptation, they contributed to the identification of Kwakwaka'wakw culture as a static relic of the past."[75]

Given the paucity of records on the subject, it is impossible to offer even a rough estimate of the number of people hired to work at the American Canoe Association encampments on a yearly basis. The cook/caterer was in charge of hiring staff for the kitchen and mess hall, so there is no record of their labour in association accounts. Similarly, some years the responsibility for arranging manual labourers was farmed out to the property owner or a local merchant.[76] The accounts for the 1900 meet at Birch Point on Lake Rosseau in Muskoka and the 1905 encampment on Sugar Island are unique for naming labourers responsible for landscaping and construction.[77] Even as attempts to find further information about the individuals listed in the accounting for the 1900 and 1905 meets have proved fruitless, such records are nonetheless instructive. They offer some sense, for instance, of the scale of the workforce, listing payments to nine and seven different individuals for manual labour, respectively. Moreover, the records from the 1905 meet specify a rate of pay for three of the workers and also the length of employment. Thomas Nicholson and Alexander Sherby worked for 19.5 days at $3.50 and $2.00 per day, respectively. Donald McLennan was paid $1.50 per day for 15 days of work. These accounts suggest that the American Canoe Association paid skilled manual labourers relatively well. According to the 1901 census, the average male clerk in Canada earned $496.49 annually, while the average production worker took home $375.00.[78] Of course, wages paid to workers at the ACA meets were only temporary.

Work at the American Canoe Association encampments, which may have been welcomed by local people, was likely one component of a larger household or family economy that existed for rural folks on both sides of the Canada-US border in the late nineteenth century.[79] Women played an important economic role in sustaining families through the production of goods such as butter, buttons, and hats; taking in boarders; and the sale of services such as laundry.[80] Joan Jensen goes so far as to suggest that farmwomen, in particular, "*expected* to undertake work that would bring in money to the household economy."[81] Such tasks were important in an era when farms existed at a midpoint on the continuum between subsistence production and the capitalist economy. Farm men were also known to take on wage labour intermittently to supplement their family incomes.[82] One of the primary sources of seasonal labour for the Ontario lumber camps was agriculturalists.[83] Conversely, the examples of Joe Vasseur and the camp cooks suggest that the ACA encampments also occasionally provided ancillary work for men engaged in seasonal resource industries.[84] Still other workers may have been employed in nearby factories. As we saw in chapter 2, few of the campsites were spatially distant from industrial production. Occupational plurality, in other words, was a likely reality for many of the women and men the ACA employed.

Just as accounts of the American Canoe Association meets offer few specifics about the women and men whose labour made the encampments possible, they are also relatively silent on encounters between the canoeists and workers. Some of the organizers' comments hint at tensions between the two groups. This friction may have resulted from differences of class, race, nationality, and location (rural versus urban). For example, although the ACA publicly praised the relationship they had with the Delaneys of Grindstone Island – the encampment was held on this site five times (in 1884, 1885, 1886, 1896, and 1897) – there was not universal satisfaction with the arrangement. In 1885 and again in 1886, the ACA's executive committee deemed the bills presented by the family to the organization "excessive" and "exorbitant," respectively.[85] Such interactions were likely frustrating for the Delaneys as well, who may have felt the ACA was trying to undercut them. Moreover, given the canoeists' penchant for pranks and debauchery, the organization may not have always made the best guests or neighbours.

The ACA's dependency on local labour was not unique. Rather, it was (and remains) characteristic of tourist economies. Dona Brown has explored the complex of tourist industries that emerged in New England over the course of the nineteenth century to accommodate, feed, and outfit the many visitors to the area.[86] At a more intimate level, J.I. Little's work demonstrates how a small group of "city folk" that summered on Lake Memphremagog around the turn of the century "relied on the easy-going local men who knew how to build boats and cabins, fix engines, and fulfill other traditionally male tasks that [the campers were] somewhat incompetent at."[87] Despite such dependencies, visitors to each of these spaces, the American Canoe Association encampments included, rarely remarked on the labours of local people that sustained them.

The American Canoe Association encampment was not just a space of material production, but of consumption as well. At various times in the period between 1880 and 1910, a canoeist could purchase goods from the camp store, views of the encampment from a photographer, handicrafts from Indigenous artisans, and canoe parts from a builder. In other words, people consumed more than landscapes, experiences, or services at the annual meets; they also purchased physical goods, some of which made the journey home with them as souvenirs of their time at the ACA gatherings. In the final section of this chapter, I consider three different groups that peddled their wares at the encampments: Indigenous artisans, commercial photographers, and boat builders. Just as the labourers on site were not created equal, nor were the vendors.

The souvenir trade was big business in the late nineteenth century, a consequence of the "rapid growth in tourism during the Victorian era."[88] Making handicrafts for white travellers was a "principal occupation of Native women along most tourist routes" and an important source of income in places where "older means of survival had been eroded."[89] The types of available crafts varied from location to location. In Niagara, Ontario, mohair items, cigar cases, and moccasins were popular, while in the province's northern communities, such as Killarney, travellers could find baskets, mats, and toy canoes made of birchbark.[90]

D.B. Goodsell, in his 1936 memoir, made passing mention of Indigenous people who sold "baskets and such" at the Willsborough Point meets in 1891 and 1892.[91] Florence Watters Snedeker recounts in *A Family Canoe Trip* how her seven-year-old son "sold his heart to dark maidens for bows and arrows and mimic canoes" at the "Indian encampment" at Caldwell en route to the 1891 meet on Lake Champlain.[92] In addition to being on the way to Lake Champlain, the Indian encampment at Caldwell, which sat at the south end of Lake George, was only a stone's throw from the sites of the 1880–2 and 1888 meets. There were also reserves near to other meet locations. Travellers to the ACA encampments on the St Lawrence that came along the river from Montreal or Cornwall would have passed and perhaps even stopped at the "Indian village" of St Regis–Akewasasne, and visitors to the 1890 meet at Jessup's Neck on Long Island coming through Southampton may have seen or visited the Shinnecock reservation there.[93] Indigenous artisans did not wait for tourists to come to them; as Melissa Otis has demonstrated, Indigenous artisans in the Adirondacks actively pursued consumers, particularly as the market for crafts became glutted in the 1890s.[94] Given the prevalence of the souvenir trade in other tourist locations, the proximity of reserves and Indian encampments to the meet locations, and the mobility of craftspeople, we can presume that Indigenous artisans were more common at the American Canoe Association encampments than these two references allow.

What did such souvenirs mean for white consumers? In the most general sense, a souvenir functions as a metonym for an experience, a way to recall a time or place after it has passed.[95] More specifically, consumers of Indigenous arts, Ruth Phillips and Christopher Steiner argue, "were motivated both by a genuine admiration for the technical expertise and aesthetic sensibility of non-Western artists and, like anthropologists, by a romantic and nostalgic desire for the 'primitive' induced by the experience of modernization."[96] Consumption was also inspired by a "suspicion of mass manufacturing and mass marketing and the desire to retrieve the authenticity belonging to the rare and the singular lost through new modes of production."[97] Finally, like the orientalist material culture so popular at the ACA encampments, Indigenous handicrafts represented exotic artefacts of an ostensibly dying race, an idea that as I have noted elsewhere had profound political consequences.

Indigenous artisans were not the only group engaged in the souvenir trade at the annual meets. The American Canoe Association encampments were also frequented by those "proletarians of creation," commercial photographers.[98] Jean Sagne has noted that in France "from 1880 onwards, photographers started to follow the crowds as they left town for spas and seaside resorts," convincing hikers "to pose for portraits in their hiking boots, knapsacks on their backs" and persuading "bathers in striped bathing costumes to have their pictures taken in front of painted backdrops showing swelling seas or a port."[99] A similar phenomenon emerged in relation to the ACA encampments, which provided commercial photographers the opportunity to sell portraits of canoe clubs and families, and views of camp landscapes and activities to members of the organization.[100] The introduction of Eastman's Kodak camera in 1888 made photographic practice accessible to a broader public, but commercial photographers remained a feature of encampment life throughout this period.[101]

Most of the commercial photographers at the American Canoe Association encampments were local studio photographers.[102] Still others selling their pictures were canoeists and amateur photographers looking to supplement their incomes while at the annual meets.[103] The most prominent photographer at the encampments, however, did not fit into either of these categories.[104] Born in the foothills of the Adirondacks, Seneca Ray Stoddard had worked as a decorative painter before turning to photography in the mid-1860s.[105] By the time he attended his first ACA encampment in 1881, on Lake George, he was a relatively well-known photographic artist in the northeast. With the exception of the 1883 meet on Stony Lake, Stoddard attended every encampment between 1881 and 1896.[106] By 1888, he had become "a feature of every ACA meet, with his camera, and his request for 'a pleasant expression, now,' or 'quiet, now, for a moment,' or 'rest where you are for another clip.'"[107] Stoddard produced large numbers of images documenting the people, places, and events of the ACA meets, which he then sold to members of the association.[108] These same photographs circulated in the canoeing press, including the yearbook and official organs of the American Canoe Association. A selection was gathered into three souvenir albums of the meets, entitled *Glimpses of the ACA*, in 1887, 1889, and 1890.[109] Some years, Stoddard set up a tent on site where he displayed and sold available photographs and albums.[110] He also advertised his views in the ACA yearbooks, as well as in canoeing-related publications such as *Forest and Stream*.[111]

As the American Canoe Association's unofficial photographer for almost two decades, Stoddard was profoundly influential in producing a particular vision of the encampments and a recognizable ACA aesthetic. Stoddard, in other words, performed not only the mechanical work necessary in creating photographic images that could be sold, but also the cultural work that constructed the ACA encampments as competitive, recreational, and social canoeing landscapes. His effectiveness in framing the experience of the meets is evident in the extent to which canoeists consumed his photographs, but also reproduced his aesthetics in their own images.[112] James Opp's writing on his family's colour slide images, while the product of a very different time and place, is nevertheless useful in thinking through the "work" that Stoddard performed as an ACA photographer.[113] Of particular interest are the ways in which Stoddard contributed to the erasure of labour and labourers from the popular memory of the annual meets by producing images that elided or obscured such subjects. The American Canoe Association that Stoddard constructed was a place of canoe competition, tent villages, and play. Even when he documented work, it was easily reimagined as something else. Consider, for example, the two photographs of the "Coon Band" he included in the 1890 version of *Glimpses* (figures 8.4 and 8.5).[114] These images suggest the three male performers are not working, for how could music making be labour? Rather, they are merely amusing the audience of white folks that surround them in one image or line up to parade behind them in another. It is all play, these photographs suggest, not work. If we consider the experience from the perspective of the musicians, however, both the event and Stoddard's photographs take on a very different meaning.

The third and final group of vendors for whom the American Canoe Association encampments were spaces of work were boat builders. For these men (and they were uniformly men), the ACA meets were places to see and be seen.[115] The races that took place during the second week of the encampment were routinely imagined as sites of friendly competition. However, they also provided an opportunity to compare the merits of different craft. J.H. Rushton, a boat builder from Canton, New York, attributed the success of his business, in part, to attendance at the ACA meets and local canoe club regattas, where he "observed the success of this or failure of that particular thing; using the knowledge thus obtained to aid us in making our work more perfect."[116] Canoe meets were also places for selling canoes. Following the ACA's 1881 meet, the *Lake George Mirror* reported that Rushton and W.P. Stephens, a builder from New Jersey, had "been crowded with work to fill orders."[117] For Canadian canoe builders, in particular, the ACA encampments provided an entry point to lucrative American markets.[118]

Builders did more than watch the races or hand out advertising flyers at the annual American Canoe Association encampments. They also provided repair services to the canoeists. Rushton was the first to recognize the need for a canoe shop on site. In 1884, he set up a large tent on the Grindstone site, in which he "offered for display and sale a full line of single and double paddles, oars, masts, sails, and rigging

8.4 S.R. Stoddard, "Arrival of the Coon Band," 1890. S.R. Stoddard, *Glimpses of the ACA* (Glens Falls, 1890).

8.5 S.R. Stoddard, "De Wattah Mellin Growin' on de Vine," 1890. S.R. Stoddard, *Glimpses of the ACA* (Glens Falls, 1890).

features."[119] The following year, the Rushton tent, which was located near to the headquarters, doubled as a repair shop. It was "fitted with a work bench," "a large supply of fittings," and a "competent man ... ready to do any kind of repair work."[120] *Forest and Stream* declared Rushton's tent a "great convenience" to which canoes were carried daily "for repairs or alterations."[121] Unidentified employees from Rushton's boat shop in Canton performed the repair work at the ACA meets.[122] In later years, other builders followed suit. In 1894, for example, the St Lawrence River Skiff, Canoe and Steam Launch Company of Clayton, New York, had a "repair and supply tent with competent men in charge," at the meet at Croton Point on the Hudson River.[123]

In myriad overlapping ways the annual American Canoe Association encampments were spaces of production and consumption, work and leisure. Local carpenters and labourers produced landscapes, Indigenous craftworkers produced baskets, and photographers produced images, all of which were consumed by the canoeists. It is unlikely that visitors to the ACA encampments would have understood the space and their experiences in these terms. As Dona Brown demonstrates, one of the sleights of hand performed by the tourist industry in the late nineteenth century was to "disguise the commercial relationship" that was at the heart of the touristic practices of consuming landscapes or experiences, so that tourism appeared as an escape from rather than a participant in the creation of "a consumer-oriented society and economy."[124] To an extent, these acts of conjuring sought to ameliorate anxieties about changes being wrought by industrial capitalism. That the American Canoe Association invited commercial vendors such as boat builders and photographers to its meets is evidence of the contradictions inherent in these practices.

8.4. and 8.5. (opposite) At the 1890 meet, the canoeists hired a trio of Black musicians from nearby Sag Harbor. The musicians served as another spectacle at the Long Island meet, alongside the minstrel show and pirate re-enactment. This trio lived on in ACA memory, aided in part by Stoddard's photographs, but also because of the song they sang. Writing in 1936, D.B. Goodsell described "Watermelon Growing on the Vine" as the melody of the meets for forty-six years. Fenimore Museum, ACA Collection, box 1.6/2, D.B. Goodsell, "A Canoeing Reminiscence" (1936).

Tourism operators, including the ACA organizers, did more than shroud the performance of consumption in a discourse of authentic experiences. They also obscured the labour that made such experiences possible. As in the broader tourist industry and the world of organized sport, the ACA encampments existed in the manner they did because of the work of women, working-class and rural whites, Black folks, French Canadians, and Indigenous peoples. Much of this work, however, was rendered invisible. The invisibility of workers at the ACA gatherings was partially a function of the related myths that the canoeist was self-sufficient and that the real work of the meet was undertaken by the organizing committee and those preparing for and participating in the regatta. In practice, however, the canoeists delegated tasks they were unable or unwilling to perform to people they could easily overlook: men and women of different socioeconomic and racialized groups. Here again, the American Canoe Association was not unique. As Thomas Andrews argues, in the late nineteenth century tourists were set up to ignore the work around them in two ways. First, if the hired help did their work properly, they would be scarcely noticed. Second, travellers were surrounded by "the sort of labor they were least likely to consider work: the household work of women and the menial labor of racialized others."[125] In their efforts to make work and workers invisible, the canoeists also sought to maintain the fiction of the ACA encampment as a space for white, middle-class men, and to a certain extent for white, middle-class women. This served to distance their sporting world from the politics of everyday life, while also ignoring the physically and likely at times emotionally demanding contributions made by workers. Ultimately, it deepened the already marginal status of the men and women who devoted their time and energies to making the annual ACA gatherings possible.

That I am able to write this chapter indicates that the organizers and members were not entirely successful in their efforts to elide workers and work from the historical record of the American Canoe Association encampments. In a photograph from the 1887 meet at Bow Arrow Point on Lake Champlain that bears much resemblance to the image that opened this chapter, the members of the Mohican Canoe Club are gathered once again in a tableau to the left of a decked canoe in full sail (figure 8.6).[126] The eye is drawn to the scene being performed by the canoeists. A closer look, however, reveals a Black man to the right of the sail of the canoe, his eyes trained directly on the camera held by George Warder. The photograph thus operates as a scene of resistance to the broader, systemic pattern of historical erasure that one encounters in the ACA archive.

8.6 George Warder, "Keys, Kanoe, Kaptor, and Kowboy," 1887. This is one of the few extant photographs from the encampments that features a person of colour (right of sail). It is unclear whether the Black man's appearance in the frame is accidental or intentional. Regardless, his presence disrupts the image of the ACA as a white, middle-class organization and begs the historian to ask deeper questions about who was on site and in what capacity. More than likely, the unidentified man was employed by the club as a cook or labourer. Fenimore Museum, ACA Collection, box 1.2/6.

Workers have not only been overlooked in accounts of the American Canoe Association encampments. They have also been marginal figures in academic writing on the history of sport. Whereas historians have capably shown how organized sport through membership systems and amateur clauses (re)produced inequitable social relations in the Victorian era, they have largely ignored the ways in which the sporting practices of the middle and upper classes, but particularly organized sport, were made possible by the work of "Others." In this way, sport historians have been complicit in sport and leisure's marginalization of labour, but also in the (re)constitution of social divisions and hierarchies along lines of class, race, and gender. To counter such tendencies, we must tell the stories of the women and men whose labours have enabled middle-class forms of leisure, to make visible the deep dependencies that organized sport historically and in the present day has on workers, many of whom occupy marginal positions in society. The goal is not only to counter the "enormous condescension of posterity," but also to draw attention to the ways in which sport is constitutive of the politics of everyday life.[127]

Conclusion

There was no official closing ceremony to mark the end of the American Canoe Association encampments. Rather, the campers drifted away, some leaving as soon as the regatta was finished, others lingering for a few days or even weeks. Trunks were repacked and tents taken down. Tent floors were disassembled and the wood sold. Luggage was ferried to the wharf, where goodbyes were said. Some of the canoeists were surely heartened by the prospect of a feather bed or a home-cooked meal, but many more were saddened by these final tasks. As one observer noted, and the caption for figure 9.1 underlines, "Making camp is delightful. Breaking camp is torture."[1]

Accounts of the encampments end almost inevitably on a melancholy note. All of the months of anticipation, the time spent seeking out routes, preparing for the races, packing trunks and boarding trains, and of course, the hours passed on the water, along the shoreline, in the nearby woods, or around the campfire, quickly came to a close:

> No more dismal contrast can be imagined than that presented by a large camp just before and just after breaking up. In the morning a row of white and parti-colored tents, each with flags flying, reached from the hill down the shore, while the beach was bright with canoes. At noon a tent or two was still standing at intervals, a few canoes partly packed lay on the beach, and a huge pile of baggage and boats was on the wharf. At sunset the last tent had disappeared, and where the turtle of the Mohicans and the twin cherubs of Springfield had gamboled together but a few hours before, the lazy sheep found sweet nourishment on old hats and newspaper, and the patient kine placidly chewed the chromos from beef and tomato cans; while above on the crown of the hill, among the ashes of the camp-fire stood "Uncle Mike," watching the last retreating paddle and wondering whether the canoeists would come back next year to Grindstone.[2]

9.1 "Packing Up – Sad Day in Camp," 1888. This is one of the few photographs that captures the end of an encampment, a rare glimpse at the sadder side of camp life and further testament to the emotional power of the annual meets. Fenimore Museum, ACA Collection, box 1.1/32.

Often it took less than a day to dismantle the site. What had once been a lively community was suddenly little more than a pile of tent floors waiting to be carted off and refuse strewn ignobly among the trees and grasses. As one reporter for the *New York Evening Post* put it the day after the close of the 1887 meet at Bow Arrow Point, "But a heap of straw remained, a broken board, a few bottles perhaps, some forgotten or discarded garment – a little trench and badly worn grass mark the spot where but yesterday there was comfort, jollity, life, and a *home*."[3]

In spite of the ephemerality of the American Canoe Association encampments, there was something enduring about the experience of attending a meet. The yearly gatherings lived on in the photographs that canoeists took or purchased from S.R. Stoddard and in the scrapbooks that some campers assembled; they were carried home in the form of camp badges and prize flags and recalled in the ensuing

Conclusion

months in newspaper articles, letters to the editor, and conversations with friends. There was also something more intangible about the experience that stayed with the canoeists. Consider the following excerpt from an account of the first Grindstone Island meet in 1884:

> Home again; back to desk and counter, to hot and dusty sidewalks, boiled shirt and stiff collar, and the grind of everyday life for another year, with a pleasant but tantalizing memory of last week; idling under the trees; the glorious stir and excitement of racing; pleasant hours by the evening camp-fires; the bright green waters, clear and beautiful, of the St Lawrence; the deep blue sky, half American half Canadian; free from smoke, except the light blue of the camp-fire; free from noise, except the distant whistle of a steamer, too far off to be unpleasant – until the drone of the city, the rattle of cart and omnibus over stones subside into a refrain of "Alouette, gentil Alouette," the brief or ledger fade from view for a moment, and we have a glimpse of camp again.[4]

This quotation speaks to the power of the encampments for the canoeists, but also to the particular place memories the ACA meets evoked.

To recall the encampment was to be transported to a place of nature, socializing, and sport. Yet, even as this writer names the St Lawrence, he is not describing a specific locale, but rather a feeling that emerged from attending an ACA meet, a sense of place based not on a physical location, but on an experience. That the physical backdrops for the encampments varied widely mattered little. The memories conjured up are of the shared elements of these spaces: the shorelines, the campfires, the snowy-white tents nestled between the trees, one's fellow canoeists. The ACA encampment, in other words, was a composite of layers of social and spatial experiences that crossed time and geography, a place given shape as much by people (the community of canoeists) and activities (canoeing, spectacles, and campfires) as by the topography of the site itself. In this way, placemaking at the ACA was unique for the ways in which it could transcend geography, so intimately was it tied to the group of people who gathered – further evidence of the centrality of community formation to the making of place – and the roster of activities. The relative coherence of this impression of the annual gatherings speaks to the success of the ACA in producing a vision of the encampments that resonated with its members, a vision that was further developed by photographers like Seneca Ray Stoddard and those who captured the meets with their pens for periodicals like *Forest and Stream*. Of course, it was not a vision without contest; drinking is just one example of the gap that existed between prescription and reality at the yearly meets.

I hope it is clear to the reader by now that the American Canoe Association encampments were more than a canoeing holiday. They were profoundly meaningful events for many of the people who attended. It is no coincidence that canoeists returned year after year. D.B. Goodsell concluded his 1936 memoir of his involvement with ACA with the following thoughts: "The camps at Sugar Island are remembered as the happiest days of my life ... It is forty years since my first meet and I still have the same enthusiasm and love of the locality that I had at first and in spite of the fact that I have travelled and seen other places."[5] What stood out about the experience? The encampments were an escape, not least from work and the heat and bustle of the city. They provided participants with opportunities to compete and achieve success. They offered a sense of community, a space in which ACA members could develop valued relationships. Last, but certainly not least, they were fun.

Without taking away from the members' enjoyment or the meaningfulness of these experiences, we cannot overlook the fact that these events were contingent upon practices of hierarchy and exclusion. Despite its claims to egalitarianism, the American Canoe Association prevented women, working-class people, Indigenous people, and people of colour from full membership. This had the dual effect of shoring up the power of white, middle- and upper-class men and reinforcing the "common-sense" assumption of these other groups as inferior, which further contributed to their marginalization in contemporary society. It was not just ACA membership practices that reinforced these social hierarchies. Canoeing contests featuring Indigenous participants, performances by Black musicians, and the canoeists' own theatrical endeavours all served to normalize and fortify social relations that privileged white masculinity. Similar ends were served by the canoeists' oversight and in some cases concealment of the workers at the encampments, many of whom lived life at the margins.

The encampments were also enabled by and furthered the reach of colonialism. Through its habitation of sites on waterways in Ontario, New York, and New England, but most notably through its purchase and occupation of Sugar Island in the St Lawrence River, the American Canoe Association participated in the displacement and dispossession of Indigenous peoples, and contributed to the transformation of the lives of rural whites. The ACA was/is not alone in the world of sport and leisure in benefiting from and contributing to colonial imperatives. Contemporary global geographies of sport are a legacy of nineteenth- and twentieth-century Euro-American imperialism.[6] From soccer (football) to cricket to big game hunting, sport was/is a powerful agent of colonialism, a means by which colonizers distinguish themselves from local populations and through which they endeavour to civilize and assimilate ostensibly savage cultures.[7] One has to look no further than to the residential schools/boarding schools so common in Canada and the United States in the nineteenth and twentieth centuries to see how sports and games contributed to the related missions of assimilation and dispossession.[8] Leisure has also historically been implicated in colonial projects. Summer camps, summer homes, and national parks all provided the impetus for the dispossession of Indigenous peoples.[9]

The interpolation of sport, leisure, and colonialism is not solely a feature of late nineteenth-century life. Scholarship on mega-events such as the Olympics and World Cup has made abundantly clear how sport continues to displace, disproportionately affecting Indigenous peoples and others at the margins.[10] Leisure pursuits are not exempt either. Recent conflicts between Indigenous wild rice harvesters and summer home owners on Pigeon Lake, a stone's throw from the site of the 1883 encampment at Juniper Island on Stony Lake, are just one example of what Indigenous activists and academics have come to call "cottage colonialism."[11] Settlers continue to use unceded Indigenous land for their sport and pleasure, often without any serious reflection on the Indigenous histories, presents, and futures of these territories. What's more, they rarely, if ever, contemplate their right to occupy certain spaces. If anything, settler "traditions" like the American Canoe Association encampments provide historical justification for access to and the occupation and control of recreational spaces.[12]

The privileges of whiteness afford a belief that the only limitations to access are financial, geographical, or temporal. This latter assumption has been evident in discussions about Thaıdene Nëné, a new national and territorial park on the East Arm of Great Slave Lake in the ancestral homelands of the Łútsël K'é Dene.[13] It is the vision of the Łútsël K'é Dene First Nation (LKDFN) that while negotiations for the creation of a protected area have involved both Parks Canada and the Government of the Northwest Territories, management and operation of the new park will be the responsibility of the community. In addition to facing opposition from the mining sector, the protected area has raised concerns among white recreationalists, primarily based in Yellowknife, that they will no longer have unfettered access to the East Arm (despite the LKDFN's assurances to the contrary).[14] An imperative of decolonization is that white settlers respect the rights of Indigenous groups to control access to their land and to articulate appropriate conduct while on their territory should access be granted, whether visitors are interested in industrial development or paddling.[15]

As I noted in the introduction to this book, the existing research on canoeing is profoundly Canadian in its orientation. This makes the example of the American Canoe Association, a transnational organization dominated by Americans, unique. In the introduction, I left the reader with the following question: How do we understand the canoe and cultures of canoeing differently when we take the encampments of the American Canoe Association as our starting point? Others have provided critical readings of the canoe that demonstrate how it has functioned symbolically to constitute the Canadian nation as white. While I agree that the canoe has been used for such cultural work, these readings overlook the multivalent nature of the small craft: the canoe is not just a symbol, nor is it the exclusive domain of Canada. The canoe is a craft that has been paddled and sailed in other times and places, giving rise to particular social and cultural formations. It has also been made meaningful in other times and places, not least in the United States in the decades around the turn of the twentieth century. If anything, the example of the American Canoe Association suggests that the use of the canoe to celebrate whiteness and to further colonial and territorial imperatives transcended the international border. The ACA is a reminder, in other words, that we cannot assume the meanings associated with a particular object. Rather, we must pay close attention to the specificities of time and place.

As a social history of sport and leisure, *Canoe and Canvas* has benefited from the research and analysis of scholars like Nancy Bouchier, Russell Field, Gillian Poulter, and Colin Howell. It has sought to extend this work by turning our attention to sport beyond the city limits, in ostensibly wild places. Questions of community, class, and gender have long been important to historians of sport in Canada. *Canoe and Canvas* confirms much of the scholarship that has come before it. It highlights, for instance, the centrality of community to understanding cultures of sport and leisure, not least because it helps us to think about the ways in which recreational practices both include and exclude. This book also reaffirms the importance of sport and leisure to middle-class identities in the decades around the turn of the twentieth century, and provides further evidence of women's negotiations of and variable inclusion in an ostensibly masculine sphere. What stands out in relation to gender in this work is the prevalence of male domesticity in a mixed-gender space, a finding that further undermines the framing of outdoor recreation as a flight from the domestic.

Less common in the analytic toolbox of Canadian sport historians are space, race, and labour, all of which are central to the interpretive frames employed in *Canoe and Canvas*. Paying close attention to the ways in which the landscapes of the ACA encampments were imagined, represented, constructed, inhabited, and governed by different kinds of people from the executive committee to member canoeists to labourers has produced a much richer and more complex picture of cultures of sport and leisure during the period covered by this study. Social histories of sport are spatial histories of the sport, if we ask the right questions. *Canoe and Canvas* brings race to the fore. Although I have worked hard to uncover the presence of Black and Indigenous people at the American Canoe Association encampments, making whiteness visible has also been a central preoccupation of this book. Careful attention to race has revealed the exclusivity of the meets, but also the complexities of sporting worlds. For all of their attempts to exclude Others, the ACA canoeists were surrounded by them. Asking questions about work was particularly fruitful in revealing how race operated at the annual encampments. Historians of sport have attended to labourers' sport, but they have had very little to say about the labours of sport beyond the professional athlete as worker. I hope future scholarship will ask questions about who makes sport possible – in all of its guises from recreational leagues to professional contests to mega-events.

The canoeists worked hard to obscure the presence of Others at the American Canoe Association encampments; they appear so infrequently in the carefully produced and archived accounts and images of the meets. Less easy to overlook is the intensity of feeling that the yearly events inspired. Even the most superficial of encounters with the historical record reveals the rich emotional geographies of the ACA encampments. This, in turn, underscores the importance of these events to those who attended, but also to those of us in the present looking back, trying to make sense of the ways in which sport and leisure figured into the lives of individuals and communities. As we explore the complex and multivalent terrain of the American Canoe Association encampments – at once spaces of canoeing, sociability, competition, intimacy, camping, nostalgia, work, community, play, belonging, and exclusion – we also better understand how sport and leisure shaped and were shaped by the broader society at the end of the long nineteenth century.

Appendix: Dates and Locations of the American Canoe Association Encampments, 1880–1910

3–6 Aug. 1880	Crosbyside Park, Lake George, Adirondacks
11–13 Aug. 1881	Canoe Islands, Lake George, Adirondacks
8–11 Aug. 1882	Canoe Islands, Lake George, Adirondacks
10–24 Aug. 1883	Juniper Island, Stony Lake, Kawarthas
1–15 Aug. 1884	Grindstone Island, Thousand Islands, St Lawrence River
25 July–8 Aug. 1885	Grindstone Island, Thousand Islands, St Lawrence River
13–27 Aug. 1886	Grindstone Island, Thousand Islands, St Lawrence River
12–26 Aug. 1887	Bow Arrow Point, Lake Champlain
10–24 Aug. 1888	Long Island, Lake George, Adirondacks
9–23 Aug. 1889	Stave Island, Thousand Islands, St Lawrence River
8–23 Aug. 1890	Jessup's Neck, Peconic Bay, Long Island
6–27 Aug. 1891	Willsborough Point, Lake Champlain
4–25 Aug. 1892	Willsborough Point, Lake Champlain
11–26 Aug. 1893	Brophy's Point, Wolfe Island, St Lawrence River/Lake Ontario
13–28 July 1894	Croton Point, Hudson River
9–23 Aug. 1895	Bluff Point, Lake Champlain
14–28 Aug. 1896	Grindstone Island, Thousand Islands, St Lawrence River
6–20 Aug. 1897	Grindstone Island, Thousand Islands, St Lawrence River
5–19 Aug. 1898	Stave Island, Thousand Islands, St Lawrence River
4–18 Aug. 1899	Hay Island, Thousand Islands, St Lawrence River

3–17 Aug. 1900	Birch Point, Lake Rosseau, Muskoka
9–23 Aug. 1901	Mudlunta Island, Thousand Islands, St Lawrence River
8–22 Aug. 1902	Chatham, Cape Cod
7–21 Aug. 1903	Sugar Island, Thousand Islands, St Lawrence River
5–19 Aug. 1904	Sugar Island, Thousand Islands, St Lawrence River
4–18 Aug. 1905	Sugar Island, Thousand Islands, St Lawrence River
10–24 Aug. 1906	Sugar Island, Thousand Islands, St Lawrence River
9–23 Aug. 1907	Sugar Island, Thousand Islands, St Lawrence River
7–21 Aug. 1908	Sugar Island, Thousand Islands, St Lawrence River
6–20 Aug. 1909	Sugar Island, Thousand Islands, St Lawrence River
12–26 Aug. 1910	Sugar Island, Thousand Islands, St Lawrence River

Notes

Preface

1 For a similar approach, see Sharon Wall, *The Nurture of Nature: Childhood, Antimodernism, and Ontario Summer Camps, 1920–1955* (Vancouver: University of British Columbia Press, 2009), 25.
2 Jessica Dunkin, "The Canoe," in *Symbols of Canada*, ed. Michael Dawson, Catherine Gidney, and Donald Wright (Toronto: Between the Lines Press, 2018), 18-29.

Introduction

1 "The Canoe Boom," *New York Times* (*NYT*), 19 June 1880. Here "birch" signifies the canoe as an "Indian" craft, a point I will return to later in this chapter.
2 Accounts of the inaugural meeting appear in "The Canoeists' Convention," *New York Evening Telegram*, 5 Aug. 1880; "The Canoe Congress,"*Forest and Stream*, 12 Aug. 1880; "The Canoe Convention," *NYT*, 17 Aug. 1880.
3 "The Canoe Congress,"*Forest and Stream*, 12 Aug. 1880.
4 Whereas the starting point is self-evident – the organization was founded and held its first encampment in 1880 – the end date requires some explanation. I might have elected to end this study in 1902, the year of the last mobile encampment of the ACA. However, I was curious about the ways in which a permanent campsite shaped the community of canoeists and the encampment as place. The First World War, which is commonly understood as marking the close of the "long nineteenth century," is perhaps the "natural" endpoint for a study of leisure in the Victorian era. But in the case of the ACA, the effects of the Great War were relatively minor, only becoming noticeable in 1918. In other words, 1910 allows us to linger with the canoeists while they settled into their permanent home

without reproducing the mythological importance later ascribed to the First World War.
5. Colin Howell, *Northern Sandlots: A Social History of Maritime Baseball* (Toronto: University of Toronto Press, 1995); Nancy B. Bouchier, *For the Love of the Game: Amateur Sport in Small-Town Ontario, 1838–1895* (Montreal and Kingston: McGill-Queen's University Press, 2003); Russell Field, "A Night at the Garden(s): A History of Professional Hockey Spectatorship in the 1920s and 1930s" (PhD dissertation, University of Toronto, 2008); Gillian Poulter, *Becoming Native in a Foreign Land: Sport, Visual Culture, and Identity in Montreal, 1840–1885* (Vancouver: UBC Press, 2009).
6. Patricia Jasen, *Wild Things: Nature, Culture, and Tourism in Ontario, 1790–1914* (Toronto: University of Toronto Press, 1995); Leslie Paris, *Children's Nature: The Rise of the American Summer Camp* (New York: New York University Press, 2008); Sharon Wall, *The Nurture of Nature: Childhood, Antimodernism, and Ontario Summer Camps, 1920–1955* (Vancouver: UBC Press, 2009); Jocelyn Thorpe, *Temagami's Tangled Wild: Race, Gender, and the Making of Canadian Nature* (Vancouver: UBC Press, 2012).
7. Michel Foucault, "Governmentality," in *The Foucault Effect: Studies in Governmentality*, ed. Graham Burchell, Colin Gordon, and Peter Miller (Chicago: University of Chicago Press, 1991), 87–104.
8. Michel de Certeau, *The Practice of Everyday Life*, trans. Steven Rendell (Berkeley: University of California Press, 1984), xi, xiv.
9. Ibid.
10. Ibid., xviii.
11. Henri Lefebvre, *The Production of Space*, trans. Donald Nicholson-Smith (Oxford: Blackwell, 1991).
12. John C. Walsh and Steven High, "Rethinking the Concept of Community," *Histoire sociale/Social History* 32, no. 64 (1999): 255–74.
13. See, e.g., Edward Said, *Orientalism* (New York: Vintage Books, 1978); Philip J. Deloria, *Playing Indian* (New Haven: Yale University Press, 1998); Paige Raibmon, *Authentic Indians: Episodes of Encounter from the Late-Nineteenth-Century Northwest Coast* (Durham: Duke University Press, 2005).
14. Iconic books documenting the history of canoes and canoeing in Canada include the following: Bruce Hodgins and Margaret Hobbs, eds., *Nastawgan: The Canadian North by Canoe & Snowshoe* (Toronto: Dundurn Press, 1987); James Raffan and Bert Horwood, eds., *Canexus: The Canoe in Canadian Culture* (Toronto: Betelguese Books, 1988); Jamie Benidickson, *Idleness, Water, and a Canoe: Reflections on Paddling for Pleasure* (Toronto: University of Toronto Press, 1997); James Raffan, *Bark, Skin, and Cedar: Exploring the Canoe in Canadian Experience* (Toronto: Harper Collins, 1999); John Jennings, Bruce W. Hodgins, and Doreen Small, eds., *The Canoe in*

Canadian Cultures (Toronto: Natural Heritage/Natural History, 1999); John Jennings,*The Canoe: A Living Tradition* (Toronto: Firefly Books, 2002).
15 Benidickson, *Idleness, Water, and a Canoe*, 3–4.
16 Bruce Erickson, *Canoe Nation: Nature, Race, and the Making of a Canadian Icon* (Vancouver: UBC Press, 2013); Misao Dean, *Inheriting a Canoe Paddle: The Canoe in Discourses of English-Canadian Nationalism* (Toronto: University of Toronto Press, 2013). See also Thorpe, *Temagami's Tangled Wild*; Andrew Baldwin, "Ethnoscaping Canada's Boreal Forest: Liberal Whiteness and Its Disaffiliation from Colonial Space," *Canadian Geographer* 53, no. 4 (2009): 427–43; Beverly Haun-Moss, "Layered Hegemonies: The Production and Regulation of Canoeing Desire in the Province of Ontario," *Topia* 7 (Spring 2002): 39–55; Bruce Braun, *The Intemperate Rainforest: Nature, Culture, and Power on Canada's West Coast* (Minneapolis: University of Minnesota Press, 2002).
17 Vaux fancied himself a historian of canoeing, publishing a series of articles on the subject in *Outing* magazine in the summer of 1887. Vaux's photographic collection fills Fenimore Museum (FM), formerly the New York State Historical Association (NYSHA), American Canoe Association (ACA) Collection, box 1.1 and box 1.2. C. Bowyer Vaux was also the author of *Canoe Handling* (New York: Forest and Stream Publishing, 1885).
18 FM, ACA Collection, box 1.5 and 1.5A, Scrapbooks.
19 Joan M. Schwartz and James R. Ryan, eds., *Picturing Place: Photography and the Geographical Imagination* (London: I.B. Tauris, 2003), 7.
20 Allan Sekula, "Photography Between Labour and Capital," in *Mining Photographs and Other Pictures, 1948–1968*, ed. Benjamin H.D. Buchloh and Robert Wilkie (Halifax: Press of the Nova Scotia College of Art and Design, 1983), 193.
21 Peter Bailey, "'A Mingled Mass of Perfectly Legitimate Pleasures': The Victorian Middle Class and the Problem of Leisure," *Victorian Studies* 21, no. 1 (1977): 7–28; David Strauss, "Toward a Consumer Culture: 'Adirondack Murray' and the Wilderness Vacation," *American Quarterly* 39, no. 2 (1987): 270–86.
22 Most contemporary authors attributed canoeing's meteoric rise to MacGregor. For accounts of the origins of "modern" canoeing, see "Canoeing," *NYT*, 22 Aug. 1871; "Paddle and Sail," *NYT*, 2 Aug. 1878; "Canoeing in the United States," *NYT*, 1 Aug. 1880; "Where Canoes Will Float," *NYT*, 2 Aug. 1891; "Annual Canoe Meet," *NYT*, 4 Aug. 1895; Hermann Dudley Murphy, "Lovers of the Canoe," *Boston Evening Transcript*, 3 Aug. 1909.
23 John MacGregor, *A Thousand Miles in the Rob Roy Canoe: On Rivers and Lakes of Europe* (London: Sampson, Low, Marlowe and Co., 1866). MacGregor's book was undoubtedly popular; by 1879, it was on its fifteenth printing.

24 M.J.D. Roberts, "Between Fame and Eccentricity: John 'Rob Roy' Macgregor, Almost Eminent Victorian," *History Australia* 2, no. 2 (2005): 36-1–36-8.
25 MacGregor's writing would have also circulated in book form in North America, but especially in Canada. William Crowley, *Rushton's Rowboats and Canoes: The 1903 Catalog in Perspective* (Blue Mountain Lake: Adirondack Museum, 1983), vi.
26 The importance of print culture in facilitating the canoe boom cannot be understated. A number of early canoeists apart from Alden had connections to publishing including Montgomery Schuyler, who worked for *Harper's*; Arthur Brentano, a member of the Brentano Family publishing house; and William P. Stephens, who eventually became the chair of the yachting and canoeing department at *Forest and Stream*. Ronald Hoffman, "The History of the American Canoe Association, 1880–1960" (PhD dissertation, Springfield College, 1967), 10–13; C. Bowyer Vaux, "History of American Canoeing, Part I," *Outing* 10, no. 3 (1887): 264.
27 Vaux, "American Canoeing, Part I," 262. Alden's work found print in the pages of *Harper's*, and later in folio form as *The Canoe and the Flying Proa, or Cheap Cruising and Safe Sailing* (New York: Harper & Brothers, 1878). In 1883, he published a work of boys' fiction, *The Cruise of the Canoe Club* (New York: Harper & Brothers, 1883).
28 Nathaniel Holmes Bishop, *Voyage of the Paper Canoe* (Boston: Lee and Shepard, 1878). George Washington Sears published a series of articles about canoeing the Adirondacks in *Forest and Stream* in the early 1880s, as well as *Woodcraft* (New York: Forest and Stream Publishing, 1884).
29 On Rushton, see Atwood Manley, *Rushton and His Times in American Canoeing* (Syracuse: Syracuse University Press, 1968); Hallie E. Bond, *Boats and Boating in the Adirondacks* (Syracuse: Syracuse University Press, 1998), 86; Vaux, "American Canoeing, Part I," 266. William P. Stephens, *Canoe and Boat Building* (New York: Forest and Stream Publishing, 1883); by 1903, the manual was on its tenth edition.
30 "Not Too Late Yet," *NYT*, 28 Dec. 1865. Emphasis added.
31 David R. Roedigger, *Working Toward Whiteness: How America's Immigrants Became White; The Strange Journey from Ellis Island to the Suburbs* (New York: Basic Books, 2005). Similar practices were employed to whiten another Indigenous activity in the same period: lacrosse. Poulter notes that promoters did not just civilize the sport, they also sought to civilize the Aboriginal participants by making them play according to white rules. Poulter, *Becoming Native*, 125–39.
32 "City and Suburban News," *NYT*, 20 Mar. 1886; "The Miniature Navy," *NYT*, 25 Apr. 1886.

33 See Frederic G. Mather, "The Evolution of Canoeing," *Outing* 5, no. 6 (1885): 414–23.
34 "Features of the Meet at Croton Point," *NYT*, 15 July 1894.
35 "Clubs and Competitions," in Benidickson, *Idleness, Water, and a Canoe*, 110–28.
36 C. Bowyer Vaux, "The Canoeing of Today," *Outing* 16, no. 2 (1890): 133.
37 The early membership of the NYCC is representative of canoe clubs more broadly. Commodore M. Roosevelt Schuyler was a merchant (and a cousin of Teddy Roosevelt); Montgomery Schuyler and John Haberton were newspaper editors; G. Livingston Morse and H. Edwards-Ficken were architects; Col. C.L. Norton was a soldier and travel writer; A. Cary Smith was a yacht designer; and J.S. Mosher, M.D., was a health officer. W.P. Stephens, "Memoirs," in *New York Canoe Club-North Shore Yacht Club Yearbook*, 1971; Vaux, "American Canoeing, Part I."
38 "The Canoe Pastime," *NYT*, 5 May 1872; "Other Canoeists of the Passaic," *NYT*, 3 Sept. 1893.
39 City of Toronto Archives (CTA), Fonds 1244, "Foot of York Street," 1910; Diane Beasley, "Walter Dean and Sunnyside: A Study of Waterfront Recreation" (MA thesis, University of Toronto, 1995); Dan Miller, "The Charles River Canoe," *Wooden Canoe* 30, no. 3 (2007): 8–15.
40 Kathy Peiss, *Cheap Amusements: Working Women and Leisure in Turn-of-the-Century New York* (Philadelphia: Temple University Press, 1986).
41 James Morton Turner, "From Woodcraft to 'Leave No Trace': Wilderness, Consumerism, and Environmentalism," *Environmental History* 7, no. 3 (2002): 462–84.

1 Organizing

1 "No Title," *Forest and Stream*, 1 Jan. 1880; "Canoeists to Hold a Convention," *New York Times* (*NYT*), 25 Feb. 1880.
2 "The Canoe Congress," *Forest and Stream*, 12 Aug. 1880; "The Canoe Congress," *Forest and Stream*, 26 Aug. 1880.
3 In the ensuing years, the Canadian contingent increased exponentially. The ACA remained the umbrella organization for Canadian canoeists until 1900, the year the Canadian Canoe Association was founded. While the number of Canadian members declined after 1900, the Northern Division continues to represent Canadian canoeists within the ACA to this day. Ronald Hoffman, "The History of the American Canoe Association, 1880–1960" (PhD dissertation, Springfield College, 1967), 47; C. Fred Johnston, *100 Years of Champions: The Canadian Canoe Association, 1900–2000* (Kingston: Canadian Canoe Association, 2003).

4 "Cruisers and the American Canoe Association," *Forest and Stream*, 13 Dec. 1883.
5 "The Canoe Congress," *Forest and Stream*, 26 Aug. 1880.
6 "City and Suburban News," *NYT*, 20 May 1880; "The Canoe Convention," *NYT*, 17 Aug. 1880.
7 Alexis de Tocqueville, *Democracy in America*, vol. 1 [1835], ed. Phillips Bradley (New York: Knopf, 1980), 191. Jeffrey McNairn argues that a similar observation could have been made of British North Americans prior to Confederation, in his *The Capacity to Judge: Public Opinion and Deliberative Democracy in Upper Canada, 1791–1854* (Toronto: University of Toronto Press, 2000), 67.
8 Leonore Davidoff and Catharine Hall, *Family Fortunes: Men and Women of the English Middle Class, 1780–1850*, rev. ed. (London: Routledge, 2002), 419.
9 Ibid., 420–1; Gerald Gamm and Robert D. Putnam, "The Growth of Voluntary Organizations in America, 1840–1940," *Journal of Interdisciplinary History* 29, no. 4 (1999): 511–57; Darren Ferry, *Uniting in Measures of Common Good: The Construction of Collective Liberal Identities in Central Canada, 1830–1900* (Montreal and Kingston: McGill-Queen's University Press, 2008).
10 C. Bowyer Vaux, "History of American Canoeing, Part I," *Outing* 10, no. 3 (1887): 262; W.P. Stephens, *Traditions and Memories of American Yachting: The 50th Anniversary Edition* (Brooklin, ME: Wooden Boat Publications, 1989), 96; Mystic Seaport Collections Research Center (MSCRC), Collection 291, vol. 2, Meeting Minutes of the Association, 12 Aug. 1881.
11 Ronald Hoffman's accounting of ACA officials indicates that the secretary was also the treasurer until 1905, when the roles of secretary and treasurer became separate positions. However, it was commonplace in association records and elsewhere to describe the officer in this role as the secretary. For the sake of consistency and also because, in later years, it was its own role, I use the term "secretary" throughout. See "Appendix B: Officers of the ACA, 1880–1960," in Hoffman, "American Canoe Association," 169–72.
12 Ibid. Although I don't have a breakdown of the number of Canadian versus American members in the same period, I would hazard a guess that the number of Canadian commodores relative to American ones was an accurate representation, if not an overrepresentation of the size of the Canadian membership.
13 Charles F. Wolters was the only person to hold the commodoreship for more than one year during the period covered by this study. He served as commodore in 1904 and 1905. It was more common for the secretary to serve consecutive terms (Nathaniel Holmes Bishop, 1880–81; Dr Charles A. Neide, 1882–86; Herb Begg, 1900–01). Ibid.

14 MSCRC, Collection 291, vol. 2, Minutes of the Annual Meeting, 23 Aug. 1883.
15 Don H. Doyle, "The Social Functions of Voluntary Associations in a Nineteenth-Century American Town," *Social Science History* 1, no. 3 (1977): 336.
16 St Lawrence County Historical Association (SLCHA), "Camp Circular for Grindstone Island" (1886).
17 There were five divisions created in the period covered by this study: (1) the Eastern Division (1886), comprised of Maine, Vermont, New Hampshire, Rhode Island, Massachusetts, and Connecticut; (2) the Central Division (1886), which consisted of the parts of the United States not covered by the other divisions; (3) the Northern Division (1887), which covered all of Canada; (4) the Atlantic Division (1888), which included the lower Hudson, Delaware, Susquehanna, and Potomac Rivers; and (5) the Western Division (1898), which covered the states of Ohio, Indiana, Illinois, Iowa, Michigan, Wisconsin, and Minnesota. *American Canoeist* (Apr. 1887); W.H.B. McClelland, ed., *American Canoe Association Yearbook* (n.p., 1916), 30.
18 "Canoe Camp at Muskoka Lake," *Rochester Democrat Chronicle*, 30 July 1900.
19 "Local Canoe Meets," *Forest and Stream*, 1 Nov. 1883. See also Marilyn R. Linton, *The Ballast Island Chronicles: A History of the Western Canoe Association and ILYA Beginnings* (Linwood: M.R. Linton, 1994).
20 This contradicts somewhat Ronald Hoffman's argument that divisions were formed solely to better meet the needs of members. See Hoffman, "American Canoe Association," 29; MSCRC, Collection 291, vol. 3, Minutes of the Annual Meeting, 7 Aug. 1885, and Meeting of the Executive Committee, 22 and 27 Aug. 1886, 12 Feb. 1887; C. Bowyer Vaux, "History of American Canoeing, Part III," *Outing* 10, no. 5 (1887): 408.
21 Retaw, *Fragments from the '88 Meet* (Montreal, 1888), 8.
22 Roger Gibbins and Loleen Berdahl, "The Roots of Western Alienation," in *Western Visions, Western Futures: Perspectives on the West in Canada*, 2nd ed. (Toronto: University of Toronto Press, 2003), 24–65.
23 Frederick L. Mix, ed., *American Canoe Association Yearbook* (New York: John C. Rankin Jr, 1888), 47–8.
24 Representation was proportional; divisions were allowed one representative for every 100 members. MSCRC, Collection 291, vol. 3, Meeting of the Executive Committee, 12 Feb. 1887.
25 Ibid., 25 Aug. 1887; Vaux, "American Canoeing, Part III," 396.
26 "Canoeing," *New York Sun*, 19 Aug. 1897.
27 Alan Trachtenberg, *The Incorporation of America: Culture and Society in the Gilded Age* (New York: Hill and Wang, 1982).
28 "Canoeists Adopt a New Policy," *NYT*, 5 Nov. 1893; MSCRC, Collection 291, box 1, folder 1, letter from Robert Wilkin to Walwin Barr, 1 Sept. 1926.

29 "Public character" is the term used by Davidoff and Hall in *Family Fortunes*. Patrick Joyce employs "publicity" in *The Rule of Freedom: Liberalism and the Modern City* (London: Verso, 2003).
30 The 1901 election results, e.g., were published in the *St Paul Globe*, 26 Aug. 1901, even as the organization had limited membership in Minnesota.
31 "The Executive Committee Meeting," *Forest and Stream*, 18 Nov. 1886; *Forest and Stream*, 23 Jan. 1887.
32 Freedom, as I discuss in chapter 4, was an important strategy of rule in the late nineteenth century that was adopted by the ACA. Joyce, *The Rule of Freedom*, 100.
33 "ACA Executive Committee Meeting," *Forest and Stream*, 20 Nov. 1890. Emphasis added.
34 Initially, only those who owned canoes could vote at the association meetings or hold office. MSCRC, Collection 291, box 10, folder 11, Constitution and By-Laws, 1 Nov. 1880.
35 Nancy B. Bouchier, *For The Love of the Game: Amateur Sport in Small-Town Ontario, 1838–1895* (Montreal and Kingston: McGill-Queen's University Press, 2003), 73.
36 "The Association Meet, Regatta Week," *Forest and Stream*, 13 Aug. 1885; MSCRC, Collection 291, vol. 3, Meeting of the Executive Committee, 7 Nov. 1885; Mix, *American Canoe Association Yearbook* (1888).
37 John H. Gilkeson Jr, *Middle-Class Providence, 1820–1940* (Princeton: Princeton University Press, 1986), 142.
38 I'm borrowing this language from Benedict Anderson, *Imagined Communities: Reflections on the Origin and Spread of Nationalism* (London: Verso, 1983).
39 Camp fees, which were in addition to association dues, were one dollar for members until 1904, and 2 dollars thereafter. MSCRC, Collection 291, vol. 4, Meeting of the Executive Committee, 15 Oct. 1904.
40 "Preparing for the Canoe Camp," *Watertown Daily Times*, 6 Aug. 1901.
41 There are no extant membership applications in the ACA archive, so it is unclear what information the organization asked of applicants.
42 MSCRC, Collection 291, vol. 3, Meeting of the Executive Committee, 23 Nov. 1889.
43 Amy Milne-Smith, *London Clubland: A Cultural History of Gender and Class in Late Victorian Britain* (New York: Palgrave Macmillan, 2011), 43–4.
44 Blackballing was a common practice in social clubs, used "for any number of reasons from the trivial to the personal," with politics being a particularly important motivation. Amy Milne-Smith, "Club Talk: Gossip, Masculinity and Oral Communities in Late Nineteenth-Century London," *Gender and History* 21, no. 1 (2009): 92; Milne-Smith, *London Clubland*, 46.
45 MSCRC, Collection 291, vol. 3, Meeting of the Executive Committee, 23 Nov. 1889.

46 See Ann Laura Stoler, "Making Empire Respectable: The Politics of Race and Sexual Morality in Twentieth-Century Colonial Cultures," *Cultural Politics* 11 (1997): 344–73; Adele Perry, *On the Edge of Empire: Gender, Race, and the Making of British Columbia* (Toronto: University of Toronto Press, 2001).
47 See chapter 3, "The Light of Publicity," in Joyce, *The Rule of Freedom*, 98–143.
48 See Patricia Vertinsky, *The Eternally Wounded Woman: Women, Doctors, and Exercise in the Late Nineteenth Century* (Toronto: St Martin's Press, 1990); Allen Guttmann, *Women's Sports: A History* (New York: Columbia University Press, 1991); M. Ann Hall, *The Girl and the Game: A History of Women's Sport in Canada* (Peterborough: Broadview Press, 2002); Andrea L. Smalley, "'Our Lady Sportsmen': Gender, Class, and Conservation in Sport Hunting Magazines, 1873–1920," *Journal of the Gilded Age and Progressive Era* 4, no. 4 (2005): 355–80.
49 Unknown, *American Canoe Association Book* (New York: Vaux and Co., 1883), 3.
50 This reflected the situation in contemporary politics. White women did not receive the right to vote and hold office at the federal level in Canada until 1918 and 1920, respectively. At the provincial level, such rights were granted anywhere between 1916 in the case of Manitoba to 1940 in the case of Quebec. By 1900, however, white women in many provinces could vote for school trustees and municipal politicians. In the United States, white women were granted federal suffrage in 1920. Heather McIvor, *Women and Politics in Canada* (Peterborough: Broadview Press, 1996), 86, 77; Alexander Keyssar, *The Right to Vote: The Contested History of Democracy in the United States* (New York: Basic Books, 2009), 175.
51 To be fair, I have only uncovered one instance where women who had put their names forward for membership were not approved. At a 1908 meeting of the Executive Committee, a motion was carried that stated: "The applications of Miss Addies Rodenstein and Miss Etta K. Thomas for associate membership be laid on the table indefinitely by reason of their ineligibility," although what was meant by "ineligibility" went unspoken. MSCRC, Collection 291, vol. 4, Meeting of the Executive Committee, 15 Aug. 1908.
52 John Sears Wright, ed., *American Canoe Association Yearbook* (n.p., 1904), 7.
53 MSCRC, Collection 291, vol. 3, Reports of the Fourth Annual Meeting, 15 Aug. 1884.
54 Ferry, *Measures of Common Good*, 16. In this way, Ferry's work provides an important contrast to McNairn's depiction of voluntary organizations as spaces of inclusive, deliberative democracy. Emphasis in original.
55 MSCRC, Collection 291, vol. 3, Meeting of the Executive Committee, 4 Nov. 1893.
56 See, e.g., "The Canoe Congress," *Forest and Stream*, 22 Jan. 1880; "The Second Day of the Regatta," *NYT*, 13 Aug. 1881; S.R. Stoddard, *Glimpses*

of the ACA (Glens Falls, 1890); O.K. Chobee, "Echoes from Stony Lake," *American Canoeist* 2, no. 8 (1883): 114; Fenimore Museum (FM), formerly the New York State Historical Association (NYSHA), American Canoe Association (ACA) Collection, box 1.1/25, "The Sneak-Box Mess: Camp of the Brooklyn Canoe Club" (1887).

57 "About Canoeing," *Lowell Daily Courier*, 11 May 1882.
58 "The Canoe Island Camp," *NYT*, 13 Aug. 1881; "Paddle Your Own Canoe," *Watertown Herald*, 10 July 1886.
59 They appear, e.g., in Stoddard, *Glimpses of the ACA* (1890); "Bathing Beach at Grindstone," in John R. Blake, ed., *American Canoe Association Yearbook* (Toronto: Bryant Press, 1897), 49; "Camp Group, Hay Island, 1899," in Herb Begg, ed., *American Canoe Association Yearbook* (New York City: Forest and Stream Publishing, 1900), insert between 46 and 47; "Canoeists' Enjoyable Time," *Daily Mail and Empire*, 9 Aug. 1900; "Opening of the A.C.A. Meet," *Boating* 2 (1906): 318.
60 J.I. Little, "Life without Conventionality: American Social Reformers as Summer Campers on Lake Memphremagog, Quebec, 1878–1905," *Journal of the Gilded Age and the Progressive Era* 9, no. 3 (2010): 299.
61 Doyle, "Social Functions," 350.
62 For a discussion of the temporal rhythms of association life, see ibid., 347.
63 Geographers refer to this as "translocality." Katherine Brickell and Ayona Datta, eds., *Translocal Geographies: Spaces, Places, Connections* (Burlington: Ashgate, 2011).
64 "Local Canoe Meets," *Forest and Stream*, 1 Nov. 1883.
65 FM, ACA Collection, box 1.6/11, "Camp Circular for Sugar Island" (1910).
66 "ACA Annual Meeting," *Peterborough Daily Review*, 14 Aug. 1883.
67 See, e.g. Charles P. Forbush, ed., *American Canoe Association Yearbook* (n.p., 1899), and Louis Reichert, ed., *American Canoe Association Yearbook* (n.p., 1912).
68 C.V. Schulyer, ed., *American Canoe Association Yearbook* (n.p., 1898), 2.
69 James C. Scott, *Seeing like a State: How Certain Schemes to Improve the Human Condition Have Failed* (New Haven: Yale University Press, 1998); Timothy Mitchell, *The Rule of Experts: Egypt, Techno-politics, Modernity* (Berkeley: University of California Press, 2002).
70 MSCRC, Collection 291, vol. 3, Meeting of the Executive Committee, 14 Nov. 1891.
71 Robert Tyson, "Laying Out the Course on Stony Lake," *American Canoeist* 2, no. 5 (1883): 66–8.
72 I explore the work of these men and Vasseur in greater detail in chapter 8.
73 Nikolas S. Rose, "Governing," in *Powers of Freedom: Reframing Political Thought* (Cambridge: Cambridge University Press, 1999), 1–60.

74 John C. Walsh, "Landscapes of Longing: Colonization and the Problem of State Formation in Canada West" (PhD dissertation, University of Guelph, 2001).
75 Trent University Archives (TUA), 77-015, James W. Fitzgerald, "Report and Diary of Burleigh Road Survey" (1860–61).
76 Katharine N. Hooke, *From Campsite to Cottage: Early Stoney Lake*, Occasional Paper 13 (Peterborough: Peterborough Historical Society, 1992).
77 J.B. Harley, *The New Nature of Maps: Essays in the History of Cartography*, ed. Paul Laxton (Baltimore: Johns Hopkins University Press, 2002), 54. See also Joyce, *The Rule of Freedom*, 36; Rose, *Powers of Freedom*, 36.
78 Richard Drayton, *Nature's Government: Science, Imperial Britain, and the 'Improvement' of the World* (New Haven: Yale University Press, 2000).
79 "Lake George Meet," *Forest and Stream*, 28 Aug. 1881; MSCRC, Collection 291, vol. 3, Meeting of the Executive Committee, 23 Nov. 1889; "The ACA Meet," *Forest and Stream*, 31 July 1890.
80 "Correspondence," *American Canoeist* 2, no. 5 (1883): 59–61; Tyson, "Laying Out the Course"; "American Canoe Association," *Peterborough Examiner*, 21 June 1883; "Canoists [sic] Again in Camp," *New York Herald*, 7 Aug. 1897; "In the Thousand Islands," *New York Tribune*, 10 July 1904; "Canoe Race," *Evening News*, 5 Aug. 1904.
81 MSCRC, Collection 291, vol. 3, Meeting of the Executive Committee, 23 Nov. 1889.
82 "The Season for Canoeing," *NYT*, 25 Mar. 1883; "A Winter Evening's Reverie," *Forest and Stream*, 11 Feb. 1886.
83 "Winter Work," *Forest and Stream*, 18 Oct. 1883.
84 McMaster University Archives (MUA), E. Pauline Johnson Fonds, box 3, files 6–10, Pauline Johnson, "Canoe and Canvas," *Rudder* (Mar. 1895): 34.
85 This is the term that canoeists use to describe their cruising equipment.
86 "Canoe Sailors in Camp," *New York Sun*, 4 Aug. 1884. The anticipation is captured in other articles, including "Canoeists Going to Sugar Island," *Rochester Democrat Chronicle*, 18 July 1908.
87 "The Canoe Association," *NYT*, 25 July 1885.
88 Announcements for the publication of the yearbook were included in the following issues of *Forest and Stream*: 21 May 1881, 29 May 1884, 12 July 1888, and 16 July 1891. Similar announcements were made in the *American Canoeist*. See, e.g., "The Association Book," *American Canoeist* 4, no. 6 (1885): 102.
89 John C. Walsh, "Performing Public Memory and Re-placing Home in the Ottawa Valley, 1900–1958," in *Placing Memory and Remembering Place in Canada*, ed. James Opp and John C. Walsh (Vancouver: UBC Press, 2010), 27, 29.
90 FM, ACA Collection, box 1.6/12, "Camp Circular for Cape Cod" (1902).

91 Joyce, *The Rule of Freedom*, 41. On maps more generally, see Harley, *New Nature of Maps*.
92 Joyce, *The Rule of Freedom*, 36.
93 Jeff Oliver, "On Mapping and Its Afterlife: Unfolding Landscapes in Northwestern North America," *World Archaeology* 43, no. 1 (2011): 68.
94 There were exceptions. Area maps for the 1888 and 1893 meets were hand drawn. George W. Hatton and C. Bowyer Vaux, eds., *American Canoe Association Yearbook* (New York: Nautical Publishing, 1889), xxix; R. Easton Burns, ed., *American Canoe Association Yearbook* (Kingston: Daily News Printing House, 1893), 9.
95 Ralph F. Brazer, ed., *American Canoe Association Yearbook* (n.p., 1891), insert between 42 and 43; *Picturesque Views and Maps of the Muskoka Lakes, Canada* (Toronto: Ralph and Smith, 1893).
96 W.G. MacKendrick, "Map of the Campsite," in Begg, *American Canoe Association Yearbook* (1900), 10; Herb Begg, ed., *American Canoe Association Yearbook* (New York City: Forest and Stream Publishing, 1901), 10.
97 Begg, *American Canoe Association Yearbook* (1901), 10.
98 William M. Carter, ed., *American Canoe Association Yearbook* (Trenton, NJ: John L. Murphy Publishing, 1887), 4.
99 Burns, *American Canoe Association Yearbook*, 9.
100 Joyce, *The Rule of Freedom*, 36.
101 Megan Davies, "Night Soil, Cesspools, and Smelly Hogs on the Streets: Sanitation, Race, and Governance in Early British Columbia," *Histoire sociale/Social History* 38, no. 75 (2005): 1–36; Stanley K. Schultz and Clay McShane, "To Engineer the Metropolis: Sewers, Sanitation, and City Planning in Late-Nineteenth-Century America," *Journal of American History* 65, no. 2 (1978): 389–411.
102 Cecilia Morgan, *'A Happy Holiday': English Canadians and Transatlantic Tourism* (Toronto: University of Toronto Press, 2008), 15.
103 Roger Chartier, "Culture as Appropriation: Popular Cultural Uses in Early Modern France, " in *Understanding Popular Culture: Europe from the Middle Ages to the Nineteenth Century*, ed. Steven L. Kaplan (Berlin: Mouton, 1984), 234.
104 Doyle, "Social Functions," 350.

2 (Dis)Placing

1 Photographs of the re-enactment appear in Fenimore Museum (FM), formerly the New York State Historical Association (NYSHA), American Canoe Association (ACA) Collection, box 1.5/3, Fred Saunders Scrapbook, Meets and Camps (1900–40).

2 This chapter has some parallels with Gillian Poulter's work on sporting cultures in nineteenth-century Montreal. Whereas Poulter focuses on acts of cultural appropriation – she considers the means by which Indigenous sports were reimagined as white Canadian practices, a subject relevant to a book on canoeing – this chapter interrogates the appropriation of space. Gillian Poulter, *Becoming Native in a Foreign Land: Sport, Visual Culture, and Identity in Montreal, 1840–1885* (Vancouver: UBC Press, 2009).

3 Edward Said, *Culture and Imperialism* (Toronto: Random House, 1993), 7.

4 Cole Harris, *Making Native Space: Colonialism, Resistance, and Reserves in British Columbia* (Vancouver: UBC Press, 2002), xvii.

5 On colonial projects targeting Indigenous peoples in Canada, see Harris, *Making Native Space*, and John Milloy, *A National Crime: The Canadian Government and the Residential School System* (Winnipeg: University of Manitoba Press, 1999). For the United States, see David Wallace Adams, *Education for Extinction: American Indians and the Boarding School Experience, 1875–1928* (Lawrence: University Press of Kansas, 1995), and Gray S. Whaley, *Oregon and the Collapse of Illahee: US Empire and the Transformation of an Indigenous World* (Chapel Hill: University of North Carolina Press, 2010).

6 Ian McKay, *Quest of the Folk: Antimodernism and Cultural Selection in Twentieth-Century Nova Scotia* (Montreal and Kingston: McGill-Queen's University Press, 1994); Dona Brown, *Inventing New England: Regional Tourism in the Nineteenth Century* (Washington, DC: Smithsonian Institution Press, 1995); Thomas G. Andrews, "'Made by Toile'? Tourism, Labor, and the Construction of the Colorado Landscape," *Journal of American History* 92, no. 3 (2005): 837–63.

7 This book contributes to the emerging field of sport tourism by providing a much-needed historical perspective to a subfield which to date has been largely focused on issues of management, rather than critical cultural studies. See critiques of the field offered by Laurence Chalip, "The Cogency of Culture in Sport Tourism Research," *Journal of Sport and Tourism* 15, no. 1 (2010): 3–5, and Paul Dimeo, "Review of *Sports Tourism: Participants, Policy and Providers*," *Tourism Management* 29 (2008): 603.

8 "Cruisers and the American Canoe Association," *Forest and Stream*, 13 Dec. 1883; "The 1884 Meet of the A.C.A.," *Outing* 3, no. 6 (1884): 464–5.

9 "The Canoe Island Camp," *New York Times* (*NYT*), 13 Aug. 1881.

10 See C. Bowyer Vaux, "History of American Canoeing, Part III," *Outing* 10, no. 5 (1887): 396.

11 "Lake George Meet," *Forest and Stream*, 25 Aug. 1881; FM, ACA Collection, box 1.5/1, "Camping on Canoe Island," *Truth*, c. 1881; C. Bowyer Vaux, "History of American Canoeing, Part II," *Outing* 10, no. 4 (1887): 396.

12 "Lake George Meet," *Forest and Stream*, 25 Aug. 1881.

13 "The 1884 Meet of the A.C.A.," *Outing* 3, no. 6 (1884): 464–5. There were, of course, contradictory opinions. According to *Forest and Stream*, Lake George was a wonderful location, easily accessible with good rail service and courses, which had already been surveyed. "The Future Camp of the American Canoe Association," *Forest and Stream*, 4 Oct. 1883.
14 Vaux, "American Canoeing, Part III," 400.
15 Ibid., 397.
16 See Appendix for a list of the exact dates and locations of the encampments from 1880 to 1910.
17 "A Permanent or Movable Camp," *American Canoeist* 3, no. 2 (1884): 31. See also "The Association Camp," *Forest and Stream*, 11 Oct. 1883.
18 Mystic Seaport Collections Research Center (MSCRC), Collection 291, vol. 2, "Record Book of the Secretary of the ACA, 1881–1893," and vol. 2, Annual Meeting, 22 Aug. 1883; "The Association Races at Stony Lake," *Forest and Stream*, 6 Sept. 1883.
19 "The Association Camp," *Forest and Stream*, 11 Oct. 1883. Rowing was notorious for its association with professionalism. See "On Canada," *American Canoeist* 2, no. 1 (1883): 1.
20 This theme of comfort was reiterated in a letter from Orange Frazer. "The ACA Camp," *Forest and Stream*, 1 Nov. 1883.
21 "The Association Camp," *Forest and Stream*, 11 Oct. 1883.
22 See, e.g., MSCRC, Collection 291, vol. 2, Meeting of the Executive Committee, 13 Nov. 1883; vol. 3, Meeting of the Executive Committee, 4 Nov. 1893.
23 MSCRC, Collection 291, vol. 2, Annual Meeting, 25 July 1894; Meeting of the Executive Committee, 12 Nov. 1894.
24 Library and Archives Canada (LAC), RG 10, vol. 2718, file 144, 001-53, letter from C.E. Britton to Hon. J.A. Smart, 6 Feb. 1901.
25 MSCRC, Collection 291, vol. 4, Meeting of the Executive Committee, 20 Oct. 1900.
26 MSCRC, Collection 291, box 23, folder 5, "Brief Synopsis of the History of St Lawrence Island" (30 Sept. 1933); LAC, RG 10, vol. 2718, file 144, 001-53.
27 "ACA Meet of 1890," *Forest and Stream*, 12 Sept. 1889.
28 MSCRC, Collection 291, vol. 2, Meeting of the Executive Committee, 4 Oct. 1884; vol. 3, Meeting of the Executive Committee, 7 Nov. 1885, and Meeting of the Executive Committee, 13 Nov. 1886; "A Site for a Saltwater Meet," *Forest and Stream*, 4 Nov. 1886; Frank H. Taylor, "The Thousand Islands," *American Canoeist* 1, no. 10 (1882): 147–8; William Whitlock, "The Next Camp," *American Canoeist* 2, no. 8 (1883): 116.
29 An excellent example of the rationale for one particular site can be found in debates over the 1890 camp. MSCRC, Collection 291, vol. 3, Executive Committee Minutes, 23 Nov. 1889.

30 In the late nineteenth century, hotels were simultaneously symbols of capitalist potential and, for many in the middling classes, emblems of "consumption and entitlement." Molly Berger, *Hotel Dreams: Luxury, Technology and Urban Ambition in America, 1829–1929* (Baltimore: Johns Hopkins University Press, 2011), 7. See also J.I. Little, "Life without Conventionality: American Social Reformers as Summer Campers on Lake Memphremagog, Quebec, 1878–1905," *Journal of the Gilded Age and the Progressive Era* 9, no. 3 (2010): 284.
31 "The 1884 Meet of the A.C.A.," *Outing* 3, no. 6 (1884): 464–5. The difficulties of finding a balance between accessibility and seclusion is well articulated in "The ACA Meet of 1888: The Camp and the Association," *Forest and Stream*, 6 Sept. 1888.
32 *Forest and Stream* described the general sentiments of the membership regarding the location of the 1884 meet as follows: "While many favor the old camp at Lake George, it is felt that the meet should if possible be held at some point more accessible to the Canadians, who now constitute so large a proportion of members." "The Association Races at Stony Lake," *Forest and Stream*, 6 Sept. 1883.
33 Ronald Hoffman, "The History of the American Canoe Association, 1880–1960" (PhD dissertation, Springfield College, 1967), 63.
34 MSCRC, Collection 291, vol. 4, "Report of the Camp Site Committee" (1902).
35 "The ACA Meet of 1890 – II," *Forest and Stream*, 6 Nov. 1890.
36 "Canoeists' Enjoyable Time," *Daily Mail and Empire*, 9 Aug. 1900; D.J. Howell, "The International Canoe Meet," *Canadian Magazine* 15, no. 6 (1900): 513–21.
37 FM, ACA Collection, box 1.1/6–1.1/23, Photographs from Grindstone Island, 1884–6; MSCRC, Collection 291, box 23, folder 2, "Camp Circular for Lake George" (1888).
38 "American Canoe Association," *Forest and Stream*, 14 Aug. 1890.
39 "The ACA Meet of 1887," *Forest and Stream*, 2 June 1887; MSCRC, Collection 291, vol. 3, Meeting of the Executive Committee, 23 Nov. 1889; "Secretary-Treasurer's Report," in Herb Begg, ed., *American Canoe Association Yearbook* (New York City: Forest and StreamPublishing, 1901), 60–1.
40 "The ACA Meet: Camp Circular," *Forest and Stream*, 10 July 1890.
41 S.R. Stoddard, *Lake George Illustrated* (Albany: Van Benthuysen & Sons, 1882), 31. See also MSCRC, Collection 291, box 23, folder 2, "Camp Circular for Lake George" (1881).
42 According to C. Bowyer Vaux, Bishop was one of a number of canoeists who "made Lake George their regular summer residence and kept canoes there." Vaux, "American Canoeing, Part II," 361.
43 David Strauss, "Toward a Consumer Culture: 'Adirondack Murray' and the Wilderness Vacation," *American Quarterly* 39, no. 2 (1997): 270–86; Jeffrey

L. Horrell, *Seneca Ray Stoddard: Transforming the Adirondack Wilderness in Text and Image* (Syracuse: Syracuse University Press, 1999); Bryant F. Tolles Jr, *Resort Hotels of the Adirondacks: The Architecture of a Summer Paradise, 1850–1950* (Lebanon: University Press of New England, 2003), 30.

44 Tolles, *Resort Hotels*, 31, 38, 40. Stoddard's guidebook lists a number of cottages and summer homes on the lake belonging to clergy, doctors, artists, and the like. Stoddard, *Lake George Illustrated*.

45 For pre-Contact history of the region, see Melissa Otis, "The Adirondacks as Indigenous Homeland," in *Rural Indigenousness: A History of Iroquoian and Algonquian Peoples of the Adirondacks* (Syracuse: Syracuse University Press, 2018), 27–56. Subsequent chapters in *Rural Indigenousness* attend to the colonial period up to the First World War. See also Karl Jacoby, *Crimes against Nature: Squatters, Poachers, Thieves, and the Hidden History of American Conservation* (Berkeley: University of California Press, 2001), 20–1.

46 Jacoby, *Crimes against Nature*, 20–1.

47 "The Canoe Congress," *Forest and Stream*, 22 Jan. 1880; Florence Watters Snedeker, *A Family Canoe Trip* (New York: Harper & Brothers, 1892), 33.

48 Otis, *Rural Indigenousness*.

49 Jacoby, *Crimes against Nature*, 26.

50 There are discrepancies in the spelling of the lake. Within the same document, you might see Stony or Stoney. I have chosen the former for the sake of consistency.

51 "Stony Lake – Letter from Commodore Edwards," *American Canoeist* 1, no. 10 (1882): 154.

52 Leanne Betasamosake Simpson, *As We Have Always Done: Indigenous Freedom Through Radical Resurgence* (Minneapolis: University of Minnesota Press, 2017).

53 Robert J. Surtees, "Land Cessions, 1763–1830," in *Aboriginal Ontario: Historical Perspectives on the First Nations*, ed. Edward S. Rogers and Donald B. Smith (Toronto: Dundurn Press, 1994), 113.

54 Christine Bentham and Katharine Hooke, *From Burleigh to Boschink: A Community Called Stony Lake* (Toronto: Natural Heritage/Natural History, 2000), 15.

55 For a broad overview of Stony Lake's development as a tourist destination/cottaging community, see Bentham and Hooke, *From Burleigh to Boschink*.

56 Vaux, "American Canoeing, Part III," 397.

57 See chapter 5, "A Trip to Stony Lake," in Susanna Moodie, *Roughing It in the Bush*, 2nd ed. (London: Richard Bentley, 1852), 84–102.

58 "The Meet," *American Canoeist* 2, no. 6 (1883): 79–83.

59 "Letter from Commodore Edwards," 154.

60 Enid L. Mallory, *Kawartha: Living on These Lakes* (Peterborough: Peterborough Publishing, 1991); Katharine N. Hooke, *From Campsite*

to Cottage: Early Stoney Lake, Occasional Paper 13 (Peterborough: Peterborough Historical Society, 1992).
61 Ken Brown, Personal Collection, Dominion Department of Indian Affairs, "Indian Land Sale Grant for Island #18," 26 May 1883.
62 Bentham and Hooke, *From Burleigh to Boschink*, 16.
63 Patricia Jasen, *Wild Things: Nature, Culture, and Tourism in Ontario, 1790–1914* (Toronto: University of Toronto Press, 1995), 66; Frank H. Taylor, "Grindstone Island and Its Surroundings," *Outing* 4, no. 1 (1884): 29–33.
64 Jasen, *Wild Things*, 77.
65 There had been a permanent Mohawk settlement at St Regis since the 1770s or 1780s. Surtees, "Land Cessions," 94.
66 See chapter 3, "Wilderness Panorama," in Jasen, *Wild Things*, 55–79.
67 Gregory S. Kealey, *Workers and Canadian History* (Montreal and Kingston: McGill-Queen's University Press, 1995), 249; Morton Schoolman and Alvin Magid, *Reindustrializing New York State: Strategies, Implications, Challenges* (Albany: State University of New York Press, 1986), 132.
68 Colin G. Calloway, *The Western Abenakis of Vermont, 1600–1800: War, Migration, and the Survival of an Indian People* (Norman: University of Oklahoma Press, 1994), 7.
69 "N'dakina – Our Homelands & People." Accessed 26 May 2016 at http://www.cowasuck.org/history/ndakina.cfm.
70 Gordon M. Day, "Abenaki Place-Names in the Champlain Valley," *International Journal of Linguistics* 47, no. 2 (1981): 144. See also Frederick Matthew Wiseman, *The Voice of the Dawn: An Autohistory of the Abenaki Nation* (Lebanon, NH: University Press of New England, 2001), and Jean L. Manore, "The Historical Erasure of an Indigenous Identity in the Borderlands: The Western Abenaki of Vermont, New Hampshire, and Quebec," *Journal of Borderland Studies* 26, no. 2 (2011): 179–96.
71 Louis M. Babcock, *Our American Resorts: For Health, Pleasure and Recreation* (Washington, DC: National News Bureau, 1883), 124.
72 Ibid.
73 "From Vergennes to Lorna Island," *Forest and Stream*, 24 May 1883; William Henry Harrison Murray, *Lake Champlain and Its Shores* (Boston: De Wolfe, Fiske, and Co., 1890), 231–5; John C. Smock, "Geologico-Geographical Distribution of the Iron Ores of the Eastern United States," *Engineering and Mining Journal* 37 (Mar. 1884): 217; Charles H. Possons, *Lake George and Lake Champlain* (Glens Falls: Chas. H. Possons, 1887), 110.
74 John A. Strong, *The Montaukett Indians of Eastern Long Island* (Syracuse: Syracuse University Press, 2001).
75 Marilyn E. Weigold, *The Long Island Sound: A History of Its People, Places, and Environment* (New York: New York University Press, 2004), 69–71, 74–9.

76 Cynthia V.A. Schaffner and Lori Zabar, "The Founding and Design of William Merrit Chase's Shinnecock Hills Summer School of Art and the Art Village," *Winterthur Portfolio* 44, no. 4 (2010): 307.
77 Richard H. Gassan, *The Birth of American Tourism: New York, the Hudson Valley, and American Culture* (Amherst: University of Massachusetts Press, 2008), 2.
78 Jasen, *Wild Things*, 58.
79 Cindy S. Aron, *Working at Play: A History of Vacations in the United States* (New York: Oxford University Press, 1999), 131; David Stradling, "We Are Still in Eden: Romanticism, Tourism, and the Power of Culture," in *The Nature of New York: An Environmental History of the Empire State* (Ithaca: Cornell University Press, 2010), 76–105.
80 George V. Hutton, *The Great Hudson River Brick Industry: Commemorating Three and One Half Centuries of Brickmaking* (Fleischmann: Purple Mountain Press, 2003).
81 James W. Oberly, *A Nation of Statesmen: The Political Culture of the Stockbridge-Munsee Mohicans, 1815–1972* (Norman: University of Oklahoma Press, 2005), 3–7.
82 Jasen, *Wild Things*, 116.
83 Robin Jarvis Brownlie, *A Fatherly Eye: Indian Agents, Government Power, and Aboriginal Resistance in Ontario, 1918–1939* (Don Mills: Oxford University Press, 2003), 4–5.
84 Jasen, *Wild Things*, 117; Peggy J. Blair, *Lament for a First Nation: The Williams Treaties in Southern Ontario* (Vancouver: UBC Press, 2008); Andrew Watson, chapter 3, "Experiences of Continuity and Change for Muskoka's First Nations," in "Poor Soils and Rich Folks: Household Economics and Sustainability in Muskoka, 1850–1920" (PhD dissertation, York University, 2014), 129–91. Testimony describing land use practices by Anishnaabeg in "cottage country" can be found in LAC, RG 10, vol. 2328, file 67071-1, and vol. 2329, file 67071-2.
85 Robin Jarvis Brownlie, "'A better citizen than lots of white men': First Nations Enfranchisement – an Ontario Case Study, 1918–1940," *Canadian Historical Review* 87, no. 1 (2006): 41.
86 Andrew Watson, "Pioneering a Rural Identity on the Canadian Shield: Tourism, Household Economies, and Poor Soils in Muskoka, Ontario, 1870–1900," *Canadian Historical Review* 98, no. 2 (2017): 261–93.
87 Patricia Jasen argues that settlement and tourism developed not in that order, as was common in most locales, but in tandem, a point echoed by Andrew Watson. Jasen, *Wild Things*, 117.
88 Ibid., 120.
89 Jack Campisi, *The Mashpee Indians: Tribe on Trial* (Syracuse: Syracuse University Press, 1991).

90 Lewis M. Alexander, "The Impact of Tourism on the Economy of Cape Cod, Massachusetts," *Economic Geography* 29, no. 4 (1953): 320–6.
91 Brown, *Inventing New England*, 11, 202, 204.
92 Henry David Thoreau, *Cape Cod* (Boston: Ticknor and Fields, 1865).
93 As quoted in Brown, *Inventing New England*, 202.
94 Jacoby, *Crimes against Nature*, 28.
95 LAC, RG 10, vol. 3044, file 236, 725-147, Letter from C.E. Britton to J.D. McLean, 16 July 1903.
96 MSCRC, Collection 291, vol. 4, "Board of Governor's Report" (1 Oct. 1907).
97 LAC, RG 10, vol. 2718, file 144, 001-53, Letter from J.C. Caldwell, Director of Indian Lands and Timber, to Allan Leja, 4 Oct. 1932. Presumably, Caldwell is drawing from the *Canadian Indian Treaties and Surrenders*, which states: "The principal members of the Mississauga tribe of the Alnwick, surrendered for sale for the benefit of the tribe, all and singular, those islands lying and situated in the Bay of Quinte, in Lake Ontario, Willis' Bay and in the River St Lawrence called 'Thousand Islands' which have not heretofore been granted or patented by the crown," as part of Surrender 77. This text was published in 1891 after the Mississauga voiced their dissent with the original treaty.
98 Blair, *Lament for a First Nation*, 43–4, 79.
99 Ibid., 44.
100 Ibid., 79–80.
101 LAC, RG 10, vol. 2718, file 144, 001-53, "Report on Sugar Island" (13 May 1885); Letter from Caldwell to Leja, 4 Oct. 1932; Affidavit signed by John McDonald, 5 Apr. 1901.
102 LAC, RG 10, vol. 2718, file 144, 001-53, Letter from George Keys to DIA, 29 Apr. 1885.
103 See letters from A.B. Cowan (Indian Land Agent) to DIA dated 16 June, 5 July, 24 July 1886; 19 May 1888; 16 May 1891 in LAC, RG 10, vol. 2718, file 144, 001-53.
104 Letter from Caldwell to Leja, 4 Oct. 1932. Accounts of Unwin's progress can be found in LAC, RG 10, vol. 1899, file 1969, and vol. 1879, file 1032. Further surveys and land valuations were conducted in the 1880s and 1890s. See Susan W. Smith, *A History of Recreation in the Thousand Islands* (Parks Canada, 1974).
105 Smith, *Recreation in the Thousand Islands*.
106 LAC, RG 10, vol. 2718, file 144, 001-53, Letter from Deputy Superintendent General of Indian Affairs to Robert W. Deane, 9 Aug. 1894, and Letter from Hayter Reed to Haldane Millar, 8 Oct. 1896.
107 Letter from Britton to Sifton, 19 Feb. 1901.
108 LAC, RG 10, vol. 2718, file 144, 001-53, Letter from J.A. Smart to Mr MacLean, 9 Feb. 1901, and letter from Unknown to the Secretary, 11 Feb. 1901.

109 LAC, RG 10, vol. 2718, file 144, 001-53, letter from Clifford Sifton to J.A. Smart, 17 June 1901.
110 Said, *Culture and Imperialism*, 7.
111 MSCRC, Collection 291, box 7, folder 1, Patent for Sugar Island, 1901.
112 Reginald Horsman, *Race and Manifest Destiny: The Origins of American Racial Anglo-Saxonism* (Cambridge: Harvard University Press, 1981), 58–9. Cole Harris's work is instructive in understanding the philosophical underpinnings of the displacement of Indigenous people from their territories, as well as the mechanisms by which colonizers reconfigured BC geographies. Harris, *Making Native Space*.
113 Herb Begg, ed., *American Canoe Association Yearbook* (New York City: Forest and Stream Publishing, 1900), 11.
114 See, e.g., Walsh, "Performing Public Memory."
115 Sharon Wall, *The Nurture of Nature: Childhood, Antimodernism, and Ontario Summer Camps, 1920–1955* (Vancouver: UBC Press, 2009), 247.
116 Strong, *The Montaukett Indians*.
117 "The Canoe Meet," *Troy Northern Budget*, 16 Aug. 1891.
118 Simpson adds that the dissemination of "the mediatory fiction of vanishing aboriginality" produced the "material and ideological conditions needed for Native Americans to disappear by the thousands." Mark Simpson, *Trafficking Subjects: The Politics of Mobility in Nineteenth-Century America* (Minneapolis: University of Minnesota Press, 2005), xiv–xv. See also Jean M. O'Brien, *Firsting and Lasting: Writing Indians Out of Existence in New England* (Minneapolis: University of Minnesota Press, 2010).
119 "Sugar Island for a Home," *Watertown Re-Union*, 29 June 1901.
120 FM, ACA Collection, box 1.5/3, Fred Saunders Scrapbook, Meets and Camps (1900–40).

3 Navigating

1 Florence Watters Snedeker, *A Family Canoe Trip* (New York: Harper & Brothers, 1892).
2 Michael Haldrup, "Laid-Back Mobilities: Second Home Holidays in Time and Space," *Tourism Geographies* 6, no. 4 (2004): 447.
3 Ibid., 434.
4 For an introduction to the mobilities literature, see Mimi Sheller and John Urry, "The New Mobilities Paradigm," *Environment and Planning A* 38 (2006): 207–26, and Tim Cresswell, *On the Move: Mobility in the Modern Western World* (London: Routledge, 2006). See also Tim Cresswell's three updates on mobilities scholarship in *Progress in Human Geography*: "Mobilities I: Catching Up," 35, no. 4 (2010): 550–8; "Mobilities II: Still," 36, no. 5 (2012): 645–53; "Mobilities III: Moving On," 38, no. 5 (2014): 712–21.

5 See, e.g., "Part I: Practices," in *Geographies of Mobilities: Practices, Spaces, Subjects*, ed. Tim Cresswell and Peter Merriman (Burlington: Ashgate, 2011), 19–96.
6 Cresswell, *On the Move*, 53–4. Cresswell cites as evidence of this particular formulation of the nomad, Walter Benjamin's *flâneur*, Michel de Certeau's *Wandersmänner*, and Gilles Deleuze and Felix Guattari's *nomad*.
7 Wolfgang Schivelbusch, *The Railway Journey: The Industrialization of Time and Space in the Nineteenth Century* (Berkeley: University of California Press, 1986), 95. Between 1865 and 1890, the number of railroad miles in the United States alone increased by more than four times. John F. Stover, *American Railroads* (Chicago: University of Chicago Press, 1997), 134.
8 James Buzard, *The Beaten Track: European Tourism, Literature, and the Ways to "Culture," 1800–1918* (Oxford: Clarendon Press, 1993), 40–1, 47–77.
9 Patricia Jasen, *Wild Things: Nature, Culture, and Tourism in Ontario, 1790–1914* (Toronto: University of Toronto Press, 1995), 20–2.
10 Karen Jones, "Review of *Trafficking Subjects*," *English Studies in Canada* 31, no. 4 (2005): 237.
11 The most common railway discount was full fare to the meet and one-third return in lieu of a full round trip fare. "A.C.A.," *American Canoeist* 4, no. 6 (1885): 87–8; Mystic Seaport Collections Research Center (MSCRC), Collection 291, box 23, folder 2, "Camp Circular for Lake George" (1888); F.L. Dunnell, ed., *American Canoe Association Yearbook* (New York: n.p., 1890), 22; Fenimore Museum (FM), formerly the New York State Historical Association (NYSHA), American Canoe Association (ACA) Collection, box 1.6/11, "Camp Circular for Sugar Island Meet" (1904).
12 See, e.g., MSCRC, Collection 291, box 23, folder 2, "Camp Circular for Lake George" (1888); FM, American Canoe Association Collection, box 1.6/11, "Camp Circular for Bluff Point" (1895).
13 E.g., "Outing for Canoeists," *New York Sun*, 1 Aug. 1897.
14 C.V. Schulyer, ed., *American Canoe Association Yearbook* (n.p., 1898), 39.
15 "Canoeing: Opens This Morning," *Daily Mail and Empire*, 3 Aug. 1900.
16 Most canoeists brought one canoe with them if any at all, although there were exceptions. M.F. Johnson, e.g., brought "three different paddling canoes" to the 1884 meet on Grindstone Island because he wanted to compete in all of the paddling races and you needed different boats to do so. C. Bowyer Vaux, "History of American Canoeing, Part III," *Outing* 10, no. 5 (1887): 406.
17 "Transportation of Canoes," *Forest and Stream*, 21 July 1881; "Canoe, Camp and Camera on Lakes George and Champlain," *Lowell Daily Courier*, 29 Aug. 1882.
18 "Report of the Committee on Railways Transportation," *Forest and Stream*, 21 June 1888.

19 E.g., see "Homeward from Stony Lake," *Forest and Stream*, 19 Feb. 1885; "The Great Canoe Meet," *Outing* 9, no. 2 (1886): 164–6.
20 "Transportation to Bow-Arrow Point," *Forest and Stream*, 14 July 1887; FM, ACA Collection, box 1.6/11, "Camp Circular for Sugar Island" (1904).
21 "Canoe Sailors in Camp," *New York Sun*, 4 Aug. 1884.
22 "Personal," *Utica Morning Herald*, 18 Aug. 1885.
23 "The Meet," *American Canoeist* 2, no. 6 (1883): 79–83; R. Easton Burns, ed., *American Canoe Association Yearbook* (Kingston: Daily News Printing House, 1893), 11.
24 References to on-site customs officials appear in "City and Vicinity: Briefs," *Watertown Re-Union*, 8 July 1885; "The Tenth Annual Meet of the American Canoe Association," *Sail and Paddle* 7, no. 9 (1889): 198–204; "Around the Pine Camp Fire," *New York Times* (*NYT*), 20 Aug. 1893; MSCRC, Collection 291, box 23, folder 2, "Camp Circular for Sugar Island" (1907); FM, ACA Collection, box 1.6/11, "Camp Circular for Sugar Island" (1910). The role of the officer is succinctly described in the 1907 circular.
25 Customs officer Comer presided at the Wolfe Island meet. "The Company Gathered," *British Daily Whig*, 11 Aug. 1893.
26 "City and Vicinity: Briefs," *Watertown Re-Union*, 8 July 1885. Delaney's appointment echoes a broader reality of nineteenth-century state formation. See, e.g., Bruce Curtis, *The Politics of Population: State Formation, Statistics, and the Census of Canada, 1840–1875* (Toronto: University of Toronto Press, 2001), and Karl Jacoby, "Part I," in *Crimes against Nature: Squatters, Poachers, Thieves, and the Hidden History of American Conservation* (Berkeley: University of California Press, 2001), 11–75.
27 "The ACA Meet," *Forest and Stream*, 10 July 1884.
28 MSCRC, Collection 291, box 23, folder 2, "Camp Circular for Sugar Island" (1907).
29 "The ACA Meet," *Forest and Stream*, 25 Aug. 1887.
30 MSCRC, Collection 291, box 23, folder 2, "Camp Circular for Lake George" (1881).
31 Prior to this, travel literature predominantly consisted of personal accounts of travel, gazetteers, and geographies. Richard H. Gassan, *The Birth of American Tourism: New York, the Hudson Valley, and American Culture* (Amherst: University of Massachusetts Press, 2008), 70–1.
32 Matt Johnston, "National Spectacle from the Boat and from the Train: Moulding Perceptions of History in American Scenic Guides of the Nineteenth Century," *University of Toronto Quarterly* 73, no. 4 (2004): 1023.
33 Ibid.; Gassan, *Birth of American Tourism*, 71; Buzard, *Beaten Track*, 67.
34 Buzard, *Beaten Track*, 67.
35 Cindy Aron, *Working at Play: A History of Vacations in the United States* (New York: Oxford University Press, 1999), 51.

36 Johnston, "National Spectacle," 1030.
37 "Musquito Fleet," *Salt Lake Herald*, 9 Aug. 1891. As so many of the newspaper articles produced about the meet were reprinted in a variety of periodicals, I am assuming, rightly or wrongly, that this article would have also appeared in newspapers closer to the location of the meet.
38 "From Chicago to Lake George," *American Canoeist* 1, no. 3 (1882): 40.
39 "Stony Lake," *Forest and Stream*, 2 Aug. 1883.
40 "Driftings," *American Canoeist* 1, no. 5 (1882): 71.
41 FM, ACA, box 1.6/2, D.B. Goodsell, "A Canoeing Reminiscence" (1936), 6.
42 I borrow this language from Mike Michael, "These Boots Are Made for Walking ...: Mundane Technology, the Body and Human-Environment Relations," *Body and Society* 6, no. 107 (2000): 107–26.
43 Haldrup, "Laid-Back Mobilities," 436; David Crouch, "Places around Us: Embodied Lay Geographies in Leisure and Tourism," *Leisure Studies* 19, no. 2 (2000): 63–76.
44 John Urry, "Social Networks, Travel and Talk," *British Journal of Sociology* 54, no. 2 (2003): 163. Emphasis in original.
45 Here I am echoing the observations of Kevin Hannam, Mimi Sheller, and John Urry, "Editorial: Mobilities, Immobilities and Moorings," *Mobilities* 1, no. 1 (2006): 12.
46 D.J. Howell, "The International Canoe Meet," *Canadian Magazine* 15, no. 6 (1900): 515.
47 Ibid. Frank Micklethwaite was a commercial photographer, based in Toronto, who migrated north to Muskoka each summer, on the heels of Toronto society. He operated a seasonal studio in Port Sandfield, where he sold photographs like this one to well-to-do cottagers, resort dwellers, and ACA members. Mike Filey and Victor Russell, *From Horse Power to Horsepower: Toronto 1890–1930* (Toronto: Dundurn Press, 1993), 20–1.
48 "The ACA Meet of 1891," *Forest and Stream*, 20 Aug. 1891. At the 1889 meet at Stave Island, e.g., canoeists were forced to wait for half a day because there were no suitable boats to the encampment. In 1890, the wait was "anywhere from six to twenty-four hours." "American Canoe Association Meet," *Forest and Stream*, 12 Sept. 1889; "The ACA Meet of 1890 – I," *Forest and Stream*, 30 Oct. 1890.
49 "The Stony Lake Meet," *Peterborough Examiner*, 16 Aug. 1883.
50 "American Canoe Association," *Forest and Stream*, 14 Aug. 1890.
51 *Forest and Stream*, 31 July 1890.
52 "American Canoe Association Meet," *Forest and Stream*, 12 Sept. 1889. A newspaper account from 1896, which celebrated the work of Frank Potter, collector of customs, hinted at the border crossing troubles experienced by Canadians attending the meets in previous years. See also "Canoists [sic] Gathering," *Rochester Democrat Chronicle*, 20 Aug. 1896.

53 "American Canoe Association Meet," *Forest and Stream*, 12 Sept. 1889.
54 "Canoeing," *Forest and Stream*, 23 Nov. 1895.
55 This echoes the conclusions drawn in Colin Howell, "Borderlands, Baselines, and Big Game: Conceptualizing the Northeast as a Sporting Region," in *New England and the Maritime Provinces: Connections and Comparisons*, ed. Stephen J. Hornsby and John G. Reid (Montreal and Kingston: McGill-Queen's University Press, 2005), 264–79.
56 See, e.g., FM, ACA Collection, box 1.6/11, "Camp Circular for Stony Lake" (1883). Alexander Wilson offers a succinct overview of the intersection of leisure and nature on both sides of the border in the pre–Second World War era in *The Culture of Nature: North American Landscapes from Disney to the Exxon Valdez* (Toronto: Between the Lines Press, 1990), 23–8.
57 See, e.g., Charles Neide, *The Canoe Aurora: A Cruise from the Adirondacks to the Gulf* (New York: Forest and Stream Publishing, 1885); Snedeker, *A Family Canoe Trip*; "Homeward Bound," *Forest and Stream*, 6 Sept. 1883; "Cruising Notes," *Forest and Stream*, 10 July 1884; "Cruising Notes," *Forest and Stream*, 24 July 1884; "The Association Meet," *Forest and Stream*, 6 Aug. 1885; "The Canoe Meet Ended," *NYT*, 28 Aug. 1886.
58 "The Great Canoe Meet," *Outing* 9, no. 2 (1886): 166; Trent University Archives (TUA), 83-014/2, Paul Vernon, "Tales of the ACA" (1940).
59 "Canoeists Break Camp," *New York Sun*, 16 Aug. 1884; FM, ACA Collection, box 1.1/28, Photographs from Lake Champlain, 1887.
60 "The Association Meet," *Forest and Stream*, 6 Aug. 1885.
61 "The Opening Days Are Not Full of Briskness," *British Daily Whig*, 11 Aug. 1893.
62 "From Vergennes to Lorna Island," *Forest and Stream*, 24 May 1883.
63 Patricia Jasen, "Close Encounters," in *Wild Things: Nature, Culture, and Tourism in Ontario, 1790–1914* (Toronto: University of Toronto Press, 1995), 133–49; Hallie E. Bond, *Boats and Boating in the Adirondacks* (Syracuse: Syracuse University Press, 1998), 57–67, 164–6.
64 Snedeker, *A Family Canoe Trip*, 27.
65 FM, ACA Collection, box 1.1/28, Photographs from Lake Champlain, 1887.
66 "From Vergennes to Lorna Island," *Forest and Stream*, 24 May 1883.
67 Snedeker, *A Family Canoe Trip*, 30, 24.
68 "Cruising Notes," *Forest and Stream*, 10 July and 24 July 1884; Snedeker, *A Family Canoe Trip*, 80–4; "Homeward from Stony Lake," *Forest and Stream*, 19 Feb. 1885.
69 Snedeker, *A Family Canoe Trip*, 24.
70 Ibid., 19–23, 30, 33, 42.
71 Joan Pau Rubies, "Travel Writing and Ethnography," in *The Cambridge Companion to Travel Writing*, ed. Peter Hulme and Tim Youngs (New York: Cambridge University Press, 2002), 242, 258.

72 George W. Stocking Jr, *Victorian Anthropology* (New York: Free Press, 1987); Lee D. Baker, *From Savage to Negro: Anthropology and the Construction of Race, 1896–1954* (Berkeley: University of California Press, 1998).
73 "Women as Canoeists," *NYT*, 10 Aug. 1892.
74 "Paddle and Sail," *NYT*, 2 Aug. 1878.
75 Meg Stanley, "More Than Just a Spare Rib but Not Quite a Whole Canoe: Some Aspects of Women's Canoe-Tripping Experiences, 1900–1940," in *Using Wilderness: Essays on the Evolution of Youth Camping in Ontario*, ed. Bruce E. Hodgins and Bernadine Dodge (Peterborough: Frost Centre for Canadian Heritage and Development Studies, 1992), 51–60.
76 "From Vergennes to Lorna Island," *Forest and Stream*, 24 May 1883; "Homeward from Stony Lake," *Forest and Stream*, 19 Feb. 1885.
77 Vernon, "Tales of the ACA."
78 Phil MacNaghten and John Urry, "Bodies of Nature: Introduction," *Body and Society* 6, no. 3–4 (2000): 8.
79 Snedeker, *A Family Canoe Trip*, 23.
80 "Great Canoe Meet," *Outing* 9, no. 2 (1886): 166.
81 "From Vergennes to Lorna Island," *Forest and Stream*, 24 May 1883; Snedeker, *A Family Canoe Trip*, 56, 68.
82 FM, ACA Collection, box 1.1/30, "Lunch Below the Sagamore, Lake George" (1887).
83 "From Vergennes to Lorna Island," *Forest and Stream*, 24 May 1883.
84 Schivelbusch, *The Railway Journey*; Michael Freeman, *Railways and the Victorian Imagination* (New Haven: Yale University Press, 1999).
85 Freeman, *Railways*, 7; Schivelbusch, *The Railway Journey*, 36.
86 Freeman, *Railways*, 23, 80.
87 Johnston, "National Spectacle," 1028.
88 "Canoeists' Annual Meet," *NYT*, 26 Aug. 1900. Emphasis added. See also C. Bowyer Vaux, "The American Canoe Association, and Its Birthplace," *Outing* 12, no. 5 (1888): 414–15.
89 C. Bowyer Vaux, "Canoe Meet at the Thousand Islands," *Outing* 14, no. 5 (1889): 345.
90 Schivelbusch, *Railway Journey*, 53–5.
91 Aron, *Working at Play*, 51.
92 "Resting at Lake George," *NYT*, 13 July 1883.
93 Aron, *Working at Play*, 51.
94 Amy Richter, *Home on the Rails: Women, the Railroad, and the Rise of Public Domesticity* (Chapel Hill: University of North Carolina Press, 2005), 66.
95 Ibid., 51–2; Aron, *Working at Play*, 51.
96 "Canoeing: Opens This Morning," *Daily Mail and Empire*, 3 Aug. 1900; "Canoists [sic] Leave for Camp," *New York Herald*, 4 Aug. 1900; "Canoeists' Annual Meet," *NYT*, 26 Aug. 1900; FM, ACA Collection, box 1.6/11, "Camp Circular for Sugar Island" (1908).

97 MSCRC, Collection 291, box 23, folder 2, "Camp Circular for Sugar Island" (1907).
98 Richter, *Home on the Rails*, 55.
99 "Canoe Sailors in Camp," *New York Sun*, 4 Aug. 1884.
100 FM, ACA Collection, box 1.6/12, ACA Atlantic Division, "Instructions to Members Attending the ACA Meet at Stave Island" (1898).
101 Richter, *Home on the Rails*, 37; Casey Blanton, "Victorian Women Travelers: Mary Kingsley," in *Travel Writing: The Self and the World* (New York: Routledge, 2002), 44–58. See, e.g., "American Canoe Association Meet: Tenth Annual," *Forest and Stream*, 22 Aug. 1889; "Musquito Fleet," *Salt Lake Herald*, 9 Aug. 1891.
102 "This an Ideal Canoe Camp," *World*, 20 Aug. 1893.
103 "Around Lake Champlain," *Forest and Stream*, 7 July 1892.
104 Richter, *Home on the Rails*, 48–9.
105 Johnston, "National Spectacle."
106 "The Meet of 1886," *Forest and Stream*, 26 Aug. 1886.
107 "Great Canoe Meet," *Outing* 9, no. 2 (1886): 164. See also "Paddle Your Own Canoe," *Forest and Stream*, 30 June 1887.
108 Johnston, "National Spectacle," 1025.
109 James Armstrong and David M. Williams, "The Steamboat and Popular Tourism," *Journal of Transport History* 26, no. 1 (2005): 61–76.
110 J.I. Little, "Scenic Tourism on the Northeastern Borderland: Lake Memphremagog's Steamboat Excursions and Resort Hotels, 1850–1900," *Journal of Historical Geography* 35, no. 4 (2009): 717, 739.
111 Vaux, "Its Birthplace," 414.
112 Goodsell, "A Canoeing Reminiscence," 2.
113 The length of such journeys ranged between a few miles and 21 miles in the case of the Muskoka meet in 1900. "Canoe Camp at Muskoka Lake," *Rochester Democrat Chronicle*, 30 July 1900.
114 FM, ACA Collection, box 1.2/28, "Steamer Valeria at ACA Camp Dock" (1898); box 1.3/6, "SS Valeria Arriving at Camp Dock" (1905); box 1.5/1, "ACA Meet and Camp" (1906); box 1.6/11, "Camp Circular for Sugar Island" (1904); "Canoeists' Annual Camp," *NYT*, 11 Aug. 1901.
115 Snedeker, *A Family Canoe Trip*, 84.
116 Ibid.
117 Ibid., 119.
118 "The 1884 Meet," *American Canoeist* 3, no. 8/9 (1884): 114.
119 Tim Youngs, *Travel Writing in the Nineteenth Century: Filling in the Blank Spaces* (London: Anthem Press, 2006), 2.
120 See, e.g., "A.C.A. Camp," *Forest and Stream*, 14 Aug. 1884; Columbine, "A Visit to the American Canoe Association," *Young Friend's Review* (1886): 67; "Canoeists in Camp," *NYT*, 9 Aug. 1890.

Notes to pages 70–4

121 "Noyac Bay Is Deserted," *NYT*, 24 Aug. 1890.
122 "The Association Meet," *Forest and Stream*, 21 Aug. 1884.
123 Haldrup, "Laid-Back Mobilities," 447.
124 Ibid. Emphasis in original.

4 Governing

1 "The Canoe Men in Camp,"*New York Times* (*NYT*), 17 Aug. 1890.
2 "Canoeing at Thousand Islands," *New York Sun*, 9 Aug. 1885; "Around the Pine Camp Fire," *NYT*, 20 Aug. 1893. For similar references, see "The Association Meet," *Forest and Stream*, 6 Aug. 1885; "Pleasant Time at the Canoe Camp," *New York Sun*, 20 Aug. 1896; "Meet of the Canoeists," *NYT*, 15 Aug. 1897; "Rowing," *Utica Observer*, 19 Aug. 1897; D.J. Howell, "The International Canoe Meet," *Canadian Magazine* 15, no. 6 (1900): 518; "Canoemen Gather at the 1000 Islands," *Watertown Re-Union*, 15 Aug. 1903.
3 "The Association Meet," *Forest and Stream*, 6 Aug. 1885; "Around the Pine Camp Fire," *NYT*, 20 Aug. 1893; "Placing More Democrats," *Boston Evening Transcript*, 17 Apr. 1913; "Obituary: Major Gen. William H. Cotton," *NYT*, 21 Apr. 1914.
4 Keith Walden, *Becoming Modern in Toronto: The Industrial Exhibition and the Shaping of a Late Victorian Culture* (Toronto: University of Toronto Press, 1997), 33.
5 McMaster University Archives (MUA), E. Pauline Johnson Collection, box 3, file 1-5, Pauline Johnson, "The American Canoe Association at Grindstone Island," *Rudder* (1896): 355–8.
6 Ibid. See also Howell, "International Canoe Meet," 513–20; "The A.C.A. Canoe Meet," *Outing* 11, no. 1 (1887): 95–6.
7 Florence Watters Snedeker, *A Family Canoe Trip* (New York: Harper & Brothers, 1892), 87.
8 Patrick Joyce, *The Rule of Freedom: Liberalism and the Modern City* (London: Verso, 2003), 1. Emphasis in original.
9 Michel Foucault, *Discipline and Punish: The Birth of the Prison*, trans. Alan Sheridan (New York City: Vintage Books, 1977); Michel Foucault, "Governmentality," in *The Foucault Effect: Studies in Governmentality*, ed. C. Gordon and P. Miller (Chicago: Chicago University Press, 1991), 87–104.
10 Walden, *Becoming Modern*, 33.
11 David M. Scobey, *Empire City: The Making and Meaning of the New York City Landscape* (Philadelphia: Temple University Press, 2003), 159.
12 P.G. Mackintosh, "'The Development of Higher Urban Life' and the Geographic Imagination: Beauty, Art, and Moral Environmentalism in Toronto, 1900–1920," *Journal of Historical Geography* 31 (2005): 689.

13 Ibid., 705. On the City Beautiful Movement, see William H. Wilson, *The City Beautiful Movement* (Baltimore: Johns Hopkins University Press, 1989).
14 Joe Hermer, *Regulating Eden: The Nature of Order in the North American Parks* (Toronto: University of Toronto Press, 2002), 46.
15 Mystic Seaport Collections Research Center (MSCRC), Collection 291, vol. 3, Meeting of the Executive Committee, 23 Nov. 1889.
16 Michel de Certeau, *The Practice of Everyday Life*, trans. Steven Rendell (Berkeley: University of California Press, 1984 [1980]); Roy Rosenzweig and Elizabeth Blackmar, *The Park and the People: A History of Central Park* (Ithaca: Cornell University Press, 1992).
17 Activity arenas are "spaces not necessarily defined by walls and roofs, but created by human action," such as a campfire circle or racecourse. They remind us that as important as the built environment is to social relations so too are the ways in which spaces are understood and used. Elizabeth C. Cromley, "Transforming the Food Axis: Houses, Tools, Modes of Analysis," *Material History Review* 44 (Fall 1996): 8–22.
18 Abigail Van Slyck, "Kitchen Technologies and Mealtime Rituals: Interpreting the Food Axis at American Summer Camps, 1890–1950," *Technology and Culture* 43, no. 4 (2002): 673–4.
19 "Last Days of the River Season," *Syracuse Evening Herald*, 30 Aug. 1896.
20 See also "The ACA Meet of 1892," *Forest and Stream*, 25 Aug. 1892; Fenimore Museum (FM), formerly the New York State Historical Association (NYSHA), American Canoe Association (ACA) Collection, box 1.2/22, Frank H. Foster, "General View of Camp Headquarters" (1892); box 1.2/25, "View of Camp from West Overlooking Eel Bay" (1897); box 1.2/26, H.C. Morse, "Headquarters from Dock" (1897); box 1.2/28, A.A. Lewis, "ACA Camp Headquarters" (1898).
21 "Their Campfires Ablaze," *NYT*, 11 Aug. 1895.
22 See "Headquarters from the Dock," in Thomas H. Stryker, ed., *American Canoe Association Yearbook* (Rome: Press of the Rome Sentinel Co., 1896), 74.
23 St Lawrence County Historical Association (SLCHA), "Camp Circular for Grindstone Island" (1886); Harry Eckford, "Camp Grindstone," *Century Magazine* 30, no. 4 (1885): 511; MSCRC, Collection 291, box 23, folder 2, "Camp Circular for Lake George" (1888).
24 "Our Trip to the A.C.A. Meet of '93," *Rockwood Review* 1, no. 7 (1894): no pp.
25 R.B. Burchard, "Back to Grindstone: The Canoe Camp," *Outing* 29, no. 2 (1896): 141; "The Annual Canoe Meet," *New York Evening Post*, 27 Aug. 1887; FM, ACA Collection, box 1.2/19, "The Mess Pavilion" (1891).
26 Other photographs of the inside of the mess can be seen in FM, ACA Collection, box 1.2/7, "General Camp Mess" (1890).

Notes to pages 77–9

27 Abigail Van Slyck, *A Manufactured Wilderness: Summer Camps and the Shaping of American Youth, 1890–1960* (Minneapolis: University of Minnesota Press, 2006), 129.
28 Van Slyck, "Kitchen Technologies," 675.
29 "ACA Meet," *Forest and Stream*, 31 July 1890.
30 "The ACA Meet: Camp Circular," *Forest and Stream*, 10 July 1890; "The ACA Meet of 1890 – II," *Forest and Stream*, 6 Nov. 1890; Robert E. Weir, *Class in America: An Encyclopedia* (Westport: Greenwood Press, 2007), 202.
31 "The ACA Meet of 1890 – II," *Forest and Stream*, 6 Nov. 1890.
32 MSCRC, Collection 291, box 23, folder 2, "Camp Circular for Lake George" (1888). See, e.g., "The Meet," *American Canoeist* 2, no. 6 (1883): 79–83.
33 "The Meet," *American Canoeist* 2, no. 6 (1883): 79–83; SLCHA, "Camp Circular for Grindstone Island" (1886); R. Easton Burns, ed., *American Canoe Association Yearbook* (Kingston: Daily News Printing House, 1893), 10.
34 "American Canoe Association Meet," *Forest and Stream*, 12 Sept. 1889.
35 "The ACA Meet of 1890 – II," *Forest and Stream*, 6 Nov. 1890; "The Meet," *American Canoeist* 2, no. 6 (1883): 79.
36 "The American Canoe Association in Canada," *Forest and Stream*, 19 Apr. 1883.
37 O.K. Chobee, "Echoes from Stony Lake," *American Canoeist* 2, no. 8 (1883): 114.
38 Lynne Marks, *Revivals and Roller Rinks: Religion, Leisure, and Identity in Late-Nineteenth-Century Small-Town Ontario* (Toronto: University of Toronto Press, 1997), 23.
39 Colin Howell, *Northern Sandlots: A Social History of Maritime Baseball* (Toronto: University of Toronto Press, 1995), 76.
40 Andrea L. Smalley, "'Our Lady Sportsmen': Gender, Class and Conservation in Sport Hunting Magazines, 1873–1920," *Journal of the Gilded Age and Progressive Era* 4, no. 4 (2005): 364.
41 Alan Hunt, "Regulating Heterosocial Space: Sexual Politics in the Early Twentieth Century," *Journal of Historical Sociology* 15, no. 1 (2002): 1–34.
42 C. Bowyer Vaux, "The American Canoe Association, and Its Birthplace," *Outing* 12, no. 5 (1888): 415.
43 "Snips from Snaps at the '89 Meet," *Forest and Stream*, 19 Sept. 1889. See also "Address Wanted," *Forest and Stream*, 17 Sept. 1891.
44 "A.C.A.," *American Canoeist* 2, no. 12 (1884): 189.
45 Ann Douglas, *The Feminization of American Culture* (New York: Knopf, 1977); Michael Kimmel, "Consuming Manhood: The Feminization of American Culture and the Recreation of the Male Body, 1832–1920," *Michigan Quarterly Review* 33 (1994): 7–36; Gail Bederman, *Manliness and Civilization: A Cultural History of Gender and Race in the United States, 1880–1917* (Chicago: University of Chicago Press, 1996).

46 Clifford Putney, *Muscular Christianity: Manhood and Sports in Protestant America* (Boston: Harvard University Press, 2003); David I. MacLeod, *Building Character in the American Boy: The Boy Scouts, YMCA and Their Forerunners, 1870–1920* (Madison: University of Wisconsin Press, 1983); Leslie Paris, *Children's Nature: The Rise of the American Summer Camp* (New York: New York University Press, 2008).

47 "The American Canoe Association in Canada," *Forest and Stream*, 19 Apr. 1883.

48 This was also to be the plan in 1888. In the end, the two camps were housed on the same island. MSCRC, Collection 291, vol. 3, Meeting of the Executive Committee, 17 Nov. 1888.

49 Cindy Aron, "The Evolution of the Middle Class," in *A Companion to Nineteenth-Century America*, ed. William Barney (New York: Blackwell, 2000), 185. Emphasis added.

50 Abigail Van Slyck, "The Lady and the Library Loafer: Gender and Public Space in Victorian America," *Winterthur Portfolio* 31, no. 4 (1996): 223.

51 Ibid., 221.

52 Susan Porter Benson, *Counter Cultures: Sales-Women, Managers, and Customers in American Department Stores, 1890–1940* (Urbana: University of Illinois Press, 1986); Katherine C. Grier, "Imagining the Parlor, 1830–1880," in *Perspectives on American Furniture*, ed. Gerald W.R. Ward (New York: W.W. Norton for the Henry Francis du Pont Winterthur Museum, 1988), 205–39; Carolyn Brucken, "In the Public Eye: Women and the American Luxury Hotel," *Winterthur Portfolio* 31, no. 4 (1996): 203–20; Galen Cranz, "Women in Urban Parks," *Signs* 5, no. 3 (1980, Supplement): S80–S85.

53 Muriel Stanley Venne, "The 'S' Word: Reclaiming 'Esquao' for Aboriginal Women," in *Unsettled Pasts: Reconceiving the West through Women's History*, ed. Sarah Carter, Lesley Erickson, Patricia Roome, and Char Smith (Calgary: University of Calgary Press, 2005), 125.

54 See, e.g., Flip, "The Lake Champlain Canoe Meet," *Outing* 11, no. 3 (1887): 262.

55 Ronald Hoffman, "The History of the American Canoe Association, 1880–1960" (PhD dissertation, Springfield College, 1967), 43.

56 Anne McClintock, *Imperial Leather: Race, Gender, and Sexuality in the Colonial Contest* (New York: Routledge, 1995), 6.

57 Linda K. Kerber, "Separate Spheres, Female Worlds, Woman's Place: The Rhetoric of Women's History," *Journal of American History* 75, no. 1 (1988): 9–39.

58 "American Canoe Association Meet," *Forest and Stream*, 12 Sept. 1889; "The Tenth Annual Meet of the American Canoe Association," *Sail and Paddle* 7, no. 9 (1889): 198; "The ACA Meet of 1890 – I," *Forest and Stream*, 30 Oct. 1890; FM, ACA Collection, box 1.6/11, "Camp Circular for Bluff Point" (1895).

59 "Canoeists at Lake George," *NYT*, 16 Aug. 1887; "The Canoeists in Camp," *NYT*, 22 Aug. 1887; "Canoeists' Annual Meet," *NYT*, 26 Aug. 1900; "The Meet in Muskoka," *Daily Mail and Empire*, 27 July 1900.
60 "Stony Lake Canoe Congress," *Peterborough Examiner*, 23 Aug. 1883.
61 Flip, "Lake Champlain Canoe Meet," 263; D'Arcy Scott, "The Annual Camp of the American Canoe Association," *Massey's Magazine* 2, no. 2 (1896): 118.
62 "Obituary," *Forest and Stream*, 15 Oct. 1885; "The ACA Meet: Camp Circular," *Forest and Stream*, 10 July 1890; "Fun with Sail and Paddle," *NYT*, 3 Aug. 1890.
63 Eckford, "Camp Grindstone," 510–11.
64 The sheet music collection at the Adirondack Experience, formerly the Adirondack Museum, is one of the best examples of this. Not only are there a number of songs linking canoeing and romance, including "We'll Paddle Our Own Canoe" and "Love's Canoe," but also many of the covers feature couples out in canoes, often at night. Thomas McMullin's article on the controversy over mixed-sex canoeing in Boston demonstrates the links between canoeing and courting and also the anxieties that surfaced from that relationship. Thomas McMullin, "Revolt at Riverside: Victorian Virtue and the Charles River Canoeing Controversy, 1903–1905," *New England Quarterly* 73, no. 5 (2000): 482–94.
65 Caspar W. Whitney, "Annual Meet of the American Canoe Association," *Harper's Weekly*, 2 Sept. 1893.
66 Robert Tyson, "Laying Out the Course on Stony Lake," *American Canoeist* 2, no. 5 (1883): 67; "The Meet," *American Canoeist* 2, no. 7 (1883): 79. Emphasis added.
67 Flip, "Lake Champlain Canoe Meet," 262.
68 See also "American Canoe Association: Thirteenth Annual Meet," *Forest and Stream*, 14 July 1892.
69 Reuben Rose-Redwood, "Rationalizing the Landscape: Superimposing the Grid upon the Island of Manhattan" (MA thesis, Pennsylvania State University, 2002); James C. Scott, "Nature and Space," in *Seeing Like a State: How Certain Schemes to Improve the Human Condition Have Failed* (New Haven: Yale University Press, 1998), 11–52.
70 "The ACA Meet of 1890 – III," *Forest and Stream*, 13 Aug. 1890.
71 "The ACA Meet, Lake George," *Forest and Stream*, 23 Aug. 1888.
72 Martin V. Melosi, *The Sanitary City: Urban Infrastructure in America from Colonial Times to the Present* (Baltimore: John Hopkins University Press, 2000).
73 There are only a handful of references to sanitary arrangements in the ACA archive. See "Local Canoe Meets," *Forest and Stream*, 1 Nov. 1883; "The 1884 Meet of the A.C.A.," *Outing* 3, no. 6 (1884): 464–5; "The ACA Meet: Camp Circular," *Forest and Stream*, 10 July 1890.

74 SLCHA, "Camp Circular for Grindstone Island" (1886); MSCRC, Collection 291, box 23, folder 2, "Camp Circular for Lake George" (1888), and 'Camp Circular for Willsborough Point" (1892).
75 SLCHA, "Camp Circular for Grindstone Island" (1886).
76 Linda Nash, *Inescapable Ecologies: A History of Environment, Disease, and Knowledge* (Berkeley: University of California Press, 2006), 18.
77 "The Canoeists' Convention," *New York Evening Telegram*, 5 Aug. 1880.
78 "The Annual Canoe Regatta," *Forest and Stream*, 21 Apr. 1881; "The Association Meet," *Forest and Stream*, 21 Aug. 1884; "ACA Regatta Rules, etc. – Suggestions," *Forest and Stream*, 27 Sept. 1888; "The ACA Meet of 1891: Race Week," *Forest and Stream*, 27 Aug. 1891.
79 "Canoeing," *New York Evening Post*, 19 Aug. 1891; Lorgnette, "A Woman at a Canoe Race," *Outing* 24, no. 6 (1894): 421–4."
80 "Canoeists in Camp," *New York Herald*, 2 Aug. 1885; "Arrivals at Canoe Camp," *NYT*, 16 Aug. 1895; "Canoeing," *New York Sun*, 10 Aug. 1899.
81 MSCRC, Collection 291, vol. 3, Meeting of the Executive Committee, 23 Nov. 1889.
82 "The ACA Meet: Race Week," *Forest and Stream*, 28 Aug. 1890.
83 My understanding and use of the term "conduct" owes much to Michel Foucault, who observes that "to 'conduct' is at the same time to 'lead' others (according to mechanisms of coercion which are, to varying degrees, strict) and a way of behaving within a more or less open field of possibilities. The exercise of power consists in guiding the possibility of conduct and putting in order the possible outcome. Basically power is less a confrontation between two adversaries or the linking of one to the other than a question of government." Michel Foucault, "The Subject and Power," *Critical Inquiry* 8 (1982): 789.
84 SLCHA, "Camp Circular for Grindstone Island" (1886).
85 Joyce, *The Rule of Freedom*, 1.
86 MSCRC, Collection 291, vol. 3, Meeting of the Executive Committee, 17 Nov. 1888.
87 Ibid., 15 Aug. 1888.
88 MSCRC, Collection 291, vol. 4, Special Meeting of the Executive Committee, 11 Aug. 1899.
89 MSCRC, Collection 291, box 23, folder 2, "Camp Circular for Lake George" (1888) and "Camp Circular for Sugar Island" (1907).
90 Examples of the ribbons can be found in the Fred Saunders Scrapbooks, FM, ACA Collection, box 1.5/1.
91 Stephen Graham and David Wood, "Digitizing Surveillance: Categorization, Space, Inequality," *Critical Social Policy* 23, no. 3 (2003): 227.

92 Walden, *Becoming Modern*, 34.
93 The circular for the 1888 meet offers a particularly detailed schedule. MSCRC, Collection 291, box 23, folder 2, "Camp Circular for Lake George" (1888).
94 Van Slyck, *A Manufactured Wilderness*, 126.
95 Marks, *Revivals and Roller Rinks*, 23–5.
96 D.J. Howell, "The International Canoe Meet," *Canadian Magazine* 15, no. 6 (1900): 515.
97 Eckford, "Camp Grindstone," 504.
98 MUA, box 9, file 27, Pauline Johnson, "Sail and Paddle," *Illustrated Buffalo Express*, c. 1893; "The Canoeists," *Rochester Democrat Chronicle*, 14 Aug. 1887; "The ACA Meet: Race Week," *Forest and Stream*, 28 Aug. 1890.
99 Both the signal officer and bugler were paid camp positions.
100 MSCRC, Collection 291, box 23, folder 2, "Camp Circular for Willsborough Point" (1892).
101 "The ACA Meet of 1890," *Forest and Stream*, 21 Aug. 1890.
102 E.P. Thompson, "Time, Work-Discipline, and Industrial Capitalism," *Past and Present* 38, no. 1 (1967): 56–97.
103 SLCHA, "Camp Circular for Grindstone Island" (1886).
104 All of these terms – "officer of the day," "police," and "pickets" – were military sobriquets. Thomas Wilhelm, *A Military Dictionary and Gazeteer*, rev. ed. (Philadelphia: L.R. Hamersly and Co., 1881). Some of the same terminology was employed at contemporary summer camps. Van Slyck, *A Manufactured Wilderness*, 131.
105 SLCHA, "Camp Circular for Grindstone Island" (1886).
106 FM, ACA Collection, box 1.6/2, D.B. Goodsell, "A Canoeing Reminiscence" (1936), 3. Bruce Curtis and Karl Jacoby make similar arguments about those employed by the nineteenth-century state to conduct censuses or enforce conservation legislation. Bruce Curtis, *The Politics of Population: State Formation, Statistics, and the Census of Canada, 1840–1875* (Toronto: University of Toronto Press, 2001); Karl Jacoby, *Crimes against Nature: Squatters, Poachers, Thieves, and the Hidden History of American Conservation* (Berkeley: University of California Press, 2001).
107 Walden, *Becoming Modern*, 32–79.
108 Ladies Days were a common occasion at exhibitions and sporting events in the late nineteenth century. See Howell, *Northern Sandlots*, 77; Walden, *Becoming Modern*, 171.
109 A sample notice from the 1888 encampment on Lake George is included in FM, ACA Collection, box 1.6/11.
110 See, e.g., "Sport on the St Lawrence," *NYT*, 28 July 1889.

111 "The Canoe Men in Camp,"*NYT*, 17 Aug. 1890; *Rochester Democrat Chronicle*, 13 Aug. 1896.
112 *Sag Harbor Express*, 14 Aug. 1890; *Sag Harbor Corrector*, 16 Aug. 1890.
113 "The ACA Meet of 1890 – III," *Forest and Stream*, 13 Nov. 1890.
114 "The ACA Meet: Race Week," *Forest and Stream*, 28 Aug. 1890; "The ACA Meet of 1891: Race Week," *Forest and Stream*, 27 Aug. 1891. Roy Rosenzweig, *Eight Hours for What We Will: Workers and Leisure in an Industrial City* (Cambridge: Cambridge University Press, 1983), 39, 68, 69, 179–80; Bryan Palmer, chapter 5, "Merchants of Their Time," in *A Culture in Conflict: Skilled Workers and Industrial Capitalism in Hamilton, Ontario, 1860–1914* (Montreal and Kingston: McGill-Queen's University Press, 1979).
115 "The ACA Meet of 1890 – I," *Forest and Stream*, 30 Oct. 1890.
116 MSCRC, Collection 291, box 23, folder 2, "Camp Circular for Sugar Island" (1907).
117 "The ACA Meet of 1890: Jessup's Neck," *Forest and Stream*, 21 Aug. 1890.
118 Other rules on the sign pertained to fires, foliage, and graffiti. FM, ACA Collection, box 1.6/12.
119 MSCRC, Collection 291, vol. 3, Letter from Commodore Stanton to the Executive Committee, 29 Apr. 1890; "The ACA Meet," *Forest and Stream*, 22 May 1890.
120 MSCRC, Collection 291, vol. 4, Meeting of the Executive Committee, 15 Oct. 1904.
121 Eckford, "Camp Grindstone," 511. Emphasis in original.
122 Craig Heron, *Booze: A Distilled History* (Toronto: Between the Lines Press, 2003), 60.
123 "Ex-Commodore Winne Given a Big Reception," *British Daily Whig*, 18 Aug. 1893.
124 Scott, "Annual Camp," 116.
125 Johnson, "Sail and Paddle."
126 Heron, *Booze*, 76.
127 Ibid., 77.
128 Vernon, "Tales of the ACA."
129 Ibid.
130 Goodsell, "A Canoeing Reminiscence," 6.
131 Vernon, "Tales of the ACA."
132 Ibid.
133 Ibid.
134 Walden, *Becoming Modern*, 44.
135 Eckford, "Camp Grindstone," 511.
136 Henri Lefebvre, *The Production of Space*, trans. Donald Nicholson-Smith (Oxford: Blackwell, 1991).

5 Domesticating

1. D'Arcy Scott, "The Annual Camp of the American Canoe Association," *Massey's Magazine* 2, no. 2 (1896): 116–17.
2. Arnold van Gennep, *The Rites of Passage* (London: Paul, 1960 [1909]); Renate Dohmen, "The Home in the World: Threshold Designs and Performative Relations in Contemporary Tamil Nadu, South India," *Cultural Geographies* 11 (2004): 7–25.
3. Keith Walden makes a similar argument about the spatial and temporal structure of the Industrial Exhibitions in *Becoming Modern in Toronto: The Industrial Exhibition and the Shaping of a Late Victorian Culture* (Toronto: University of Toronto Press, 1997), 26.
4. Dohmen, "Home in the World," 23.
5. The two encampments on Willsborough Point on Lake Champlain in 1891 and 1892 were three weeks long.
6. Alison Blunt and Robyn Dowling, *Home* (London: Routledge, 2006), 2.
7. Ibid., 23.
8. Michael Egan, "Wrestling Teddy Bears: Wilderness Masculinity as Invented Tradition in the Pacific Northwest," *Gender Forum* 15 (2006). Accessed 19 Mar. 2012: http://www.genderforum.org/issues/gender-roomours-i/wrestling-teddy-bears/; Ben Jordan, "'Conservation of Boyhood': Boy Scouting's Modest Manliness and Natural Resource Conservation, 1910–1930," *Environmental History* 15 (2010): 612–42. This line of thinking owes much to Roderick Nash, *Wilderness and the American Mind* (New Haven: Yale University Press, 2001 [1967]).
9. Examples of this growing body of work on "exclusively male domesticities outside the home" include Jane Rendell, "The Clubs of St James's: Places of Public Patriarchy – Exclusivity, Domesticity and Secrecy," *Journal of Architecture* 4 (1999): 167–89; Amy Milne-Smith, "A Flight to Domesticity? Making a Home in the Gentleman's Clubs of London, 1880–1914," *Journal of British Studies* 45 (2006): 796–818; Phillip Gordon Mackintosh and Clyde R. Forsberg, "Performing the Lodge: Masonry, Masculinity, and Nineteenth-Century North American Moral Geography," *Journal of Historical Geography* 35 (2009): 451–72; Quintin Colville, "Corporate Domesticity and Idealised Masculinity; Royal Naval Officers and Their Shipboard Home, 1918–1939," *Gender & History* 21, no. 3 (2009): 499–519.
10. "The Meet of 1886," *Forest and Stream*, 26 Aug. 1886.
11. D.J. Howell, "The International Canoe Meet," *Canadian Magazine* 15, no. 6 (1900): 515.
12. "The Meet of 1886," *Forest and Stream*, 26 Aug. 1886.
13. "ACA Annual Meeting," *Peterborough Daily Review*, 14 Aug. 1883.

14 An exception to this can be found in "Around the Pine Camp Fire," *New York Times* (*NYT*), 20 Aug. 1893.
15 "ACA Camp," *Forest and Stream*, 14 Aug. 1884; Fenimore Museum (FM), formerly the New York State Historical Association (NYSHA), American Canoe Association (ACA) Collection, box 1.2/15, "Mending Sails, Canoe Sailors' Row," 1890; "The Canoe Men in Camp,"*NYT*, 17 Aug. 1890. Electricity was an anomaly in the camp at least until the late 1890s, if not after.
16 See, e.g., "The Canoe Island Camp,"*NYT*, 13 Aug. 1881; "The ACA Meet, Lake George," *Forest and Stream*, 23 Aug. 1888; Retaw, *Fragments from the '88 Meet* (Montreal, 1888), 13; "Some More Snips from and Another Snap at the '89 Meet," *Forest and Stream*, 24 Oct. 1889; "The Canoe Men in Camp," *NYT*, 17 Aug. 1890; "The ACA Meet of 1890: Jessup's Neck," *Forest and Stream*, 21 Aug. 1890; FM, ACA Collection, box 1.2/11, "Camp of the Ianthe Canoe Club," 1890.
17 Elizabeth Fee, Theodore M. Brown, Jan Lazarus, and Paul Theerman, "Baxter Street Then," *American Journal of Public Health* 92, no. 5 (2002): 753.
18 Wendy Roy, "Visualizing Labrador: Maps, Photographs, and Geographical Naming in Mina Hubbard's *A Woman's Way through Unknown Labrador*," *Studies in Canadian Literature* 29, no. 1 (2004): 24, 26–7.
19 Paul Carter, *The Road to Botany Bay: An Exploration of Landscape and History* (New York: Knopf, 1988), 67.
20 Catherine Nash, "Irish Placenames: Postcolonial Locations," *Transactions of the Institute of British Geographers* 24, no. 4 (1999): 457.
21 "Beautiful Sugar Island: New Home of the ACA," *Sail and Sweep* 2, no. 9 (1903): 364–6.
22 "The Canoe Men in Camp,"*NYT*, 17 Aug. 1890; MSCRC, Collection 291, box 23, folder 2, "Camp Circular for Willsborough Point" (1892); D.J. Howell, "The International Canoe Meet," *Canadian Magazine* 15, no. 6 (1900): 513–20; FM, ACA Collection, box 1.6/11, "Camp Circular for Sugar Island" (1904).
23 "Stony Lake Canoe Congress," *Peterborough Examiner*, 23 Aug. 1883; "The Association Meet," *Forest and Stream*, 21 Aug. 1884.
24 R.B. Burchard, "Back to Grindstone: The Canoe Camp," *Outing* 29, no. 2 (1896): 141.
25 Abigail Van Slyck, *A Manufactured Wilderness: Summer Camps and the Shaping of American Youth, 1890–1960* (Minneapolis: University of Minnesota Press, 2006), 131.
26 FM, ACA Collection, box 1.1/27, "Dinner Time in the Mess Tent" (1898).
27 "Paddling Their Own Canoes on the St Lawrence," *Syracuse Daily Standard*, 31 May 1896.
28 "ACA Annual Meeting," *Peterborough Daily Review*, 14 Aug. 1883; St Lawrence County Historical Association (SLCHA), "Camp Circular for Grindstone Island" (1886); "In Brief," *Utica Daily Press*, 11 Aug. 1906.

29 "ACA Annual Meeting," *Peterborough Daily Review*, 18 Aug. 1883; "The ACA Meet, Lake George," *Forest and Stream*, 23 Aug. 1888; "Opening of the A.C.A. Meet," *Boating* (Sept. 1906): 18.
30 "The ACA Meet," *Forest and Stream*, 25 Aug. 1887.
31 "American Canoe Association: Twenty-First Annual Meet," *Forest and Stream*, 1 Sept. 1900.
32 "Pleasures of the Canoe Camp," *NYT*, 22 July 1894; FM, ACA Collection, box 1.2/4, "A Typical ACA Squaw Camp" (1890), and box 1.5A, Scrapbook of Walwin Barr (c. 1905–date unknown).
33 See Lady Mary Anne Barker, *The Bedroom and Boudoir* (London: Macmillan, 1878).
34 Conevery Bolton Valencius, *The Health of the Country: How American Settlers Understood Themselves and Their Land* (New York: Basic Books, 2002), 95–6, 112–13.
35 Scott, "Annual Camp," 117; "Pleasures of the Canoe Camp," *NYT*, 22 July 1894; "The Association Meet," *Forest and Stream*, 21 Aug. 1884.
36 FM, ACA Collection, box 1.1/5, "Mess Time in the Canadian Camp" (1883); box 1.1/16, "Camp of the Brooklyn Canoe Club" (1886).
37 "The ACA Meet of 1888: The Camp and the Association," *Forest and Stream*, 6 Sept. 1888.
38 "The ACA Meet of 1891," *Forest and Stream*, 20 Aug. 1891; FM, ACA Collection, box 1.1/5, "Mess Time in the Canadian Camp" (1883); box 1.1/16, "Camp of the Brooklyn Canoe Club" (1886); box 1.1/24, "Camp of the Deowainsta Canoe Club, Rome, NY" (1887).
39 Frederick L. Mix, ed., *American Canoe Association Yearbook* (New York: John C. Rankin Jr, 1888).
40 "Club Uniforms at the Meet," *Forest and Stream*, 18 June 1885.
41 Jennifer Craik, *Uniforms Exposed: From Conformity to Transgression* (Oxford: Berg, 2005), 45.
42 Mix, *American Canoe Association Yearbook*, 50.
43 "Canoe Sailors in Camp," *New York Sun*, 4 Aug. 1884.
44 "The ACA Meet of 1888," *Forest and Stream*, 6 Sept. 1888. See also "The ACA Meet, Lake George," *Forest and Stream*, 23 Aug. 1888.
45 Retaw, *Fragments*, 17–18; FM, ACA Collection, box 1.2/24, "A Camp Group at Bluff Point" (1895); box 1.3/1, "Louis Drake" (1910).
46 "The Great Canoe Meet," *Outing* 9, no. 2 (1886): 164–6.
47 "The 1884 Meet," *American Canoeist* 3, no. 8/9 (1884): 113. See also "ACA Camp," *Forest and Stream*, 14 Aug. 1884.
48 "The Canoe Men in Camp," *NYT*, 17 Aug. 1890.
49 Diana Crane, *Fashion and Its Social Agendas: Class, Gender, and Identity in Clothing* (Chicago: University of Chicago Press, 2000), 5.
50 FM, ACA Collection, box 1.1, 1.2, and 1.3, Photographs, 1880–1910. See also Retaw, *Fragments*, 17.

51 "Canoists [sic] Break Camp," *New York Sun*, 29 July 1894.
52 Patricia A. Cunningham, *Reforming Women's Fashion, 1850–1920: Politics, Health, and Art* (Kent: Kent State University Press, 2003).
53 Pauline Johnson, "Canoe and Canvas: The A.C.A. Meets in Canadian Waters," *Saturday Night*, 2 Sept. 1893.
54 C. Boyer Vaux, "Canoeing: The Ninth Annual Meet of the A.C.A.," *Outing* 13, no. 1 (1888): 74. See also Burchard, "Back to Grindstone," 138–43.
55 Brent Shannon, "Fashion, Masculinity, and the Cultivation of the Male Consumer in Britain, 1860–1914," *Victorian Studies* 46, no. 4 (2004): 613.
56 Textual and photographic accounts of tent interiors can be found in Flip, "Lake Champlain Canoe Meet"; FM, ACA Collection, box 1.1/27, "Scene Along the Shore" (1887); "Canoists [sic] Break Camp," *New York Sun*, 29 July 1894; FM, ACA Collection, box 1.2/18, "Camp of the Mohican Canoe Club" (1891), and box 1.3/2, "ACA Meet, Sugar Island" (1911).
57 Gulen Cevik, "American Style or Turkish Chair: The Triumph of Bodily Comfort," *Journal of Design History* 23, no. 4 (2010): 371.
58 Karen Halttunen, "From Parlor to Living Room: Domestic Space and the Culture of Personality," in *Consuming Visions: Accumulation and Display of Goods in America, 1880–1920*, ed. Simon J. Bronner (New York: W.W. Norton, 1989), 164–5. On the subject of comfort and the American home, see Katherine C. Grier, *Culture and Comfort: Parlor Making and Middle-Class Identity, 1850–1930* (London: Smithsonian Institution Press, 1997).
59 Halttunen, "Parlor to Living Room," 181, 188.
60 Ibid., 166–7.
61 Ibid., 167.
62 Ibid., 168.
63 Elizabeth Collins Cromley, "Sleeping Around: A History of Beds and Bedrooms," *Journal of Design History* 3, no. 1 (1990): 8. Emphasis in original.
64 "The Bedroom and Its Individuality," *Craftsman*, 9 Feb. 1906, as quoted in Cromley, "Sleeping Around," 8.
65 Cromley, "Sleeping Around."
66 Trent University Archives (TUA), 83-014/2, Paul Vernon, "Tales of the ACA" (1940).
67 J.I. Little, "Life without Conventionality: American Social Reformers as Summer Campers on Lake Memphremagog, Quebec, 1878–1905," *Journal of the Gilded Age and the Progressive Era* 9, no. 3 (2010): 282.
68 Columbine, "A Visit to the American Canoe Association," *Young Friend's Review* (1886): 68.
69 Daniel Freund, "The Battle for a Brighter America: A Social History of Natural Light, 1850–1935," (PhD dissertation, Columbia University, 2008).

70 William F. Bynum, *Science and the Practice of Medicine in the Nineteenth Century* (Cambridge: Cambridge University Press, 1994); Valencius, *Health of the Country*, 110–17. The belief in the remedial effects of sunshine and "the hygiene of fresh air" were both expressions of a more common faith in the "redeeming power of nature" to promote physical and moral health that the ACA encampments shared with sanatoria and "fresh air" camps. Annmarie Adams and Stacie Burke, "'Not a Shack in the Woods': Architecture for Tuberculosis in Muskoka and Toronto," *Canadian Bulletin of Medical History* 23, no. 2 (2006): 429–55; Phillip G. Mackintosh and Richard Anderson, "The *Toronto Star* Fresh Air Fund: Transcendental Rescue in a Modern City, 1900–1915," *Geographical Review* 99, no. 4 (2009): 540.

71 Paige Raibmon, "Living on Display: Colonial Visions of Aboriginal Domestic Space," *BC Studies* 140 (2003): 71.

72 Mary Douglas and Baron Isherwood, *The World of Goods: Towards an Anthropology of Consumption* (New York: W.W. Norton, 1979); Richard Wrightman Fox and T. Jackson Lears, eds., *The Culture of Consumption: Critical Essays in American History, 1880–1980* (New York: Pantheon Books, 1983); William Leach, *Land of Desire: Merchants, Power, and the Rise of a New American Culture* (New York: Pantheon Books, 1993); Walden, *Becoming Modern*; Donica Belisle, *Retail Nation: Department Stores and the Making of Modern Canada* (Vancouver: UBC Press, 2011).

73 Jessica Dunkin, "Manufacturing Landscapes: Place and Community at Glen Bernard Camp, 1924–1933," *Histoire sociale/Social History* 45, no. 89 (2012): 99. See also Leslie Paris, *Children's Nature: The Rise of the American Summer Camp* (New York: New York University Press, 2008), 103.

74 "The ACA Meet of 1890: Jessup's Neck," *Forest and Stream*, 21 Aug. 1890.

75 "Tents," *Forest and Stream*, 20 Dec. 1883. See also "The Canoe Men in Camp: Some of the Delights at Jessup's Neck," *NYT*, 17 Aug. 1890.

76 "Some More Snips from and Another Snap at the '89 Meet," *Forest and Stream*, 24 Oct. 1889.

77 Ibid.

78 Vernon, "Tales of the ACA."

79 FM, ACA Collection, box 1.5/4, Scrapbook of Thomas Hale (c. 1890–1900).

80 "The ACA Meet of 1890: Jessup's Neck," *Forest and Stream*, 21 Aug. 1890; "The ACA Meet of 1890 – III," *Forest and Stream*, 13 Nov. 1890.

81 Sydney Krause, "Penn's Elm and Edgar Huntly: Dark 'Instruction to the Heart,'" *American Literature* 66, no. 3 (1994): 464–5.

82 I consider acts of cultural appropriation like playing Indian and donning blackface in more detail in chapter 6.

83 Paige Raibmon, *Authentic Indians: Episodes of Encounter from the Late-Nineteenth-Century Northwest Coast* (Durham: Duke University Press, 2005), 124.

84 Frederick Jackson Turner, "The Significance of the Frontier in American History," *Annual Report of the American Historical Association for the Year 1893* (Washington, DC: Government Printing Office, 1894), 199–227.
85 Raibmon, *Authentic Indians*, 123. Curtis Hinsley refers to this as the "dehistoricized Indian," a product of the "end of Indian history." Curtis Hinsley, "Zunis and Brahmins: Cultural Ambivalence in the Gilded Age," in *Romantic Motives: Essays on Anthropological Sensibility*, ed. George W. Stocking Jr (Madison: University of Wisconsin Press, 1989), 170.
86 Edward Said, *Orientalism* (New York: Vintage Books, 1978), 2–3.
87 Leach, *Land of Desire*; Robert Rydell, *All the World's a Fair: Visions of Empire at American International Expositions, 1876–1916* (Chicago: University of Chicago Press, 1987). See also John Tchen, *New York before Chinatown: Orientalism and the Shaping of American Culture, 1776–1882* (Baltimore: Johns Hopkins University Press, 1999).
88 Leach, *Land of Desire*, 104.
89 Although he developed this line of thought in *Orientalism*, Said expands on these ideas further in his *Culture and Imperialism* (Toronto: Random House, 1993).
90 Kristin Hoganson, "Buying into Empire: American Consumption at the Turn of the Twentieth Century," in *Colonial Crucible: Empire in the Making of the Modern American State*, ed. Alfred McCoy and Francisco Antonio Scarano (Madison: University of Wisconsin Press, 2009), 249.
91 See "Pleasures of the Canoe Camp," *NYT*, 22 July 1894; FM, ACA Collection, box 1.2/30, "Visitors at Commodore Thorn's Camp" (1899).
92 J.I. Little, "Life without Conventionality: American Social Reformers as Summer Campers on Lake Memphremagog, Quebec, 1878–1905," *Journal of the Gilded Age and the Progressive Era* 9, no. 3 (2010): 283.
93 Martin Francis, "The Domestication of the Male? Recent Research on Nineteenth- and Twentieth-Century British Masculinity," *Historical Journal* 45, no. 3 (2002): 642.
94 Little, "Life without Conventionality," 283.
95 Angel Kwolek-Folland, "The Elegant Dugout: Domesticity and Moveable Culture in the United States, 1870–1900," *American Studies* 25, no. 2 (1984): 21–37.
96 Ibid., 35.
97 See, e.g., "Pleasures of the Canoe Camp," *NYT*, 22 July 1894; "The Canoe Men in Camp,"*NYT*, 17 Aug. 1890; Retaw, *Fragments*, 14. Karen Halttunen argues, "Such tongue-in-cheek identification of the summerhouse piazza as a 'parlor' and its nearby grove of trees as a 'drawing room' was clearly intended to undercut the formality of Victorian middle-class social life." Halttunen, "Parlor to Living Room," 158. However, I think such

naming was also about cultivating the encampments as a homeplace. Beyond legitimizing their presence on the sites, conceiving of the encampments as home belied the canoeists' deep attachment to the place.

98 "The ACA Meet of 1888: The Camp and the Association," *Forest and Stream*, 6 Sept. 1888.
99 "Around the Pine Camp Fire," *NYT*, 20 Aug. 1893.
100 David Schuster, *Neurasthenic Nation: America's Search for Health, Happiness, and Comfort, 1869–1920* (New Brunswick: Rutgers University Press, 2011).
101 Gail Bederman, *Manliness and Civilization: A Cultural History of Gender and Race in the United States, 1880–1917* (Chicago: University of Chicago Press, 1995), 25.
102 Ibid.
103 Halttunen, "Parlor to Living Room," 157–89.

6 Inhabiting

1 A typical day at the annual meeting is described in "ACA Camp," *Forest and Stream*, 14 Aug. 1884, and Retaw, *Fragments from the '88 Meet* (Montreal, 1888), 14–15.
2 Michael Haldrup, "Laid-Back Mobilities: Second Home Holidays in Time and Space," *Tourism Geographies* 6, no. 4 (2004): 445.
3 "The ACA Meet of 1890: Jessup's Neck," *Forest and Stream*, 21 Aug. 1890.
4 I owe this idea of a "micro-journey" to Jessica Dunkin and Bryan S.R. Grimwood, "Mobile Habitations in Canoe-scapes," in *Lifestyle Mobilities and Corporealities*, ed. Tara Duncan, Scott Cohen, and Maria Thulemark (Aldershot: Ashgate, 2013), 171–2.
5 "The ACA Meet of 1891," *Forest and Stream*, 20 Aug. 1891.
6 John C. Walsh and Steven High, "Rethinking the Concept of Community," *Histoire sociale/Social History* 32, no. 64 (1999): 255–74.
7 Abigail Van Slyck, *A Manufactured Wilderness: Summer Camps and the Shaping of American Youth, 1890–1960* (Minneapolis: University of Minnesota Press, 2006), 126.
8 "The ACA Meet of 1888: The Camp and the Association," *Forest and Stream*, 6 Sept. 1888.
9 In 1890, mess tent meals were offered on a sliding scale. "The ACA Meet of 1890 – II," *Forest and Stream*, 6 Nov. 1890.
10 *American Canoeist* 3, no. 8 (1884): 64.
11 Mystic Seaport Collections Research Center (MSCRC), Collection 291, box 23, folder 2, "Camp Circular for Lake George" (1888).
12 Not only is the description here more elaborate for the midday meal, but also on those occasions where separate prices were provided, dinner was

the most expensive. At the 1892 meet, dinner was 50 cents, while breakfast or supper were 35 cents. MSCRC, Collection 291, box 23, folder 2, "Camp Circular for Willsborough Point" (1892).

13 Canned goods were not a significant part of middle-class diets until the 1920s. Ruth Schwartz Cowan, "The 'Industrial Revolution' in the Home: Household Technology and Social Change in the 20th Century," *Technology and Culture* 17, no. 1 (1976): 8.

14 Fenimore Museum (FM), formerly the New York State Historical Association (NYSHA), American Canoe Association (ACA) Collection, box 1.1/24, "Camp of the Mohican Canoe Club, Albany, NY" (1887).

15 "ACA Meet," *Forest and Stream*, 31 July 1890; "The ACA Meet of 1890: Jessup's Neck," *Forest and Stream*, 21 Aug. 1890.

16 "Ready for the Races," *Syracuse Evening Herald*, 23 Aug. 1896.

17 Jeff Wiltse, *Contested Waters: A Social History of Swimming Pools in America* (Chapel Hill: University of North Carolina Press, 2007), 13, 4; Christopher Love, "Swimming and Gender in the Victorian World," in *A Social History of Swimming in England, 1800–1918: Splashing in the Serpentine* (London: Routledge, 2008), 19–35.

18 Love, *Social History of Swimming*, 20; Wiltse, *Contested Waters*, 9. See also Ken Cruikshank and Nancy Bouchier, "'Dirty Spaces': Environment, the State and Recreational Swimming in Hamilton Harbour, 1870–1946," *Sport History Review* 29, no. 1 (1998): 67.

19 Perhaps somewhat surprisingly given the recreational culture of the era, I have only found two references to hunting at the encampments, one in anticipation of the 1883 meet and one following it. "Correspondence," *American Canoeist* 2, no. 4 (1883): 59–61; "Stony Lake Canoe Congress," *Peterborough Examiner*, 23 Aug. 1883.

20 Other references to fishing can be found in W.S. Buell, "The American Canoe Association – The Meet of '99," *Outing* 35, no. 1 (1899): 87–9; FM, ACA Collection, box 1.6/2, D.B. Goodsell, "A Canoeing Reminiscence" (1936), 15–16.

21 "The Stony Lake Meet," *Peterborough Examiner*, 16 Aug. 1883.

22 "A Preliminary Business Meeting of the Association," *Peterborough Daily Review*, 22 Aug. 1883.

23 "The Stony Lake Meet," *Peterborough Examiner*, 16 Aug. 1883. See also "Around the Pine Camp Fire," *New York Times* (*NYT*), 20 Aug. 1893; "New Mab Is a Flyer," *New York Sun*, 22 Aug. 1896; John R. Blake, ed., *American Canoe Association Yearbook* (Toronto: Bryant Press, 1897), 48. Women's enthusiasm for and participation in fishing excursions at the encampments was part of a broader interest in piscatorial pursuits among the "gentle sex" in the late nineteenth century. David McMurray, "Rivaling the Gentleman in the Gentle Art: The Authority of the Victorian Woman Angler," *Sport History Review* 39, no. 2 (2008): 99–126.

24 William Knight, "'Our Sentimental Fisheries': Angling and State Fisheries Administration in 19th Century Ontario" (MA thesis, Trent University, 2006), 102.
25 Buell, "The Meet of '99," 87. See also "Around the Pine Camp Fire," *NYT*, 20 Aug. 1893, and *Forest and Stream*, 5 Sept. 1896.
26 FM, ACA Collection, box 1.5A, Scrapbook of Walwin Barr (c. 1905–date unknown).
27 For picnics, see "The ACA Meet," *Forest and Stream*, 23 Aug. 1883; FM, ACA Collection, box 1.2/1, "Picnic Lunch on a Cruise" (1889); Library and Archives Canada (LAC), R2730-1-0-E, "A Group at the American Canoe Association Camp at Gananoque, St Lawrence River" (1893).
28 "The ACA Meet, Lake George," *Forest and Stream*, 23 Aug. 1888.
29 Harry Eckford, "Camp Grindstone," *Century Magazine* 30, no. 4 (1885): 506; "The Canoe Men in Camp," *NYT*, 17 Aug. 1890; "Canoeing," *New York Sun*, 10 Aug. 1899.
30 "Canoe Race," *Evening News*, 5 Aug. 1904.
31 FM, ACA Collection, box 1.2/25, "Fun in Camp, A Base Ball Game" (1897).
32 "Canoeists Win at Baseball," *NYT*, 15 Aug. 1895; *Milwaukee Journal*, 21 Aug. 1897.
33 "The ACA Meet of 1892," *Forest and Stream*, 25 Aug. 1892. Boxing, wrestling, and tumbling are also mentioned in a brief account of the 1898 encampment. See "Thousand Islands," *Brooklyn Daily Eagle*, 14 Aug. 1898.
34 Kevin B. Wamsley and David Whitson, "Celebrating Violent Masculinities: The Boxing Death of Luther McCarty," *Journal of Sport History* 25, no. 3 (1998): 420–1.
35 "The ACA Meet of 1890: Jessup's Neck," *Forest and Stream*, 21 Aug. 1890; "Annual Canoe Meet," *NYT*, 4 Aug. 1895; FM, ACA Collection, box 1.5/4, Scrapbook of Thomas Hale, "Bluff Point, Lake Champlain, NY" (1895), and box 1.6/19, "Paddling among the Thousand Islands: Whiling Away the Days at Sugar Island" (1904).
36 FM, ACA Collection, box 1.2/23, "An Afternoon at Squaw Camp" (1894).
37 Ibid., box 1.1/26, "Camp of the Springfield Canoe Club" (1887); box 1.2/6, "A Little Music at the Mohican Camp" (1890); box 1.2/18, "Mohican Club" (1891); box 1.5/4, Scrapbook of Thomas Hale, "Camp Group Croton Point" (1894).
38 McMaster University Archives (MUA), E. Pauline Johnson Collection, box 3, file 1–5, Pauline Johnson, "The American Canoe Association at Grindstone Island," *Rudder* (Dec. 1896): 355–8.
39 "Fun for the Canoeists," *NYT*, 21 Aug. 1891. Reports of large campfires are included in "Canoeists Break Camp," *New York Sun*, 16 Aug. 1884; "The ACA Meet, Lake George," *Forest and Stream*, 23 Aug. 1888; "The Canoe Meet," *Troy Northern Budget*, 16 Aug. 1891.

40 Visitors planning to attend the 1907 meet were urged to bring instruments for the "camp orchestra." MSCRC, Colledtion 291, box 23, folder 2, "Camp Circular for Sugar Island" (1907).
41 "Our Trip to the A.C.A. Meet of '93," *Rockwood Review* 1, no. 6 (1894): n.p.
42 "The Association Meet," *Forest and Stream*, 21 Aug. 1884; "Canoeists Break Camp," *New York Sun*, 16 Aug. 1884. See also FM, ACA Collection, box 1.6/21, "A Reminiscence of Grindstone Island, 1884"; "Fun for the Canoeists," *NYT*, 22 Aug. 1890; "Tents All Pitched," *New York World*, 7 Aug. 1892; *Forest and Stream*, 1 Sept. 1892.
43 Hallie E. Bond, Joan Jacobs Brumberg, and Leslie Paris, *"A Paradise for Boys and Girls": Children's Camps in the Adirondacks* (Syracuse: Syracuse University Press, 2006), 48. In addition to alluding to the power of the shared experience of the campfire, Sharon Wall's analysis of Council Rings at children's camps highlights the spiritual aspects of the campfire. Sharon Wall, *The Nurture of Nature: Childhood, Antimodernism, and Ontario Summer Camps, 1920–1955* (Vancouver: UBC Press, 2009), 224–8.
44 "The ACA Meet of 1890 – III," *Forest and Stream*, 13 Aug. 1890; "The ACA Meet of 1891: Race Week," *Forest and Stream*, 27 Aug. 1891; "At the Canoe Camp," *New York Sun*, 25 Aug. 1896.
45 "Like a Serpent of Fire," *New York World*, 26 Aug. 1887; "Fun for the Canoeists," *NYT*, 22 Aug. 1890.
46 "Fun for the Canoeists," *NYT*, 22 Aug. 1890.
47 See Susan Lee Johnson, "Bulls, Bears, and Dancing Boys: Race, Gender, and Leisure in the California Gold Rush," *Radical History Review* 60 (1994): 25–6; Adele Perry, *On the Edge of Empire: Gender, Race, and the Making of British Columbia* (Toronto: University of Toronto Press, 2001), 29–30.
48 MSCRC, Collection 291, vol. 3, Meeting of the Executive Committee, 17 Nov. 1888.
49 "The ACA Meet of 1890 – III," *Forest and Stream*, 13 Aug. 1890.
50 "The Association Meet," *Forest and Stream*, 6 Aug. 1885; "The Annual Canoe Meet," *New York Evening Post*, 27 Aug. 1887; Ronald Hoffman, "The History of the American Canoe Association, 1880–1960" (PhD dissertation, Springfield College, 1967), 123.
51 "Noyac Bay Is Deserted," *NYT*, 24 Aug. 1890.
52 Goodsell, "A Canoeing Reminiscence," 6.
53 "Holidaying in the West," *Quebec Saturday Budget*, 7 Aug. 1897.
54 E.g., see "ACA Annual Meeting," *Peterborough Daily Review*, 21 Aug. 1883; "Sunday at the Canoe Camp," *NYT*, 8 Aug. 1892; FM, ACA Collection, box 1.1/29, "Divine Service" (1887); box 1.2/21, Henry D. Marsh, "Divine Service in Camp" (1891); box 1.5A, Scrapbook of Walwin Barr, "Divine Service, Sugar Island" (1907 and 1910).

55 "The Lake Champlain Canoe Meet," *Outing* 11, no. 3 (1887): 264.
56 D.J. Howell, "The International Canoe Meet," *Canadian Magazine* 15, no. 6 (1900): 516.
57 "The ACA Meet of 1890: Jessup's Neck," *Forest and Stream*, 21 Aug. 1890.
58 "Brooklyn's Social World," *New York Tribune*, 20 May 1900.
59 Eva L. Moffat, *The Ancestors of Daniel Freeman Britton of Westmoreland and Gananoque, 1808–1807* (n.p., 1953), 128; "Canoes and Canoeing," *New York Sun*, 11 June 1894.
60 "Canoes and Canoeing," *New York Sun*, 11 June 1894.
61 See "ACA Weddings," *Forest and Stream*, 26 June 1909. It is not clear whether or not they met through the ACA. However, images from Barr's personal album suggest a developing relationship between the young couple over the course of their presence at the Sugar Island encampments. FM, ACA Collection, box 1.5A, Scrapbook of Walwin Barr.
62 Trent University Archives (TUA), 83-014/2, Paul Vernon, "Tales of the ACA" (1940).
63 Steven Maynard, "Queer Musings on Masculinity and History," *Labour/Le Travail* 42 (Fall 1998): 191.
64 Ibid.; George Chauncey, *Gay New York: Gender, Urban Culture, and the Making of the Gay Male World, 1890–1994* (New York: Basic Books, 1994).
65 John Ibson, *Picturing Men: A Century of Male Relationships in Everyday American Photography* (Chicago: University of Chicago Press, 2006).
66 Maynard, "Queer Musings," 183–97.
67 Steven Maynard, "Rough Work and Rugged Men: The Social Construction of Masculinity in Working-Class History," *Labour/Le Travail* 23 (1989): 168. See, e.g., Arthur N. Gilbert, "Buggery and the British Navy, 1700–1861," *Journal of Social History* 10 (1976): 72–98; Judith C. Brown, "Lesbian Sexuality in Renaissance Italy: The Case of Sister Benedetta Carlini," *Signs* 9, no. 4 (1984): 751–8; Martha Vicinus, "Distance and Desire: English Boarding School Friendships, 1870–1920," *Signs* 9, no. 4 (1984): 600–22.
68 Photographic evidence of these excursions includes FM, ACA Collection, box 1.1/4, "All Ready for a Cruise" (1883); box 1.1/10, "Steamer Magic at ACA Camp" (1885); box 1.1/37, "A Thousand Island Sightseeing Trip" (1889).
69 Cecilia Morgan, *'A Happy Holiday': English Canadians and Transatlantic Tourism* (Toronto: University of Toronto Press, 2008), 15–16.
70 Haldrup, "Laid-back Mobilities," 447. Emphasis in original.
71 Ibid., 436.
72 J.I. Little, "Scenic Tourism on the Northeastern Borderland: Lake Memphremagog's Steamboat Excursions and Resort Hotels, 1850–1900," *Journal of Historical Geography* 35, no. 4 (2009): 716–42.

73 Hal K. Rothman, "Selling the Meaning of Place: Entrepreneurship, Tourism, and Community Transformation in the Twentieth-Century American West," *Pacific Historical Review* 65, no. 4 (1996): 526.
74 "The ACA Meet," *Forest and Stream*, 25 Aug. 1887; "Canoeists Go on Cruises," *NYT*, 12 Aug. 1895.
75 "The Old Van Cortlandt Manor," *NYT*, 22 July 1894.
76 Patricia Jasen, *Wild Things: Nature, Culture, and Tourism in Ontario, 1790–1914* (Toronto: University of Toronto Press, 1995), 7.
77 Rothman, "Selling the Meaning of Place," 526. See also Cindy S. Aron, *Working at Play: A History of Vacations in the United States* (New York: Oxford University Press, 1999), 132.
78 T. Jackson Lears, *No Place of Grace: Antimodernism and the Transformation of American Culture, 1880–1920* (Chicago: University of Chicago Press, 1994 [1981]).
79 E.g., "The ACA Meet," *Forest and Stream*, 23 Aug. 1883; FM, ACA Collection, box 1.2/1, "Picnic Lunch on a Cruise" (1888); "Snips from Snaps at the '89 Meet," *Forest and Stream*, 19 Sept. 1889; "The ACA Meet of 1892," *Forest and Stream*, 8 Sept. 1892; FM, ACA Collection, box 1.5A, Scrapbook of Walwin Barr.
80 "The 1884 Meet," *American Canoeist* 3, no. 8/9 (1884): 115.
81 "The Association Meet," *Forest and Stream*, 6 Aug. 1885.
82 Vernon, "Tales of the ACA."
83 Janet Miron, *Prisons, Asylums, and the Public: Institutional Visiting in the Nineteenth Century* (Toronto: University of Toronto Press, 2011).
84 Blake, *American Canoe Association Yearbook*, 72.
85 Mera Flaumenhaft, *The Civic Spectacle: Essays on Drama and Community* (London: Rowman and Littlefield, 1994), 1.
86 Don Handelman, *Models and Mirrors: Towards an Anthropology of Public Events* (Cambridge: Cambridge University Press, 1989), 15–16.
87 "A.C.A. Annual Meeting," *Peterborough Daily Review*, 23 Aug. 1883; MSCRC, Collection 291, box 23, folder 2, "Camp Circular for Lake George" (1888).
88 "The Association Meet," *Forest and Stream*, 6 Aug. 1885.
89 Flip, "Lake Champlain Canoe Meet," *Outing* 11, no. 3 (1887): 264.
90 See also "Canoeists on the St Lawrence," *Utica Daily Press*, 12 Aug. 1898; "Canoeists Enjoying Camp Life," *New York Sun*, 14 Aug. 1901; "Canoeists in Camp," *Syracuse Daily Journal*, 9 Aug. 1905.
91 "What They Did at Stony Lake of an Evening," *American Canoeist* 2, no. 8 (1883): 125. See also Eckford, "Camp Grindstone," 499, and "The Association Meet," *Forest and Stream*, 6 Aug. 1885.
92 Keith Walden, *Becoming Modern in Toronto: The Industrial Exhibition and the Shaping of a Late Victorian Culture* (Toronto: University of Toronto Press, 1997), 37.

Notes to pages 131–4

93 Mel Watkins, "Foreword," in *Inside the Minstrel Mask: Readings in Nineteenth-Century Blackface Minstrelsy*, ed. Annemarie Bean, James Vernon Hatch, and Brooks Macnamara (Hanover: University Press of New England, 1996), ix; Alexander Saxton, *The Rise and Fall of the White Republic: Class Politics and Mass Culture in Nineteenth-Century America* (London: Verso, 2003), 165.
94 Robert C. Toll, *Blacking Up: The Minstrel Show in America* (New York: Oxford University Press, 1974), 30–1, 52.
95 Ibid., 53.
96 Stump speech referenced in "ACA Annual Meeting," *Peterborough Daily Review*, 18 Aug. 1883.
97 Leslie Paris, *Children's Nature: The Rise of the American Summer Camp* (New York: New York University Press, 2008), 191.
98 Greg Dening, *Performances* (Chicago: University of Chicago Press, 1996), 105.
99 Paris, *Children's Nature*, 191.
100 Robert Taft, *Photography and the American Scene* (New York: Dover, 1964), 352–3.
101 R.B. Burchard, "Canoeing," *Outing* 29, no. 1 (1896): 84. See also "New Mab Is a Flyer," *New York Sun*, 22 Aug. 1896.
102 "The ACA Meet of 1892," *Forest and Stream*, 25 Aug. 1892. A program for the tableaux is included in FM, ACA Collection, box 1.6/12.
103 R.B. Burchard, "Back to Grindstone: The Canoe Camp," *Outing* 29, no. 2 (1896): 141.
104 "The Association Meet," *Forest and Stream*, 21 Aug. 1884.
105 "Canoeists Break Camp," *New York Sun*, 16 Aug. 1884.
106 Paige Raibmon, *Authentic Indians: Episodes of Encounter from the Late-Nineteenth-Century Northwest Coast* (Durham: Duke University Press, 2005), 73. See esp. chapter 3, "Theatres of Contact: The Kwakwaka'wakw at the Fair," 50–73.
107 C. Bowyer Vaux, "The Canoeing of To-Day: Second Paper," *Outing* 16, no. 3 (1890): 215. There may also have been a circus in 1898. See "At the Canoe Association Camp," *New York Tribune*, 9 Aug. 1898.
108 Vaux, "Canoeing of To-Day," 216.
109 "The Tenth Annual Meet of the American Canoe Association," *Sail and Paddle* 7, no. 9 (1889): 200.
110 Janet M. Davis, *The Circus Age: Culture and Society under the American Big Top* (Chapel Hill: University of North Carolina Press, 2002), 10.
111 Ibid., 26.
112 "The ACA Meet of 1891," *Forest and Stream*, 20 Aug. 1891.
113 Images of the spectacle were included in the 1901, 1902, and 1904 Yearbooks. Herb Begg, ed., *American Canoe Association Yearbook* (New York City: Forest and Stream Publishing, 1901), 37; Francis Johnson Burrage, ed., *American*

Canoe Association Yearbook (n.p., 1902), 74; John Sears Wright, ed., *American Canoe Association Yearbook* (n.p., 1904), insert between 30 and 31.
114 Howell, "International Canoe Meet," 520.
115 John R. Haddad, "The Wild West Turns East: Audience, Ritual, and Regeneration in Buffalo Bill's Boxer Uprising," *American Studies* 49, no. 3/4 (2008): 5–38.
116 Ibid., 5–6.
117 Ibid., 8.
118 For more on the midway, see Walden, *Becoming Modern*, 286–91; Robert Rydell, *All the World's a Fair: Visions of Empire at American International Expositions, 1876–1916* (Chicago: University of Chicago Press, 1987), 40–1, 55–68.

7 Competing

1 "Canoeists on Lake George," *New York Sun*, 11 Aug. 1882. Emphasis added.
2 Columbine, "A Visit to the American Canoe Association," *Young Friend's Review* (1886): 68.
3 E. Pauline Johnson, "Princes of the Paddle," *Toronto Saturday Night* (9 Sept. 1893): 6.
4 Lorgnette, "A Woman at a Canoe Race," *Outing* 24, no. 6 (1894):422. See, e.g., Fenimore Museum (FM), formerly the New York State Historical Association (NYSHA), American Canoe Association (ACA) Collection, box 1.2/8, S.R. Stoddard, "Visitors' Day, Main Dock" (1890); box 1.2/20, S.R. Stoddard, "Willsborough Point, Visitors Day" (1891).
5 Retaw, *Fragments from the '88 Meet* (Montreal, 1888), 24.
6 My approach draws inspiration from Greg Dening's artful account of the mutiny on the Bounty. Greg Dening, *Mr Bligh's Bad Language: Passion, Power and Theatre on the Bounty* (Cambridge: Cambridge University Press, 1992). See also Greg Dening, *Performances* (Chicago: University of Chicago Press, 1996); Keith Walden, *Becoming Modern in Toronto: The Industrial Exhibition and the Shaping of a Late Victorian Culture* (Toronto: University of Toronto Press, 1997); John C. Walsh, "Performing Public Memory and Re-placing Home in the Ottawa Valley, 1900–1958," in *Placing Memory and Remembering Place in Canada*, ed. James Opp and John C. Walsh (Vancouver: UBC Press, 2010), 25–56.
7 Jamie Benidickson, *Idleness, Water, and a Canoe: Reflections on Paddling for Pleasure* (Toronto: University of Toronto Press, 1997), 110. See also C. Fred Johnston, "Canoe Sport in Canada: Anglo-American Hybrid?" in *Canexus: The Canoe in Canadian Culture*, ed. James Raffan and Bert Horwood (Toronto: Betelguese Books, 1988), 59–60.
8 Anna Jameson, *Winter Studies and Summer Rambles in Canada* (New York: Wiley and Putnam, 1839), 294.

Notes to pages 139–41

9 Carolyn Podruchny, *Making the Voyageur World: Travelers and Traders in the North American Fur Trade* (Toronto: University of Toronto Press, 2006), 184–7.
10 Jean Murray Cole, "Kawartha Lakes Regattas," in *Nastawgan: The Canadian North by Canoe & Snowshoe*, ed. Bruce W. Hodgins and Margaret Hobbs (Toronto: Dundurn Press, 1987), 203–10.
11 Gillian Poulter, *Becoming Native in a Foreign Land: Sport, Visual Culture, and Identity in Montreal, 1840–1885* (Vancouver: UBC Press, 2009), 28.
12 *Halifax Free Press*, 11 July 1826; *Halifax Nova Scotian*, 24 Aug. 1836; *Peterborough Examiner*, 15 Sept. 1859.
13 Adele Perry, *On the Edge of Empire: Gender, Race, and the Making of British Columbia* (Toronto: University of Toronto Press, 2001); Ann Laura Stoler, *Carnal Knowledge and Imperial Power: Race and the Intimate in Colonial Rule* (Berkeley: University of California Press, 2002).
14 Peter L. Lindsay, "The Impact of Military Garrisons on the Development of Sport in British North America," *Canadian Journal of History of Sport and Physical Education* 1, no. 1 (1970): 33. See also Benidickson, *Idleness*, 111.
15 Johnston, "Canoe Sport in Canada," 63–4.
16 "Canoeing," *Ottawa*, 21 July 1900; "Canoeing," *Ottawa Citizen*, 28 July 1902; "Canoeing," *Ottawa Daily Citizen*, 27 July 1903; "Canoeing," *Ottawa Citizen*, 6 July 1906.
17 "The A.C.A. Canoe Meet," *Outing* 11, no. 1 (1887): 95–6; "Discussed in Canoe Camp," *New York Times* (*NYT*), 15 Aug. 1892.
18 See, e.g., "Along the St Lawrence," *New York Tribune*, 28 July 1901.
19 W.P. Stephens, *Traditions and Memories of American Yachting: The 50th Anniversary Edition* (Brooklin: Wooden Boat Publications, 1989), 1–5.
20 John Rousmaniere, *The America's Cup 1851–1983* (London: Pelham Books, 1983).
21 Key texts on amateurism in Canada, the United States, and Great Britain include the following: Alan Metcalfe, "The Growth of Organized Sport and the Development of Amateurism in Canada, 1807–1914," in *Not Just a Game: Essays in Canadian Sport Sociology*, ed. Jean Harvey and Hart Cantelon (Ottawa: University of Ottawa Press, 1988), 33–50; S.W. Pope, "Amateurism and American Sports Culture: The Invention of an Athletic Tradition in the United States, 1870–1900," *International Journal of the History of Sport* 13, no. 3 (1996): 290–309; Dilwyn Porter and Stephen Wagg, eds., *Amateurism in British Sport: It Matters Not Who Won or Lost?* (London: Taylor and Francis, 2007).
22 "Features of the Meet at Croton Point, on the Hudson," *NYT*, 15 July 1894.
23 "A Year's Work," *NYT*, 8 June 1881. See also Harry Eckford, "Camp Grindstone," *Century Magazine* 30, no. 4 (1885): 502; Cruiser, "The 'Musquito' Fleet," *Gloversville Daily Leader*, 14 Aug. 1891; Caspar W. Whitney, "Annual Meet of the American Canoe Association," *Harper's Weekly*, 2 Sept. 1893.

24 Mary O. Furner refers to the late nineteenth century as a "professionalization period" in *Advocacy and Objectivity: A Crisis in the Professionalization of American Social Science, 1865–1905* (New Brunswick: Transaction Publishers, 2011), xi.
25 Tara Magdalinski, *Sport, Technology, and the Body: The Nature of Performance* (New York: Routledge, 2000), 16.
26 Bruce Kidd, *The Struggle for Canadian Sport* (Toronto: University of Toronto Press, 1996), 33.
27 Clark Davis, "The Corporate Reconstruction of Middle-Class Manhood," in *The Middling Sorts: Explorations in the History of the American Middle Class*, ed. Burton Bledstein and Robert D. Johnston (New York: Routledge, 2001), 201–2.
28 Kidd, *Struggle for Canadian Sport*, 33.
29 Porter and Wagg, *Amateurism in British Sport*, 4.
30 Kidd, *Struggle for Canadian Sport*, 27.
31 Ibid., 28.
32 Ibid.
33 Mary Louise Adams, *Artistic Impressions: Figure Skating, Masculinity, and the Limits of Sport* (Toronto: University of Toronto Press, 2011), 168.
34 Mystic Seaport Research Collections Center (MSCRC), Collection 291, box 23, folder 2, "Camp Circular for Lake George" (1881); William M. Carter, ed., *American Canoe Association Yearbook* (Trenton, NJ: John L. Murphy Publishing, 1887), 29.
35 J.N. MacKendrick, "The Definition of an Amateur," *Forest and Stream*, 6 Nov. 1890.
36 "The ACA Meet of 1890 – II," *Forest and Stream*, 6 Nov. 1890. See also "Discussed in Canoe Camp," *NYT*, 15 Aug. 1892.
37 Colin Howell, *Blood, Sweat, and Cheers: Sport and the Making of Modern Canada* (Toronto: University of Toronto Press, 2001), 63.
38 MSCRC, Collection 291, vol. 4, Special Meeting of the Executive Committee, 11 Aug. 1899, and Meeting of the Executive Committee, 27 July 1903.
39 E.B. Edwards, "The Meet," *American Canoeist* 2, no. 6 (1883): 82.
40 "Notes About the Meet," *Forest and Stream*, 20 Aug. 1885.
41 "American Canoe Association," *Forest and Stream*, 28 Aug. 1884. Other races were introduced with similar ends. See "The Annual Canoe Meet," *New York Evening Post*, 27 Aug. 1887; "Paddling Their Own Canoes on the St Lawrence," *Syracuse Daily Standard*, 31 May 1896.
42 "The Canoe Association," *NYT*, 25 July 1885.
43 "The Perfect Canoe," *Harper's New Monthly Magazine* 56 (1877–78): 754–5; "About Canoeing," *Lowell Daily Courier*, 11 May 1882.
44 Robert Rydell, *All the World's a Fair: Visions of Empire at American International Expositions, 1876–1916* (Chicago: University of Chicago Press, 1987), 4.

45 Ibid., 5.
46 "A Year's Work," *NYT*, 8 June 1881.
47 Bernard Lightman, ed., *Victorian Science in Context* (Chicago: University of Chicago Press, 1997).
48 A 2011 exhibition, entitled "The Perfect Canoe?," at the Antique Boat Museum in Clayton, NY, captured the thrust of this project. As the title suggests, there was no single answer to the question of the perfect canoe.
49 MSCRC, Collection 291, vol. 3, Regatta Committee Report, 1890.
50 Alan Trachtenberg, *The Incorporation of America: Culture and Society in the Gilded Age* (New York: Hill and Wang, 1982), 38.
51 Ibid., 39.
52 Magdalinski, *Sport, Technology*, 16.
53 George P. Douglass, ed., *American Canoe Association Yearbook* (Newark: Press of the Holbrook Printing Co., 1894), 14.
54 "The Meet of 1884," *Forest and Stream*, 8 Nov. 1883.
55 Robert Tyson, "The Sailing Regulations of the American Canoe Association," *Outing* 3, no. 4 (1884): 296.
56 "The Canoes of 1884," *Forest and Stream*, 4 Sept. 1884.
57 "The Regatta Programme for 1886," *Forest and Stream*, 8 Oct. 1885.
58 "The ACA Meet: Race Week," *Forest and Stream*, 28 Aug. 1890.
59 "Canoeing," *Toronto Daily Mail*, 12 July 1881.
60 "Lake George Meet," *Forest and Stream*, 25 Aug. 1881.
61 "The Meet," *American Canoeist* 2, no. 6 (1883): 82. Emphasis added.
62 "Prizes for 1886," *Forest and Stream*, 25 Feb. 1886.
63 "ACA Annual Meeting," *Peterborough Daily Review*, 20 Aug. 1883. A detailed list of donations can also be found in "The Association Meet," *Forest and Stream*, 6 Aug. 1885.
64 "Canoeists in Camp," *Auburn Morning Dispatch*, 23 Aug. 1886.
65 Alan Metcalfe, "The Meaning of Amateurism: A Case Study of Canadian Sport, 1884–1970," *Canadian Journal of the History of Sport* 26, no. 2 (1995): 33.
66 I recognize that what on the surface appeared to oppose modernity was often deeply entangled in and committed to its development. Sharon Wall, *The Nurture of Nature: Childhood, Antimodernism, and Ontario Summer Camps, 1920–1955* (Vancouver: UBC Press, 2009), 4–5.
67 "The Meet of 1886: Race Week," *Forest and Stream*, 2 Sept. 1886.
68 See chapter IX of the Bylaws, entitled "Duties of the Regatta Committee." Douglass, *American Canoe Association Yearbook*, 13.
69 MSCRC, Collection 291, vol. 4, Meeting of the Executive Committee, 15 Nov. 1902; "Canoe Association Changes," *NYT*, 25 Oct. 1903.
70 "Racing in Canoes," *New York Evening Post*, 9 Nov. 1897.
71 "Fun with Sail and Paddle," *NYT*, 3 Aug. 1890.
72 "Correspondence," *American Canoeist* 2, no. 1 (1883): 27.

73 MSCRC, Collection 291, vol. 3, Annual Meeting, 27 Aug. 1886.
74 "The ACA Meet of 1891," *Forest and Stream*, 20 Aug. 1891.
75 "At the Canoe Camp," *Buffalo Morning Express*, 15 Aug. 1899; "Commodore Is Here," *Post Express*, 23 Aug. 1904.
76 "The Association Meet," *Forest and Stream*, 6 Aug. 1885.
77 "Racing in Canoes," *New York Evening Post*, 9 Nov. 1897.
78 "Canoe Racing on Lake George and Trotting in Rochester," *New York Sun*, 12 Aug. 1882; "American Canoe Association," *New York Herald*, 16 Aug. 1886; "Canoe Racing," *NYT*, 29 Sept. 1889.
79 "Racing in Canoes," *New York Evening Post*, 9 Nov. 1897.
80 "With Sails and Paddles," *New York Herald*, 23 Aug. 1886.
81 E.L.F., "The Canoe Meet," *Buffalo Daily Courier*, 25 Aug. 1886; "The Canoe Fleet Disbanded," *New York Herald*, 28 Aug. 1886.
82 "Canoeing," *New York Sun*, 10 Aug. 1899.
83 W.S. Buell, "The American Canoe Association – The Meet of '99," *Outing* 35, no. 1 (1899): 88.
84 Richard Schneirov, Shelton Stromquist, and Nick Salvatore, eds., *The Pullman Strike and the Crisis of the 1890s: Essays on Labor and Politics* (Chicago: University of Illinois Press, 1999).
85 "Canoe Race Flat Failure," *Rochester Democrat Chronicle*, 13 Aug. 1899.
86 Hoffman, "American Canoe Association," 47; "Canoeing," *Forest and Stream*, 7 Apr. 1900.
87 "The Canoeists' Convention," *New York Evening Telegram*, 5 Aug. 1880.
88 "Canoeing," *New York Evening Post*, 19 Aug. 1891; Lorgnette, "A Woman," 421–4; "Canoeists in Camp," *New York Herald*, 2 Aug. 1885; "Arrivals at Canoe Camp," *NYT*, 16 Aug. 1895; "Canoeing," *New York Sun*, 10 Aug. 1899.
89 "The Thousand Isles," *NYT*, 25 Aug. 1889.
90 "The Canoe Men's Holiday," *NYT*, 14 Aug. 1881.
91 Roberta Park, "Sport, Gender, and Society in Transatlantic Victorian Perspective," *International Journal of the History of Sport* 24, no. 12 (2007): 1572.
92 Patricia Vertinsky, *The Eternally Wounded Woman: Women, Doctors, and Exercise in the Late Nineteenth Century* (Toronto: St Martin's Press, 1990).
93 Patricia Marks, *Bicycles, Bangs, and Bloomers: The New Woman in the Popular Press* (Lexington: University of Kentucky Press, 1990); Lois Banner, *American Beauty: A Social History through Two Centuries of the American Idea, Ideal, and Image of the Beautiful Woman* (New York: Knopf, 1983).
94 Kathleen E. McCrone, "Women's Sport and Dress Reform," in *Playing the Game: Sport and the Physical Emancipation of English Women, 1870–1914* (Lexington: University of Kentucky Press, 1988), 216–46.

95 Colin Howell, *Northern Sandlots: A Social History of Maritime Baseball* (Toronto: University of Toronto Press, 1995), 81–2.
96 Susan K. Cahn, *Coming on Strong: Gender and Sexuality in Twentieth-Century Women's Sport* (New York: Free Press, 1994), 28–9.
97 M. Ann Hall, *The Girl and the Game: A History of Women's Sport in Canada* (Peterborough: Broadview Press, 2002), 20.
98 Kidd, *Struggle for Canadian Sport*, 27.
99 MSCRC, Collection 291, vol. 3, Regatta Committee Report, 1890.
100 "The Canoe Men in Camp," *NYT*, 17 Aug. 1890.
101 Thomas H. Stryker, ed., *American Canoe Association Yearbook* (Rome: Press of the Rome Sentinel Co., 1896), 60–1.
102 "Canoeists Greatly Interested," *NYT*, 25 Aug. 1891. These same races were part of the program in 1897 and 1898 as well. "Canoeing," *Outing* 31, no. 1 (1897): 97; "Canoe Races for Women," *NYT*, 11 Aug. 1898.
103 Stryker, *American Canoe Association Yearbook*; MSCRC, Collection 291, vol. 4, Special Meeting of the Executive Committee, 11 Aug. 1899.
104 "The ACA Meet of 1891: Race Week," *Forest and Stream*, 27 Aug. 1891.
105 Howell, *Northern Sandlots*, 86.
106 "The Second Day of the Regatta," *NYT*, 13 Aug. 1881.
107 Poulter, *Becoming Native*, 131.
108 There are a few exceptions. See, e.g., Fred Mason, "R. Tait McKenzie's Medical Work and Early Exercise Therapies for People with Disabilities," *Sport History Review* 39, no. 1 (2008): 45–70, and Steve Bailey, *Athlete First: A History of the Paralympic Movement* (London: Wiley, 2008).
109 "The Canoe Beat the Skiff," *NYT*, 15 Aug. 1893.
110 W.P. Stephens, "The Past and Future of American Canoeing, 1880–1900," *Forest and Stream*, 6 Jan. 1900; C. Bowyer Vaux, "The Canoeing of Today," *Outing* 16, no. 2 (1890): 135.
111 Maurice D. Wilt, "Canoeing under Sail" in *Sailing Craft*, ed. Edwin J. Schoettle (New York: Macmillan, 1928), n.p.; FM, ACA Collection, box 1.1/20, Photographs from Grindstone Island, 1886; box 1.1/33, Photographs from Lake George, 1888; box 1.2/6, Photographs from Jessup's Neck, 1890.
112 Stephens, *Traditions and Memories*, 172.
113 "The Canoe Camp," *Lowell Courier*, 25 Aug. 1888; "The ACA Meet: Race Week," *Forest and Stream*, 28 Aug. 1890; McMaster University Archives (MUA), box 9, file 27, Pauline Johnson, "Sail and Paddle," *Illustrated Buffalo Express*, c. 1893; "Fine Sport in Canoes," *NYT*, 1 July 1895.
114 "The ACA Meet: Race Week," *Forest and Stream*, 28 Aug. 1890.
115 Allen Guttmann, *From Ritual to Record: The Nature of Modern Sports* (New York: Columbia University Press, 1978).
116 Howell, *Blood, Sweat, and Cheers*, 89.

Notes to pages 153–6

117 Timothy Mitchell, *Colonising Egypt* (Berkeley: University of California Press, 1991).
118 Retaw, *Fragments*, 3.
119 "The Meet of 1884," *Forest and Stream*, 8 Nov. 1883; "The Association Meet," *Forest and Stream*, 21 Aug. 1884; "American Canoe Association," *Forest and Stream*, 28 Aug. 1884; "ACA Regatta Rules, etc. – Suggestions," *Forest and Stream*, 27 Sept. 1888. The line-up of officials depended, in part, on the availability of volunteers. There appears to have been some difficulty in arranging for race officials, particularly among the "non-racing men," which may explain the overlap between competitors and officials.
120 "ACA Regatta Rules, etc. – Suggestions," *Forest and Stream*, 27 Sept. 1888.
121 David A. Poe, "The Status of the Clerk of the Course," *Forest and Stream*, 10 Aug. 1889; "ACA Regatta Rules, etc. – Suggestions," *Forest and Stream*, 27 Sept. 1888; "American Canoe Association," *Forest and Stream*, 28 Aug. 1884.
122 "American Canoe Association," *Forest and Stream*, 28 Aug. 1884; "American Canoe Association," *Forest and Stream*, 14 Oct. 1886.
123 Tyson, "Sailing Regulations," 297; FM, ACA Collection, box 1.1/22, "Viewing the Corpse" (1886).
124 "Argonauts Take Canoing [sic] Shield," *New York Herald*, 20 Aug. 1901; "Canoe Crews' Close Races," *NYT*, 21 Aug. 1902.
125 "Canoeing," *New York Sun*, 15 Aug. 1897; "Races at the Canoe Camp," *Brooklyn Daily Eagle*, 26 Aug. 1896.
126 "At the Canoe Camp," *New York Sun*, 25 Aug. 1896.
127 "Programme of the ACA Regatta," *Forest and Stream*, 8 Jan. 1885.
128 "The Meet of 1886: Race Week," *Forest and Stream*, 2 Sept. 1886.
129 Johnson, "Princes of the Paddle," 6.
130 Lorgnette, "A Woman," 421.
131 As there are no photographs of the women's races, it is difficult to know what they would have worn to compete. The only extant regatta photograph (at least to my knowledge) with female competitors features two women wearing long skirts and long-sleeved blouses in the midst of a jousting duel. Lawrence E. Zuk, ed., *American Canoe Association 100th Anniversary Yearbook* (Concord: Minutemen Printing Corp., 1980), 13.
132 Douglass, *American Canoe Association Yearbook*, 17.
133 "Notes About the Meet," *Forest and Stream*, 20 Aug. 1885; "The ACA Meet: Race Week," *Forest and Stream*, 28 Aug. 1890.
134 "The ACA Meet of 1891: Race Week," *Forest and Stream*, 27 Aug. 1891.
135 "The Association Meet," *Forest and Stream*, 21 Aug. 1884.
136 "Notes About the Meet," *Forest and Stream*, 20 Aug. 1885.
137 "The Association Races at Stony Lake," *Forest and Stream*, 6 Sept. 1883.
138 Buell, "The Meet of '99," 88.
139 Douglass, *American Canoe Association Yearbook*, 14.

140 "Pleasant Time at the Canoe Camp," *New York Sun*, 20 Aug. 1896.
141 "Exciting Contests at the ACA Encampment," *Brooklyn Daily Eagle*, 19 Aug. 1902.
142 "The Association Meet," *Forest and Stream*, 21 Aug. 1884.
143 "Last Days of the River Season," *Syracuse Evening Herald*, 30 Aug. 1896; "The Races at Gananoque," *Montreal Gazette*, 16 Aug. 1899.
144 "At Grindstone Island," *Rochester Democrat Chronicle*, 26 Aug. 1886; "The Meet of 1886: Race Week," *Forest and Stream*, 2 Sept. 1886.
145 Douglass, *American Canoe Association Yearbook*, 16–17.
146 Lorgnette, "A Woman," 422; Flip, "Lake Champlain Canoe Meet," *Outing* 11, no. 3 (1887): 263.
147 See, e.g., FM, ACA Collection, box 1.1/25, "Watching the Trophy Race from West Shore" (1887).
148 "Canoes on Kill Von Kull," *NYT*, 25 June 1882.
149 "Canoe Racing on Lake George," *New York Sun*, 10 Aug. 1882.
150 R.B. Burchard, "The Real Canoeing," *Outing* 36, no. 1 (1899): 79.
151 "The Canoe Meeting,"*NYT*, 20 Aug. 1881.
152 "The Association Races at Stony Lake," *Forest and Stream*, 6 Sept. 1883.
153 Unknown, *American Canoe Association Book* (New York: Vaux and Co., 1883), 20.
154 Douglass, *American Canoe Association Yearbook*, 17.
155 Ibid., 16.
156 "The ACA Meet: Race Week," *Forest and Stream*, 28 Aug. 1890.
157 Lorgnette, "A Woman," 424.

8 Working

1 Fenimore Museum (FM), formerly the New York State Historical Association (NYSHA), American Canoe Association (ACA) Collection, box 1.1/24, "Work and Fun in Camp" (1887).
2 Theodore Corbett, *The Making of American Resorts: Saratoga Springs, Ballston Spa, Lake George* (Piscataway: Rutgers University Press, 2001).
3 Patricia Jasen, "Close Encounters," in *Wild Things: Nature, Culture, and Tourism in Ontario, 1790–1914* (Toronto: University of Toronto Press, 1995), 133–49; Tina Loo, "Of Moose and Men: Hunting for Masculinities in British Columbia, 1880–1939," *Western Historical Quarterly* 32, no. 3 (2001): 296–319; Karl Jacoby, *Crimes against Nature: Squatters, Poachers, Thieves, and the Hidden History of American Conservation* (Berkeley: University of California Press, 2001); Scott E. Giltner, *Hunting and Fishing in the New South: Black Labor and White Leisure after the Civil War* (Baltimore: Johns Hopkins University Press, 2008); Anne Gilbert Coleman, "The Rise of the House of Leisure: Outdoor Guides, Practical

Knowledge, and Industrialization," *Western Historical Quarterly* 42, no. 4 (2011): 436–57.
4 The intersections between the history of sport and labour history have largely centred on working-class leisure or labour organizing/disputes in professional sport. See, e.g., Martin H. Blatt and Martha K. Norkunas, eds., *Work, Recreation, and Culture: Essays in American Labor History* (New York: Garland, 1996); Lynne Marks, *Revivals and Roller Rinks: Religion, Leisure, and Identity in Late-Nineteenth-Century Small-Town Ontario* (Toronto: University of Toronto Press, 1997); Gerald Gems, "Welfare Capitalism and Blue-Collar Sport: The Legacy of Labour Unrest," *Rethinking History* 5, no. 1 (2001): 43–58. Historians of tourism have been more attune to questions of labour and leisure. See, e.g., Karen Dubinsky, *The Second Greatest Disappointment: Honeymooners, Heterosexuality, and the Tourist Industry at Niagara Falls* (Toronto: Between the Lines Press, 1999); Cecilia Morgan, "Porters, Guides, and Middle-Class Tourists," in *'A Happy Holiday': English Canadians and Transatlantic Tourism* (Toronto: University of Toronto Press, 2008), 31–58; Thomas G. Andrews, "'Made by Toile'? Tourism, Labor, and the Construction of the Colorado Landscape," *Journal of American History* 92, no. 3 (2005): 837–63; LouAnn Wurst, "'Human Accumulations': Class and Tourism at Niagara Falls," *International Journal of Historical Archaeology* 15, no. 2 (2011): 254–66.
5 Wurst, "Human Accumulations," 256–7.
6 Andrews, "Made by Toile," 837, 840.
7 Ibid., 841.
8 One exception to this appears in Charles Britton's letter to the Department of Indian Affairs (DIA) regarding the purchase of Sugar Island. He notes that the ACA "gives employment to our labouring men, boatmen, tent makers, etc. and also largely increases the patronage of our River Boats and in many other ways increases business on the River." Library and Archives Canada (LAC), RG 10, vol. 2718, file 144, 001–53, Letter from C.E. Britton to Hon. Clifford Sifton, 19 Feb. 1901.
9 Robert Tyson, "Laying Out the Course on Stony Lake," *American Canoeist* 2, no. 5 (1883): 66–8.
10 Peter Bailey, *Leisure and Class in Victorian England: Rational Recreation and the Contest for Control, 1830–1885* (Buffalo: University of Toronto Press, 1978).
11 J.I. Little, "Life without Conventionality: American Social Reformers as Summer Campers on Lake Memphremagog, Quebec, 1878–1905," *Journal of the Gilded Age and the Progressive Era* 9, no. 3 (2010): 290.
12 For more on paternalism in industrial labour relations, see Daniel J. Walkowitz, *Worker City, Company Town* (Urbana: University of Illinois Press, 1978); Jacquelyn Dowd Hall, James L. Leloudis, Robert Rodgers

Notes to pages 164–6

Korstad, Mary Murphy, Lu Ann Jones, and Christopher B. Daly, *Like a Family: The Making of a Southern Cottage Mill World* (Chapel Hill: University of North Carolina Press, 1987).

13 Vladimir Kapor, *Local Colour: A Travelling Concept* (Bern: Peter Lang, 2009), 132.
14 D.J. Howell, "The International Canoe Meet," *Canadian Magazine* 15, no. 6 (1900): 513–20.
15 Andrews, "Made by Toile," 848; Morgan, 'A Happy Holiday,' 7. See also Dubinsky, *The Second Greatest Disappointment*, 74–83.
16 "The ACA Meet," *Forest and Stream*, 31 July 1884; "The Association Meeting," *Forest and Stream*, 21 Aug. 1884; "The Executive Committee Meeting," *Forest and Stream*, 18 Nov. 1886; "The ACA Meet, Lake George," *Forest and Stream*, 23 Aug. 1888.
17 "1908 Meet," in Oscar J. West, ed., *American Canoe Association Yearbook* (Chicago: Press of De Land, Coles and Putnam, 1909), 48.
18 "Secretary Treasurer's Report, 1904," in H.M. Stewart, ed., *American Canoe Association Yearbook* (Rochester: Morrison's Press, 1905), 47.
19 Trent University Archives (TUA), 83-014/2, Paul Vernon, "Tales of the ACA" (1940).
20 Susan Williams estimates that almost 25% of all American households, urban and suburban, had help in 1880. Susan Williams, *Savory Suppers and Fashionable Feasts: Dining in Victorian America* (Knoxville: University of Tennessee Press, 1996), 153. See also Eric W. Sager, "The Transformation of the Canadian Domestic Servant, 1871–1931," *Social Science History* 31, no. 4 (2007): 512–13.
21 "At the Canoe Camp: The Fishing and Swimming Is Fine – Laying a Course," *British Daily Whig*, 15 Aug. 1893.
22 W.P. Stephens, *Traditions and Memories of American Yachting: The 50th Anniversary Edition* (Brooklin: Wooden Boat Publications, 1989), 173; FM, ACA Collection, box 1.6/2, D.B. Goodsell, "A Canoeing Reminiscence" (1936), 2.
23 FM, ACA Collection, box 1.5/3, Fred Saunders Scrapbook, Meets and Camps (1900–40).
24 "A Permanent Camp," *Forest and Stream*, 18 Dec. 1890.
25 "The Great Canoe Meet," *Outing* 9, no. 2 (1886): 164–6; C. Bowyer Vaux, "The American Canoe Association, and Its Birthplace," *Outing* 12, no. 5 (1888): 410–21.
26 "Canoe Sailors in Camp," *New York Sun*, 4 Aug. 1884.
27 Beth Tompkins Bailey, *Pullman Porters and the Rise of Protest Politics in Black America, 1925–1945* (Chapel Hill: University of North Carolina Press, 2001).
28 Andrews, "Made by Toile," 849.
29 Bailey, *Pullman Porters*, 19, 22.

30 Ian McKay, *Quest of the Folk: Antimodernism and Cultural Selection in Twentieth-Century Nova Scotia* (Montreal and Kingston: McGill-Queen's University Press, 1994).
31 Florence Watters Snedeker, *A Family Canoe Trip* (New York: Harper & Brothers, 1892), 30.
32 Ibid., 24.
33 See, e.g., the time the family spent with Mr Windham on Lake George. Ibid., 37–42.
34 Cindy S. Aron, *Working at Play: A History of Vacations in the United States* (New York: Oxford University Press, 1999), 176–7.
35 The article described Jackman as an "experienced carpenter with a good staff of assistants." "Snips from Snaps at the '89 Meet," *Forest and Stream*, 19 Sept. 1889.
36 "The ACA Meet of 1892," *Forest and Stream*, 8 Sept. 1892.
37 Rare examples include "The Meet of 1884," *Forest and Stream*, 8 Nov. 1883; "The Executive Committee Meeting," *Forest and Stream*, 18 Nov. 1886; *Forest and Stream*, 25 Feb. 1892.
38 See, e.g., "The Lively Canoeists Are Coming Out in Numbers," *British Daily Whig*, 12 Aug. 1893.
39 St Lawrence County Historical Association (SLCHA), "Camp Circular for Grindstone Island" (1886).
40 See, e.g., "Merry Days on the River," *Syracuse Daily Standard*, 15 Aug. 1897; Charles P. Forbush, ed., *American Canoe Association Yearbook* (n.p., 1899); William A. Furman, ed., *American Canoe Association Yearbook* (Trenton, NJ: State Gazette Print, 1907).
41 This move to professionalize the oversight of food services while continuing to use marginal labour for supporting tasks in the kitchen and dining hall was echoed in summer camps, although in a somewhat later period. Abigail Van Slyck, *A Manufactured Wilderness: Summer Camps and the Shaping of American Youth, 1890–1960* (Minneapolis: University of Minnesota Press, 2006), 137–43. On young women and the family economy, albeit in an urban context, see Bettina Bradbury, *Working Families: Age, Gender, and Daily Survival in Industrializing Montreal* (Toronto: University of Toronto Press, 1993), 118–51.
42 On servers at the 1890 and 1893 meets, see Goodsell, "A Canoeing Reminiscence," 3, and *British Daily Whig*, 15 Aug. 1893.
43 Wurst, "Human Accumulations," 257.
44 Flip, "The Lake Champlain Canoe Meet," *Outing* 11, no. 3 (1887): 262.
45 Goodsell, "A Canoeing Reminiscence," 4.
46 R.B. Burchard, "Back to Grindstone: The Canoe Camp," *Outing* 29, no. 2 (1896): 141. Having found no records from the caterers, I have no way of knowing if the servers were instructed to avoid any kind of indiscretion or if they chose to remain distant.

47 C. Bowyer Vaux, "Canoe Meet at the Thousand Islands," *Outing* 14, no. 5 (1889): 348.
48 Vernon, "Tales of the ACA."
49 "To Camp on Bow Arrow Point," *Brooklyn Daily Eagle*, 6 Aug. 1887.
50 "The ACA Meet: Camp Circular," *Forest and Stream*, 10 July 1890; Adam Tomczik, "'He-Men Could Talk to He-Men in He-Men Language': Lumberjack Work Culture in Maine and Minnesota, 1840–1940," *Historian* 70, no. 4 (2008): 706.
51 "The ACA Meet: Camp Circular," *Forest and Stream*, 10 July 1890.
52 FM, ACA Collection, box 1.1/25, S.R. Stoddard, "The Sneak-Box Mess: Camp of the Brooklyn Canoe Club," 1887. The caption borrows from Nathaniel Holmes Bishop, *Four Months in a Sneak Box* (Boston: Lee and Shepard, 1879).
53 It's not clear whether the Black man in the photograph is Frank Baker, as no name is given. "To Camp on Bow Arrow Point," *Brooklyn Daily Eagle*, 6 Aug. 1887.
54 Van Slyck, *A Manufactured Wilderness*, 129.
55 "The ACA Meet of 1888: The Camp and the Association," *Forest and Stream*, 6 Sept. 1888; FM, ACA Collection, box 1.6/11, "A Trip with the Knickerbockers" (1883–84).
56 O.K. Chobee, "Echoes from Stony Lake," *American Canoeist* 2, no. 8 (1883): 115.
57 Magda Fahrni, "'Ruffled'.Mistresses and 'Discontented' Maids: Respectability and the Case of Domestic Service, 1880–1914," *Labour/Le Travail* 39 (Spring 1997): 70.
58 Ibid., 72.
59 Ibid., 70.
60 "Canoeists Break Camp," *New York Sun*, 16 Aug. 1884.
61 Schroeder argues there was a "coon song craze" in the 1890s. Patricia R. Schroeder, "Passing for Black: Coon Songs and the Performance of Race," *Journal of American Culture* 33, no. 2 (2010): 139.
62 D.B. Goodsell outlined the circumstances of the event in "A Canoeing Reminiscence," 3. Photographs of the band were also included in S.R. Stoddard, *Glimpses of the ACA* (Glens Falls, 1890).
63 Johnson has attracted much scholarly attention, particularly in the decade around the turn of the twenty-first century. See, e.g., Marilyn J. Rose, "Pauline Johnson: New World Poet," *British Journal of Canadian Studies* 12, no. 2 (1997): 298–307; Janice Fiamengo, "Reconsidering Pauline," *Canadian Literature* 167 (2000): 174–6; Jennifer I.M. Reid, "'Fair Descendant of the Mohawk': Pauline Johnson as an Ontological Marker," in *Historical Papers 2001*, ed. Bruce L. Guenther (Canadian Society of Church History, 2001), 5–21; Charlotte Gray, *Flint and Feather: The Life and Times of E. Pauline Johnson, Tekahionwake* (Toronto: HarperFlamingo, 2002); Sabine Milz, "'Publica(c)

tion': E. Pauline Johnson's Publishing Venues and Their Contemporary Significance," *Studies in Canadian Literature/Études en littérature canadienne* 29, no. 1 (2004): 127–45. On her performances, I turned to Veronica Strong-Boag and Carole Gerson, "Literature, Performance, and Reception," in *Paddling Her Own Canoe: The Times and Texts of E. Pauline Johnson (Tekahionwake)* (Toronto: University of Toronto Press, 2000), 100–34.

64 Johnson had intentions to attend the 1894 meet, but poor weather and health kept her away. She was in camp at the 1896 meet. Archives of Ontario, F1173, Letter from Pauline Johnson to Mr O'Brien, 20 June c. 1894, and Letter from Pauline Johnson to Mr O'Brien, 23 Aug. c. 1894. *Forest and Stream*, 5 Sept. 1896.

65 "Around the Pine Camp Fire," *New York Times (NYT)*, 20 Aug. 1893.

66 "The Second Day of the Regatta," *NYT*, 13 Aug. 1881.

67 "The Canoe Congress," *Forest and Stream*, 22 Jan. 1880.

68 I borrow this notion of authenticity from Paige Raibmon, *Authentic Indians: Episodes of Encounter from the Late-Nineteenth-Century Northwest Coast* (Durham: Duke University Press, 2005), 3–9.

69 Gillian Poulter, *Becoming Native in a Foreign Land: Sport, Visual Culture, and Identity in Montreal, 1840–1885* (Vancouver: UBC Press, 2009).

70 Schroeder, "Passing for Black," 143; Raibmon, *Authentic Indians*, 51.

71 Milz, "Publica(c)tion," 130.

72 Raibmon, *Authentic Indians*, 72; Schroeder, "Passing for Black," 143.

73 Schroeder, "Passing for Black," 143.

74 Ibid., 139.

75 Raibmon, *Authentic Indians*, 72–3.

76 See, e.g., "The ACA Meet of 1887," *Forest and Stream*, 2 June 1887; FM, ACA Collection, box 1.6/11, "Camp Circular for Sugar Island" (1910).

77 "Executive Committee Meeting," *Forest and Stream*, 3 Nov. 1900; Mystic Seaport Collections Research Center (MSCRC), Collection 291, vol. 4, "Camp Site Committee Report, 1906."

78 Graham S. Lowe, "Class, Job, and Gender in the Canadian Office," *Labour/Le Travail* 10 (Autumn 1982): 11.

79 Marjorie Cohen, *Women's Work, Markets and Economic Development in Nineteenth-Century Ontario* (Toronto: University of Toronto Press, 1988); Nancy Grey Osterud, *Bonds of Community: The Lives of Farm Women in Nineteenth-Century New York* (Ithaca: Cornell University Press, 1991).

80 See, e.g., Joan M. Jensen, "Cloth, Butter, and Boarders: Women's Household Production for the Market," *Review of Radical Political Economics* 12 (1980): 14–24; Thomas Dublin, *Transforming Women's Work: New England Lives in the Industrial Revolution* (Ithaca: Cornell University Press, 1994); Sally Ann McMurry, *Transforming Rural Life: Dairying Families and Agricultural Change* (Baltimore: Johns Hopkins University Press, 1995).

81 Jensen, "Cloth, Butter, and Boarders," 15. Emphasis added.
82 Joy Parr, "Ontario Agricultural Wage Labour in Historical Perspective," *Labour/Le Travail* 15 (Spring 1985): 91–103; Rusty Bittermann, "Farm Households and Wage Labour in the Northeastern Maritimes in the Early 19th Century," *Labour/Le Travail* 31 (Spring 1993): 13–45.
83 Ian Radforth, *Bushworkers and Bosses: Logging in Northern Ontario, 1900–1980* (Toronto: University of Toronto Press, 1987), 27–9.
84 Ibid., 26–7.
85 "The Executive Committee Meeting," *Forest and Stream*, 12 Nov. 1885; "The Executive Committee Meeting," *Forest and Stream*, 18 Nov. 1886.
86 Dona Brown, *Inventing New England: Regional Tourism in the Nineteenth Century* (Washington, DC: Smithsonian Institution Press, 1995).
87 Little, "Life without Conventionality," 289.
88 Ruth B. Phillips and Christopher B. Steiner, "Art, Authenticity, and Baggage of Cultural Encounter," in *Unpacking Culture: Art and Commodity in Colonial and Postcolonial Worlds*, ed. Ruth B. Phillips and Christopher B. Steiner (Berkeley: University of California Press, 1999), 9.
89 Jasen, *Wild Things*, 70, 97.
90 Ibid., 50, 97.
91 Goodsell, "A Canoeing Reminiscence," 5.
92 Snedeker, *A Family Canoe Trip*, 33. According to Melissa Otis, "Indian encampments" were common around Lake George throughout the nineteenth century. There was also a store in the town run by an Abenaki couple, Angeline Sarah Kaziah-Otondosonne (1851–1925) and Norman Frank Johnson (1852–1919). See Melissa Otis, "At Home in the Adirondacks: A History of Indigenous and Euroamerican Interactions, 1776–1920" (PhD dissertation, University of Toronto, 2013), 95, 179, 214–15; "Basketmaking Indians of Lake George," *NYT*, 8 Sept. 1912.
93 Jasen, *Wild Things*, 70.
94 See Otis, "Performing Native Culture: Marketing Art, Acting, and Educating Newcomers in the Adirondacks," in "At Home in the Adirondacks," 208–51.
95 Beverly Gordon, "The Souvenir: Messenger of the Extraordinary," *Journal of Popular Culture* 20, no. 3 (1986): 135.
96 Phillips and Steiner, "Art, Authenticity, and Baggage," 12.
97 Ibid.
98 Bernard Edelman, *Ledroit Saisi par la Photographie* (Paris: François Maspéro, 1973), as quoted in Allan Sekula, "Photography Between Labour and Capital," in *Mining Photographs and Other Pictures, 1948–1968*, ed. Benjamin H.D. Buchloh and Robert Wilkie (Halifax: Press of the Nova Scotia College of Art and Design, 1983), 194.
99 Jean Sagne, "All Kinds of Portraits: The Photographer's Studio," in *A New History of Photography*, ed. Michael Frizot (Koln: Konneman, 1998), 120.

100 "ACA Annual Meeting," *Peterborough Daily Review*, 21 Aug. 1883.
101 Mary Warner Marien, *Photography: A Cultural History*, 2nd ed. (Upper Saddle River: Prentice Hall, 2006), 168–9.
102 See, e.g., "ACA Annual Meeting: A Quiet Sunday on the Lake – An Impressive and Appropriate Service," *Peterborough Daily Review*, 21 Aug. 1883.
103 Occupational plurality was common among photographers also. See, e.g., Carol J. Williams, *Framing the West: Race, Gender, and the Photographic Frontier in the Pacific Northwest* (New York: Oxford University Press, 2003).
104 Much has been written about Stoddard's association with the Adirondacks and the wilderness ideal. However, only Stoddard's biographer has paid any attention to his involvement with the American Canoe Association. See Maitland C. De Sormo, *Seneca Ray Stoddard: Versatile Camera-Artist* (Saranac Lake: Adirondack Yesteryears, 1972). See also Jeffrey L. Horrell, *Seneca Ray Stoddard: Transforming the Adirondack Wilderness in Text and Image* (Syracuse: Syracuse University Press, 1999); Frank H. Goodyear, III, "A Wilderness for Men: The Adirondacks in the Photographs of Seneca Ray Stoddard," in *Gender and Landscape: Renegotiating Morality and Space*, ed. Lorraine Dowler, Josephine Carubia, and Bonj Szczygiel (London: Routledge, 2005), 124–42.
105 Horrell, *Seneca Ray Stoddard*, 43–5.
106 When he stopped attending, the ACA appointed an official photographer. A.A. Lewis held this post in 1897 and 1898. C.V. Schulyer, ed., *American Canoe Association Yearbook* (n.p., 1898), 2; Charles P. Forbush, ed., *American Canoe Association Yearbook* (n.p., 1899), 3.
107 Vaux, "Its Birthplace," 418.
108 Other photographers at the meets offered similar goods and services, although not to the same degree as Stoddard. E.g., a number advertised stock images of the encampments, including Frank H. Foster of Lebanon, NH.
109 S.R. Stoddard, *Glimpses of the ACA* (Glens Falls, 1886); S.R. Stoddard, *Glimpses of the ACA* (Glens Falls, 1887); S.R. Stoddard, *Glimpses of the ACA* (Glens Falls, 1890).
110 I uncovered two images that support this hypothesis. They depict display boards of photographs and *Glimpses* put together for the 1887 meet. FM, ACA Collection, box 1.1/29.
111 There are, e.g., advertisements for Stoddard's images in "Camp Photos," *Forest and Stream*, 14 Sept. 1882; George W. Hatton and C. Bowyer Vaux, eds., *American Canoe Association Yearbook* (New York: Nautical Publishing, 1889), xxi; *Sail and Paddle* 7, no. 1 (1889): n.p.; Ralph F. Brazer, ed., *American Canoe Association Yearbook* (New York: n.p., 1891), 73; Charles E. Cragg, ed., *American Canoe Association Yearbook* (Port Henry: Press of the Essex County Publishing Co., 1895), 80.

112 A review of other scrapbooks included in the ACA Collection proves this point. See, e.g., FM, ACA Collection, box 1.5/4, Scrapbook of Thomas Hale (c. 1891–1900); box 1.5A, Scrapbook of Walwin Barr (c. 1905–date unknown).
113 James Opp, "Finding the View: Landscape, Place, and Colour Slide Photography in Southern Alberta," in *Placing Memory and Remembering Place in Canada*, ed. James Opp and John C. Walsh (Vancouver: UBC Press, 2010), 271–90.
114 S.R. Stoddard, *Glimpses of the ACA* (Glens Falls, 1890).
115 It is not clear how many builders were in attendance at a given meet. We know, however, that at the 1888 encampment on Lake George, the builders in camp included J.H. Rushton of Canton, NY, George Ruggles of Rochester, NY, Nelson Bowdish of Skaneateles, NY, and Mr Spencer (either of Lowell, MA, or Hartford, CT). "The ACA Meet, Lake George," *Forest and Stream*, 23 Aug. 1888.
116 Atwood Manley, *Rushton and His Times in American Canoeing* (Syracuse: Syracuse University Press, 1968), 97.
117 As quoted in ibid., 71.
118 Ken Brown, *The Canadian Canoe Company and the Early Peterborough Canoe Factories* (Peterborough: Cover to Cover, 2011), 15.
119 Manley, *Rushton and His Times*, 96.
120 "The Association Meet," *Forest and Stream*, 6 Aug. 1885.
121 "The ACA Meet, Lake George," *Forest and Stream*, 23 Aug. 1888.
122 Manley, *Rushton and His Times*, 71, 123, 47.
123 George P. Douglass, ed., *American Canoe Association Yearbook* (Newark: Press of the Holbrook Printing Co., 1894), 7.
124 Brown, *Inventing New England*, 6.
125 Andrews, "Made by Toile," 848.
126 FM, ACA Collection, box 1.2/26, "Keys, Kanoe, Kaptor, and Kowboy" (1887).
127 E.P. Thompson, *The Making of the English Working Class* (London: V. Gollanz, 1963), 12.

Conclusion

1 "The Annual Canoe Meet," *New York Evening Post*, 27 Aug. 1887.
2 "The Association Meet," *Forest and Stream*, 6 Aug. 1885. Interestingly, this word picture of the ACA encampments asks us to consider the longer histories of the encampment sites beyond the annual meetings, to inquire about, e.g., the workers who stay behind.
3 "The Annual Canoe Meet," *New York Evening Post*, 27 Aug. 1887. Emphasis added.

4 "The Association Meet," *Forest and Stream*, 21 Aug. 1884.
5 Fenimore Museum (FM), formerly the New York State Historical Association (NYSHA), American Canoe Association (ACA) Collection, box 1.6/2, D.B. Goodsell, "A Canoeing Reminiscence" (1936), 13.
6 Allen Guttmann, *Games & Empires: Modern Sports and Cultural Imperialism* (New York: Columbia University Press, 1994).
7 C.L.R. James, *Beyond a Boundary* (London: Hutchinson, 1963); J.A. Mangan, *The Games Ethic and Imperialism: Aspects of the Diffusion of an Ideal* (London: Viking, 1986); John Mackenzie, *The Empire of Nature: Hunting, Conservation, and British Imperialism* (Manchester: Manchester University Press, 1988); Laura Fair, "Kickin' It: Leisure, Politics and Football in Colonial Zanzibar, 1900s–1950s," *Africa* 67, no. 2 (1997): 224–51; Greg Gillespie, *Hunting for Empire: Narratives of Sport in Rupert's Land, 1840–70* (Vancouver: UBC Press, 2007).
8 John Bloom, *To Show What an Indian Can Do: Sports at Native American Boarding Schools* (Minneapolis: University of Minnesota Press, 2005); Janice Forsyth, "Bodies of Meaning: Sports and Games at Canadian Residential Schools," in *Aboriginal Peoples and Sport in Canada: Historical Foundations and Contemporary Issues*, ed. Janice Forsyth and Audrey Giles (Vancouver: UBC Press, 2013), 15–34.
9 Sharon Wall, *The Nurture of Nature: Childhood, Antimodernism, and Ontario Summer Camps, 1920–1955* (Vancouver: UBC Press, 2009); Andrew Watson, "Poor Soils and Rich Folks: Household Economies and Sustainability in Muskoka, 1850–1920" (PhD dissertation, York University, 2014); Stan Steves, ed., *Indigenous Peoples, National Parks and Protected Areas: New Paradigm Linking Conservation, Culture and Rights* (Tuscon: University of Arizona Press, 2014).
10 Maurice Roche, *Mega-Events and Modernity: Olympics and Expos in the Growth of Global Culture* (London: Routledge, 2000); Helen Jefferson Lenskyj, *Inside the Olympic Industry: Power, Politics, and Activism* (Albany: State University of New York Press, 2000); Libby Porter, "Planning Displacement: The Real Legacy of Major Sporting Events," *Planning Theory & Practice* 10, no. 3 (2009): 395–9; Jules Boykoff, "The Anti-Olympics," *New Left Review* 67 (2011): 41–59.
11 Drew Hayden Taylor, "Wild Rice Fight: Cottagers Versus Indians," *Now Toronto*, 1 Nov. 2015. Accessed 1 June 2016: https://nowtoronto.com/news/wild-rice-fight-cottagers-versus-indians/; Lisa Jackson, "Canada's Wild Rice Wars," *Aljazeera*, 20 Feb. 2016. Accessed 1 June 2016: http://www.aljazeera.com/indepth/features/2016/02/canada-wild-rice-wars-160217083126970.html.
12 Again, we can look to the example of Rice Lake to see how settlers deploy their "traditional" use of the land as cottagers to justify their

continued occupation of the shorelines and their right to dictate Indigenous harvesting practices.

13 Thaidene Nene means "land of our ancestors" in Dënesųłné (Chipewyan), the language of the Łutsël K'é Dene. "Thaidene Nene FAQ." Accessed 2 June 2016: http://landoftheancestors.ca/downloads/thaidene-nene-faq-v4.pdf.

14 In the community's own words: "It is not LKDFN's intention to restrict others' access and enjoyment of the natural wonders of Thaidene Nene: as the keepers of Thaidene Nene, the Łutsël K'é Denesoline have the responsibility to act as stewards of the land and as host to visitors." "Thaidene Nene FAQ."

15 With respect to the latter, the Łutsël K'é Dene developed a code of conduct for visitors. This set of guidelines, in the band's words, "educate[s] visitors about our expectations for respectful travel within our ancestral homeland." It also "reaffirms Denesoline self-determination and autonomy in land governance and tourism management." Allison P. Holmes, Bryan S.R. Grimwood, Lauren J. King, and the Lutsel K'e Dene First Nation, "Creating an Indigenized Visitor Code of Conduct: The Development of Denesoline Self-Determination for Sustainable Tourism," *Journal of Sustainable Tourism* 24, no. 8–9 (2016): 1177–93.

Bibliography

PRIMARY SOURCES

Unpublished

Fenimore Museum (FM), formerly the New York State Historical Association (NYSHA), Cooperstown, New York

American Canoe Association Collection

Mystic Seaport Collections Research Center (MSCRC), Mystic, Connecticut

Collection 291, American Canoe Association

St Lawrence County Historical Association (SLCHA), Canton, New York

John Henry Rushton Collection

McMaster University Archives (MUA), Hamilton, Ontario

E. Pauline Johnson Fonds

Trent University Archives (TUA), Peterborough, Ontario

83-014 Stoney Lake: American Canoe Association

Library and Archives Canada (LAC), Ottawa, Ontario

MG30-C-27 W.L. Scott Fonds
RG 10 Department of Indian Affairs
R2936 John Harold Micklethwaite Fonds

Personal Collections

MacKendrick Family Photograph Albums and Family Letter Collections, Milford, Connecticut, and Windermere, Ontario

I also consulted select materials at Adirondack Experience, formerly the Adirondack Museum (Blue Mountain Lake, New York), the Canadian Museum of Science and Technology (Ottawa, Ontario), and the City of Toronto Archives (Toronto, Ontario).

Published

American Canoe Association Yearbook (1881–1910).
Alden, W.L. *The Canoe and the Flying Proa, or Cheap Cruising and Safe Sailing.* New York: Harper and Brothers Publishers, 1878.
– *The Cruise of the Canoe Club.* New York: Harper and Brothers, 1883.
Babcock, Louis M. *Our American Resorts: For Health, Pleasure and Recreation.* Washington, DC: National News Bureau, 1883.
Barker, Lady Mary Anne. *The Bedroom and Boudoir.* London: Macmillan, 1878.
Bishop, Nathaniel Holmes. *The Voyage of the Paper Canoe.* Boston: Lee and Shepard, 1878.
– *Four Months in a Sneak Box.* Boston: Lee and Shepard, 1879.
Jameson, Anna. *Winter Studies and Summer Rambles in Canada.* New York: Wiley and Putnam, 1839.
MacGregor, John. *A Thousand Miles in the Rob Roy Canoe: On Rivers and Lakes of Europe.* London: Sampson, Low, Marlowe and Co., 1866.
Mallory, Enid L. *Kawartha: Living on These Lakes.* Peterborough: Peterborough Publishing, 1991.
Moodie, Susanna. *Roughing It in the Bush, or Life in Canada.* 2nd ed. London: Richard Bentley, 1852.
Murray, William Henry Harrison. *Lake Champlain and Its Shores.* Boston: De Wolfe, Fiske, and Co., 1890.
Neide, Charles. *The Canoe Aurora: A Cruise from the Adirondacks to the Gulf.* New York: Forest and Stream Publishing, 1885.
Picturesque Views and Maps of the Muskoka Lakes, Canada. Toronto: Ralph, Smith and Co., 1893.
Possons, Charles H. *Lake George and Lake Champlain.* Glens Falls, 1887.
Retaw. *Fragments from the '88 Meet.* Montreal, 1888.
Sears, George Washington. *Woodcraft.* New York: Forest and Stream Publishing, 1884.
Smock, John C. "Geologico-Geographical Distribution of the Iron Ores of the Eastern United States." *Engineering and Mining Journal* 37 (Mar. 1884): 130–44.

Snedeker, Florence Watters. *A Family Canoe Trip*. New York: Harper and Brothers, 1892.

Stephens, W.P. *Canoe and Boat Building*. New York: Forest and Stream Publishing, 1883.

– *Traditions and Memories of American Yachting: The 50th Anniversary Edition*. Brooklin: Wooden Boat Publications, 1989.

Stoddard, S.R. *Lake George Illustrated*. Albany: Van Benthuysen and Sons, 1882.

– *Glimpses of the ACA*. Glens Falls, 1887.

– *Glimpses of the ACA*. Glens Falls, 1889.

– *Glimpses of the ACA*. Glens Falls, 1890.

Thoreau, Henry David. *Cape Cod*. Boston: Ticknor and Fields, 1865.

Tocqueville, Alexis de. *Democracy in America*, vol. 1 [1835], ed. Phillips Bradley. New York: Knopf, 1980.

Turner, Frederick Jackson. "The Significance of the Frontier in American History." In *Annual Report of the American Historical Association for the Year 1893*, 188–227. Washington, DC: Government Printing Office, 1894.

Vaux, C. Bowyer. *Canoe Handling*. New York: Forest and Stream Publishing, 1885.

Wilhelm, Thomas. *A Military Dictionary and Gazeteer.* Rev. ed. Philadelphia: L.R. Hamersly and Co., 1881.

Wilt, Maurice D. "Canoeing under Sail." In *Sailing Craft*, ed. Edwin J. Schoettle, n.p. New York: Macmillian, 1928.

Zuk, Lawrence E., ed. *American Canoe Association 100th Anniversary Yearbook*. Concord: Minuteman Printing Corp., 1980.

Newspapers and Periodicals

American Canoeist (1882–1887)
Forest and Stream (1873–1910)
New York Times (1872–1910)
Outing Magazine (1884–1900)

Note: Included here are newspaper and periodical sources that I consulted in depth. Any other newspapers or magazines from which I drew material are cited in the notes.

SECONDARY SOURCES

Adams, Annmarie, and Stacie Burke. "'Not a Shack in the Woods': Architecture for Tuberculosis in Muskoka and Toronto." *Canadian Bulletin of Medical History* 23, no. 2 (2006): 429–55.

Adams, David Wallace. *Education for Extinction: American Indians and the Boarding School Experience, 1875–1928*. Lawrence: University Press of Kansas, 1995.

Adams, Mary Louise. *Artistic Impressions: Figure Skating, Masculinity, and the Limits of Sport*. Toronto: University of Toronto Press, 2011.

Alexander, Lewis M. "The Impact of Tourism on the Economy of Cape Cod, Massachusetts." *Economic Geography* 29, no. 4 (1953): 320–6.

Andrews, Thomas G. "'Made by Toile'? Tourism, Labor, and the Construction of the Colorado Landscape." *Journal of American History* 92, no. 3 (2005): 837–63.

Armstrong, James, and David M. Williams. "The Steamboat and Popular Tourism." *Journal of Transport History* 26, no. 1 (2005): 61–76.

Aron, Cindy S. *Working at Play: A History of Vacations in the United States*. New York: Oxford University Press, 1999.

– "The Evolution of the Middle Class." In *A Companion to Nineteenth-Century America*, ed. William Barney, 178–91. New York: Blackwell, 2000.

Bailey, Beth Tompkins. *Pullman Porters and the Rise of Protest Politics in Black America, 1925–1945*. Chapel Hill: University of North Carolina Press, 2001.

Bailey, Peter. "'A Mingled Mass of Perfectly Legitimate Pleasures': The Victorian Middle Class and the Problem of Leisure." *Victorian Studies* 21, no. 1 (1977): 7–28.

– *Leisure and Class in Victorian England: Rational Recreation and the Contest for Control, 1830–1885*. Buffalo: University of Toronto Press, 1978.

Bailey, Steve. *Athlete First: A History of the Paralympic Movement*. London: Wiley, 2008.

Baker, Lee D. *From Savage to Negro: Anthropology and the Construction of Race, 1896–1954*. Berkeley: University of California Press, 1998.

Baldwin, Andrew. "Ethnoscaping Canada's Boreal Forest: Liberal Whiteness and Its Disaffiliation from Colonial Space." *Canadian Geographer* 53, no. 4 (2009): 427–43.

Banner, Lois. *American Beauty: A Social History through Two Centuries of the American Idea, Ideal, and Image of the Beautiful Woman*. New York: Knopf, 1983.

Beasley, Diane. "Walter Dean and Sunnyside: A Study of Waterfront Recreation." MA thesis, University of Toronto, 1995.

Bederman, Gail. *Manliness and Civilization: A Cultural History of Gender and Race in the United States, 1880–1917*. Chicago: University of Chicago Press, 1995.

Belisle, Donica. *Retail Nation: Department Stores and the Making of Modern Canada*. Vancouver: UBC Press, 2011.

Benidickson, Jamie. *Idleness, Water, and a Canoe: Reflections on Paddling for Pleasure*. Toronto: University of Toronto Press, 1997.

Benson, Susan Porter. *Counter Cultures: Sales-Women, Managers, and Customers in American Department Stores, 1890–1940*. Urbana: University of Illinois Press, 1986.

Bentham, Christine, and Katharine Hooke. *From Burleigh to Boschink: A Community Called Stony Lake*. Toronto: Natural Heritage/Natural History, 2000.

Berger, Molly. *Hotel Dreams: Luxury, Technology and Urban Ambition in America, 1829–1929*. Baltimore: Johns Hopkins University Press, 2011.

Bittermann, Rusty. "Farm Households and Wage Labour in the Northeastern Maritimes in the Early 19th Century." *Labour/Le Travail* 31 (1993): 13–45.

Blair, Peggy J. *Lament for a First Nation: The Williams Treaties in Southern Ontario*. Vancouver: UBC Press, 2008.

Blanton, Casey. *Travel Writing: The Self and the World*. New York: Routledge, 2002.

Blatt, Martin H., and Martha K. Norkunas, eds. *Work, Recreation, and Culture: Essays in American Labor History*. New York: Garland, 1996.

Bloom, John. *To Show What an Indian Can Do: Sports at Native American Boarding Schools*. Minneapolis: University of Minnesota Press, 2005.

Blunt, Alison, and Robyn Dowling. *Home*. London: Routledge, 2006.

Bond, Hallie E. *Boats and Boating in the Adirondacks*. Syracuse: Syracuse University Press, 1998.

Bond, Hallie E, Joan Jacobs Brumberg, and Leslie Paris. *A Paradise for Boys and Girls: Children's Camps in the Adirondacks*. Syracuse: Syracuse University Press, 2006.

Bouchier, Nancy B. *For the Love of the Game: Amateur Sport in Small-Town Ontario, 1838–1895*. Montreal and Kingston: McGill-Queen's University Press, 2003.

Boykoff, Jules. "The Anti-Olympics." *New Left Review* 67 (2011): 41–59.

Bradbury, Bettina. *Working Families: Age, Gender, and Daily Survival in Industrializing Montreal*. Toronto: University of Toronto Press, 1993.

Braun, Bruce. *The Intemperate Rainforest: Nature, Culture, and Power on Canada's West Coast*. Minneapolis: University of Minnesota Press, 2002.

Brickell, Katherine, and Ayona Datta, eds. *Translocal Geographies: Spaces, Places, Connections*. Burlington: Ashgate, 2011.

Brown, Dona. *Inventing New England: Regional Tourism in the Nineteenth Century*. Washington, DC: Smithsonian Institution Press, 1995.

Brown, Judith C. "Lesbian Sexuality in Renaissance Italy: The Case of Sister Benedetta Carlini." *Signs* 9, no. 4 (1984): 751–8.

Brown, Ken. *The Canadian Canoe Company and the Early Peterborough Canoe Factories*. Peterborough: Cover to Cover, 2011.

Brownlie, Robin Jarvis. *A Fatherly Eye: Indian Agents, Government Power, and Aboriginal Resistance in Ontario, 1918–1939*. Don Mills: Oxford University Press, 2003.

– "'A better citizen than lots of white men': First Nations Enfranchisement – An Ontario Case Study, 1918–1940." *Canadian Historical Review* 87, no. 1 (2006): 29–52.

Brucken, Carolyn. "In the Public Eye: Women and the American Luxury Hotel." *Winterthur Portfolio* 31, no. 4 (1996): 203–20.

Buzard, James. *The Beaten Track: European Tourism, Literature, and the Ways to "Culture," 1800–1918*. Oxford: Clarendon Press, 1993.

Bynum, William F. *Science and the Practice of Medicine in the Nineteenth Century.* Cambridge: Cambridge University Press, 1994.

Cahn, Susan K. *Coming on Strong: Gender and Sexuality in Twentieth-Century Women's Sport.* New York: Free Press, 1994.

Calloway, Colin G. *The Western Abenakis of Vermont, 1600–1800: War, Migration, and the Survival of an Indian People.* Norman: University of Oklahoma Press, 1994.

Campisi, Jack. *The Mashpee Indians: Tribe on Trial.* Syracuse: Syracuse University Press, 1991.

Carter, Paul. *The Road to Botany Bay: An Exploration of Landscape and History.* New York: Knopf, 1988.

Certeau, Michel de. *The Practice of Everyday Life.* Translated by Steven Rendell. Berkeley: University of California Press, 1984 [1980].

Cevik, Gulen. "American Style or Turkish Chair: The Triumph of Bodily Comfort." *Journal of Design History* 23, no. 4 (2010): 367–85.

Chalip, Laurence. "The Cogency of Culture in Sport Tourism Research." *Journal of Sport and Tourism* 15, no. 1 (2010): 3–5.

Chartier, Roger. "Culture as Appropriation: Popular Cultural Uses in Early Modern France." In *Understanding Popular Culture: Europe from the Middle Ages to the Nineteenth Century*, ed. Steven L. Kaplan, 229–53. Berlin: Mouton, 1984.

Chauncey, George. *Gay New York: Gender, Urban Culture, and the Making of the Gay Male World, 1890–1994.* New York: Basic Books, 1994.

Cohen, Marjorie. *Women's Work, Markets, and Economic Development in Nineteenth-Century Ontario.* Toronto: University of Toronto Press, 1988.

Cole, Jean Murray. "Kawartha Lakes Regattas." In *Nastawgan: The Canadian North by Canoe & Snowshoe*, ed. Bruce W. Hodgins and Margaret Hobbs, 203–10. Toronto: Dundurn Press, 1987.

Coleman, Anne Gilbert. "The Rise of the House of Leisure: Outdoor Guides, Practical Knowledge, and Industrialization." *Western Historical Quarterly* 42, no. 4 (2011): 436–57.

Colville, Quintin. "Corporate Domesticity and Idealised Masculinity: Royal Naval Officers and Their Shipboard Home, 1918–1939." *Gender and History* 21, no. 3 (2009): 499–519.

Corbett, Theodore. *The Making of American Resorts: Saratoga Springs, Ballston Spa, Lake George.* Piscataway: Rutgers University Press, 2001.

Cowan, Ruth Schwartz. "The 'Industrial Revolution' in the Home: Household Technology and Social Change in the 20th Century." *Technology and Culture* 17, no. 1 (1976): 1–23.

Craik, Jennifer. *Uniforms Exposed: From Conformity to Transgression.* Oxford: Berg, 2005.

Crane, Diana. *Fashion and Its Social Agendas: Class, Gender, and Identity in Clothing.* Chicago: University of Chicago Press, 2000.

Cranz, Galen. "Women in Urban Parks." *Signs* 5, no. 3 (1980, Supplement): S80–S85.
Cresswell, Tim. *On the Move: Mobility in the Modern Western World*. London: Routledge, 2006.
– "Mobilities I: Catching Up." *Progress in Human Geography* 35, no. 4 (2010): 550–8.
– "Mobilities II: Still." *Progress in Human Geography* 36, no. 5 (2012): 645–53.
– "Mobilities III: Moving On." *Progress in Human Geography* 38, no. 5 (2014): 712–21.
Cresswell, Tim, and Peter Merriman, eds. *Geographies of Mobilities: Practices, Spaces, Subjects*. Burlington: Ashgate, 2011.
Cromley, Elizabeth Collins. "Sleeping Around: A History of Beds and Bedrooms." *Journal of Design History* 3, no. 1 (1990): 1–17.
– "Transforming the Food Axis: Houses, Tools, Modes of Analysis." *Material History Review* 44 (1996): 8–22.
Crouch, David. "Places around Us: Embodied Lay Geographies in Leisure and Tourism." *Leisure Studies* 19, no. 2 (2000): 63–76.
Crowley, William. *Rushton's Rowboats and Canoes: The 1903 Catalog in Perspective*. Blue Mountain Lake: Adirondack Museum, 1983.
Cruikshank, Ken, and Nancy Bouchier. "'Dirty Spaces': Environment, the State and Recreational Swimming in Hamilton Harbour, 1870–1946." *Sport History Review* 29, no. 1 (1998): 59–76.
Cunningham, Patricia A. *Reforming Women's Fashion, 1850–1920: Politics, Health, and Art*. Kent: Kent State University Press, 2003.
Curtis, Bruce. *The Politics of Population: State Formation, Statistics, and the Census of Canada, 1840–1875*. Toronto: University of Toronto Press, 2001.
Davidoff, Leonore, and Catharine Hall. *Family Fortunes: Men and Women of the English Middle Class, 1780–1850*. Rev. ed. London: Routledge, 2002.
Davies, Megan. "Night Soil, Cesspools, and Smelly Hogs on the Streets: Sanitation, Race, and Governance in Early British Columbia." *Histoire sociale/Social History* 38, no. 75 (2005): 1–36.
Davis, Clark. "The Corporate Reconstruction of Middle-Class Manhood." In *The Middling Sorts: Explorations in the History of the American Middle Class*, ed. Burton Bledstein and Robert D. Johnston, 201–16. New York: Routledge, 2001.
Davis, Janet M. *The Circus Age: Culture and Society under the American Big Top*. Chapel Hill: University of North Carolina Press, 2002.
Day, Gordon M. "Abenaki Place-Names in the Champlain Valley." *International Journal of Linguistics* 47, no. 2 (1981): 143–71.
Dean, Misao. *Inheriting a Canoe Paddle: The Canoe in Discourses of English-Canadian Nationalism*. Toronto: University of Toronto Press, 2013.
Deloria, Philip J. *Playing Indian*. New Haven: Yale University Press, 1998.
Dening, Greg. *Mr Bligh's Bad Language: Passion, Power and Theatre on the Bounty*. Cambridge: Cambridge University Press, 1992.

– *Performances*. Chicago: University of Chicago Press, 1996.

De Sormo, Maitland C. *Seneca Ray Stoddard: Versatile Camera-Artist*. Saranac Lake: Adirondack Yesteryears, 1972.

Dimeo, Paul. "Review of *Sports Tourism: Participants, Policy and Providers*." *Tourism Management* 29 (2008): 603.

Dohmen, Renate. "The Home in the World: Threshold Designs and Performative Relations in Contemporary Tamil Nadu, South India." *Cultural Geographies* 11 (2004): 7–25.

Douglas, Ann. *The Feminization of American Culture*. New York: Knopf, 1977.

Douglas, Mary, and Baron Isherwood. *The World of Goods: Towards an Anthropology of Consumption*. New York: W.W. Norton, 1979.

Doyle, Don H. "The Social Functions of Voluntary Associations in a Nineteenth-Century American Town." *Social Science History* 1, no. 3 (1977): 333–55.

Drayton, Richard. *Nature's Government: Science, Imperial Britain, and the "Improvement" of the World*. New Haven: Yale University Press, 2000.

Dubinsky, Karen. *The Second Greatest Disappointment: Honeymooners, Heterosexuality, and the Tourist Industry at Niagara Falls*. Toronto: Between the Lines Press, 1999.

Dublin, Thomas. *Transforming Women's Work: New England Lives in the Industrial Revolution*. Ithaca: Cornell University Press, 1994.

Dunkin, Jessica. "Manufacturing Landscapes: Place and Community at Glen Bernard Camp, 1924–1933." *Histoire sociale/Social History* 45, no. 89 (2012): 79–113.

– "The Canoe." In *Symbols of Canada*, ed. Michael Dawson, Catherine Gidney, and Donald Wright, 18-29. Toronto: Between the Lines Press, 2018.

Dunkin, Jessica, and Bryan S.R. Grimwood. "Mobile Habitations in Canoescapes." In *Lifestyle Mobilities and Corporealities*, eds. Tara Duncan, Scott Cohen, and Maria Thulemark, 159–75. Aldershot: Ashgate, 2013.

Egan, Michael. "Wrestling Teddy Bears: Wilderness Masculinity as Invented Tradition in the Pacific Northwest." *Gender Forum* 15 (2006). Accessed 19 Mar. 2012: http://www.genderforum.org/issues/gender-roomours-i/wrestling-teddy-bears/.

Erickson, Bruce. *Canoe Nation: Nature, Race, and the Making of a Canadian Icon*. Vancouver: UBC Press, 2013.

Fahrni, Magda. "'Ruffled' Mistresses and 'Discontented' Maids: Respectability and the Case of Domestic Service, 1880–1914," *Labour/Le Travail* 39 (1997): 69–97.

Fair, Laura. "Kickin' It: Leisure, Politics and Football in Colonial Zanzibar, 1900s–1950s." *Africa* 67, no. 2 (1997): 224–51.

Fee, Elizabeth, Theodore M. Brown, Jan Lazarus, and Paul Theerman. "Baxter Street Then." *American Journal of Public Health* 92, no. 5 (2002): 753.

Ferry, Darren. *Uniting in Measures of Common Good: The Construction of Collective Liberal Identities in Central Canada, 1830–1900*. Montreal and Kingston: McGill-Queen's University Press, 2008.

Fiamengo, Janice. "Reconsidering Pauline." *Canadian Literature* 167 (2000): 174–6.

Field, Russell. "A Night at the Garden(s): A History of Professional Hockey Spectatorship in the 1920s and 1930s." PhD dissertation, University of Toronto, 2008.

Filey, Mike, and Victor Russell. *From Horse Power to Horsepower: Toronto 1890–1930*. Toronto: Dundurn Press, 1993.

Flaumenhaft, Mera. *The Civic Spectacle: Essays on Drama and Community*. London: Rowman and Littlefield, 1994.

Forsyth, Janice. "Bodies of Meaning: Sports and Games at Canadian Residential Schools." In *Aboriginal Peoples and Sport in Canada: Historical Foundations and Contemporary Issues*, ed. Janice Forsyth and Audrey Giles, 15–34. Vancouver: UBC Press, 2013.

Foucault, Michel. *Discipline and Punish: The Birth of the Prison*. Translated by Alan Sheridan. New York City: Vintage Books, 1977.

– "The Subject and Power." *Critical Inquiry* 8, no. 4 (1982): 777–95.

– "Governmentality." In *The Foucault Effect: Studies in Governmentality*, ed. Graham Burchell, Colin Gordon, and Peter Miller, 87–104. Chicago: University of Chicago Press, 1991.

Fox, Richard Wrightman, and T. Jackson Lears, eds. *The Culture of Consumption: Critical Essays in American History, 1880–1980*. New York: Pantheon Books, 1983.

Francis, Martin. "The Domestication of the Male? Recent Research on Nineteenth- and Twentieth-Century British Masculinity." *Historical Journal* 45, no. 3 (2002): 637–52.

Freeman, Michael. *Railways and the Victorian Imagination*. New Haven: Yale University Press, 1999.

Freund, Daniel. "The Battle for a Brighter America: A Social History of Natural Light, 1850–1935." PhD dissertation, Columbia University, 2008.

Furner, Mary O. *Advocacy and Objectivity: A Crisis in the Professionalization of American Social Science, 1865–1905*. New Brunswick: Transaction Publishers, 2011.

Gamm, Gerald, and Robert D. Putnam. "The Growth of Voluntary Organizations in America, 1840–1940." *Journal of Interdisciplinary History* 29, no. 4 (1999): 511–57.

Gassan, Richard H. *The Birth of American Tourism: New York, the Hudson Valley, and American Culture*. Amherst: University of Massachusetts Press, 2008.

Gems, Gerald. "Welfare Capitalism and Blue-Collar Sport: The Legacy of Labour Unrest." *Rethinking History* 5, no. 1 (2001): 43–58.

Gibbins, Roger, and Loleen Berdahl. *Western Visions, Western Futures: Perspectives on the West in Canada*. 2nd ed. Toronto: University of Toronto Press, 2003.

Gilbert, Arthur N. "Buggery and the British Navy, 1700–1861." *Journal of Social History* 10 (1976): 72–98.

Gilkeson, John H., Jr. *Middle-Class Providence, 1820–1940*. Princeton: Princeton University Press, 1986.

Gillespie, Greg. *Hunting for Empire: Narratives of Sport in Rupert's Land, 1840–70*. Vancouver: UBC Press, 2007.

Giltner, Scott E. *Hunting and Fishing in the New South: Black Labor and White Leisure after the Civil War*. Baltimore: Johns Hopkins University Press, 2008.

Goodyear, III, Frank H. "A Wilderness for Men: The Adirondacks in the Photographs of Seneca Ray Stoddard." In *Gender and Landscape: Renegotiating Morality and Space*, ed. Lorraine Dowler, Josephine Carubia, and Bonj Szczygiel, 124–42. London: Routledge, 2005.

Gordon, Beverly. "The Souvenir: Messenger of the Extraordinary." *Journal of Popular Culture* 20, no. 3 (1986): 135–46.

Graham, Stephen, and David Wood. "Digitizing Surveillance: Categorization, Space, Inequality." *Critical Social Policy* 23, no. 3 (2003): 227–48.

Gray, Charlotte. *Flint and Feather: The Life and Times of E. Pauline Johnson, Tekahionwake*. Toronto: HarperFlamingo, 2002.

Grier, Katherine C. "Imagining the Parlor, 1830–1880." In *Perspectives on American Furniture*, ed. Gerald W.R. Ward, 205–39. New York: W.W. Norton for the Henry Francis du Pont Winterthur Museum, 1988.

– *Culture and Comfort: Parlor Making and Middle-Class Identity, 1850–1930*. London: Smithsonian Institution Press, 1997.

Guttmann, Allen. *From Ritual to Record: The Nature of Modern Sports*. New York: Columbia University Press, 1978.

– *Women's Sports: A History*. New York: Columbia University Press, 1991.

– *Games & Empires: Modern Sports and Cultural Imperialism*. New York: Columbia University Press, 1994.

Haddad, John R. "The Wild West Turns East: Audience, Ritual, and Regeneration in Buffalo Bill's Boxer Uprising." *American Studies* 49, no. 3/4 (2008): 5–38.

Haldrup, Michael. "Laid-Back Mobilities: Second Home Holidays in Time and Space." *Tourism Geographies* 6, no. 4 (2004): 434–55.

Hall, Jacquelyn Dowd, James L. Leloudis, Robert Rodgers Korstad, Mary Murphy, Lu Ann Jones, and Christopher B. Daly. *Like a Family: The Making of a Southern Cottage Mill World*. Chapel Hill: University of North Carolina Press, 1987.

Hall, M. Ann. *The Girl and the Game: A History of Women's Sport in Canada*. Peterborough: Broadview Press, 2002.

Halttunen, Karen. "From Parlor to Living Room: Domestic Space and the Culture of Personality." In *Consuming Visions: Accumulation and Display of Goods in America, 1880–1920*, ed. Simon J. Bronner, 157–89. New York: W.W. Norton, 1989.

Handelman, Don. *Models and Mirrors: Towards an Anthropology of Public Events*. Cambridge: Cambridge University Press, 1989.

Hannam, Kevin, Mimi Sheller, and John Urry. "Editorial: Mobilities, Immobilities and Moorings." *Mobilities* 1, no. 1 (2006): 1–22.

Harley, J.B. *The New Nature of Maps: Essays in the History of Cartography*. Edited by Paul Laxton. Baltimore: Johns Hopkins University Press, 2002.

Harris, Cole. *Making Native Space: Colonialism, Resistance, and Reserves in British Columbia*. Vancouver: UBC Press, 2002.

Haun-Moss, Beverly. "Layered Hegemonies: The Production and Regulation of Canoeing Desire in the Province of Ontario." *Topia* 7 (Spring 2002): 39–55.

Hermer, Joe. *Regulating Eden: The Nature of Order in the North American Parks*. Toronto: University of Toronto Press, 2002.

Heron, Craig. *Booze: A Distilled History*. Toronto: Between the Lines Press, 2003.

Hinsley, Curtis M. "Zunis and Brahmins: Cultural Ambivalence in the Gilded Age." In *Romantic Motives: Essays on Anthropological Sensibility*, ed. George W. Stocking Jr, 169–207. Madison: University of Wisconsin Press, 1989.

Hodgins, Bruce, and Margaret Hobbs, eds. *Nastawgan: The Canadian North by Canoe and Snowshoe*. Toronto: Dundurn Press, 1987.

Hoffman, Ronald. "The History of the American Canoe Association, 1880–1960." PhD dissertation, Springfield College, 1967.

Hoffmann, Charles. *The Depression of the Nineties: An Economic History*. Westport: Greenwood, 1970.

Hoganson, Kristin. "Buying into Empire: American Consumption at the Turn of the Twentieth Century." In *Colonial Crucible: Empire in the Making of the Modern American State*, ed. Alfred McCoy and Francisco Antonio Scarano, 248–59. Madison: University of Wisconsin Press, 2009.

Holmes, Allison P., Bryan S.R. Grimwood, Lauren J. King, and the Lutsel K'e Dene First Nation. "Creating an Indigenized Visitor Code of Conduct: The Development of Denesoline Self-Determination for Sustainable Tourism." *Journal of Sustainable Tourism* 24, no. 8–9 (2016): 1177–93.

Hooke, Katharine N. *From Campsite to Cottage: Early Stoney Lake*. Occasional Paper 13. Peterborough: Peterborough Historical Society, 1992.

Horrell, Jeffrey L. *Seneca Ray Stoddard: Transforming the Adirondack Wilderness in Text and Image*. Syracuse: Syracuse University Press, 1999.

Horsman, Reginald. *Race and Manifest Destiny: The Origins of American Racial Anglo-Saxonism*. Cambridge: Harvard University Press, 1981.

Howell, Colin. *Northern Sandlots: A Social History of Maritime Baseball*. Toronto: University of Toronto Press, 1995.

– *Blood, Sweat, and Cheers: Sport and the Making of Modern Canada*. Toronto: University of Toronto Press, 2001.
– "Borderlands, Baselines, and Big Game: Conceptualizing the Northeast as a Sporting Region." In *New England and the Maritime Provinces: Connections and Comparisons*, ed. Stephen J. Hornsby and John G. Reid, 264–79. Montreal and Kingston: McGill-Queen's University Press, 2005.
Hunt, Alan. "Regulating Heterosocial Space: Sexual Politics in the Early Twentieth Century." *Journal of Historical Sociology* 15, no. 1 (2002): 1–34.
Hutton, George V. *The Great Hudson River Brick Industry: Commemorating Three and One Half Centuries of Brickmaking*. Fleischmann: Purple Mountain Press, 2003.
Ibson, John. *Picturing Men: A Century of Male Relationships in Everyday American Photography*. Chicago: University of Chicago Press, 2006.
Jacoby, Karl. *Crimes against Nature: Squatters, Poachers, Thieves, and the Hidden History of American Conservation*. Berkeley: University of California Press, 2001.
James, C.L.R. *Beyond a Boundary*. London: Hutchinson, 1963.
Jasen, Patricia. *Wild Things: Nature, Culture, and Tourism in Ontario, 1790–1914*. Toronto: University of Toronto Press, 1995.
Jennings, John. *The Canoe: A Living Tradition*. Toronto: Firefly Books, 2002.
Jennings, John, Bruce W. Hodgins, and Doreen Small, eds, *The Canoe in Canadian Cultures*. Toronto: Natural Heritage/Natural History, 1999.
Jensen, Joan M. "Cloth, Butter, and Boarders: Women's Household Production for the Market." *Review of Radical Political Economics* 12 (1980): 14–24.
Johnson, Susan Lee. "Bulls, Bears, and Dancing Boys: Race, Gender, and Leisure in the California Gold Rush." *Radical History Review* 60 (1994): 5–37.
Johnston, C. Fred. "Canoe Sport in Canada: Anglo-American Hybrid?" in *Canexus: The Canoe in Canadian Culture*, ed. James Raffan and Bert Horwood, 59–71. Toronto: Betelgeuse Books, 1988.
– *100 Years of Champions: The Canadian Canoe Association, 1900–2000*. Kingston: Canadian Canoe Association, 2003.
Johnston, Matt. "National Spectacle from the Boat and from the Train: Moulding Perceptions of History in American Scenic Guides of the Nineteenth Century." *University of Toronto Quarterly* 73, no. 4 (2004): 1021–35.
Jones, Karen. "Review of *Trafficking Subjects*." *English Studies in Canada* 31, no. 4 (2005): 235–7.
Jordan, Ben. "'Conservation of Boyhood': Boy Scouting's Modest Manliness and Natural Resource Conservation, 1910–1930." *Environmental History* 15 (2010): 612–42.
Joyce, Patrick. *The Rule of Freedom: Liberalism and the Modern City*. London: Verso, 2003.
Kapor, Vladimir. *Local Colour: A Travelling Concept*. Bern: Peter Lang, 2009.
Kealey, Gregory S. *Workers and Canadian History*. Montreal and Kingston: McGill-Queen's University Press, 1995.

Kerber, Linda K. "Separate Spheres, Female Worlds, Woman's Place: The Rhetoric of Women's History." *Journal of American History* 75, no. 1 (1988): 9–39.

Keyssar, Alexander. *The Right to Vote: The Contested History of Democracy in the United States.* New York: Basic Books, 2009.

Kidd, Bruce. *The Struggle for Canadian Sport.* Toronto: University of Toronto Press, 1996.

Kimmel, Michael S. "Consuming Manhood: The Feminization of American Culture and the Recreation of the Male Body, 1832–1920." *Michigan Quarterly Review* 33 (1994): 7–36.

Knight, William. "'Our Sentimental Fisheries': Angling and State Fisheries Administration in 19th Century Ontario." MA thesis, Trent University, 2006.

Krause, Sydney. "Penn's Elm and Edgar Huntly: Dark 'Instruction to the Heart.'" *American Literature* 66, no. 3 (1994): 463–84.

Kwolek-Folland, Angel. "The Elegant Dugout: Domesticity and Moveable Culture in the United States, 1870–1900." *American Studies* 25, no. 2 (1984): 21–37.

Leach, William. *Land of Desire: Merchants, Power, and the Rise of a New American Culture.* New York: Pantheon Books, 1993.

Lears, T. Jackson. *No Place of Grace: Antimodernism and the Transformation of American Culture, 1880–1920.* Chicago: University of Chicago Press, 1994 [1981].

Lefebvre, Henri. *The Production of Space.* Translated by Donald Nicholson-Smith. Oxford: Blackwell, 1991 [1974].

Lenskyj, Helen J. *Inside the Olympic Industry: Power, Politics, and Activism.* Albany: State University of New York Press, 2000.

Lightman, Bernard, ed. *Victorian Science in Context.* Chicago: University of Chicago Press, 1997.

Lindsay, Peter L. "The Impact of Military Garrisons on the Development of Sport in British North America." *Canadian Journal of History of Sport and Physical Education* 1, no. 1 (1970): 33–44.

Linton, Marilyn R. *The Ballast Island Chronicles: A History of the Western Canoe Association and ILYA Beginnings.* Linwood: M.R. Linton, 1994.

Little, J.I. "Scenic Tourism on the Northeastern Borderland: Lake Memphremagog's Steamboat Excursions and Resort Hotels, 1850–1900." *Journal of Historical Geography* 35, no. 4 (2009): 716–42.

– "Life without Conventionality: American Social Reformers as Summer Campers on Lake Memphremagog, Quebec, 1878–1905." *Journal of the Gilded Age and the Progressive Era* 9, no. 3 (2010): 281–311.

Loo, Tina. "Of Moose and Men: Hunting for Masculinities in British Columbia, 1880–1939." *Western Historical Quarterly* 32, no. 3 (2001): 296–319.

Love, Christopher. *A Social History of Swimming in England, 1800–1918: Splashing in the Serpentine.* London: Routledge, 2008.

Lowe, Graham S. "Class, Job, and Gender in the Canadian Office." *Labour/Le Travail* 10 (Autumn 1982): 11.

Mackenzie, John. *The Empire of Nature: Hunting, Conservation, and British Imperialism*. Manchester: Manchester University Press, 1988.

Mackintosh, Phillip Gordon. "'The Development of Higher Urban Life' and the Geographic Imagination: Beauty, Art, and Moral Environmentalism in Toronto, 1900–1920." *Journal of Historical Geography* 31 (2005): 688–722.

Mackintosh, Phillip Gordon, and Richard Anderson. "The *Toronto Star* Fresh Air Fund: Transcendental Rescue in a Modern City, 1900–1915." *Geographical Review* 99, no. 4 (2009): 539–62.

Mackintosh, Phillip Gordon, and Clyde R. Forsberg. "Performing the Lodge: Masonry, Masculinity, and Nineteenth-Century North American Moral Geography." *Journal of Historical Geography* 35 (2009): 451–72.

MacLeod, David I. *Building Character in the American Boy: The Boy Scouts, YMCA and Their Forerunners, 1870–1920*. Madison: University of Wisconsin Press, 1983.

Macnaghten, Phil, and John Urry. "Bodies of Nature: Introduction." *Body and Society* 6, no. 3–4 (2000): 1–11.

Magdalinski, Tara. *Sport, Technology, and the Body: The Nature of Performance*. New York: Routledge, 2000.

Mangan, J.A. *The Games Ethic and Imperialism: Aspects of the Diffusion of an Ideal*. London: Viking, 1986.

Manley, Atwood. *Rushton and His Times in American Canoeing*. Syracuse: Syracuse University Press, 1968.

Manore, Jean L. "The Historical Erasure of an Indigenous Identity in the Borderlands: The Western Abenaki of Vermont, New Hampshire, and Quebec." *Journal of Borderland Studies* 26, no. 2 (2011): 179–96.

Marien, Mary Warner. *Photography: A Cultural History*. 2nd ed. Upper Saddle River: Prentice Hall, 2006.

Marks, Lynne. *Revivals and Roller Rinks: Religion, Leisure, and Identity in Late-Nineteenth-Century Small-Town Ontario*. Toronto: University of Toronto Press, 1997.

Marks, Patricia. *Bicycles, Bangs, and Bloomers: The New Woman in the Popular Press*. Lexington: University of Kentucky Press, 1990.

Mason, Fred. "R. Tait McKenzie's Medical Work and Early Exercise Therapies for People with Disabilities." *Sport History Review* 39, no. 1 (2008): 45–70.

Maynard, Steven. "Rough Work and Rugged Men: The Social Construction of Masculinity in Working-Class History." *Labour/Le Travail* 23 (1989): 159–69.

– "Queer Musings on Masculinity and History." *Labour/Le Travail* 42 (1998): 183–97.

McClintock, Anne. *Imperial Leather: Race, Gender, and Sexuality in the Colonial Contest*. New York: Routledge, 1995.

McCrone, Kathleen E. *Playing the Game: Sport and the Physical Emancipation of English Women, 1870–1914*. Lexington: University of Kentucky Press, 1988.
McIvor, Heather. *Women and Politics in Canada*. Peterborough: Broadview Press, 1996.
McKay, Ian. *Quest of the Folk: Antimodernism and Cultural Selection in Twentieth-Century Nova Scotia*. Montreal and Kingston: McGill-Queen's University Press, 1994.
McMullin, Thomas A. "Revolt at Riverside: Victorian Virtue and the Charles River Canoeing Controversy, 1903–1905." *New England Quarterly* 73, no. 3 (2000): 482–94.
McMurray, David. "Rivaling the Gentleman in the Gentle Art: The Authority of the Victorian Woman Angler." *Sport History Review* 39, no. 2 (2008): 99–126.
McMurry, Sally Ann. *Transforming Rural Life: Dairying Families and Agricultural Change*. Baltimore: Johns Hopkins University Press, 1995.
McNairn, Jeffrey L. *The Capacity to Judge: Public Opinion and Deliberative Democracy in Upper Canada, 1791–1854*. Toronto: University of Toronto Press, 2000.
Melosi, Martin V. *The Sanitary City: Urban Infrastructure in America from Colonial Times to the Present*. Baltimore: Johns Hopkins University Press, 2000.
Metcalfe, Alan. "The Growth of Organized Sport and the Development of Amateurism in Canada, 1807–1914." In *Not Just a Game: Essays in Canadian Sport Sociology*, ed. Jean Harvey and Hart Cantelon, 33–50. Ottawa: University of Ottawa Press, 1988.
– "The Meaning of Amateurism: A Case Study of Canadian Sport, 1884–1970." *Canadian Journal of the History of Sport* 26, no. 2 (1995): 33–48.
Michael, Mike. "These Boots Are Made for Walking ...: Mundane Technology, the Body and Human-Environment Relations." *Body and Society* 6, no. 107 (2000): 107–26.
Miller, Dan. "The Charles River Canoe." *Wooden Canoe* 30, no. 3 (2007): 8–15.
Milloy, John. *A National Crime: The Canadian Government and the Residential School System*. Winnipeg: University of Manitoba Press, 1999.
Milne-Smith, Amy. "A Flight to Domesticity? Making a Home in the Gentleman's Clubs of London, 1880–1914." *Journal of British Studies* 45 (2006): 796–818.
– "Club Talk: Gossip, Masculinity and Oral Communities in Late Nineteenth-Century London." *Gender and History* 21, no. 1 (2009): 86–106.
– *London Clubland: A Cultural History of Gender and Class in Late Victorian Britain*. New York: Palgrave Macmillan, 2011.
Milz, Sabine. "'Publica(c)tion': E. Pauline Johnson's Publishing Venues and Their Contemporary Significance." *Studies in Canadian Literature/Études en littérature canadienne* 29, no. 1 (2004): 127–45.
Miron, Janet. *Prisons, Asylums, and the Public: Institutional Visiting in the Nineteenth Century*. Toronto: University of Toronto Press, 2011.

Mitchell, Timothy. *Colonising Egypt*. Berkeley: University of California Press, 1991.
– *The Rule of Experts: Egypt, Techno-politics, Modernity*. Berkeley: University of California Press, 2002.
Moffat, Eva L. *The Ancestors of Daniel Freeman Britton of Westmoreland and Gananoque, 1808–1807*. n.p., 1953.
Morgan, Cecilia. *"A Happy Holiday": English Canadians and Transatlantic Tourism*. Toronto: University of Toronto Press, 2008.
Nash, Catherine. "Irish Placenames: Postcolonial Locations." *Transactions of the Institute of British Geographers* 24, no. 4 (1999): 457–80.
Nash, Linda. *Inescapable Ecologies: A History of Environment, Disease, and Knowledge*. Berkeley: University of California Press, 2006.
Nash, Roderick. *Wilderness and the American Mind*. New Haven: Yale University Press, 2001 [1967].
Oberly, James W. *A Nation of Statesmen: The Political Culture of the Stockbridge-Munsee Mohicans, 1815–1972*. Norman: University of Oklahoma Press, 2005.
O'Brien, Jean M. *Firsting and Lasting: Writing Indians Out of Existence in New England*. Minneapolis: University of Minnesota Press, 2010.
Oliver, Jeff. "On Mapping and Its Afterlife: Unfolding Landscapes in Northwestern North America." *World Archaeology* 43, no. 1 (2011): 66–85.
Opp, James. "Finding the View: Landscape, Place, and Colour Slide Photography in Southern Alberta." In *Placing Memory and Remembering Place in Canada*, ed. James Opp and John C. Walsh, 271–90. Vancouver: UBC Press, 2010.
Osterud, Nancy Grey. *Bonds of Community: The Lives of Farm Women in Nineteenth-Century New York*. Ithaca: Cornell University Press, 1991.
Otis, Melissa. "At Home in the Adirondacks: A History of Indigenous and Euroamerican Interactions, 1776–1920." PhD dissertation, University of Toronto, 2013.
– *Rural Indigenousness: A History of Iroquoian and Algonquian Peoples of the Adirondacks*. Syracuse: Syracuse University Press, 2018.
Palmer, Bryan. *A Culture in Conflict: Skilled Workers and Industrial Capitalism in Hamilton, Ontario, 1860–1914*. Montreal and Kingston: McGill-Queen's University Press, 1979.
Paris, Leslie. *Children's Nature: The Rise of the American Summer Camp*. New York: New York University Press, 2008.
Park, Roberta. "Sport, Gender, and Society in Transatlantic Victorian Perspective." *International Journal of the History of Sport* 24, no. 12 (2007): 1570–1603.
Parr, Joy. "Ontario Agricultural Wage Labour in Historical Perspective." *Labour/Le Travail* 15 (1985): 91–103.
Peiss, Kathy. *Cheap Amusements: Working Women and Leisure in Turn-of-the-Century New York*. Philadelphia: Temple University Press, 1986.

Perry, Adele. *On the Edge of Empire: Gender, Race, and the Making of British Columbia*. Toronto: University of Toronto Press, 2001.
Petersen, Stephen. "Tableaux." In *Encyclopedia of Nineteenth-Century Photography*, ed. John Hannavy, 1373–5. London: Routledge, 2013.
Phillips, Ruth B. and Christopher B. Steiner, eds. *Unpacking Culture: Art and Commodity in Colonial and Postcolonial Worlds*. Berkeley: University of California Press, 1999.
Podruchny, Carolyn. *Making the Voyageur World: Travelers and Traders in the North American Fur Trade*. Toronto: University of Toronto Press, 2006.
Pope, S.W. "Amateurism and American Sports Culture: The Invention of an Athletic Tradition in the United States, 1870–1900." *International Journal of the History of Sport* 13, no. 3 (1996): 290–309.
Porter, Dilwyn, and Stephen Wagg, eds. *Amateurism in British Sport: It Matters Not Who Won or Lost?* London: Taylor and Francis, 2007.
Porter, Libby. "Planning Displacement: The Real Legacy of Major Sporting Events." *Planning Theory & Practice* 10, no. 3 (2009): 395–9.
Poulter, Gillian. *Becoming Native in a Foreign Land: Sport, Visual Culture, and Identity in Montreal, 1840–1885*. Vancouver: UBC Press, 2009.
Putney, Clifford. *Muscular Christianity: Manhood and Sports in Protestant America*. Boston: Harvard University Press, 2003.
Radforth, Ian. *Bushworkers and Bosses: Logging in Northern Ontario, 1900–1980*. Toronto: University of Toronto Press, 1987.
Raffan, James. *Bark, Skin, and Cedar: Exploring the Canoe in Canadian Experience*. Toronto: Harper Collins, 1999.
Raffan, James, and Bert Horwood, eds. *Canexus: The Canoe in Canadian Culture*. Toronto: Betelguese Books, 1988.
Raibmon, Paige. "Living on Display: Colonial Visions of Aboriginal Domestic Space." *BC Studies* 140 (2003): 69–89.
– *Authentic Indians: Episodes of Encounter from the Late-Nineteenth-Century Northwest Coast*. Durham: Duke University Press, 2005.
Reid, Jennifer I.M. "'Fair Descendant of the Mohawk': Pauline Johnson as an Ontological Marker." In *Historical Papers 2001*, ed. Bruce L. Guenther, 5–21. Canadian Society of Church History, 2001. https://historicalpapers.journals.yorku.ca/index.php/historicalpapers/article/viewFile/39317/35647
Rendell, Jane. "The Clubs of St James's: Places of Public Patriarchy – Exclusivity, Domesticity and Secrecy." *Journal of Architecture* 4 (1999): 167–89.
Richter, Amy. *Home on the Rails: Women, the Railroad, and the Rise of Public Domesticity*. Chapel Hill: University of North Carolina Press, 2005.
Roberts, M.J.D. "Between Fame and Eccentricity: John 'Rob Roy' Macgregor, Almost Eminent Victorian." *History Australia* 2, no. 2 (2005): 36-1–36-8.
Roche, Maurice. *Mega-Events and Modernity: Olympics and Expos in the Growth of Global Culture*. London: Routledge, 2000.

Roedigger, David R. *Working Toward Whiteness: How America's Immigrants Became White; The Strange Journey from Ellis Island to the Suburbs*. New York: Basic Books, 2005.
Rose, Marilyn J. "Pauline Johnson: New World Poet." *British Journal of Canadian Studies* 12, no. 2 (1997): 298–307.
Rose, Nikolas. *Powers of Freedom: Reframing Political Thought*. Cambridge: Cambridge University Press, 1999.
Rose-Redwood, Reuben. "Rationalizing the Landscape: Superimposing the Grid upon the Island of Manhattan." MA thesis, Pennsylvania State University, 2002.
Rosenzweig, Roy. *Eight Hours for What We Will: Workers and Leisure in an Industrial City*. Cambridge: Cambridge University Press, 1983.
Rosenzweig, Roy, and Elizabeth Blackmar. *The Park and the People: A History of Central Park*. Ithaca: Cornell University Press, 1992.
Rothman, Hal K. "Selling the Meaning of Place: Entrepreneurship, Tourism, and Community Transformation in the Twentieth-Century American West." *Pacific Historical Review* 65, no. 4 (1996): 525–57.
Rousmaniere, John. *The America's Cup 1851–1983*. London: Pelham Books, 1983.
Roy, Wendy. "Visualizing Labrador: Maps, Photographs, and Geographical Naming in Mina Hubbard's *A Woman's Way through Unknown Labrador*." *Studies in Canadian Literature* 29, no. 1 (2004): 13–34.
Rubies, Joan Pau. "Travel Writing and Ethnography." In *The Cambridge Companion to Travel Writing*, ed. Peter Hulme and Tim Youngs, 242–60. New York: Cambridge University Press, 2002.
Rydell, Robert. *All the World's a Fair: Visions of Empire at American International Expositions, 1876–1916*. Chicago: University of Chicago Press, 1987.
Sager, Eric W. "The Transformation of the Canadian Domestic Servant, 1871–1931." *Social Science History* 31, no. 4 (2007): 509–37.
Sagne, Jean. "All Kinds of Portraits: The Photographer's Studio." In *A New History of Photography*, ed. Michael Frizot, 102–22. Cologne: Konneman, 1998.
Said, Edward. *Orientalism*. New York: Vintage, 1978.
– *Culture and Imperialism*. Toronto: Random House, 1993.
Saxton, Alexander. *The Rise and Fall of the White Republic: Class Politics and Mass Culture in Nineteenth-Century America*. London: Verso, 2003.
Schaffner, Cynthia V.A., and Lori Zabar. "The Founding and Design of William Merrit Chase's Shinnecock Hills Summer School of Art and the Art Village." *Winterthur Portfolio* 44, no. 4 (2010): 303–50.
Schivelbusch, Wolfgang. *The Railway Journey: The Industrialization of Time and Space in the Nineteenth Century*. Berkeley: University of California Press, 1986.
Schneirov, Richard, Shelton Stromquist, and Nick Salvatore, eds. *The Pullman Strike and the Crisis of the 1890s: Essays on Labor and Politics*. Chicago: University of Illinois Press, 1999.

Schoolman, Morton, and Alvin Magid. *Reindustrializing New York State: Strategies, Implications, Challenges.* Albany: State University of New York Press, 1986.

Schroeder, Patricia R. "Passing for Black: Coon Songs and the Performance of Race." *Journal of American Culture* 33, no. 2 (2010): 139–53.

Schultz, Stanley K., and Clay McShane. "To Engineer the Metropolis: Sewers, Sanitation, and City Planning in Late-Nineteenth-Century America." *Journal of American History* 65, no. 2 (1978): 389–411.

Schuster, David. *Neurasthenic Nation: America's Search for Health, Happiness, and Comfort, 1869–1920.* New Brunswick: Rutgers University Press, 2011.

Schwartz, Joan M., and James R. Ryan, eds. *Picturing Place: Photography and the Geographical Imagination.* London: I.B. Tauris, 2003.

Scobey, David M. *Empire City: The Making and Meaning of the New York City Landscape.* Philadelphia: Temple University Press, 2003.

Scott, James C. *Seeing like a State: How Certain Schemes to Improve the Human Condition Have Failed.* New Haven: Yale University Press, 1998.

Sekula, Allan. "Photography between Labour and Capital." In *Mining Photographs and Other Pictures, 1948–1968*, ed. Benjamin H.D. Buchloh and Robert Wilkie, 193–268. Halifax: Press of the Nova Scotia College of Art and Design, 1983.

Shannon, Brent. "Fashion, Masculinity, and the Cultivation of the Male Consumer in Britain, 1860–1914." *Victorian Studies* 46, no. 4 (2004): 597–630.

Sheller, Mimi, and John Urry. "The New Mobilities Paradigm." *Environment and Planning A* 38 (2006): 207–26.

Simpson, Leanne Betasamosake. *As We Have Always Done: Indigenous Freedom Through Radical Resurgence.* Minneapolis: University of Minnesota Press, 2017.

Simpson, Mark. *Trafficking Subjects: The Politics of Mobility in Nineteenth-Century America.* Minneapolis: University of Minnesota Press, 2005.

Smalley, Andrea L. "'Our Lady Sportsmen': Gender, Class, and Conservation in Sport Hunting Magazines, 1873–1920." *Journal of the Gilded Age and Progressive Era* 4, no. 4 (2005): 355–80.

Smith, Susan W. *A History of Recreation in the Thousand Islands.* Parks Canada, 1974.

Stanley, Meg. "More Than Just a Spare Rib but Not Quite a Whole Canoe: Some Aspects of Women's Canoe-Tripping Experiences, 1900–1940." In *Using Wilderness: Essays on the Evolution of Youth Camping in Ontario*, ed. Bruce E. Hodgins and Bernadine Dodge, 51–60. Peterborough: Frost Centre for Canadian Heritage and Development Studies, 1992.

Steves, Stan, ed. *Indigenous Peoples, National Parks and Protected Areas: New Paradigm Linking Conservation, Culture and Rights.* Tuscon: University of Arizona Press, 2014.

Stocking, George W., Jr. *Victorian Anthropology.* New York: Free Press, 1987.

Stoler, Ann Laura. "Making Empire Respectable: The Politics of Race and Sexual Morality in Twentieth-Century Colonial Cultures." *Cultural Politics* 11 (1997): 344–73.

– *Carnal Knowledge and Imperial Power: Race and the Intimate in Colonial Rule*. Berkeley: University of California Press, 2002.
Stover, John F. *American Railroads*. Chicago: University of Chicago Press, 1997.
Stradling, David. *The Nature of New York: An Environmental History of the Empire State*. Ithaca: Cornell University Press, 2010.
Strauss, David. "Toward a Consumer Culture: 'Adirondack Murray' and the Wilderness Vacation." *American Quarterly* 39, no. 2 (1987): 270–86.
Strong, John A. *The Montaukett Indians of Eastern Long Island*. Syracuse: Syracuse University Press, 2001.
Strong-Boag, Veronica, and Carole Gerson. *Paddling Her Own Canoe: The Times and Texts of E. Pauline Johnson (Tekahionwake)*. Toronto: University of Toronto Press, 2000.
Surtees, Robert J. "Land Cessions, 1763–1830." In *Aboriginal Ontario: Historical Perspectives on the First Nations*, ed. Edward S. Rogers and Donald B. Smith, 92–121. Toronto: Dundurn Press, 1994.
Taft, Robert. *Photography and the American Scene*. New York: Dover, 1964.
Tchen, John. *New York before Chinatown: Orientalism and the Shaping of American Culture*. Baltimore: Johns Hopkins University Press, 1999.
Thompson, E.P. *The Making of the English Working Class*. London: V. Gollanz, 1963.
– "Time, Work-Discipline, and Industrial Capitalism." *Past and Present* 38, no. 1 (1967): 56–97.
Thorpe, Jocelyn. *Temagami's Tangled Wild: Race, Gender and the Making of Canadian Nature*. Vancouver: UBC Press, 2012.
Toll, Robert C. *Blacking Up: The Minstrel Show in America*. New York: Oxford University Press, 1974.
Tolles, Bryant F., Jr. *Resort Hotels of the Adirondacks: The Architecture of a Summer Paradise, 1850–1950*. Lebanon: University Press of New England, 2003.
Tomczik, Adam. "'He-Men Could Talk to He-Men in He-Men Language': Lumberjack Work Culture in Maine and Minnesota, 1840–1940." *Historian* 70, no. 4 (2008): 697–715.
Trachtenberg, Alan. *The Incorporation of America: Culture and Society in the Gilded Age*. New York: Hill and Wang, 1982.
Turner, James Morton. "From Woodcraft to 'Leave No Trace': Wilderness, Consumerism, and Environmentalism." *Environmental History* 7, no. 3 (2002): 462–84.
Urry, John. "Social Networks, Travel and Talk." *British Journal of Sociology* 54, no. 2 (2003): 155–75.
Valencius, Conevery Bolton. *The Health of the Country: How American Settlers Understood Themselves and Their Land*. New York: Basic Books, 2002.
van Gennep, Arnold. *The Rites of Passage*. London: Paul, 1960 [1909].
Van Slyck, Abigail. "The Lady and the Library Loafer: Gender and Public Space in Victorian America." *Winterthur Portfolio* 31, no. 4 (1996): 221–42.

- "Kitchen Technologies and Mealtime Rituals: Interpreting the Food Axis at American Summer Camps, 1890–1950." *Technology and Culture* 43, no. 4 (2002): 668–92.
- *A Manufactured Wilderness: Summer Camps and the Shaping of American Youth, 1890–1960*. Minneapolis: University of Minnesota Press, 2006.

Venne, Muriel Stanley. "The 'S' Word: Reclaiming 'Esquao' for Aboriginal Women." In *Unsettled Pasts: Reconceiving the West through Women's History*, ed. Sarah Carter, Lesley Erickson, Patricia Roome, and Char Smith, 123–8. Calgary: University of Calgary Press, 2005.

Vertinsky, Patricia. *The Eternally Wounded Woman: Women, Doctors, and Exercise in the Late Nineteenth Century*. Toronto: St Martin's Press, 1990.

Vicinus, Martha. "Distance and Desire: English Boarding School Friendships, 1870–1920." *Signs* 9, no. 4 (1984): 600–22.

Walden, Keith. *Becoming Modern in Toronto: The Industrial Exhibition and the Shaping of a Late Victorian Culture*. Toronto: University of Toronto Press, 1997.

Walkowitz, Daniel J. *Worker City, Company Town*. Urbana: University of Illinois Press, 1978.

Wall, Sharon. *The Nurture of Nature: Childhood, Antimodernism, and Ontario Summer Camps, 1920–1955*. Vancouver: UBC Press, 2009.

Walsh, John C. "Landscapes of Longing: Colonization and the Problem of State Formation in Canada West." PhD dissertation, University of Guelph, 2001.
- "Performing Public Memory and Re-placing Home in the Ottawa Valley, 1900–1958." In *Placing Memory and Remembering Place in Canada*, ed. James Opp and John C. Walsh, 25–56. Vancouver: UBC Press, 2010.

Walsh, John C., and Steven High. "Rethinking the Concept of Community." *Histoire sociale/Social History* 32, no. 64 (1999): 255–74.

Wamsley, Kevin B., and David Whitson. "Celebrating Violent Masculinities: The Boxing Death of Luther McCarty." *Journal of Sport History* 25, no. 3 (1998): 419–31.

Watkins, Mel. "Foreward." In *Inside the Minstrel Mask: Readings in Nineteenth-Century Blackface Minstrelsy*, ed. Annemarie Bean, James Vernon Hatch, and Brooks Macnamara, ix–x. Hanover: University Press of New England, 1996.

Watson, Andrew. "Poor Soils and Rich Folks: Household Economics and Sustainability in Muskoka, 1850–1920." PhD dissertation, York University, 2014.
- "Pioneering a Rural Identity on the Canadian Shield: Tourism, Household Economies, and Poor Soils in Muskoka, Ontario, 1870–1900," *Canadian Historical Review* 98, no. 2 (2017): 261–93.

Weigold, Marilyn E. *The Long Island Sound: A History of Its People, Places, and Environment*. New York: New York University Press, 2004.

Weir, Robert E. *Class in America: An Encyclopedia*. Westport: Greenwood Press, 2007.

Whaley, Gray S. *Oregon and the Collapse of Illahee: US Empire and the Transformation of an Indigenous World*. Chapel Hill: University of North Carolina Press, 2010.

Williams, Carol J. *Framing the West: Race, Gender, and the Photographic Frontier in the Pacific Northwest*. New York: Oxford University Press, 2003.

Williams, Susan. *Savory Suppers and Fashionable Feasts: Dining in Victorian America*. Knoxville: University of Tennessee Press, 1996.

Wilson, Alexander. *The Culture of Nature: North American Landscapes from Disney to the Exxon Valdez*. Toronto: Between the Lines Press, 1990.

Wilson, William H. *The City Beautiful Movement*. Baltimore: Johns Hopkins University Press, 1989.

Wiltse, Jeff. *Contested Waters: A Social History of Swimming Pools in America*. Chapel Hill: University of North Carolina Press, 2007.

Wiseman, Frederick Matthew. *The Voice of the Dawn: An Autohistory of the Abenaki Nation*. Lebanon, NH: University Press of New England, 2001.

Wurst, LouAnn. "'Human Accumulations': Class and Tourism at Niagara Falls." *International Journal of Historical Archaeology* 15, no. 2 (2011): 254–66.

Youngs, Tim. *Travel Writing in the Nineteenth Century: Filling in the Blank Spaces*. London: Anthem Press, 2006.

Index

Page numbers in italics refer to illustrations.

accountability and transparency, 18–19, 200n30
activities. *See* conduct, regulation of; daily routines and activities; excursions; spectacles
activity arenas, 74, 83, 220n17
Adams, Mary Louise, 142
Adirondack Mountains, 3, 31, 33, 38, 39, 42, 44, 175, 176. *See also* Lake George
advertisements, 12, 89–90
alcohol consumption, 11, 73, 89, *91*, *92*, 93–4
Alden, William L., 12, 196n27
Algonquian peoples, 39, 42, 43
Alnwick Band (Alderville First Nation), 45, 47, 211n97
amateurism and professionalism: amateur ideal, 141–2; concerns with professionalism, 140–1; generalism and, 143; prizes and, 145–6; technology and, 144–5; tension between, 142–3, 146–7
American Canoe Association (ACA): about, 14, 15–16, 31; administrative structure, 16–17, 18, 198nn11–13, 199n24; Canadian members, 16, 37, 147, 149, 197n3; constitution, bylaws, and other rules, 17; establishment and inaugural meet, 3, 15; fees, 19, 200n39; geographical divisions, 17–18, 199n17, 199n20; membership, 19–22, 31, 200n41; as transnational organization, 9, 23, 25, 41, 147, 188; transparency and accountability, 18–19; uniqueness of, 22; as voluntary association, 16, 22, 31; voting rights, 200n34; "whitening" of canoe by, 13. *See also* communication; encampments; membership
American Canoeist, 57, 79, 164, 203n88
Andrews, Thomas G., 162, 165, 166, 180
Anishnaabeg (Ojibwe) people, 43, 44
Archibald, Charles, 149
Aron, Cindy, 79, 167
associations, voluntary, 16, 21, 22, 31, 201n54
audience. *See* spectators

Baden-Powell, Warrington, 102, 148
baggage handlers and porters, 166
Bailey, Beth Tompkins, 166
Baker, Frank, 168, 251n53
Barr, Walwin, 10, 125, 237n61
baseball, 7, 78, 121, 136, 151

bathing, 83, 86; suits (costumes), 119, 120, 137, 155. *See also* swimming
Bederman, Gail, 115
bedroom, 108, 115
Begg, Herb, 29
Benidickson, Jamie, 9
Billings (cook), 170
Bishop, Nathaniel Holmes, 12, 15, 23, 34, 39, 169, 171–2, 207n42
black(s), *181*, 189; cooks and valets, 22, 170; hired to landscape, cook, clean, and entertain, 6; male staff, 168; melodies, 122; musicians, *179*, 186; performers, 131, 172; workers, 180. *See also* people of colour; race
blackballing, 200n44
blackness, performing, 131
Bluff Point, Lake Champlain meet (1895), *28*, 41
Blunt, Alison, 97
boat builders, 12, 177, 179, 255n115
Bouchier, Nancy, 6, 188
bourgeois, 170–1; masculine, 13; recreationists, 60; sport, canoeing as, 139; Victorian(s), 45, 73 107. *See also* middle class
Bow Arrow Point, Lake Champlain meet (1887): breaking camp, 184; Divine Services, 124; labour depicted in photographs, 160, *169*, 169–70, 180, *181*; ladies' camp, 82; travel to, 55–6, 60
Bowdish, Nelson, 255n115
boxing, 121
Brentano, Arthur, 196n26
British Daily Whig, 91, 165
Britton, Clara, 124
Britton, Commodore Charles Edward, 36, 46, 248n8
Britton, Mary Alice, 124
Brooklyn Canoe Club, 99, 111, 168, *169*

Brophy's Point. *See* Wolfe Island meet (1893)
Brown, Dona, 174, 179
Burchard, R.B., 100, 132, 157, 168
Butler, Paul, 93, 152, 165–6

Caldwell, J.C., 211n97
Cameron, Kenneth, 152
campfire(s), 93, 111, 121–3, *122*, 124, 127, 158, 183, 185, 236n43; entertainment, 48, 49, 123; part of daily rhythm (schedule), 5, 15, 87, 117, 118, 121, 159; singing songs around, 136; single-sex, 123
campsite rules, 75, 79, 83, 86, 89, 90, 95; for women, 82
camp store, 25, 27, 74, 76, 78, 84, 90–1, 100, 162, 165, 174; introduced in 1883, 23; run by local merchants, 77
Canadian Canoe Association, 5, 149, 197n3
canoe and canoeing: "birch" signifier, 193n1; boom in, 3, 11–12, 196n26; as camp activity, 120; class and, 13; regulation of, 145; scholarship on, 9, 187–8; technology, 144–5, 243n48; as urban pursuit, 13; "whitening" of, 12–13
canoe cruising, 60–4; about, 13–14, 60; camping along the way, 60–1, *61*; environmental and social experiences, 63; participants, 60; sailing and paddling methods, 63–4; tourism during, 64; use of other transport methods while, 61–2; women in, 60, 63
Canoe Islands, Lake George meets (1881–2): complaints about, 34–5, 206n13; Indigenous canoe races, 151; regatta, 137, *154*; travel to, 57
canoe racing, 3, 5, 78, 120, 137–40, 143–4, 159. *See also* race(s); regattas

Cape Cod, 44
Cape Cod meet (1902), 37, 44, 80, 147, 156
Chartier, Roger, 31
Chauncey, George, 125
Chinese spectacles, 134–5
Chipp, Agnes Marion, 10
Chobee, O.K., 170
Christianity and Divine Services, 87, 124
circulars: early, 60; encampment, 10, 16, 28; as guidebooks, 27; maps produced for, 29, 85; previewed mess tent offerings, 119; provided route, schedule, and fare information, 25, 54, 56, 86; transportation, 66, 70
circus, 118, 133, *134*, 135, 239n107
City Beautiful movement, 74
civilization: advanced, 115, 132; a gendered concept, 115; material markers of, 110; and nature 111; a racial concept, 115, 132; and savagery, 115, 135; wildness and, 100. *See also* domestication
class, 39, 53, 72, 89, 136, 149, 163, 170–1, 173, 188; about, 5–6; and amateurism and professionalism, 141–2; canoeing and, 13; leisure, 65; membership and, 19–21; reinforcement of, 186; train travel and, 66; and visitors to camp, 89–91. *See also* labour; middle class; respectability; upper class; working class
Clementi, Vincent, 35
clothing, 102–7; club uniforms, 104–5; effeminate concerns for men, 106–7; informal, 105; military-influenced uniforms, 102–4, *104*; "negro," 131; during regattas, 137; for women, 106, 137, 246n131. *See also* bathing: suits

Clytie (canoe cruiser), 60, 64
Cody, William "Buffalo Bill," 135
colonialism: cottage, 187, 256n12; dispossession by, 9, 33–4, 40, 47, 186; by sport, 186–7; by tourism, 24–5. *See also* Indigenous peoples
Comer (customs officer), 214n25
commodore(), 16–17, 18, 20, 22, 75, 103, 130, 131, 146, 158, 198nn12–13. *See also individual commodores by name*
Commodore's Review, 130, 131
communication: for accountability and transparency, 18–19, 200n30; alternative sources of, 31; of campsite rules, 86; circulars and yearbooks, 26–7, 29, 31, 203n88; maps, 27, *28*, 29, *30*, *85*, 204n94; reprints in periodicals, 215n37; by transportation committee, 54
community formation: about, 8–9, 185, 188; amateurism and professionalism, 146; campfires, *122*, 123; domestication and, 116; inhabiting and, 126, 136; membership practices, 19–22, 31; policing boundaries and, 91; regattas, 159; shared living, 109; spectacles, 118, 130, *134*, 135
conduct, regulation of: about, 84, 89; communication of rules, 86; daily and weekly schedules, 87–9, 117; gatekeeping role of registration, 75, 86–8, *87*, 98, 108; offsite conduct, 86; rules enforcement, 89, 225n104; use of term, 224n83; visitors and outsiders, 89–91. *See also* alcohol consumption; campsite rules; daily routines and activities
consumption: about, 161–2, 174; boat builders, 177, 179, 255n115; commercial photography, 175–6,

254n106, 254n108; souvenir trade, 174–5; tourism's disguise of, 179. *See also* labour
"Coon Band," 122, 171, 177, *178*, 251nn61–2
Cotton, Commodore Colonel William H., 72, 108–9
Coubert, L.L., 62
Craik, Jennifer, 103–4
Crane, Diana, 105
Cresswell, Tim, 213n6
Crosby, Francis G., 15
Crosbyside Hotel, 34, 76
Cross, Manley, 165
Croton Point, Hudson River meet (1894): boat builders, 179; campfires, 121; excursion to Old Van Cortlandt Manor, 127; regatta, 140–1, 155; street lights, 98; travel to, 57; women's clothing at, 106. *See also* Hudson River Valley
Crow, Mr, and son Willie, 24, 164
Curtis, Bruce, 225n106
customs officials, 25, 55, 57, 59, 75, 100, 214n25

Daily Mail and Empire, 54
daily routines and activities: about, 118–19, 136; bathing and swimming, 119–20; daily and weekly schedules, 87–9, 117; as inhabiting, 117–18; leisurely social interactions, 121; romantic heterosexual relationships, 82, 124–5, 126, 237n61; same-sex relationships, *104*, 125–6; sports, 121, 235n33. *See also* campfires; conduct, regulation of; excursions; spectacles; *particular activities*
dances, 123
Davidoff, Leonore, 16, 200n29
Davis, Clark, 141

Davis, Janet, 133
Dean, Misao, 9
De Certeau, Michel, 8
Delaney, Michael, 55, 214n26
Delaney family, 76–7, 168, 173–4
Delmonico's (New York restaurant), 77
Dening, Greg, 131–2, 240n6
Deseronto Canoe Club, 168
disabilities, competitors with, 152
displacement. *See* colonialism; encampment sites; Indigenous peoples; Sugar Island
Divine Services, 87, 124
D. McElveney and Sons (catering company), 168
domestication: about, 96–7, 115–16; arrival at camp, 75, 86–8, *87*, 96, 97–8, 108; camp amenities, 100; camp as home, 97, 232n97; concerns and anxieties about, 114–15; exterior decorations, 111, *112*, 113; gender and, 113–14; Japanese lanterns, 113; mobility and, 114; neighbourhoods, 99–100; street names and features, 98–9, *99*; tents, 100–2, 107–11. *See also* clothing; kitchen; mess tents; tents
domestic servants, 165–6, 170–1, 249n20
Dowling, Robyn, 97
Doyle, Don, 22
Dufflin, Joseph, 151

Eckford, Harry, 81, 91, 94
Edwards, Commodore Elihu Burritt (E.B.), 23, 24, 35, 40, 143, 146, 163
Edwards-Ficken, H., 197n37
electricity, 98, 228n15; absence of, 113
encampments: about, 3, 4–6, 10–11, 188–9; archival materials, 9–10; attendance, 5, 7, 37; attractions of, 5; breaking camp, 183–4, *184*;

dispossession of Indigenous peoples, 9, 33–4, 47–9, 186; enduring nature of experiences, 184–6, 255n2; fees and costs, 19, 200n39; gender, class, and race, 5–6, 130, 132, *134*, 135, 140, 142, 160, 170–1, 173, 181; inaugural meet, 15, 23; order and control, 7–8; placemaking and community formation, 8–9; spatial theory and, 7. *See also* campfires; class; consumption; daily routines and activities; domestication; encampment governance and organization; encampment sites; excursions; labour; regattas; spectacles; travel; women; *specific meets*

encampment governance and organization: about, 23, 31–2, 73, 94–5; daily and weekly schedules, 88–9, 117; freedom and, 72–3, 75, 86, 200n32; gatekeeping functions of arrival process, 75, 86–8, *87*, 98, 107–8; governmentality, 8, 73, 95, 159; layout and design, 74–5, 82–3, 98; maps, 27, *28*, 29, *30*, *85*, 204n94; member preparation for camp, 25–6; military references, 72; moral environmentalism and, 73–4, 83; organizing committees, 23, 163; racecourse preparation, 83–4, *85*, 150; sanitation and cleanliness, 29, 74, 83; segregation of women's camp, 79–82, 222n48; site construction and preparation, 25, 74, 164–5; site selection, 23–4, 36–8, 207n32; site surveying, 24–5, 83–4, 163, 164; travel preparations, 25; yearly reproduction of, 84. *See also* camp store; communication; conduct, regulation of; headquarters; kitchen; mess tents

encampment sites: about, 33–4, 48–50; accessibility, 36–7; acquisition of Sugar Island, 36, 45, 46–7; aesthetics, 37; Cape Cod, 44; criteria for, 36–8; economic and social richness of, 44–5; Hudson River Valley, 42–3; Lake Champlain, 41–2; Lake George, 34–5, 39; Long Island, 42; map, 4; mobile encampments, 35; Muskoka, 43–4; permanent location discussions, 35–6; reimagination of for tourism and leisure, 38; Stony Lake, 39–40; Thousand Islands, 40–1

environmental: concerns, 84, 85, 150, 156; experiences, 63, 64; history, 6; opportunities, 60

environmentalism, moral, 73–4, 83

Erickson, Bruce, 9

ethnic (minorities), 21, 67, 133

excursions, 126–30; formal excursions, 127; informal outings, 127–9; role and organization of, 118, 126–7; social nature of, 129–30

Fahrni, Magda, 170
Ferry, Darren, 16, 21, 201n54
Field, Russell, 6, 188
fishing, 12, 40, 44, 45, 115, 118, 120, 127, 136, 234n23
Fitzgerald, George, 120
Fitzgerald, James W., 24, 163
Flip (female camper), 82, 130
Forest and Stream: on amateur definition, 142; on boxing match, 121; on buoymen, 153; on camp meals, 119; on canoe regulation, 145; on domestication, 114; on inaugural meet, 15, 23; on Lake George site, 206n13; on nighttime pranks, 123; on permanent campsite, 35–6; on

racing, 147, 152, 156; on return travel, 70; on signal system, —; on Stony Lake site, 207n32; on tents, 102; on train travel, 67; on Willsborough Point site, 118; yearbook announcements in, 203n88
Foster, Frank H., 254n108
Foucault, Michel, 7–8, 224n83
Francis, Martin, 113–14, 116
Frazer, Orange, 57
Fredericks, Gertrude, 124–5
Freedom, 78, 107, 131, 142; afforded by the meets, 72, 75, 105; rule through, 73, 86, 94–5; sense of, 72–3, 75, 200n32; spaces of, 75, 94; travel and, 54, 64
Freeman, Michael, 64–5
Furner, Mary O., 242n24

Gamm, Gerald, 16
Gard, Gertrude, 125, 237n61
Gassan, Richard, 42
gender, 53, 115, *134*; binary affirmed, 134; boundaries and the circus, 134; and canoe trips, 63; civilization and, 115; colonialism and, 80; domestication and, 110, 113–14; hierarchies of race and, 130, 140, 181; masculinity, 20, 97, 106, 186; prescribed roles, 73; shaped the social, cultural, and physical landscapes of the meets, 6, 7, 123; spectacles and, 130, 133–4, 136; and sporting ability, 13, 160, 188. *See also* clothing; middle-class: men; sexuality and intimacy; upper–class: men; women
geographical divisions, ACA, 17–18, 199n17, 199n20
Gibson, Robert W., 160
Glimpses of the ACA (souvenir albums), 112, 176–9

Goodsell, D.B., 68, 93, 168, 174–5, 186, 251n62
governance. *See* encampment governance and organization
governmentality, 8, 73, 95, 159
Graham, Stephen, 88
Grindstone Island meets (1884–6, 1896–7): aesthetics of, 37; alcohol consumption, 93; arrival by steamboat, 55, 69–70; boat builders at, 177, 179; campfire music, 122; campsite rules, 86; clothing, 105; excursions, 128, 129, *129*; meals and mess tent, 76–7, 100, *103*, 168; memories of, 185; military reference for, 72; regatta, 143, 147, 153–4, 156, 157; return home from, 55, 70; Seavey's spectacle, 171; tensions with Delaney family, 173–4; travel to, 57–8, 60
guidebooks, 29, 39, 42, 53, 56–7, 70; circulars functioned as, 27; subgenre of travel literature, 56. *See also* circulars

Haag, Mr, 20
Haberton, John, 197n37
Haddad, John, 135
Haldrup, Michael, 52–3, 117, 126–7
Hale, Thomas J., 10
Hall, Catharine, 16, 200n29
Halttunen, Karen, 107, 232n97
Handelman, Don, 130
Hannam, Kevin, 215n45
Harley, J.B., 25
Harris, Cole, 33, 212n112
Haudenosaunee people, 39, 43, 44
Hay Island meet (1899), 86, 149
headquarters, encampment, 27, 74–6, *76*, 80, 84, 86, 90, 98, 100, *104*, 117, 121, 131, *138*, 179; camp bulletin board at, 86; codebooks sold at,

88; sacred space on Sundays, 124; secretary's tent at, 98; as space of order and discipline, *138*
Heighway, A.E., 152, 157
Heron, Craig, 91, 93
Hinsley, Curtis, 232n85
Hoffman, Ronald, 198n11, 199n20
Hoganson, Kristin, 113
homosocial: encounters, 135; intimacies, *104*; locales, 97; masculine space, 78, 126; world of the encampments, 123
hotel(s), 36, 39, 41, 77, 79, 86, 89, 101, 115, 155, 168, 207n30; luxury, 39; resort, 40, 42; workers, 162
Hotel Champlain, 28
Howell, Colin, 6, 78, 153, 188
Howell, D.J., 124
Hudson River Valley, 42–3. *See also* Croton Point, Hudson River meet (1894)
hunting, 78, 160–1, 186, 234n19

Ianthe Canoe Club, 98, 158
Ibson, John, 125
Illuminated Parade, 130–1
Indigenous peoples: ACA acknowledgments of dispossession, 47–9; in Adirondack Mountains, 39, 175; appropriation from, 9; canoe associated with, 12; canoe racing, 139; displacement of, 39–40, 41, 42, 43, 45–6, 47, 48; lacrosse, 196n31; at Lake George, 39, 175, 253n92; participation in sports and races, 140, 151, 152, 171–2; "re-enactment" of Sugar Island purchase and, 33, 48–9, *49*; romanticization of, 111, 113; souvenir trade and, 174–5; in spectacles, 132–3

Industrial Exhibition, 89, 94
inhabiting, 10, 12, 110, 117–36; definition/meaning of, 53, 118, 126. *See also* daily routines and activities; domestication; excursions; spectacles
International Challenge Cup, 140, 146, 148

Jabberwock Canoe Club, 60, 61, *61*, 64
Jackman (carpenter), 167, 250n35
Jacoby, Karl, 44, 225n106
Jameson, Anna, 139
Jasen, Patricia, 7, 41, 127, 210n87
Jensen, Joan, 173
Jessup's Neck meet (1890): alcohol forbidden at, 91; campfire music, 122; clothing at, 105; dances, 123; field mice, 110; Indigenous invisibility at, 48; intimacy between men and women, 124; kitchen, 77; layout and design, 82–3; nighttime pranks, 123–4; "pleasant walks," 117; regatta, *138*, 158; shell designs, 111, *112*; site preparation, 74; supply issues, 37; travel to, 59, 215n48; visitors to, 90
Johnson, Emily Pauline (Tekahionwake): on alcohol consumption, 93; attendance at meets, 252n64; on campfires, 121; "Canoe and Canvas" series, 26; on clothing, 106, 137; description of meets, 72; "Indian Poetess," 21; membership, 21–2; performances by, 171, 172; scholarly attention to, 251n63; on signal system, 88; travel to Wolfe Island, 66–7
Johnson, M.F., 155, 156, 213n16
Johnson, Norman Frank, 253n92
Johnston, Matt, 65
Jones, Ford, 59

Jones, Karen, 54
Joyce, Patrick, 20, 27, 29, 73, 86, 200n29
Juniper Island. *See* Stony Lake meet (1883)

Kanien'kehá:ka (Mohawk) people, 39, 41, 132, 209n65
Kaziah-Otondosonne, Angeline Sarah, 253n92
Keys, George, 46
Kidd, Bruce, 142
kitchen, 25, 76, 77, 102, 115, 119, 165; staff and chores, 167, 168, *169*, 170, 172. *See also* meals; mealtimes; mess tents
Knappe, Emil, 155
Knickerbocker Canoe Club, 59, 98, 166, 170
Krause, Sydney, 111
Kwolek-Folland, Angel, 114

labour: about, 6, 160–1, 162–3; baggage handlers and porters, 166; "Coon Band," 122, 171, 177, *178*; domestic servants, 165–6, 170–1, 249n20; for entertainment, 171–2; erasure through photography, 177; future scholarship areas, 189; invisible nature of, 162–3, 180–2, *181*, 186; as leisure, 160–1; by local people, 166–7; meal preparation and wait staff, 167–70, *169*, 250n41, 250n46; onsite during meets, 167; by organizing committee, 23, 163; permeability of encampment boundaries and, 170–1; portrayals of labourers, 163–4; records and acknowledgment of, 172–3, 248n8; site construction and preparation, 25, 74, 164–5; site surveying, 24–5, 83–4, 163, 164; sport and, 181–2, 248n4; tensions with, 173–4; tourism and, 174, 179–80; wages and employment opportunities, 173. *See also* consumption
lacrosse, 196n31
Ladies Days, 78, 89, 225n108
Lake Champlain, 41–2, 127. *See also* Bluff Point, Lake Champlain meet (1895); Bow Arrow Point, Lake Champlain meet (1887); Willsborough Point, Lake Champlain meets (1891–2)
Lake George: alcohol forbidden at, 91; background, 39; inaugural encampment (1880), 15, 23; Indigenous communities, 39, 175, 253n92; summer residences, 39, 207n42, 208n44; travel to, 57. *See also* Adirondack Mountains; Canoe Islands, Lake George meets (1881–2); Long Island, Lake George meet (1888)
Lake George Canoe Club, 57
Lake George Mirror, 177
Lake Memphremagog encampments, 67, 114, 163, 174
lanterns, oriental, *101*, 107, 113, 121, 123, 130
Lefebvre, Henri, 8, 95
Lewis, A.A., 254n106
Lindsay, Peter, 140
Little, James, 60
Little, J.I., 67, 109, 114, 127, 163, 174
living room, 107, 116. *See also* parlour
Long Island, 42. *See also* Jessup's Neck meet (1890)
Long Island, Lake George meet (1888): aesthetics of Long Island, 37; breaking camp, *184*; campsite rules, 86; clothing at, 106; domestication, 114; layout and design, 83; travel to, 57

Longworth, Nicholas, 34
Lowell Daily Courier, 22
Łútsël K'é Dene First Nation (LKDFN), 187, 257nn14–15

MacGregor, John "Rob Roy," 3, 11–12, 195nn22–3, 196n25
Mack, W.C., 156
MacKendrick, Commodore William Gordon (W.G.), 29, 152
MacKendrick, John Noble, 142
maps, 24, 26, 27, *28*, 29, *30*, *85*, 204n94; area and site, 28–9; course, 85; route, 70
Marks, Lynne, 78
Mashpee people, 44
Massey's Magazine, 96
May, Louis H., 124
Maynard, Steven, 125
McClintock, Anne, 80
McCracken, Mr, 24, 164
McDonald, James, 46
McLennan, Donald, 173
McMullin, Thomas, 223n64
McNairn, Jeffrey, 198n7, 201n54
meals, 61, 76, 77, 102, *103*, 117, 126, 136, 159, 167, 168, 183; and meal fees, 119, 233n9, 233n12; sharing, 61, 126; wine at, 91. *See also* kitchen; mess tents
mealtimes, 83, 88, 100, 118, 119
membership: age and, 22; applications, 200n41; class and, 19–21; exclusivity of, 31; fees, 19; race and, 21–2; women, 6, 21, 201n51
mess tents: canned goods, 234n13; domestication and organization, 76–7, 100, *101*, *103*. *See also* kitchen; meals; mealtimes
Metcalfe, Alan, 146
Michael, Mike, 215n42

Michi Saagiig Nishnaabeg (Mississauga) people, 39–40, 41, 45–6, 47
Micklethwaite, Frank, 58, *59*, 215n47
middle class, 12, 16, 20, 34, 35, 79, 81, 88, 91, 93, 97, 103, 105, 107, 115, 120, 132, 135, 144, 165, 166, 170, *181*, 182; men, white, 6, 7, 11, 13, 19, 21, 22, 31, 54, 113, 116, 118, 134, 143, 160, 186; respectability, 81, 84, 94, 126; women, white, 7, 31, 150
Miller, Mr, 60
Milne-Smith, Amy, 20
Milz, Sabine, 172
minstrel shows, 118, 131–2, 133, 135, 172, *180*
mobility, 35, 58, 114; among athletes, 35; scholars, 53
Mohawk. *See* Kanien'kehá:ka (Mohawk) people
Mohican Canoe Club, 101, 170, 180
Mohican people, 43
Montauk people, 42
Montreal Pedestrian Club, 142–3
Moodie, Susanna, 40
moral environmentalism, 73–4, 83
Morgan, Cecilia, 31, 126
Morse, G. Livingston, 197n37
Mosher, J.S., 197n37
Mudlunta Island meet (1901), 19, 29, *30*, 41
Munsee people, 43
Muntz, R.G., 155
Murray, "Adirondack," 39
music: canoeing and romance linked in, 223n64; "Coon Band," 122, 171, 177, *178*, 251nn61–2; for entertainment, 121–3, 236n40
Muskoka, 43–4
Muskoka meet (1900): arrival at camp, 97–8; attendance,

37; Chinese spectacle, 134–5; complaints about site, 37, 165; daily schedule, 88; displacement of Indigenous peoples, 47–8; excursion to Bala Falls, 127, *128*; labour records, 172; map, 29; regatta spectators, 157; travel to, 54, 58, *59*, 65, 218n113

naming, as an act of power, 98–9
Narragansett Boat Club, 19
Nash, Linda, 83
nature, restorative power of, 109–10, 231n70
Nauset people, 44
navigating, 51–71. *See also* travel
Neide, Charles, 60, 62, 79, 125
neurasthenia, 115
New York Canoe Club, 3, 13, 105, 197n37
New York Evening Post, 184
New York Sun, 66, 72, 106, 125, 132, 137, 149
New York Times: on canoe boom, 3, 12; on Canoe Islands, Lake George, 34; on disabled competitor, 152; on inaugural meet, 15; on Jessup's Neck clothing, 105; military references for camps, 72; on off-season canoeing, 26; on Pauline Johnson performance, 171; on regattas, 151; "whitening" of canoe and, 13
New York Tribune, 124
Nicholson, Thomas, 173
Norton, C.L., 197n37

Old Van Cortlandt Manor, 127
Oliver, Jeff, 27
Oliver, Robert Shaw, 72
Opp, James, 177

organization, 15–32. *See* American Canoe Association; encampment governance and organization
orientalism, 113
Otis, Melissa, 175, 253n92
Outing (magazine), 13

Paddling Trophy Race, *138*
Paris, Leslie, 7, 131, 132
parlour, 102, 107, 116, 127; dining, 100. *See also* living room
Parmalee, Mrs, 60
Peebles, Mrs, 80
Petersen, Stephen, *112*
people of colour, 6, 66, 161, *169*, 177, *181*; always at the margins, 31; barred from full ACA membership, 186; entertainers, 171; men, 21, 168; and work, *161*. *See also* race
Phillips, Ruth, 175
photography: archival collection, 10; commercial, 175–6, 254n103; erasure of labour by, 177; at meets, 254n106, 254n108. *See also* Micklethwaite, Frank; Stoddard, Seneca Ray
placemaking, 8–9, 32, 38, 50, 70, 126, 185
Podruchny, Carolyn, 139
Potter, Frank, 215n52
Poulter, Gillian, 6, 151–2, 172, 188, 196n31, 205n2
pranks, nighttime, 123–4
privacy, 36, 108–9, 126
professionalism, 140–1, 242n24. *See also* amateurism and professionalism
Putnam, Robert D., 16

race, *134*, 173, 176, 181; and class, 135, 142; intersection with gender, 80, 115, 130, 140; mixed, 168; shaped the social, cultural, and physical landscapes of the ACA encampments, 6–7; and spectacles, 132; stereotypes, 133. *See also* black(s); people of colour; whites(s)

race(s): about, 5–6, 8, 17, 25, 88, 117, 119, 142, 143, 157, 177, 189; advertising of, 89; Chinese spectacles, 134–5; entertainment and, 122–3, 171–2; as events, 152; impromptu, 146; "Indian," 140, 151, 152; informal (scratch or scrub), 120, 156; meal preparation and, 168–70; media accounts of, 10; members only could compete, 21–2, 35, 87; minstrel shows and, 131–2, 172; as national canoeing championships, 7; novelty, 148; officials, 153, 246n119; paddling, 15, 38, *138*, 147, 151, 154, 155, 157 158; participation in sports and, 151–2; preparation for, 160, 161, 183; prizes for, 145; reinforcement of, 186; rowing, 137, 140; technological advancement and, 144; women's, 151, 152; yachting, 84, 140. *See also* canoe racing; regattas

racecourse, 24, 34, 38, 53, 74, 85, 137, *138*, 147, 150, *154*, 163; preparation, 83–4, *85*, 150; surveying of, 24

Radforth, Ian, 125

Raibmon, Paige, 9, 110, 113, 132, 172, 252n68

railroad, 29, 42, 54, 56, 79; guides, 67; as progress, 53, 139; reshaped time and space, 65. *See also* trains

Rathbun, Commodore F.S., 125

regattas: about, 137–9, 158–9; bureaucracy, organization, and rules, 17, 25, 147; canoe regulations, 145; canoe technology and, 144–5, 243n48; criticisms and protest system, 149, 157–8; disabled competitors, 152; failure to finish, 157; generalism, 143; history of, 139–40; Indigenous participation, 140, 151, 171–2; layout and design of racecourses, 83–4, *85*, 150; obstacles during, 156–7; paddling race at Jessup's Neck, *138*; participation issues, 147–8; preparation by participants, 26, 155; prizes and rewards, 140, 145–6, 148, 158; professionalism and amateurism concerns, 140–1, 142–3, 146–7; program development, 147, 148; race and, 151; race officials, 153, 246n119; racing styles, 155–6; The Record contest, 143; role within meets, 143; site requirements, 38; as spectacle, 137, 148; starting methods, 155; types and schedule of races, 153–4; women and, 5, 150, 151, 246n131. *See also* spectators

respectability, *154*; anxieties about, 78, 80; commitment to, 22, 92; markers of, 124; marriage, men, and, 82; middle class, 81, 84, 94, 126; notions (ideas) of, 20, 66, 79

ribbons, ACA, 86–7, *87*

Richter, Amy, 67

Robert's Rock Hotel, 61

Rodenstein, Addies, 201n51

Roediger, David, 12

Rogers, Commodore Lieutenant-Colonel Henry Cassady, 20, 40, 72

Roy, Wendy, 98–9

Rubies, Joan Pau, 62

Ruggles, George, 255n115

Rushton, J.H., 12, 177, 179, 255n115

Ryan, James, 10

Rydell, Robert, 144

Sagne, Jean, 175–6
Said, Edward, 9, 33, 47, 113, 232n89
same-sex relationships, *104*, 125–6
sanitation, 29; arrangements, 23, 25, 29, 84; infrastructure, 74, 83
Saunders, Commodore Fred, 10, 48, *49*
Schivelbusch, Wolfgang, 64–5
Schoeder, Patricia R., 251n61
Schuyler, C. Valentine, 124
Schuyler, Montgomery, 196n26, 197n37
Schuyler, M. Roosevelt, 197n37
Schuyler, Mrs, 121
Schwartz, Joan, 10
Scott, D'Arcy, 93, 96
Scoville, Mr, 74
Sears, George Washington (Nessmuk), 12, 196n28
Seavey, Lafayette W., 121, 132, 133–5
Seavey, Mr and Mrs, 80
secretary, ACA, 17, 75, 86–7, 198n11
Sekula, Allan, 10
servants, domestic, 165–6, 170–1, 249n20
sewing machine advertisement (Wheeler and Wilson), 12
sexuality and intimacy: canoes and, 223n64; heterosexual relationships, 82, 124–5, 126, 237n61; same-sex and homosocial relationships, *104*, 125–6
Shannon, Brent, 106
shell designs, 111, *112*
Sheller, Mimi, 215n45
Sherby, Alexander, 173
Shinnecock people, 42, 48, 175
Sifton, Clifford, 46–7
Simpson, Mark, 48, 212n118
Skinner, Alderman, 165
Smalley, Andrea, 78
Smith, A. Cary, 197n37

Snedeker, Florence Watters: on canoe travel to Willsborough Point meet, 51–2, *52*, 60–1, 62, 63–4, 68; description of encampment, 72–3; on Indigenous souvenirs, 175; on local people, 166–7
souvenir trade, 174–5
spatial theory, 7–8
Spaulding, Oliver Lyman, 59
spectacles, 130–5; Chinese, 134–5; circus, 133, *134*, 239n107; Commodore's Review and Illuminated Parade, 130–1; Indigenous peoples in, 132–3; by Lafayette Seavey, 132, 133–5; lake monster, 133–4; minstrel shows, 131–2, 172; organization of, 130; purpose of, 130, 135; regattas as, 137, 148
spectators, 5, 11, 16, 84, 85, 94, 121, 123, 130, 131, 133, 135, 147, 148–51, 152–3, *154*, *155*, 156–7, 158, 171
Spencer, Mr, 255n115
sport: amateurism, 141–3; colonialism of, 186–7; critical approaches in, 6, 188–9; during encampments, 121, 235n33; and gender, 13, 160, 188; labour and, 181–2, 248n4; professionalism, 140–1; tourism, 7, 34; women and, 150
squaw, use of term, 79
Squaw Point, 29, 79–80, *81*, 111, *112*, 122. *See also* women: ladies' camp
Stave Island meets (1889, 1898): camp store, 77; circus, 133; mess tent, 100, *101*; onsite labour, 167; rain during, 110; regatta, *85*, 148; ribbons for attendees, *87*; travel to, 59–60, 215n48
steamboats, 67–70, *69*, 71, 127
Steiner, Christopher, 175

Stephens, William P. (W.P.), 12, 152, 177, 196n26
Stewart, Walter, 102, 148
Stewart, William J., 124–5
St Lawrence River, 120
St Lawrence River Skiff, Canoe and Steam Launch Company, 179
Stockbridge-Munsee people, 43
Stoddard, Seneca Ray: at encampments, 176–7, 185, 254n104; Lake George guidebook, 39, 208n44; photographs by, *99, 112, 138, 154, 155,* 169–70, *178*
Stony Lake, 39–40
Stony Lake meet (1883): camp mobility and, 35; centipedes, 110; fishing, 120; Illuminated Parade, 130; intimacy between men and women, 82; ladies' camp, 78, 79–80; length of, 23; location issues, 37; site survey, 24, 163, 164; spelling, 208n50; travel to, 59, 62
Sugar Island: acquisition of, 36, 45, 46–7; customs official at, 55; displacement of Indigenous peoples, 45–6, 47, 48; labour records, 172; "re-enactment" of purchase, 33, 48–9, *49*; site preparation, 165; white inhabitants, 46
surveying, 24–5, 83–4, 163, 164
swimming, 119–20, 136. *See also* bathing
Syracuse Daily Standard, 100
Syracuse Evening Herald, 119

Tahamont, Louis, 151
Taylor, Frank, 57–8, 128
technological modernity, 144–5
temperance, 91, 94. *See also* alcohol consumption
tennis, 121

tents, 107–11; display of interiors, 109–10; domestication of, 107–8, *108, 109*; for housing campers, 100–2; intrusion of nature, 110–11; lack of privacy, 108–9
Thaidene Nëné National Park Reserve, 187, 257nn13–15
Thomas, Etta K., 201n51
Thompson, E.P., 89
Thoreau, Henry David, 44
Thorpe, Jocelyn, 7
Thousand Islands, 40–1
Tocqueville, Alexis de, 16
Toker, Mrs E.J., 80
Toronto Canoe Club, 54, 66
tourism, 6, 40, 53, 64, 126: Adirondack Mountains, 39; Cape Cod, 44; colonialism and, 24–5; as escape, 179; guidebooks and advice, 56–7, 214n31; heritage, 127; Hudson River Valley, 42–3; industry, 45; labour and, 174, 179–80; Long Island, 42; Muskoka, 43–4; operators, 180; opportunities for work, 39, 50; resort, 42; settlement and, 210n87; spaces of, 38; sport, 7, 34; summer, 44; Thousand Islands, 41; while canoe cruising, 64
Trachtenberg, Alan, 144–5
trains, 64–7; and class and gender, 66–7; discounts, 54, 213n11; embodied experience of, 65–6, 71; rail development, 213n7; scholarship on, 64–5; social experiences, 67. *See also* railroad
transparency and accountability, 18–19, 200n30
travel: about, 52–3, 70–1; assistance from transportation committee, 25, 54, 55–6, 57; baggage handlers and porters, 166; by canoe, 13–14, 60–4; delays, 58–9, 215n48; evolution

of transportation network, 53–4; guidebooks and advice, 56–7, 214n31; individual responsibility for, 56; international border crossings and customs officials, 25, 55, 59–60, 214n25, 215n52; last stage to camp, 68, 218n113; methods of, 58; navigating and, 52–3; proximity and time, 57–8; return home from camps, 70; by steamboat, 67–70, *69*, 71, 127; by train, 64–7, 71, 213n7, 213n11; transportation of canoes and other goods, 54–5, 213n16. *See also* canoe cruising; excursions; railroad; Snedeker, Florence Watters; trains
travel writing, 39, 62. *See also* circulars
Turner, Frederick Jackson, 113
Tyson, Robert, 24, 163, 164, 170

Unwin, Charles, 46
upper class, 93, 142, 161, 166, 181; men, white, 6, 186
Urry, John, 58, 215n45

Valencius, Conevery, 102
Van Slyck, Abigail, 75, 79, 100, 170
Vasseur, Joe, 24, 163, 170
Vaux, C. Bowyer, 10, 13, 65, 67–8, 78, 106, 156, 157, 195n17, 207n42
Venne, Muriel Stanley, 79
Vernon, Paul, 63, 93, 94, 108–9, 110, 125, 128
Vesper Canoe Club, 93
visitors to the encampments, 5, 75, 87, 89–91, 94, 95, 104, 121, 132, 179; as challenge to organizers, 11, 73, 89; day, 95, 117, 118; limit, 170; undesirable, 91
voluntary associations, 16, 21, 22, 31, 201n54

voyageur communities, 139

Walden, Keith, 88, 89, 94, 227n3
Wall, Sharon, 7, 47, 236n43
Wallace, Mr, 15
Walsh, John, 26
Wampanoag Nation, 44
Warder, George, 91, *92*, 160, *161*, 180
Watertown Daily Times, 19
Watertown Re-Union, 48
Watson, Andrew, 210n87
Weller, Mr, 156
Western Abenaki people, 39, 41
Western Canoe Association, 17–18
Wheeler and Wilson sewing machine advertisement, 12
white(s), 31, 42, 46, 83, 115, 116, 133, 134, 143, 151; ACA as, 6–7, 9, 19, 21, 118, 142, *181*; audiences, 172, 177; Canadian nation as, 188; consumers, 175; identified by name, 170; minstrelsy, 131; practices of sport and leisure, 34, 97; rural, 11, 161, 171, 180, 186; settlers/settlements, 24, 33, 40, 43, 45, 50, 111, 187; spaces of order and play, 22, 135; sport hunters, 160; superiority, 47, 152, 186; values, 150; women workers, 168; women's participation in regattas, 140; whiteness, 136, 141, 188, 189; as privilege, 80, 132, 186
"whitening of the canoe," 12–13, 144
Whitney, Casper, 82
Wilkin, Robert J., 94, 103
Williams, Susan, 249n20
Willsborough Point, Lake Champlain meets (1891–2): boxing match, 121; displacement of Indigenous peoples, 48; length of, 227n5; onsite labour, 167; regatta, 147–8, 155; social encounters

and, 118; souvenir trade, 175; spectacles, 132, 133–4; travel to, 56–7, 58
Wilson, Alexander, 216n56
Wiltse, Jeff, 119–20
Winne, Commodore, 93
Wolfe Island meet (1893): alcohol consumption, 93–4; campfire music, 121–2; domestication of, 115; excursion, 128–9; map, 29; military references to, 72; nighttime pranks, 124; travel to, 57, 60, 66–7
Wolters, Charles F., 198n13
women: in camp organization, 23; canoe travel, 60, 63; clothing, 106, 137, 246n131; economic role, 173; fishing, 234n23; inclusion in camp life, 78–9; Indigenous racing, 140; ladies' camp, 23, 29, 78–82, 111, *112*, 113, 126; Ladies Days, 225n108; meal wait staff, 168; membership, 6, 21, 31, 201n51; prize giving by, 158; regattas and, 5, 150, 151, 246n131; romantic relationships, 82, 124–5, 126, 237n61; segregated spaces for, 79–82, 222n48; sport and, 150; Squaw Point flag, 80, *81*, 111; travel expectations, 66–7; voting rights, 201n50. *See also* gender
Wood, David, 88
work. *See* consumption; labour
working class, 6, 31, 66, 90, 141, 146, 161, 180, 186
World's Fairs, 132–3, 144, 145, 172
Wulsin, Lucien, 34
Wurst, LouAnn, 168

yachting, 26, 72, 140, 144; clubs, 16; races, 84, 137
Youngs, Tim, 70